HARCOURT

Math

INTERVENTION
SKILLS

Grade 2

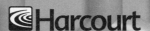

Harcourt

Orlando   Austin   Chicago   NewYork   Toronto   London   San Diego

Visit *The Learning Site!*
www.harcourtschool.com

CONTENTS

▶ **Using *Intervention • Skills*** .... **IN**ix

▶ **Chapter Correlations** .... **IN**xi

▶ **Check What You Know**

Chapter 1 .... **IN1**

Chapter 2 .... **IN2**

Chapter 3 .... **IN3**

Chapter 4 .... **IN4**

Chapter 5 .... **IN5**

Chapter 6 .... **IN6**

Chapter 7 .... **IN7**

Chapter 8 .... **IN8**

Chapter 9 .... **IN9**

Chapter 10 .... **IN10**

Chapter 11 .... **IN11**

Chapter 12 .... **IN12**

Chapter 13 .... **IN13**

Chapter 14 .... **IN14**

Chapter 15 .... **IN15**

Chapter 16 .... **IN16**

Chapter 17 .... **IN17**

Chapter 18 .... **IN18**

Chapter 19 .... **IN19**

Chapter 20 .... **IN20**

Chapter 21 .... **IN21**

Chapter 22 .... **IN22**

Chapter 23 .... **IN23**

Chapter 24 .... **IN24**

Chapter 25 .... **IN25**

Chapter 26 .... **IN26**

Chapter 27 .... **IN27**

Chapter 28 .... **IN28**

Chapter 29 .... **IN29**

Chapter 30 .... **IN30**

Answers **IN31**

Skills

Number Sense, Concepts, and Operations: Number Sense and Place Value

1 Exploring Tens **IN41**

2 Exploring Tens and Ones to 100 .... **IN45**

3 Even and Odd Numbers **IN49**

4 Skip Count by 2's, 5's, and 10's on a Hundred Chart **IN53**

5 Order on a Number Line **IN57**

6 Tens **IN61**

7 Tens and Ones to 100 .... **IN65**

8 Understand Place Value **IN69**

9 Order Numbers to 100 .... **IN73**

Number Sense, Concepts, and Operations: Whole Number Addition

10 Count On to Add **IN79**

11 Doubles and Doubles Plus One **IN83**

12 Make a Ten **IN87**

13 Mental Math to Add Tens **IN91**

14 Add Tens and Ones **IN95**

15 Regroup Ones as Tens **IN99**

16 Model 2-Digit Addition **IN103**

17 Add 2-Digit Numbers **IN107**

18 Algebra: Add 3 Numbers **IN111**

19 Practice 2-Digit Addition **IN115**

▶ Number Sense, Concepts, and Operations: Whole Number Subtraction

20	Count Back to Subtract	**IN121**
21	Algebra: Relate Addition and Subtraction	**IN125**
22	Practice the Facts	**IN129**
23	Mental Math to Subtract Tens	**IN133**
24	Subtract Tens and Ones	**IN137**
25	Regroup Tens as Ones	**IN141**
26	Model 2-Digit Subtraction	**IN145**
27	Subtract 2-Digit Numbers	**IN149**
28	Practice 2-Digit Subtraction	**IN153**

▶ Number Sense, Concepts, and Operations: Money

29	Count Groups of Coins	**IN159**
30	Count Collections	**IN163**
31	Value of a Quarter	**IN167**
32	Value of Half Dollars and Dollars	**IN171**
33	Compare Values of Coins	**IN175**
34	Make Equal Amounts	**IN179**

▶ Number Sense, Concepts, and Operations: Whole Number Multiplication

| 35 | Counting Equal Groups | **IN185** |

▶ Number Sense, Concepts, and Operations: Fractions

36	Halves	**IN191**
37	Fourths	**IN195**
38	Thirds	**IN199**
39	Parts of a Group	**IN203**

Measurement

40   Read a Clock **IN209**

41   Tell Time to the Hour **IN213**

42   Make Reasonable Estimates: One Minute **IN217**

43   Use a Calendar **IN221**

44   Compare Lengths **IN225**

45   Use Nonstandard Units **IN229**

46   Use a Balance **IN233**

47   Pounds **IN237**

48   Use Nonstandard Units to Measure Capacity **IN241**

49   Centimeters **IN245**

50   Kilograms **IN249**

51   Liters **IN253**

Geometry and Spatial Sense

52   Give and Follow Directions **IN259**

53   Plane Shapes on Solid Figures **IN263**

54   Sort and Identify Plane Shapes **IN267**

55   Solid Figures **IN271**

56   Sort Solid Figures by Attributes **IN275**

57   Symmetry **IN279**

58   Slides and Turns **IN283**

Algebraic Thinking, Patterns, and Functions

59   Algebra: Greater Than **IN289**

60   Algebra: Less Than **IN293**

61   Algebra: Use Symbols to Compare **IN297**

62   Algebra: Describe and Extend Patterns **IN301**

63   Algebra: Pattern Units **IN305**

64   Compare Numbers: $>$, $<$, and $=$ **IN309**

Data Analysis and Probability

65   Read Tally Tables **IN315**

66   Make Bar Graphs **IN319**

67   Use Data from a Bar Graph **IN323**

68   Interpret Data **IN327**

69   Certain or Impossible **IN331**

Answers **IN335**

Check What You Know Enrichment

▶ Chapter 1 Secret Numbers • Numbers to 50.................................... **IN373**

Fishing for Pairs • Tens and Ones.. **IN374**

▶ Chapter 2 Number Mix-Up • Skip Counting................................ **IN375**

True or False Skip Counting • Skip Count............................ **IN376**

▶ Chapter 3 What Animal Am I? • Numbers to 50.......................... **IN377**

Lucky Duck Factory • Order on a Number Line.................... **IN378**

▶ Chapter 4 Playground Picture Graphs • Sort and Classify............ **IN379**

Charting Colors • Graphs.. **IN380**

▶ Chapter 5 Count Dot-to-Dot • Addition.................................... **IN381**

Adding in Circles • Addition.. **IN382**

▶ Chapter 6 Fact Match • Related Facts.. **IN383**

Math Path • Subtract.. **IN384**

▶ Chapter 7 Number Puzzle • Numbers to 100.............................. **IN385**

What's Missing? • Addition.. **IN386**

▶ Chapter 8 Secret Path • Addition.. **IN387**

Addition Pairs • Addition.. **IN388**

▶ Chapter 9 What Number Am I? • Subtraction............................ **IN389**

How Many are Left? • Subtraction...................................... **IN390**

▶ Chapter 10 Subtraction Riddle • Subtraction.............................. **IN391**

Compare Differences • Subtraction...................................... **IN392**

▶ Chapter 11 Puzzling Addition • Addition.................................... **IN393**

Subtraction Wheels • Subtraction.. **IN394**

▶ Chapter 12 Coin Values • Money.. **IN395**

Do I Have Enough? • Money.. **IN396**

▶ Chapter 13 Coin Choices • Money.. **IN397**

How Can I Pay? • Money.. **IN398**

▶ Chapter 14 What Time Is It? • Time.. **IN399**

Time to Begin • Time.. **IN400**

▶ Chapter 15 Timing is Everything! • Time.................................... **IN401**

Pick a Day • Calendars.. **IN402**

▶ Chapter 16   Map Maker • Follow Directions **IN403**
                  Jellybean Taste Test • Interpret Data **IN404**

▶ Chapter 17   Yes, Maybe, No • Certain or Impossible **IN405**
                  Bag It! • Likely and Unlikely **IN406**

▶ Chapter 18   Find the Shapes • Plane Shapes **IN407**
                  Draw the Shapes • Plane Shapes **IN408**

▶ Chapter 19   Solid Animals • Solid Figures **IN409**
                  Chart the Shapes • Solid Figures **IN410**

▶ Chapter 20   Slide and Turn It • Slides and Turns **IN411**
                  Symmetry Shelves • Symmetry **IN412**

▶ Chapter 21   Whose Bracelet? • Describe Patterns **IN413**
                  Necklace Makers • Extend Patterns **IN414**

▶ Chapter 22   Put Them in Order • Length **IN415**
                  How Long Is It? • Length **IN416**

▶ Chapter 23   How Much Can it Hold? • Capacity **IN417**
                  Weight Game • Weight **IN418**

▶ Chapter 24   Small Measures • Centimeters **IN419**
                  Measuring at the Library • Kilograms **IN420**

▶ Chapter 25   Addition A to Z • Add 3 Numbers **IN421**
                  On a Roll • Add 3 Numbers **IN422**

▶ Chapter 26   Thirds, Halves, Fourths • Parts of a Whole **IN423**
                  Which One Is Right? • Parts of Groups **IN424**

▶ Chapter 27   Ring the Numbers • Numbers to 100 .... **IN425**
                  Place Value Riddles • Numbers to 100 .... **IN426**

▶ Chapter 28   Get in Order! • Numbers to 100 .... **IN427**
                  You Make the Number • Numbers to 100 .... **IN428**

▶ Chapter 29   Number Play • Addition **IN429**
                  Coded Subtraction • Subtraction **IN430**

▶ Chapter 30   Circus Ring Addition • Repeated Addition **IN431**
                  Make Them Equal • Equal Shares **IN432**

Answers **IN433**

Using *Intervention • Skills*

The *Intervention • Skills* will help you accommodate the diverse skill levels of students in your class and prepare students to work successfully on grade-level content by targeting the prerequisite skills for *each chapter* in the program. The following questions and answers will help you make the best use of this rich resource.

How can I determine which skills a student or students should work on?

Before beginning each chapter, have students complete the "Check What You Know" page in the Student Edition. This page targets the prerequisite skills necessary for success in the chapter. A student's performance on this page will allow you to diagnose skill weaknesses and prescribe appropriate interventions. *Intervention • Skills* lessons are tied directly to each of the skills assessed. The *Check What You Know Enrichment* activities are also correlated to the skills targeted on the "Check What You Know" page. A chart at the beginning of each chapter correlates the skill assessed to the appropriate intervention materials. The chart appears in the HARCOURT MATH Teacher Edition.

In what format are the *Intervention • Skills* materials?

A. **Copying masters** provide the skill development and skill practice on reproducible pages. These pages in the *Intervention • Skills Teacher's Guide with Copying Masters* can be used by individual students or small groups. You can also allow students to record their answers on copies of the pages. This guide provides teaching suggestions for skill development, as well as an alternative teaching strategy for students who continue to have difficulty with a skill. Sixty pages of *Check What You Know Enrichment* activities provide additional practice of these skills.

B. **CD-ROM** provides the skill development and practice in an interactive format. *Check What You Know Enrichment* activities are provided as printable PDF files.

Are manipulative activities included in the intervention resources?

The teaching strategies included in the teacher's materials for the *Intervention • Skills* lessons do require manipulatives, easily gathered classroom objects or copying masters from the *Teacher's Resource Book*. Since these activities are designed for only those students who show deficits in their skill development, the quantity of manipulatives will be small. For many activities, you may substitute materials, such as squares of paper for counters, coins for two-color counters, and so on.

How can I organize my classroom so that I have time and space to help students who show a need for these intervention strategies and activities?

You may want to set up a Math Skill Center with a folder for each of your students. Based on a student's performance on the *Check What You Know* page, assign appropriate skills by marking the student's record folder. The student can then work through the intervention materials, record the date of completion, and place the completed work in a folder for your review. You may wish to assign students to a partner, assign a small group to work together, or have a specified time during the day to meet with one or more of the individuals or small groups to assess their progress and to provide direct instruction. You may wish to assign *Check What You Know Enrichment* activities to those who perform satisfactorily on the *Check What You Know* pages.

How are the lessons structured?

Each skill begins with a model or an explanation with a model. The first section of exercises, titled *Try These,* provides 2–4 exercises that allow students to move toward doing the work independently. A student who has difficulty with the *Try These* exercises might benefit from the Alternative Teaching Strategy activity for that skill described in this Teacher's Guide before they attempt the *Practice on Your Own* page. The *Practice on Your Own* page provides an additional model for the skill and scaffolded exercises, which gradually remove prompts. Scaffolding provides a framework within which the student can achieve success for the skill. At the end of the *Practice on Your Own*, there is a *Quiz*. The *Quiz* provides 2–4 problems that check the student's proficiency in the skill. Guidelines for success are provided in the teacher's materials.

Intervention • Skills
Chapter Correlations

Number Sense, Concepts, and Operations
Number Sense and Place Value

Skill Number	Skill Title	Chapter Correlation
1	Exploring Tens	1
2	Exploring Tens and Ones to 100	1
3	Even and Odd Numbers	2
4	Skip Count by 2's, 5's, and 10's on a Hundred Chart	2
5	Order on a Number Line	3
6	Tens	27
7	Tens and Ones to 100	27
8	Understand Place Value	27
9	Order Numbers to 100	28

Whole Number Addition

Skill Number	Skill Title	Chapter Correlation
10	Count On to Add	5
11	Doubles and Doubles Plus One	5
12	Make a Ten	7
13	Mental Math to Add Tens	7
14	Add Tens and Ones	7
15	Regroup Ones as Tens	8
16	Model 2-Digit Addition	8
17	Add 2-Digit Numbers	11
18	Algebra: Add 3 Numbers	25
19	Practice 2-Digit Addition	29

Whole Number Subtraction

Skill Number	Skill Title	Chapter Correlation
20	Count Back to Subtract	6
21	Algebra: Relate Addition and Subtraction	6
22	Practice the Facts	9
23	Mental Math to Subtract Tens	9
24	Subtract Tens and Ones	9
25	Regroup Tens as Ones	10
26	Model 2-Digit Subtraction	10
27	Subtract 2-Digit Numbers	11
28	Practice 2-Digit Subtraction	29

Money

Skill Number	Skill Title	Chapter Correlation
29	Count Groups of Coins	12
30	Count Collections	12
31	Value of a Quarter	12
32	Value of Half Dollars and Dollars	12
33	Compare Values of Coins	13
34	Make Equal Amounts	13

Whole Number Multiplication

Skill Number	Skill Title	Chapter Correlation
35	Counting Equal Groups	30

Fractions

Skill Number	Skill Title	Chapter Correlation
36	Halves	26
37	Fourths	26
38	Thirds	26
39	Parts of a Group	26

Measurement

Skill Number	Skill Title	Chapter Correlation
40	Read a Clock	14
41	Tell Time to the Hour	14
42	Make Reasonable Estimates: One Minute	15
43	Use a Calendar	15
44	Compare Lengths	22
45	Use Nonstandard Units	22
46	Use a Balance	23
47	Pounds	23
48	Use Nonstandard Units to Measure Capacity	23
49	Centimeters	24
50	Kilograms	24
51	Liters	24

Geometry and Spatial Sense

Skill Number	Skill Title	Chapter Correlation
52	Give and Follow Directions	16
53	Plane Shapes on Solid Figures	18
54	Sort and Identify Plane Shapes	18
55	Solid Figures	19
56	Sort Solid Figures by Attributes	19
57	Symmetry	20
58	Slides and Turns	20

Algebraic Thinking, Patterns, and Functions

Skill Number	Skill Title	Chapter Correlation
59	Algebra: Greater Than	3
60	Algebra: Less Than	3
61	Algebra: Use Symbols to Compare	3
62	Algebra: Describe and Extend Patterns	21
63	Algebra: Pattern Units	21
64	Compare Numbers: >, <, and =	28

Data Analysis and Probability

Skill Number	Skill Title	Chapter Correlation
65	Read Tally Tables	4
66	Make Bar Graphs	4
67	Use Data from a Bar Graph	16
68	Interpret Data	16
69	Certain or Impossible	17

Name _____

Check What You Know

Tens

Count by tens. Write the number.

1.

___ tens   ___ fifty

2.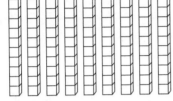

___ tens   ___ ninety

3.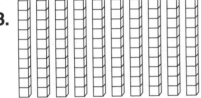

___ tens   ___ one hundred

Tens and Ones to 100

Write how many tens and ones. Write the number.

4.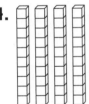

___ tens ___ ones = ___

5.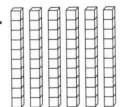

___ tens ___ ones = ___

6.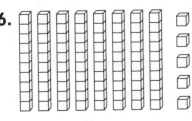

___ tens ___ ones = ___

7.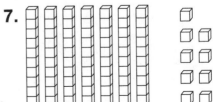

___ tens ___ ones = ___

Check What You Know
Even and Odd Numbers

Use to show each number. Circle even or odd.

I.	I	even	odd	2.	2	even	odd
3.	3	even	odd	4.	4	even	odd
5.	5	even	odd	6.	6	even	odd
7.	7	even	odd	8.	8	even	odd

Skip Count by 2s, 5s, and 10s

Skip count. Write how many.

9.

    2 ____ ____ ____ ____ ____ ____

10.

    5 ____ ____ ____ ____ ____ ____

11.

    10 ____ ____ ____ ____ ____ ____

Name _____

Check What You Know

● Greater Than

Use to show each number.
Circle the greater number. Write the numbers.

1. ☆ 28   ☆ 36   **2.** ☆ 41   ☆ 14

_____ is greater than _____   _____ is greater than _____

_____ > _____   _____ > _____

Less Than

Use to help.
Circle the number that is less. Write the numbers.

3. ♡ 52   ♡ 50   **4.** ♡ 86   ♡ 68

_____ is less than _____   _____ is less than _____

_____ < _____   _____ < _____

Use Symbols to Compare

Compare the numbers.
Use to show each number. Draw the
▱. Write <, >, or = in the box.

5.   32 ☐ 35   **6.**   63 ☐ 36

Order on a Number Line

Write the missing number that is just before,
between, or just after.

7. 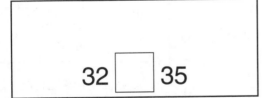   **8.**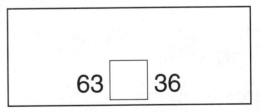

Name _____

Check What You Know

Read Tally Tables

Favorite Fruit		Total
Apples	~~IIII~~ I	6
Grapes	~~IIII~~ IIII	9

Use the tally table to answer these questions.

1. How many children chose apples? _____

2. How many children chose grapes? _____

3. Which fruit did most children choose? _____

Make Bar Graphs

Color the bar graph to match the tally marks.

Favorite Snack		Total
Pretzels	~~IIII~~	5
Popcorn	~~IIII~~ ~~IIII~~	10
Raisins	III	3

Use the graph to answer the questions.

4. How many children chose popcorn? _____

5. How many more children chose pretzels than raisins?

_____

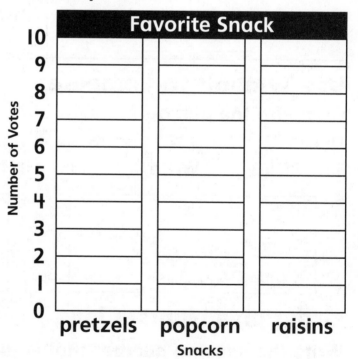

© Harcourt

Name _____

Check What You Know

Count On to Add

Circle the greater number.

Use the number line. Count on to add.

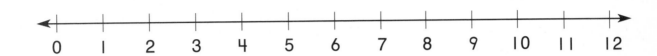

1. $4 + 3 =$ _____
2. $2 + 8 =$ _____
3. $3 + 9 =$ _____

4. $3 + 6 =$ _____
5. $7 + 1 =$ _____
6. $7 + 2 =$ _____

7. $9 + 2 =$ _____
8. $8 + 3 =$ _____
9. $2 + 6 =$ _____

10. $1 + 8 =$ _____
11. $5 + 3 =$ _____
12. $1 + 9 =$ _____

Doubles and Doubles Plus 1

Write the sum.

13. $4 + 4 =$ _____, so $4 + 5 =$ _____

14. $0 + 0 =$ _____, so $0 + 1 =$ _____

15. $5 + 5 =$ _____, so $5 + 6 =$ _____

16. $3 + 3 =$ _____, so $3 + 4 =$ _____

17. $2 + 2 =$ _____, so $2 + 3 =$ _____

Check What You Know

Count Back to Subtract

Use the number line to count back. Write the difference.

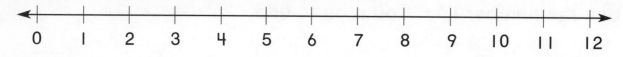

0 1 2 3 4 5 6 7 8 9 10 11 12

1. 6
   −3

2. 10
   − 1

3. 11
   − 3

4. 9
   −2

5. 8
   −2

6. 5
   −1

7. 7
   −1

8. 11
   − 2

9. 9
   −3

10. 8
    −3

11. 10
    − 2

12. 7
    −2

13. 7
    −3

14. 9
    −1

15. 8
    −1

16. 6
    −2

17. 10
    − 3

18. 12
    − 3

Relate Addition and Subtraction

Write each sum or difference.
Circle the related facts in each row.

19. 9 − 5 = _____   9 − 6 = _____   4 + 5 = _____

20. 4 + 4 = _____   12 − 4 = _____   8 + 4 = _____

21. 11 − 7 = _____   4 + 7 = _____   5 + 6 = _____

22. 7 + 3 = _____   5 + 5 = _____   10 − 3 = _____

© Harcourt

Name _____

Check What You Know

Addition Facts to 18

Use a ten frame and ● to find the sum.

1. 4
   + 9

2. 8
   + 7

3. 2
   + 9

4. 9
   + 8

5. 4
   + 8

6. 6
   + 5

7. 8
   + 6

8. 7
   + 5

9. 6
   + 9

10. 5
    + 8

Mental Math to Add Tens

Add.

11. 60
    + 30

12. 50
    + 10

13. 20
    + 60

14. 40
    + 30

15. 20
    + 20

16. 30
    + 30

17. 20
    + 70

18. 20
    + 50

19. 10
    + 40

20. 30
    + 50

Add Tens and Ones

Use Workmat 3 and ▨ to add.
Write the sum.

21.

tens	ones
6	3
+	4

tens	ones

22.

tens	ones
2	2
+	3

tens	ones

Name _____

Check What You Know
Regroup Ones as Tens

Use Workmat 3 and ⬚⬚⬚⬚⬚⬚ ▢.

Show.	Add.	Do you need to regroup? Circle Yes or No.	How many tens and ones?
1. 46	5	Yes　　No	_____ tens _____ ones
2. 22	4	Yes　　No	_____ tens _____ ones
3. 19	8	Yes　　No	_____ tens _____ ones

Model 2-Digit Addition

Use Workmat 3 and ⬚⬚⬚⬚⬚⬚ ▢. Add.

4.

tens	ones
□	
3	6
+ 1	5

Workmat

Tens	Ones

5.

tens	ones
□	
4	2
+ 3	8

Workmat

Tens	Ones

6.

tens	ones
□	
3	2
+ 1	9

Workmat

Tens	Ones

7.

tens	ones
□	
1	4
+ 2	4

Workmat

Tens	Ones

© Harcourt

Name _____

Check What You Know
Subtraction Facts to 18

Subtract.

1. 18 − 9

2. 8 − 7

3. 13 − 7

4. 14 − 5

5. 9 − 4

6. 16 − 7

7. 15 − 8

8. 7 − 5

9. 8 − 6

10. 17 − 9

Mental Math to Subtract Tens

Subtract.

11. 60 − 50

12. 80 − 60

13. 70 − 30

14. 50 − 30

15. 40 − 20

16. 90 − 60

17. 70 − 10

18. 80 − 40

19. 90 − 40

20. 60 − 30

Subtract Tens and Ones

Use Workmat 3 and 🎲 to subtract.
Write the difference.

21.

tens	ones
4	6
−	4

tens	ones

22.

tens	ones
3	9
−	3

tens	ones

Check What You Know

Regroup Tens as Ones

Use Workmat 3 and ▭▭▭▭▭▭ ▯.

Show.	Subtract.	Do you need to regroup? Circle Yes or No.	How many tens and ones are left?
1. 57	9	Yes No	____ tens ____ ones
2. 35	4	Yes No	____ tens ____ ones
3. 22	7	Yes No	____ tens ____ ones

Model 2-Digit Subtraction

Use Workmat 3 and ▭▭▭▭▭▭ ▯.

4.

tens	ones
□	□
2	3
− 1	4

Workmat

Tens	Ones

5.

tens	ones
□	□
4	5
− 2	5

Workmat

Tens	Ones

6.

tens	ones
□	□
3	5
− 1	4

Workmat

Tens	Ones

7.

tens	ones
□	□
5	1
− 3	6

Workmat

Tens	Ones

© Harcourt

Name _____

Check What You Know

Add 2-Digit Numbers

Add. Regroup if you need to.

1.	tens	ones
	2	8
+	4	7

2.	tens	ones
	3	7
+	1	5

3.	tens	ones
	6	5
+		4

4.	tens	ones
	4	0
+	5	6

5.	tens	ones
	1	6
+	6	8

6.		
	3	5
+	3	5

7.		
	1	5
+	4	9

8.		
	8	9
+		7

9.		
	7	3
+	1	4

10.		
	5	9
+	3	2

Subtract 2-Digit Numbers

Subtract. Regroup if you need to.

11.	tens	ones
	3	5
−	2	7

12.	tens	ones
	6	2
−		6

13.	tens	ones
	2	4
−	1	3

14.	tens	ones
	9	1
−	4	8

15.	tens	ones
	7	7
−	5	9

16.		
	4	8
−		9

17.		
	8	0
−	4	7

18.		
	5	5
−	1	3

19.		
	2	6
−	2	4

20.		
	9	3
−	7	6

Check What You Know

Count Groups of Coins

Count. Write the amount.

1.

_____ ¢, _____ ¢, _____ ¢, _____ ¢, _____ ¢, _____ ¢ ☐ ¢

Count Collections

Count. Write the amount.

2.

3.

Value of a Quarter

Count on from the quarter. Write the total amount.

4.

_____ ¢, _____ ¢, _____ ¢, _____ ¢, _____ ¢ ☐ ¢

Value of Half Dollars and Dollars

Draw the coins. Write how many.

5. Show how many quarters
   equal a dollar.

_____ quarters = 1 dollar

Name _____

Check What You Know

Compare Values of Coins

Count each group of coins. Circle the amount that is greater.

1.

_____ ¢

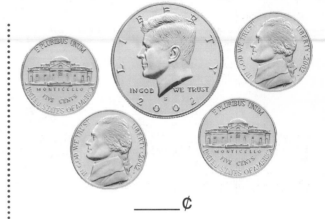
_____ ¢

2.

_____ ¢

_____ ¢

Make Equal Amounts

Use coins. Show the amount in two ways.
Draw the coins. Circle the way that uses fewer coins.

3.

4.
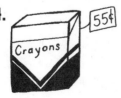

© Harcourt

Check What You Know
Read a Clock

Use a . Show each time. Trace the hour hand. Write the time.

1.

_____ o'clock

2.

_____ o'clock

3.

_____ o'clock

4.

_____ o'clock

5.

_____ o'clock

6.

_____ o'clock

Tell Time to the Hour

Use a . Show each time. Write the time.

7.

8.

9.

10.

11.
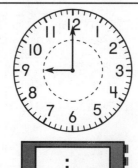

12.
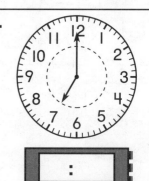

© Harcourt

Name _____

Check What You Know

⬤ Make Reasonable Estimates: One Minute

About how long would it take?
Circle your estimate. Then act it out to check.

1. read a book	2. write a letter	3. snap your fingers

more than a minute	more than a minute	more than a minute
less than a minute	less than a minute	less than a minute

Use a Calendar

⬤ **Fill in the calendar for this month.**
Use the calendar to answer the questions.

Sunday	Monday	Tuesday	Wednesday	Thursday	Friday	Saturday

4. How many days are in the month? _____

5. What day of the week is the twenty-third? _____

6. What is the date of the third Tuesday? _____

⬤ 7. What is the date of the first Monday? _____

Name _____

Check What You Know

Give and Follow Directions

Follow the directions in order.
Draw the path. Write the name.

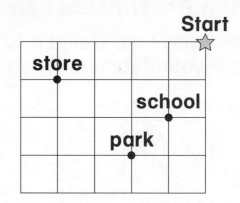

1. Go left 4. Go down 3.
   Go right 2. Where are you?

_____

Interpret Data

Use the graph to answer the questions.

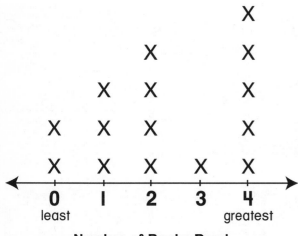

2. What is the least
   number of books
   that children read?   _____

3. What is the greatest
   number of books
   that children read?   _____

Use Data from a Bar Graph: Interpret Data

Use the bar graph to answer the question.

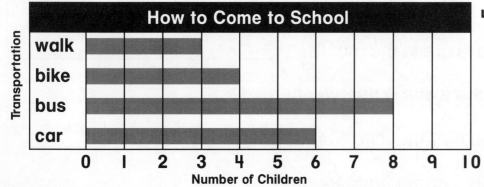

4. How many
   more children
   get to school
   by bus than
   by bike?

_____

© Harcourt

Name _____

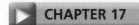

Check What You Know

Certain or Impossible

Mark an X to tell if pulling the cube shown from the bowl is certain or impossible.

	Certain	Impossible
1.		
2.		
3.		
4.		
5.		

© Harcourt

Check What You Know
Plane Shapes on Solid Figures

**Use solids. Trace around each one.
Write the name of the shape you drew.**

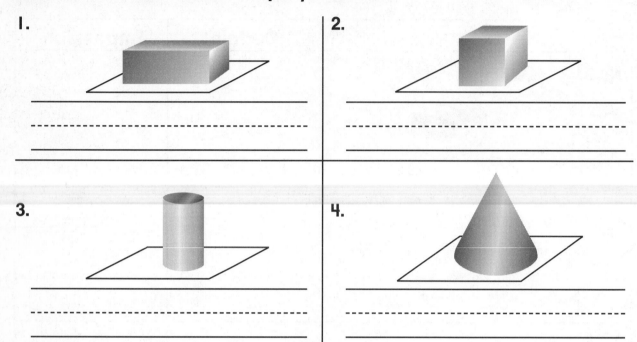

1.

_____
- - - - - - - - - - - - - - -
_____

2.

_____
- - - - - - - - - - - - - - -
_____

3.

_____
- - - - - - - - - - - - - - -
_____

4.

_____
- - - - - - - - - - - - - - -
_____

Sort and Identify Plane Shapes

**Use ◀▌red▐ to trace each side.
Use ◀▌blue▐ to circle each vertex.
Write how many sides and vertices there are.**

5.

____ sides

____ vertices

6.

____ sides

____ vertices

7.

____ sides

____ vertices

8.

____ sides

____ vertices

Name _____

Check What You Know

Solid Figures

Use solids.

1. Color each solid that will stack.

2. Color each solid that will roll.

3. Color each solid that will slide.

Sort Solid Figures by Attributes

Use solids. Circle the pictures that match the sentence.

4. These solids have 6 faces.

5. This solid has 5 vertices.

Check What You Know

Symmetry

Draw a line of symmetry to show two matching parts.

I.

2.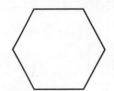

3.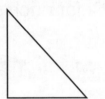

4.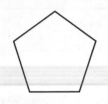

5.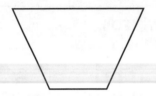

6.

Slides and Turns

Circle **slide** or **turn** to name the move.

7.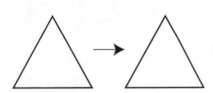

slide   turn

8.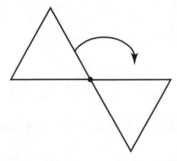

slide   turn

9.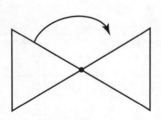

slide   turn

10.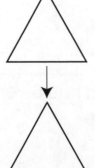

slide   turn

Name _____

Check What You Know

Describe and Extend Patterns

Find the pattern. Then color to continue it.

1.

2.

3.

4.

Pattern Units

Use the pictures. Circle the pattern unit.

5.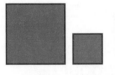

6.

7.

Check What You Know
Compare Length and Height
Circle the object to answer the question.

1. Which is longer?

2. Which is shorter?

3. Which is longest?

4. Which is longer?

Use Nonstandard Units

Circle the unit you would use to measure.
Then measure.

	Object	Unit	Measurement
5.			about _____
6.			about _____
7.			about _____

© Harcourt

Check What You Know

Use a Balance

About how many ⬭ does it take to balance?

Use real objects, a ⟍△⟋ , and ⬭.
Estimate. Then measure.

Object	Estimate.	Measure.
1.	about _____ ⬭	about _____ ⬭
2.	about _____ ⬭	about _____ ⬭

Pounds

Look at the object. Circle the better estimate.

Object	Estimate.
3.	about 1 pound about 10 pounds

Use Nonstandard Units to Measure Capacity

Use the real containers and a ⟍▱ .
Estimate. Then measure.

Container	Estimate	Measurement
4.	about _____ ⟍▱	about _____ ⟍▱
5.	about _____ ⟍▱	about _____ ⟍▱

© Harcourt

Check What You Know

Centimeters

Use real objects and a centimeter ruler.
Estimate. Then measure.

	Object	Estimate	Measurement
1.		about _____ centimeters	about _____ centimeters
2.		about _____ centimeters	about _____ centimeters

Kilograms

Circle the unit you would use to measure each object.

3.	4.	5.
 grams kilograms	 grams kilograms	 grams kilograms

Liters

Estimate whether the container holds less or more than a liter.
Then use a liter bottle to measure.

	Container	Estimate.	Measure.
6.		less than ⊟ more than ⊟	less than ⊟ more than ⊟
7.		less than ⊟ more than ⊟	less than ⊟ more than ⊟

Name _____

Check What You Know

Add 3 Numbers

Group the addends in two different ways.
Circle the addends you add first. Write the sum.

1. $7 + 5 + 3 =$ _____ $7 + 5 + 3 =$ _____

2. $5 + 5 + 2 =$ _____ $5 + 5 + 2 =$ _____

3. $9 + 8 + 1 =$ _____ $9 + 8 + 1 =$ _____

4. $4 + 3 + 5 =$ _____ $4 + 3 + 5 =$ _____

Write the sum.

5.	6.	7.	8.	9.	10.
6	4	2	4	6	8
3	5	2	3	6	1
+1	+4	+2	+6	+3	+3

11.	12.	13.	14.	15.	16.
1	7	5	1	3	8
4	3	2	2	3	2
+9	+5	+6	+3	+9	+7

17.	18.	19.	20.	21.	22.
5	9	7	3	1	6
5	8	2	4	1	4
+5	+1	+7	+5	+9	+6

Name _____

Check What You Know

Halves

Find the shapes that show halves. Color $\frac{1}{2}$.

1.

Fourths

Color one part. Circle the fraction.

2.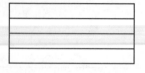

$\frac{1}{2}$ $\frac{1}{4}$

3.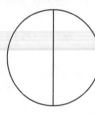

$\frac{1}{2}$ $\frac{1}{4}$

4.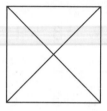

$\frac{1}{2}$ $\frac{1}{4}$

Thirds

Color one part. Circle the fraction.

5.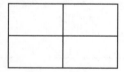

$\frac{1}{3}$ $\frac{1}{2}$ $\frac{1}{4}$

6.

$\frac{1}{3}$ $\frac{1}{2}$ $\frac{1}{4}$

7.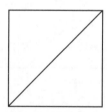

$\frac{1}{3}$ $\frac{1}{2}$ $\frac{1}{4}$

Parts of a Group

Color to show each fraction.

8. $\frac{1}{4}$

9. $\frac{1}{3}$

Name _____

Check What You Know

Tens

Write how many tens.
Then write how many ones.

1.

_____ tens = _____ ones

2.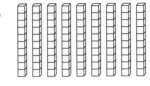

_____ tens = _____ ones

3.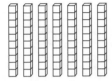

_____ tens = _____ ones

Tens and Ones to 100

Write how many tens and ones in three different ways.

4.

_____ tens _____ ones = _____

_____ + _____ = _____

_____

5.

_____ tens _____ ones = _____

_____ + _____ = _____

_____

Understand Place Value

Circle the value of the underlined digit.

6.	3<u>4</u> 4 or 40	7.	4<u>5</u> 5 or 50	8.	5<u>7</u> 7 or 70
9.	<u>8</u>0 8 or 80	10.	9<u>2</u> 2 or 20	11.	<u>9</u>1 9 or 90

Check What You Know

Compare Numbers: >, <, and =

Write greater than, less than, or equal to.
Then write >, <, or =.

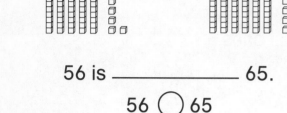

1.

56 is _____ 65.

56 ◯ 65

2.

41 is _____ 14.

41 ◯ 14

3. 24 is _____ 24.

24 ◯ 24

4. 35 is _____ 53.

35 ◯ 53

Order Numbers to 100

Write the missing numbers.

5. 16, 17, 18, _____, _____, 21, 22, _____, _____

6. 95, 94, 93, _____, 91, _____, 89, _____, _____

7. 72, 73, _____, 75, _____, 77, _____, 79, _____

8. 44, 43, 42, _____, _____, _____, _____, 37, 36

9. 35, 36, _____, _____, 39, 40, _____, _____, 43

10. 66, 65, 64, _____, _____, _____, 60, _____, 58

© Harcourt

Name _____

Check What You Know

Practice 2-Digit Addition

Add.

1. 46 +32	2. 18 +71	3. 11 +39	4. 95 + 4	5. 25 +29
6. 54 + 6	7. 16 +68	8. 40 + 2	9. 37 +24	10. 14 +83
11. 78 + 5	12. 55 +18	13. 53 +27	14. 44 + 8	15. 24 +67

Practice 2-Digit Subtraction

**Circle the problems in which you will need to regroup.
Then subtract.**

16. 64 −32	17. 50 − 1	18. 86 −28	19. 49 −18	20. 37 −15
21. 33 −30	22. 75 −48	23. 61 − 5	24. 98 −78	25. 42 −36
26. 94 −64	27. 54 − 2	28. 76 −27	29. 84 −56	30. 23 −21

© Harcourt

Check What You Know
Counting Equal Groups

Use ⬛. Draw them.
Write how many in all.

---

1. Make 3 groups.
Put 3 ⬛ in each group.

How many in all? _____

2. Make 5 groups.
Put 2 ⬛ in each group.

How many in all? _____

---

3. Make 2 groups.
Put 3 ⬛ in each group.

How many in all? _____

4. Make 4 groups.
Put 3 ⬛ in each group.

How many in all? _____

© Harcourt

Name _____

Check What You Know

Tens

Count by tens. Write the number.

1.
$\underline{5}$ tens $\underline{50}$ fifty

2.
$\underline{9}$ tens $\underline{90}$ ninety

3.
$\underline{10}$ tens $\underline{100}$ one hundred

Tens and Ones to 100

Write how many tens and ones. Write the number.

4. $\underline{4}$ tens $\underline{2}$ ones = $\underline{42}$

5. $\underline{6}$ tens $\underline{7}$ ones = $\underline{67}$

6. $\underline{8}$ tens $\underline{5}$ ones = $\underline{85}$

7. $\underline{7}$ tens $\underline{9}$ ones = $\underline{79}$

Name _____

Check What You Know

Even and Odd Numbers

Use ⬤ to show each number. Circle even or odd.

1.	1	even	(odd)	2.	2	(even)	odd
3.	3	even	(odd)	4.	4	(even)	odd
5.	5	even	(odd)	6.	6	(even)	odd
7.	7	even	(odd)	8.	8	(even)	odd

Skip Count by 2s, 5s, and 10s
Skip count. Write how many.

9. 2 $\underline{4}$ $\underline{6}$ $\underline{8}$ $\underline{10}$ $\underline{12}$ $\underline{14}$

10. 5 $\underline{10}$ $\underline{15}$ $\underline{20}$ $\underline{25}$ $\underline{30}$ $\underline{35}$

11. 10 $\underline{20}$ $\underline{30}$ $\underline{40}$ $\underline{50}$ $\underline{60}$ $\underline{70}$

Name _____

Check What You Know

Greater Than

Use ▭▭▭ ▫ to show each number.
Circle the greater number. Write the numbers.

1. 28 (36)
$\underline{36}$ is greater than $\underline{28}$
$\underline{36} > \underline{28}$

2. (41) 14
$\underline{41}$ is greater than $\underline{14}$
$\underline{41} > \underline{14}$

Less Than

Use ▭▭▭ ▫ to help.
Circle the number that is less. Write the numbers.

3. 52 (50)
$\underline{50}$ is less than $\underline{52}$
$\underline{50} < \underline{52}$

4. 86 (68)
$\underline{68}$ is less than $\underline{86}$
$\underline{68} < \underline{86}$

Use Symbols to Compare

Compare the numbers.
Use ▭▭▭ ▫ to show each number. Draw the ▭▭▭ ▫. Write <, >, or = in the box.

Check children's drawings.

5. 32 $\boxed{<}$ 35

6. 63 $\boxed{>}$ 36

Order on a Number Line

Write the missing number that is just before, between, or just after.

7. $\boxed{68}$ 69

8. 29 $\boxed{30}$ 31

Name _____

Check What You Know

Read Tally Tables

Favorite Fruit		Total
Apples	ЖН I	6
Grapes	ЖН IIII	9

Use the tally table to answer these questions.

1. How many children chose apples? $\underline{6}$

2. How many children chose grapes? $\underline{9}$

3. Which fruit did most children choose? $\underline{grapes}$

Make Bar Graphs

Color the bar graph to match the tally marks.

Favorite Snack		Total
Pretzels	ЖН	5
Popcorn	ЖН ЖН	10
Raisins	III	3

Use the graph to answer the questions.

4. How many children chose popcorn? $\underline{10}$

5. How many more children chose pretzels than raisins? $\underline{2}$

Favorite Snack

© Harcourt

Check What You Know
Count On to Add
Circle the greater number.
Use the number line. Count on to add.

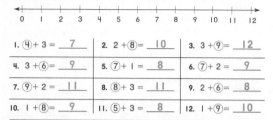

1. (4)+ 3 = __7__ | 2. 2 +(8)= __10__ | 3. 3 +(9)= __12__
4. 3 +(6)= __9__ | 5. (7)+ 1 = __8__ | 6. (7)+ 2 = __9__
7. (9)+ 2 = __11__ | 8. (8)+ 3 = __11__ | 9. 2 +(6)= __8__
10. 1 +(8)= __9__ | 11. (5)+ 3 = __8__ | 12. 1 +(9)= __10__

Doubles and Doubles Plus 1
Write the sum.

13. 4 + 4 = __8__ , so 4 + 5 = __9__

14. 0 + 0 = __0__ , so 0 + 1 = __1__

15. 5 + 5 = __10__ , so 5 + 6 = __11__

16. 3 + 3 = __6__ , so 3 + 4 = __7__

17. 2 + 2 = __4__ , so 2 + 3 = __5__

Check What You Know
Count Back to Subtract
Use the number line to count back. Write the difference.

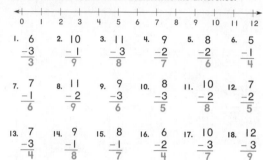

1. 6 −3 / 3 | 2. 10 −1 / 9 | 3. 11 −3 / 8 | 4. 9 −2 / 7 | 5. 8 −2 / 6 | 6. 5 −1 / 4
7. 7 −1 / 6 | 8. 11 −2 / 9 | 9. 9 −3 / 6 | 10. 8 −3 / 5 | 11. 10 −2 / 8 | 12. 7 −2 / 5
13. 7 −3 / 4 | 14. 9 −1 / 8 | 15. 8 −1 / 7 | 16. 6 −2 / 4 | 17. 10 −3 / 7 | 18. 12 −3 / 9

Relate Addition and Subtraction
Write each sum or difference.
Circle the related facts in each row.

19. (9 − 5 = __4__) | 9 − 6 = __3__ | (4 + 5 = __9__)
20. 4 + 4 = __8__ | (12 − 4 = __8__) | (8 + 4 = __12__)
21. (11 − 7 = __4__) | (4 + 7 = __11__) | 5 + 6 = __11__
22. (7 + 3 = __10__) | 5 + 5 = __10__ | (10 − 3 = __7__)

Check What You Know
Addition Facts to 18
Use a ten frame and ● to find the sum.

1. 4 +9 / 13 | 2. 8 +7 / 15 | 3. 2 +9 / 11 | 4. 9 +8 / 17 | 5. 4 +8 / 12
6. 6 +5 / 11 | 7. 8 +6 / 14 | 8. 7 +5 / 12 | 9. 6 +9 / 15 | 10. 5 +8 / 13

Mental Math to Add Tens
Add.

11. 60 +30 / 90 | 12. 50 +10 / 60 | 13. 20 +60 / 80 | 14. 40 +30 / 70 | 15. 20 +20 / 40
16. 30 +30 / 60 | 17. 20 +70 / 90 | 18. 20 +50 / 70 | 19. 10 +40 / 50 | 20. 30 +50 / 80

Add Tens and Ones
Use Workmat 3 and to add.
Write the sum.

21.
tens	ones
6	3
+	4
6	7

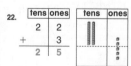

22.
tens	ones
2	2
+	3
2	5

Check What You Know
Regroup Ones as Tens
Use Workmat 3 and .

Show.	Add.	Do you need to regroup? Circle Yes or No.	How many tens and ones?
1. 46	5	(Yes) No	__5__ tens __1__ ones
2. 22	4	Yes (No)	__2__ tens __6__ ones
3. 19	8	(Yes) No	__2__ tens __7__ ones

Model 2-Digit Addition
Use Workmat 3 and . Add.

4.
tens	ones
1	
3	6
+ 1	5
5	1

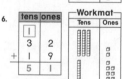

5.
tens	ones
1	
4	2
+ 3	8
8	0

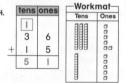

6.
tens	ones
1	
3	2
+ 1	9
5	1

7.
tens	ones
1	4
+ 2	4
3	8

Name _____

Check What You Know

Subtraction Facts to 18
Subtract.

1. 18 − 9 = 9
2. 8 − 7 = 1
3. 13 − 7 = 6
4. 14 − 5 = 9
5. 9 − 4 = 5

6. 16 − 7 = 9
7. 15 − 8 = 7
8. 7 − 5 = 2
9. 8 − 6 = 2
10. 17 − 9 = 8

Mental Math to Subtract Tens
Subtract.

11. 60 − 50 = 10
12. 80 − 60 = 20
13. 70 − 30 = 40
14. 50 − 30 = 20
15. 40 − 20 = 20

16. 90 − 60 = 30
17. 70 − 10 = 60
18. 80 − 40 = 40
19. 90 − 40 = 50
20. 60 − 30 = 30

Subtract Tens and Ones
Use Workmat 3 and ⊙ to subtract.
Write the difference.

21.

tens	ones
4	6
−	4
4	2

22.

tens	ones
3	9
−	3
3	6

Name _____

Check What You Know

Regroup Tens as Ones
Use Workmat 3 and ▭▭▭ ▱.

Show.	Subtract.	Do you need to regroup? Circle Yes or No.	How many tens and ones are left?
1. 57	9	(Yes) No	4 tens 8 ones
2. 35	4	Yes (No)	3 tens 1 ones
3. 22	7	(Yes) No	1 tens 5 ones

Model 2-Digit Subtraction
Use Workmat 3 and ▭▭▭ ▱.

4.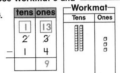

tens	ones
1	13
2	3
− 1	4
	9

5.

tens	ones
4	5
− 2	5
2	0

6.

tens	ones
3	5
− 1	4
2	1

7.

tens	ones
4	11
5	1
− 3	6
1	5

Name _____

Check What You Know

Add 2-Digit Numbers
Add. Regroup if you need to.

1.
tens	ones
1	
2	8
+ 4	7
7	5

2.
tens	ones
1	
3	7
+ 1	5
5	2

3.
tens	ones
6	5
+	4
6	9

4.
tens	ones
4	0
+ 5	6
9	6

5.
tens	ones
1	
1	6
+ 6	8
8	4

6.
tens	ones
1	
3	5
+ 3	5
7	0

7.
tens	ones
1	
1	5
+ 4	9
6	4

8.
tens	ones
1	
8	9
+	7
9	6

9.
tens	ones
7	3
+ 1	4
8	7

10.
tens	ones
1	
5	9
+ 3	2
9	1

Subtract 2-Digit Numbers
Subtract. Regroup if you need to.

11.
tens	ones
2	15
3	5
− 2	7
	8

12.
tens	ones
5	12
6	2
−	6
5	6

13.
tens	ones
2	4
− 1	3
1	1

14.
tens	ones
8	11
9	1
− 4	8
4	3

15.
tens	ones
6	17
7	7
− 5	9
1	8

16.
tens	ones
3	18
4	8
−	9
3	9

17.
tens	ones
7	10
8	0
− 4	7
3	3

18.
tens	ones
5	5
− 1	3
4	2

19.
tens	ones
2	6
− 2	4
	2

20.
tens	ones
8	13
9	3
− 7	6
1	7

Name _____

Check What You Know

Count Groups of Coins
Count. Write the amount.

1.

5 ¢, 10 ¢, 15 ¢, 16 ¢, 17 ¢, 18 ¢   18 ¢

Count Collections
Count. Write the amount.

2.    27 ¢

3.   45 ¢

Value of a Quarter
Count on from the quarter. Write the total amount.

4.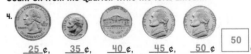

25 ¢, 35 ¢, 40 ¢, 45 ¢, 50 ¢   50 ¢

Value of Half Dollars and Dollars
Draw the coins. Write how many.

5. Show how many quarters equal a dollar.

4 quarters = 1 dollar

© Harcourt

Chapter 13

Name _____ ▶ **CHAPTER 13**

Check What You Know

Compare Values of Coins
Count each group of coins. Circle the amount that is greater.

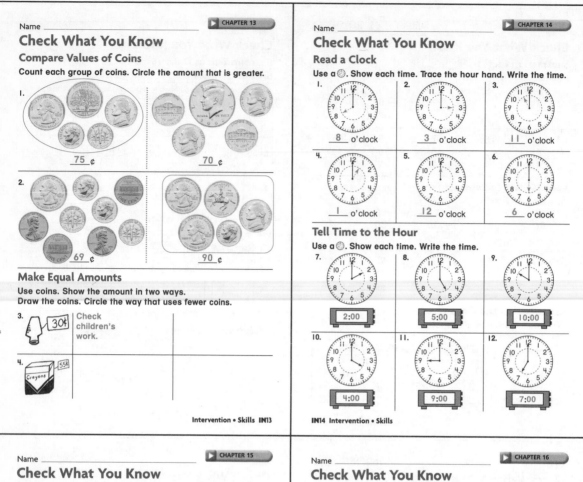

1. 75 ¢   70 ¢

2. 69 ¢   90 ¢

Make Equal Amounts
Use coins. Show the amount in two ways.
Draw the coins. Circle the way that uses fewer coins.

3. 30¢   Check children's work.

4. Crayons 55¢

Intervention • Skills **IN13**

Chapter 14

Name _____ ▶ **CHAPTER 14**

Check What You Know

Read a Clock
Use a ⊙. Show each time. Trace the hour hand. Write the time.

1. __8__ o'clock
2. __3__ o'clock
3. __11__ o'clock
4. __1__ o'clock
5. __12__ o'clock
6. __6__ o'clock

Tell Time to the Hour
Use a ⊙. Show each time. Write the time.

7. 2:00
8. 5:00
9. 10:00
10. 4:00
11. 9:00
12. 7:00

IN14 Intervention • Skills

Chapter 15

Name _____ ▶ **CHAPTER 15**

Check What You Know

Make Reasonable Estimates: One Minute
About how long would it take?
Circle your estimate. Then act it out to check.

1. read a book
(more than a minute)
less than a minute

2. write a letter
(more than a minute)
less than a minute

3. snap your fingers
more than a minute
(less than a minute)

Use a Calendar
Fill in the calendar for this month.
Use the calendar to answer the questions.
Check children's work.

Sunday	Monday	Tuesday	Wednesday	Thursday	Friday	Saturday

4. How many days are in the month? _____

5. What day of the week is the twenty-third? _____

6. What is the date of the third Tuesday? _____

7. What is the date of the first Monday? _____

Intervention • Skills **IN15**

Chapter 16

Name _____ ▶ **CHAPTER 16**

Check What You Know

Give and Follow Directions
Follow the directions in order.
Draw the path. Write the name.

1. Go left 4. Go down 3.
   Go right 2. Where are you?

   __park__

Interpret Data
Use the graph to answer the questions.

2. What is the least number of books that children read? __0__

3. What is the greatest number of books that children read? __4__

Use Data from a Bar Graph: Interpret Data
Use the bar graph to answer the question.

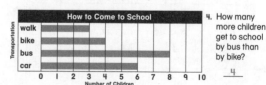

4. How many more children get to school by bus than by bike? __4__

IN16 Check What You Know

IN34 Intervention • Skills

© Harcourt

Name _____

Check What You Know
Certain or Impossible
Mark an X to tell if pulling the cube shown from the bowl is certain or impossible.

		Certain	Impossible
I.	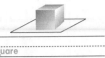	X	
2.	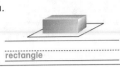	X	
3.	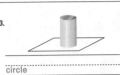		X
4.	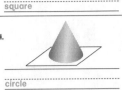	X	
5.			X

Name _____

Check What You Know
Plane Shapes on Solid Figures
Use solids. Trace around each one.
Write the name of the shape you drew.

1.
rectangle

2.
square

3.
circle

4.
circle

Sort and Identify Plane Shapes
Use [red] to trace each side.
Use [blue] to circle each vertex.
Write how many sides and vertices there are.

Check children's work.

5. _4_ sides
_4_ vertices

6. _3_ sides
_3_ vertices

7. _4_ sides
_4_ vertices

8. _6_ sides
_6_ vertices

Name _____

Check What You Know
Solid Figures
Use solids.

1. Color each solid that will stack.

2. Color each solid that will roll.

3. Color each solid that will slide.

Sort Solid Figures by Attributes
Use solids. Circle the pictures that match the sentence.

4. These solids have 6 faces.

5. This solid has 5 vertices.

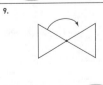

Name _____

Check What You Know
Symmetry
Draw a line of symmetry to show two matching parts. Possible answers are given for Exercises 1, 2, 4, and 6.

1.
2.
3.
4.
5.
6.

Slides and Turns
Circle **slide** or **turn** to name the move.

7.
(slide)   turn

8.
slide   (turn)

9.
slide   (turn)

10.
(slide)   turn

© Harcourt

Intervention • Skills **IN35**

Check What You Know (Chapter 21)

Describe and Extend Patterns

Find the pattern. Then color to continue it.

1. △ ▲ △ ▲ △ ▲ △ △   white black

2. ● ○ ● ● ○ ● ○ ○   gray white black

3. ⬡ ⬡ ⬡ ⬡ ⬡ ⬡ ⬡ ⬡   gray gray black

4. ▮ ▯ ▯ ▮ ▮ ▯ ▯ ▮   black white

Pattern Units

Use the pictures. Circle the pattern unit.

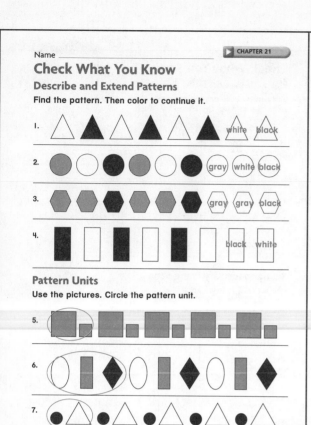

5.

6.

7.

Check What You Know (Chapter 22)

Compare Length and Height

Circle the object to answer the question.

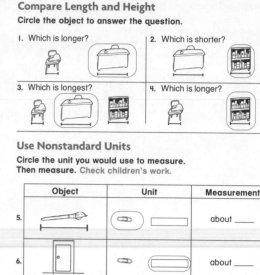

1. Which is longer?

2. Which is shorter?

3. Which is longest?

4. Which is longer?

Use Nonstandard Units

Circle the unit you would use to measure.
Then measure. Check children's work.

Object	Unit	Measurement
5.	⬭ ▭	about _____
6.	⬭ ▭	about _____
7.	⬭ ▭	about _____

Check What You Know (Chapter 23)

Use a Balance

About how many ⬭ does it take to balance?

Use real objects, a ⟁, and ⬭.
Estimate. Then measure. Check children's work.

Object	Estimate.	Measure.
1.	about ___ ⬭	about ___ ⬭
2.	about ___ ⬭	about ___ ⬭

Pounds

Look at the object. Circle the better estimate.

Object	Estimate.
3.	about 1 pound / (about 10 pounds)

Use Nonstandard Units to Measure Capacity

Use the real containers and a ⬕.
Estimate. Then measure. Check children's work.

Container	Estimate	Measurement
4.	about ___ ⬕	about ___ ⬕
5.	about ___ ⬕	about ___ ⬕

Check What You Know (Chapter 24)

Centimeters

Use real objects and a centimeter ruler.
Estimate. Then measure. Check children's work.

Object	Estimate	Measurement
1.	about ___ centimeters	about ___ centimeters
2.	about ___ centimeters	about ___ centimeters

Kilograms

Circle the unit you would use to measure each object.

3. grams (kilograms)
4. (grams) kilograms
5. (grams) kilograms

Liters

Estimate whether the container holds less or more than a liter.
Then use a liter bottle to measure. Estimates will vary.

Container	Estimate.	Measure.
6.	less than / more than	less than / (more than)
7.	less than / more than	(less than) / more than

© Harcourt

Name _____

Check What You Know
Add 3 Numbers

Group the addends in two different ways.
Circle the addends you add first. Write the sum.

Circled addends may vary.

1. ⑦ + 5 + ③ = __15__   7 + ⑤ + ③ = __15__

2. ⑤ + ⑤ + 2 = __12__   5 + ⑤ + ② = __12__

3. 9 + ⑧ + ① = __18__   ⑨ + ⑧ + 1 = __18__

4. 4 + ③ + ⑤ = __12__   ④ + 3 + ⑤ = __12__

Write the sum.

5.	6.	7.	8.	9.	10.
6	4	2	4	6	8
3	5	2	3	6	1
+1	+4	+2	+6	+3	+3
10	13	6	13	15	12

11.	12.	13.	14.	15.	16.
1	7	5	1	3	8
4	3	2	2	3	2
+9	+5	+6	+3	+9	+7
14	15	13	6	15	17

17.	18.	19.	20.	21.	22.
5	9	7	3	1	6
5	8	2	4	1	4
+5	+1	+7	+5	+9	+6
15	18	16	12	11	16

Name _____

Check What You Know
Halves

Check children's work.

Find the shapes that show halves. Color $\frac{1}{2}$.

1.

Fourths

Color one part. Circle the fraction.

2.   3.   4.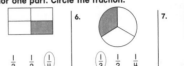

$\frac{1}{2}$ ④ $\frac{1}{4}$ ②$\frac{1}{2}$ $\frac{1}{4}$ $\frac{1}{2}$ ④$\frac{1}{4}$

Thirds

Color one part. Circle the fraction.

5.   6.   7.

$\frac{1}{3}$ $\frac{1}{2}$ ④$\frac{1}{4}$ ③$\frac{1}{3}$ $\frac{1}{2}$ $\frac{1}{4}$ $\frac{1}{3}$ ②$\frac{1}{2}$ $\frac{1}{4}$

Parts of a Group

Color to show each fraction. Check children's work.

8. $\frac{1}{4}$ 9. $\frac{1}{3}$

Name _____

Check What You Know
Tens

Write how many tens.
Then write how many ones.

1.   __4__ tens = __40__ ones

2.   __9__ tens = __90__ ones

3.   __7__ tens = __70__ ones

Tens and Ones to 100

Write how many tens and ones in three different ways.

4.   5.

__7__ tens __5__ ones = __75__   __4__ tens __8__ ones = __48__

__70__ + __5__ = __75__   __40__ + __8__ = __48__

__75__   __48__

Understand Place Value

Circle the value of the underlined digit.

6. 3̲4	7. 4̲5	8. 5̲7
④ or 40	⑤ or 50	⑦ or 70
9. 8̲0	10. 9̲2	11. 9̲1
8 or ⑧⓪	② or 20	9 or ⑨⓪

Name _____

Check What You Know
Compare Numbers: >, <, and =

Write greater than, less than, or equal to.
Then write >, <, or =.

1.   2.

56 is __less than__ 65.   41 is __greater than__ 14.

56 ⊂ 65   41 ⊃ 14

3. 24 is __equal to__ 24.   4. 35 is __less than__ 53.

24 ⊜ 24   35 ⊂ 53

Order Numbers to 100

Write the missing numbers.

5. 16, 17, 18, __19__, __20__, 21, 22, __23__, __24__

6. 95, 94, 93, __92__, 91, __90__, 89, __88__, __87__

7. 72, 73, __74__, 75, __76__, 77, __78__, 79, __80__

8. 44, 43, 42, __41__, __40__, __39__, __38__, 37, 36

9. 35, 36, __37__, __38__, 39, 40, __41__, __42__, 43

10. 66, 65, 64, __63__, __62__, __61__, 60, __59__, 58

Check What You Know

Practice 2-Digit Addition
Add.

1. 46 +32 78	2. 18 +71 89	3. 11 +39 50	4. 95 + 4 99	5. 25 +29 54
6. 54 + 6 60	7. 16 +68 84	8. 40 + 2 42	9. 37 +24 61	10. 14 +83 97
11. 78 + 5 83	12. 55 +18 73	13. 53 +27 80	14. 44 + 8 52	15. 24 +67 91

Practice 2-Digit Subtraction
Circle the problems in which you will need to regroup.
Then subtract.

16. 64 −32 32	17. ⁴10 50 − 1 49	18. ⁷16 86 −28 58	19. 49 −18 31	20. 37 −15 22
21. 33 −30 3	22. ⁶15 75 −48 27	23. ⁵11 61 − 5 56	24. 98 −78 20	25. ³12 42 −36 6
26. 94 −64 30	27. 54 − 2 52	28. ⁶16 76 −27 49	29. ⁷14 84 −56 28	30. 23 −21 2

Check What You Know

Counting Equal Groups
Use ⬛. Draw them.
Write how many in all.

1. Make 3 groups. Put 3 ⬛ in each group. Children will draw 3 groups of 3 squares. How many in all? ___9___	2. Make 5 groups. Put 2 ⬛ in each group. Children will draw 5 groups of 2 squares. How many in all? ___10___
3. Make 2 groups. Put 3 ⬛ in each group. Children will draw 2 groups of 3 squares. How many in all? ___6___	4. Make 4 groups. Put 3 ⬛ in each group. Children will draw 4 groups of 3 squares. How many in all? ___12___

Number Sense, Concepts, and Operations

Number Sense and Place Value

Skill 1

Exploring Tens

Using Skill 1

OBJECTIVE Use models to make groups of 10; count by tens; write multiples of 10

Have children point to the title of the lesson. Read it aloud.

Distribute the connecting cubes to groups of children.

Say: **Count out 10 cubes. Connect them to make 1 train.**

Ask: **How many cubes did you use?** (10) **How many trains of ten did you make?** (1)

Read Step 1 together.
Ask: **How many tens are you supposed to make?** (2) Have the children point to each cube in Step 1 as they count aloud. Explain that each train has 10 cubes or 10 ones.

Say: **Look at Step 2. How many trains of ten do you see?** (2) Have children trace the dotted 2 on the answer line.

Have the children look at Step 3. Ask: **How many ones were used to make 1 train?** (10) Say: **Since there are 2 trains of ten, let's count by tens–10, 20.** Ask: **How do you read the number that has 2 tens?** (twenty) Have children point to the number word. Ask: **How do you write the number twenty?** (20) Have children trace over the dotted 20 in Step 3.

TRY THESE These exercises give children practice putting objects into groups of ten so they can count by tens to find how many. They will also prepare children for the work they will encounter in the **Practice on Your Own** section. Encourage children to summarize each exercise with a sentence frame.

MATERIALS connecting cubes

- **Exercise 1**   <u>3</u> groups of 10 make <u>3</u> tens. <u>3</u> tens = <u>30</u>.

- **Exercise 2**   <u>4</u> groups of 10 make <u>4</u> tens. <u>4</u> tens = <u>40</u>.

PRACTICE ON YOUR OWN Review the example at the top of the page. As children work, encourage them to summarize each step using the sentence frame: <u>5</u> groups of 10 make <u>5</u> tens. <u>5</u> tens = <u>50</u>.

QUIZ Determine if children can make groups of 10, count by tens, and write the number. Success is indicated by 1 out of 1 correct responses. Children who successfully complete **Practice on Your Own** and **Quiz** are ready to move to the next skill.

COMMON ERRORS

- Children may not be able to count accurately to 10.

- Children may not make the connection between counting tens and writing the number.

Children who made more than 1 error in the **Practice on Your Own**, or who were not successful in the **Quiz** section, may benefit from the **Alternative Teaching Strategy** on the next page.

Alternative Teaching Strategy

10 Minutes

OBJECTIVE Identify groups that show 10; count, read, and write by tens.

MATERIALS connecting cubes, digit cards 1–9

Display 10 single connecting cubes in a row.

Say: **Help me count my cubes.** Point to each cube and count in chorus: 1, 2, 3, 4, 5, 6, 7, 8, 9, 10.

Now connect the cubes. As you connect each one, lead another counting chorus. Ask: **How many cubes did we use?** (10) **How many groups of 10 did we make?** (1)

Distribute the connecting cubes.

Direct each child to make an additional 10-cube train and continue as a whole class. Have individual children bring their trains to the front of the class. Lay each train against the original one to check that children have counted correctly.

As each child contributes his or her train, ask: **How many groups of 10 do we have now?** (2 or 3 or 4 and so on) **How many cubes did we use altogether to make this many groups of 10?** (20 or 30 or 40 and so on)

Display all the groups of 10. As you point to each train, have children count by 10s to discover how many cubes you used in all.

Have children work in pairs. Have a volunteer draw a digit card at random, for example 5. Have the volunteer instruct the class using this sentence frame: "Show me 5 groups of 10."

Have children work in pairs to build that number of groups of 10. As they connect the cubes, have them lay the trains side-by-side to be sure that each train has exactly 10 cubes.

As children finish, check the work of each pair.

Say: **I'm looking for 5 groups of 10. I see 5 groups of ten. Please count by tens.**

Have children count orally as you point to each group of 10 cubes. (10, 20, 30, 40, 50)

Ask: **How many cubes did you use in all?** (50)

Be sure to check the work of each pair of children and ask each pair the question.

Repeat as time allows with other digit cards.

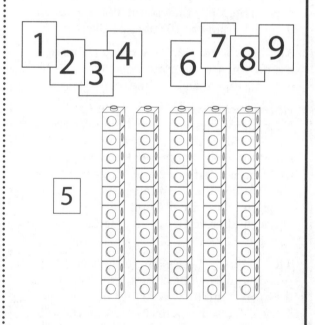

© Harcourt

Grade 2
Skill

1

Exploring Tens

Use  to make tens. Draw the tens. Count by tens. Write the number.

Step 1
Make 2 tens.

Think:
10 ones = 1 ten

☐☐☐☐☐☐☐☐☐☐

Step 2

How many tens are there?

☐☐☐☐☐☐☐☐☐☐

2 ___ tens

Step 3
Count by tens.
Write the number.

Think:
2 groups of 10 make
☐☐☐☐☐☐☐☐☐☐ *2 tens*
☐☐☐☐☐☐☐☐☐☐ *2 tens = 20*

20
2 ___ tens = _____
twenty

Try These

Use  to make tens. Count by tens. Write the number.

1 Make 3 tens.

☐☐☐☐☐☐☐☐☐☐
☐☐☐☐☐☐☐☐☐☐
☐☐☐☐☐☐☐☐☐☐

30
3 ___ tens = _____
thirty

2 Make 4 tens.

☐☐☐☐☐☐☐☐☐☐
☐☐☐☐☐☐☐☐☐☐
☐☐☐☐☐☐☐☐☐☐
☐☐☐☐☐☐☐☐☐☐

___ tens = _____
forty

Go to the next side. →

Practice on Your Own

Use **to make tens. Draw the tens. Count by tens.**
Write the number.

Make 5 tens.

_____5_____ tens   =   ___50___
                                      fifty

Use **to make tens. Draw the tens. Count by tens.**
Write the number.

1 Make 6 tens.

_____6_____ tens   =   ___60___
                                      sixty

2 Make 8 tens.

_____ tens   =   _____
                                      eighty

3 Make 9 tens.

_____ tens   =   _____
                                      ninety

▶ **Quiz**

Use **to make tens. Draw the tens. Count by tens.**
Write the number.

4 Make 7 tens.

_____ tens   =   _____
                                      seventy

© Harcourt

15 Minutes

Using Skill 2

OBJECTIVE Identify tens and ones and write numbers to 100

MATERIALS base-ten blocks (2 tens, 4 ones) for each child

You may wish to have children use base-ten blocks to model the example. Recall with children that 10 ones blocks equal 1 ten rod.

Example
In Step 1, have children look at the tens blocks. Ask: **How many tens blocks do you see?** (2)

How many tens do you write? (2 tens)

Have children model the tens.

In Step 2, have children look at the ones blocks. Ask: **How many ones blocks do you see?** (4) **How many ones do you write?** (4 ones)

Have children model the ones.

In Step 3, discuss what the model shows. You have 2 tens and 4 ones.

Continue with these questions: **How many tens do you have?** (2 tens) **How many ones?** (4 ones) **What number can you write for 2 tens 4 ones?** (24)

TRY THESE These exercises prepare children for identifying tens and ones and writing 2-digit numbers to 100 they will encounter on the **Practice on Your Own** page.

- **Exercise 1** Identify tens and ones and write 23.

- **Exercise 2** Identify tens and ones and write 31.

- **Exercise 3** Identify tens and ones and write 44.

PRACTICE ON YOUR OWN You may wish to review the example at the top of the page. Exercises 1–6 provide practice with identifying tens and ones and writing 2-digit numbers to 100 using pictorial models.

QUIZ Determine if children can identify tens and ones and write 2-digit numbers to 100. Success is indicated by 2 out of 3 correct responses.

Children who successfully complete **Practice on Your Own** and **Quiz** are ready to move to the next skill.

COMMON ERRORS

- Children may reverse the tens and ones digits when writing 2-digit numbers.

- Children may have difficulty counting by tens and ones and recording the tens and ones in numbers greater than 50.

If a child makes an error in more than 2 exercises on the **Practice on Your Own**, or is not successful on the **Quiz** section, you may wish to have the child model the problems with you using base-ten blocks. Encourage the child to model the tens first, before modeling the ones. You may wish to review the concepts with numbers between, 11–15. The child may also benefit from the **Alternative Teaching Strategy** on the next page.

15 Minutes

Alternative Teaching Strategy

OBJECTIVE Use base-ten blocks to identify tens and ones

MATERIALS index cards, base-ten blocks (5 tens, 9 ones) for each pair

Have children work with a partner. Distribute index cards and base-ten blocks to each pair. Have one child fold an index card in half. Call out a number between 11 and 19 and ask the child to write the numeral on the left side of the index card.

Next, have the partner model the number with base-ten blocks. Tell partners to write their number as tens and ones on the right half of the index card.

When partners have filled in both sides of the index card, have them read the number and the tens and ones on their card.

Repeat the activity calling out numbers between 20 and 29, then with numbers through 50.

As children demonstrate understanding, continue with numbers through 100. Have partners exchange roles for every other number.

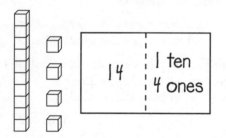

© Harcourt

Exploring Tens and Ones to 100

Grade 2 Skill 2

Remember: ten ones = 10

Write how many tens and ones.

Write how many tens.

Write how many ones.

Write the number.

|2| tens

2 tens |4| ones

2 tens 4 ones = 24

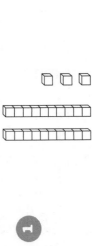

Try These

Write how many tens and ones. Write the number.

1 |2| tens |3| ones = 23

2 ⬜ tens ⬜ ones = ⬜

3 ⬜ tens ⬜ ones = ⬜

Go to the next side.

Practice on Your Own   Skill 2

Write how many tens and ones. Write the number.

 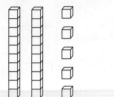   

| 5 | tens | 4 | ones | = | 54 |

Write how many tens and ones. Write the number.

1   **2**   **3**

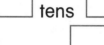

2	tens	5	ones

= 25

☐ tens ☐ ones

= ☐

☐ tens ☐ ones

= ☐

Write the number.

4   **5**   **6**

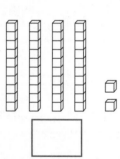

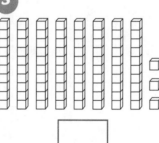

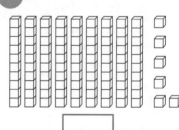

☐   ☐   ☐

▶ **Quiz**

Write the number.

7 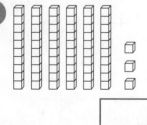   **8** 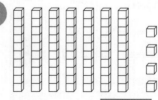   **9**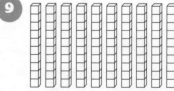

☐   ☐   ☐

Using Skill 3

OBJECTIVE Identify even and odd numbers

MATERIALS for each child:
15 connecting cubes

Review the meaning of a *pair*. Then distribute 15 connecting cubes to each child. Write 6 on the board.

Say: **Count out 6 individual cubes. Make as many pairs as you can.** Give children time to complete the task.

Ask: **How many pairs are you able to make?** (3) **Do you have any cubes left over?** (no) **What does this tell you about the number 6?** (It is an even number.) Write *even* below the number 6. Place pairs of cubes aside.

Write 7 on the board. Say: **Now count out 7 individual cubes. Make as many pairs as you can.** Give children time to complete the task.

Ask: **How many pairs are you able to make?** (3) **Do you have any cubes left over?** (yes, 1) **What does having one cube left over tell you about the number 7?** (It is an odd number.) Write *odd* below the number 7.

Say: **Now take all your cubes apart. Choose a number between 1 and 15. Count out that many cubes and make pairs.**

Ask: **Is your number even or odd? How do you know?** (Possible answers: The number is even because I made pairs with no left over cubes; the number is odd because I made pairs with 1 cube left over.)

TRY THESE In Exercises 1–3 children model and identify even and odd numbers.

- **Exercises 1–3** Children use cubes to show each number, pair them up, and circle even or odd.

PRACTICE ON YOUR OWN Review the chart with children. Encourage them to explain how they know that 4 is an even number and 5 is an odd number. Guide them to recognize and identify the patterns they see. Have them complete the pattern on the chart. Exercises 1–8 give children practice determining whether numbers are even or odd.

QUIZ Determine if children can identify even and odd numbers. Success is indicated by 3 out of 4 correct responses.

Children who successfully complete **Practice on Your Own** and **Quiz** are ready to move to the next skill.

COMMON ERRORS

- Children may confuse the terms *even* and *odd*.

- Children may forget to make pairs or connect more than 2 cubes per pair.

Children who made more than 2 errors in **Practice on Your Own**, or who were not successful in the **Quiz** section, may benefit from the **Alternative Teaching Strategy** on the next page.

© Harcourt

Alternative Teaching Strategy

OBJECTIVE Model and identify even and odd numbers

MATERIALS for each child: 1 set of 10 index cards with random numbers from 1–20 and dots depicting the number on one side and the words *even, odd* on the other side; marker

For each child, prepare and distribute a set of 10 index cards on which there is a written number from 1–20 and a representative number of dots. Have the children place the cards face down in front of them.

Say: **Choose a card.**

Say: **Read the number and count the dots on the card. Then circle as many pairs of dots as you can and decide if the number is odd or even.** Remind children that two dots make up a pair. Give children time to complete the task.

Say: **Hold your number up if you have a dot left over?** (Answers will vary.)

Ask: **When you make pairs and have 1 dot left over, what is the number?** (odd)

Say: **Hold your number up if you have pairs with no dots left over.**

Ask: **When you make pairs and have no dots left over, what is the number?** (even)

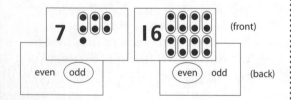

Repeat this process with the rest of your cards. Be sure to circle even or odd on the back of the card.

Say: **Now sort your cards into two piles— even and odd.** Give children time to complete the task. Observe as they work and offer assistance as necessary.

Say: **After you sort the cards into two groups, look at the stack of even numbers.** Ask: **What pattern do you see?** (All of the numbers show a 0, 2, 4, 6, or 8 in the ones place.)

Say: **Look at the stack of odd numbers.** Ask: **What pattern do you see?** (All of the numbers show a 1, 3, 5, 7, or 9 in the ones place.)

For more practice, you can have the children pair up and use the cards as flashcards. Have one child flash the number side of the card with the paired up dots or in some cases, with a left over dot. The other child should say whether the number and pattern they see indicates an even number or an odd number. The other child should provide feedback. If the answer is correct, they can keep the card, if it is incorrect, the child places it in the back of the stack. Keep playing until all ten cards are gone.

Continue play until both partners have had a turn.

© Harcourt

Grade 2
Skill
3

Even and Odd Numbers

What pattern can you find in even and odd numbers?

Think: An **even** number of objects can be grouped into pairs.

_9_

Think: An **odd** number of objects has one left over.

_7_

Try These

Use ☐ to show each number.
Circle *even* or *odd*.

1 5   even   (odd)

2 9   even   odd

3 8   even   odd

Go to the next side.

Practice on Your Own

Color to continue the pattern.

1	2	3	4	5	6	7	8	9	10
11	12	13	14	15	16	17	18	19	20
21	22	23	24	25	26	27	28	29	30
31	32	33	34	35	36	37	38	39	40
41	42	43	44	45	46	47	48	49	50

What pattern can you find in even and odd numbers?
Write *even* or *odd*.
You can use ◻ to help.

1 Are the numbers in gray shaded boxes even or odd?

(even)　odd

2 Are the numbers in white boxes even or odd?

even　odd

3 15　even　odd

4 16　even　odd

5 20　even　odd

6 17　even　odd

7 19　even　odd

8 22　even　odd

▶ Quiz

What pattern can you find in even and odd numbers?
Use ◻ to show each number.
Circle *even* or *odd*.

9 18　even　odd

10 13　even　odd

11 21　even　odd

12 14　even　odd

20 Minutes

Using Skill 4

OBJECTIVE Skip count by 2's, 5's, and 10's on a hundred chart

MATERIALS 40 classroom objects (such as crayons); hundred chart (transparency with overhead projector) or chart paper; marker, crayon

Display 4 groups of 10 crayons (or other classroom objects). Have children observe the arrangement of the objects. Ask: **How are these objects arranged?** (in 4 groups of 10)

Ask: **How can this arrangement help you count them better?** (You can count by tens instead of counting one-by-one.)

Say: **Let's count the crayons by tens—10, 20, 30, 40. So, there are 40 crayons in all or 4 groups of 10 crayons.**

Display a hundred chart on the overhead or on chart paper. Ask children to count by tens again. Have a volunteer use a marker to cross out the numbers as the class counts them aloud.

Ask: **What pattern do you see?** (Possible answer: All of the crossed out numbers end with 0.)

Now take the crayons and make 8 groups of 5. Have children observe this new arrangement. Ask: **How can this arrangement help you count them better?** (Now you can count by fives.)

Say: **Let's count the crayons by fives—5, 10, 15, 20, 25, 30, 35, 40. So, there are 40 crayons in all or 8 groups of 5 crayons.**

Direct children's attention back to the hundred chart. Ask them to count by fives again. Have a volunteer circle the numbers as the class counts them aloud.

Ask: **What pattern do you see?** (Possible answer: all of the circled numbers end in 5 or 0)

TRY THESE In Exercises 1–2 children practice skip counting by tens and fives using a hundred chart.

- **Exercise 1**   Skip count by tens and cross out the numbers you say.

- **Exercise 2**   Skip count by fives and circle the numbers you say.

PRACTICE ON YOUR OWN Have children study the hundred chart. Encourage them to conclude that all of the even numbers are missing. Have children fill in the missing numbers. Exercises 1–2 provide practice skip counting by twos and finding patterns.

QUIZ Determine if children can skip count by tens, fives and twos. Success is indicated by 3 out of 4 correct responses.

Children who successfully complete **Practice on Your Own** and **Quiz** are ready to move on to the next skill.

COMMON ERRORS

- Children may forget to count every other number when skip counting by twos.

- Children may forget to use the patterns for skip counting by fives and tens.

Children who made an error in the **Practice on Your Own,** or who were not successful in the **Quiz** section may also benefit from the **Alternative Teaching Strategy** on the next page.

© Harcourt

Alternative Teaching Strategy

15 Minutes

OBJECTIVE Model skip counting by twos, fives, and tens

MATERIALS for each pair: 50 connecting cubes; hundred chart; crayon or marker

Have children form pairs. Provide each pair with 50 connecting cubes and a hundred chart. Instruct children to make pairs with their 50 connecting cubes. Have one child hold up their model of a pair so children can see that a pair equals 2.

After all of the cubes have been paired, ask the children to push them aside and place one pair in front of them.

Ask: **How many cubes are in front of you?** (2) Say: **Shade the box with the number 2 in it on your hundred chart.**

Have the children place a second pair of cubes next to their first pair.

Ask: **What is the best way to count the number of cubes in front of you?** (by twos)

Say: **Let's count the cubes by twos–2, 4. Shade the box with the number 4 in it on the hundred chart.** Have partners take turns adding another pair of cubes to the count. After each new pair has been added, have them count by twos together (from the beginning) until they reach 50. Instruct them to shade each box with the number they say on the hundred chart.

Say: **After you count by twos to 50 and shade the boxes of these numbers on your hundred chart, look for a pattern.**

When groups finish counting by twos, have them share their responses with the class.

Ask: **What patterns can you find?** (Possible answers: All of the numbers are even. All of the numbers end in 2, 4, 6, 8, or 0.)

Ask: **Which number box did you shade in last?** (50) **Following the pattern, what number would you shade in next?** (52) **after that?** (54)

Using the 50 connecting cubes, have the pairs follow the same process to demonstrate skip counting by tens and fives. When counting by tens, have children cross out the numbers, when counting by fives, have them circle the numbers.

After each skip count, focus children's attention on finding patterns. Discuss their findings with the class.

Encourage children to continue counting by twos, fives and tens from 50–100 in the same way.

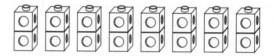

1	2	3	4	5	6	7	8	9	10
11	12	13	14	15	16	17	18	19	20
21	22	23	24	25	26	27	28	29	30
31	32	33	34	35	36	37	38	39	40
41	42	43	44	45	46	47	48	49	50
51	52	53	54	55	56	57	58	59	60
61	62	63	64	65	66	67	68	69	70
71	72	73	74	75	76	77	78	79	80
81	82	83	84	85	86	87	88	89	90
91	92	93	94	95	96	97	98	99	100

© Harcourt

Skip Count by 2's, 5's, and 10's on a Hundred Chart

Grade 2 **Skill** 4

1	2	3	4	5	6	7	8	9	~~10~~
11	12	13	14	15	16	17	18	19	~~20~~
21	22	23	24	25	26	27	28	29	~~30~~
31	32	33	34	35	36	37	38	39	~~40~~
41	42	43	44	45	46	47	48	49	~~50~~
51	52	53	54	55	56	57	58	59	60
61	62	63	64	65	66	67	68	69	70
71	72	73	74	75	76	77	78	79	80
81	82	83	84	85	86	87	88	89	90
91	92	93	94	95	96	97	98	99	100

Write the missing numbers.

Look at the tens. What pattern do you see?

The tens all have a 0 in the ones place.

Look at the fives. What pattern do you see?

The fives have a 5 or a 0 in the ones place.

Try These

1 Count by tens.
   Cross out the numbers you say.

2 Count by fives.
   Circle the numbers you say.

 Go to the next side.

Practice on Your Own

Skill 4

Write the missing numbers.

1	2	3	4	5	6	7	8	9	10
11	12	13	14	15	16	17	18	19	20
21	22	23	24	25	26	27	28	29	30
31	32	33	34	35	36	37	38	39	40
41	42	43	44	45	46	47	48	49	50
51	52	53	54	55	56	57	58	59	60
61	62	63	64	65	66	67	68	69	70
71	72	73	74	75	76	77	78	79	80
81	82	83	84	85	86	87	88	89	90
91	92	93	94	95	96	97	98	99	100

Skip count by twos. Use the hundred chart.

1 Count by twos.
Start at 2. Count to 20.

Use ✏ to shade the boxes of the numbers you say.

2 Count by twos.
Start at 82. Count to 100.

Use ✏ to shade the boxes of the numbers you say.

▶ Quiz

Skip count by tens, fives, and twos. Use the hundred chart.

3 Count by tens.
Start at 30. Count to 80.
Cross out the numbers you say.

4 Count by fives.
Start at 35. Count to 70.
Circle the numbers you say.

5 Count by twos.
Start at 42. Count to 56.

Use ✏ to shade the boxes of the numbers you say.

6 Count by twos.
Start at 22. Count to 38.

Use ✏ to shade the boxes of the numbers you say.

Using Skill 5

OBJECTIVE Find the number that comes *just before, between,* or *just after* given numbers

MATERIALS number line

Draw a number line from 20 to 30 on the board to model the example. Have children touch each number on the number line as they say the numbers aloud. Focus children's attention on the number line on the page.

Point to the number 25 on the number line. Ask: **What number comes *just before* 25?** (24) Point out that 24 is one less than 25 so it is just before 25. Have children write 24 in the box.

Point to the number 25 again. Ask: **What number comes just after 25?** (26) Point out that 26 is one more than 25 so it is just after 25. Have children write 26 in the box.

Then point to the numbers 24 and 26. Ask: **What number is *between* 24 and 26?** (25)

Guide children to follow the number line. Say: **25 is between 24 and 26. So 25 is one more than 24 and one less than 26.**

TRY THESE Exercises 1–2 give children practice in writing the number that is *just before, between,* or *just after,* to prepare them for the exercises in the **Practice on Your Own** section.

• **Exercise 1**   Write the number that is *just before.*

• **Exercise 2**   Write the number that is *between.*

PRACTICE ON YOUR OWN Review the example at the top of the page. In Exercises 1–4, children use a number line to identify numbers that are *just before, between,* and *just after* given numbers.

Have children recall the meaning of *just before, between,* and *just after.*

QUIZ Determine if children can correctly identify a number that comes *just before, between,* or *just after* a given number. Success is indicated by 3 out of 4 correct responses.

Children who successfully complete **Practice on Your Own** and **Quiz** are ready to move to the next skill.

COMMON ERRORS

• Children may confuse the terms *just before, between,* and *just after.*

• Children may have difficulty counting beyond 20.

If a child makes more than 1 error in the **Practice on Your Own** section, have the child redo the exercises while you observe. Determine if the child confuses the vocabulary terms or has difficulty counting beyond 20. The child may also benefit from the **Alternative Teaching Strategy** on the next page.

© Harcourt

Alternative Teaching Strategy

OBJECTIVE Use numeral cards to find numbers that are *just before*, *between*, and *just after*

Before working with the number line, have children complete a short activity with numeral cards.

Choose 3 cards, for example 7, 8, and 9. Mix them up and have the children put them in counting order.

As children are working, confirm their decisions. Say: **I see that you put 7** *before* **8. Then you put 9** *after* **8. Now I can see that 8 is** *between* **7 and 9.**

8	9	7
7	8	9

Repeat with other sets of 3 numbers until children are proficient in the concept of ordering with numeral cards. Then focus children's attention on the number line.

MATERIALS for each child: numeral cards 1–20, number line 0–20, paper for recording

Choose a numeral card, for example the number 18. Prompt children to point to the number 18 on the number line. While a child is touching the number 18, ask:

What number is *just before* **18?** (17)

What number is *just after* **18?** (19)

So, 18 is *between* **what two numbers?** (17 and 19)

Direct children to write the numbers in order on their recording sheet.

Have children repeat the activity. As children gain proficiency, have them work independently.

© Harcourt

IN58 Intervention • Skills

Grade 2
Skill 5

© Harcourt

Order on a Number Line

Write the missing number that is just before, between, or just after.

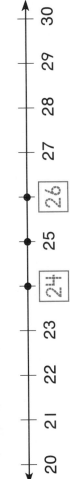

20 21 22 23 [24] 25 [26] 27 28 29 30

24 is just **before** 25.

25 is **between** 24 and 26.

26 is just **after** 25.

Try These

Write the missing number that is just before, between, or just after.

1

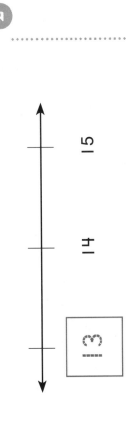

[3]   14   15

2

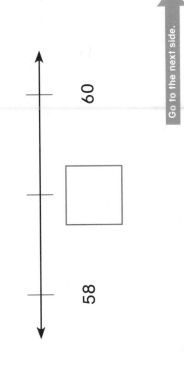

58   [   ]   60

Go to the next side.

Practice on Your Own

Skill 5

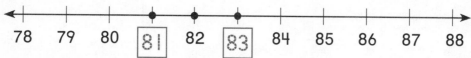

78 79 80 [81] 82 [83] 84 85 86 87 88

81 is just **before** 82. 82 is **between** 81 and 83. 83 is just **after** 82.

Write the missing number that is just before, between, or just after.

1

42 [43] 44

2

76 77 [ ]

3

[ ] 11 12

4

39 [ ] 41

▶ **Quiz**

Write the missing number that is just before, between, or just after.

5

[ ] 92 93

6

79 80 [ ]

7

75 76 [ ]

8

[ ] 24 25

© Harcourt

Using Skill 6

OBJECTIVE Identify and count groups of ten and the equivalent number of ones

Distribute 2 ten-frames, 20 beans, 2 tens rods, and 20 ones to each child. Have children use the materials to model the examples.

Say: **Count the squares in one ten-frame.**
Ask: **How many squares are there?** (10)
What number do you count by when using a ten-frame? (10)

Say: **Place 1 bean in each square.**
Ask: **How many ones (beans) did you use to make 1 ten?** (10) **How many groups of ten did you make?** (1)
Say: **You just showed that 1 ten equals 10 ones.**

Ask: **In what other way can you show 1 ten?** (with a rod) **How do you know?** (1 rod has 10 ones)

Have children count the ones in the rod and use the ones blocks to show that 1 ten equals 10 ones.

Ask: **What number can you count by when you use rods?** (10)

Follow a similar procedure to model 2 tens equal 20 ones. First have children place beans in two ten-frames.

Ask: **How many tens are there?** (2)
Say: **You know that 1 ten equals 10 ones, so what do 2 tens equal?** (2 tens equal 20 ones) Have children count aloud by tens and ones.

Say: **Using your rods, show 2 tens.**
Ask: **How many tens are there?** (2) **How many ones are there?** (20) Have children count by tens or by ones to show how they know that 2 tens equal 20 ones.

MATERIALS ten-frames, beans, and base-ten blocks (tens and ones)

TRY THESE These exercises help children count groups of ten and then write the equivalent number of ones.

- **Exercise 1**   Count 3 groups of ten.
- **Exercise 2**   Count 6 groups of ten.
- **Exercise 3**   Count 5 groups of ten.

PRACTICE ON YOUR OWN Review the examples at the top of the page. In Exercises 1–4 children write the number of tens and the equivalent number of ones.

QUIZ Determine if children can identify and count tens and write the equivalent number of ones. Success is indicated by 2 out of 2 correct responses.

Children who successfully complete **Practice on Your Own** and **Quiz** are ready to move to the next skill.

COMMON ERRORS

- Children may not make the connection between counting the number of tens and writing the number of ones they represent.

- Children may forget that 1 ten equals 10 ones.

If a child makes more than 1 error in the **Practice on Your Own**, or was not successful in the **Quiz** section, work through an exercise together. Ask the child to count the blocks in one rod (10) and then to count by 10s to determine how many ones equal the total number of tens in the exercise. The child may benefit from the **Alternative Teaching Strategy** on the next page.

Alternative Teaching Strategy

OBJECTIVE Model groups of tens and identify the equivalent number of ones

Distribute the connecting cube trains to children.

Say: **Look carefully at your cube train. You can say it is 1 group of ten, or 1 ten.**
Ask: **Why do you think this is so?** (It is made of 10 cubes.) Have children take the cubes apart and count them.

Say: **You can say that 1 ten equals 10 ones.**

Write *1 ten = 10 ones* on the board.

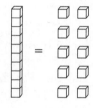

Say: **Now put the cubes together again.**
Ask: **How many tens do you each have?** (1 ten). **How many ones are in 1 ten?** (10)

Have two children stand together, each holding up a cube train.
Ask: **How many tens are there now?** (2 tens)

Have children count the number of ones in the two trains.
Ask: **How many ones are there?** (20)

Write *2 ten = 20 ones* on the board.

Say: **You can count by ones, or you can count by 10s.**
Ask: **Why can you count by 10s?** (There are 10 ones in 1 ten.)

MATERIALS one connecting cube train of 10 cubes for each child

Provide sentence frames on the board that say:

_____ tens = _____ ones

Repeat the activity as time allows, calling on children to display 3 to 10 tens trains at a time. Ask the children to determine how many tens and how many ones each set of tens equals. Have volunteers take turns recording the numbers to complete the sentences for everyone to read aloud.

Tens

© Harcourt

1 ten = 10 ones

2 tens = 20 ones

Try These

Write how many tens. Then write how many ones.

1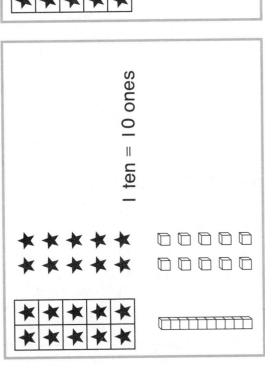

3 — tens = 30 — ones

2

—— tens = —— ones

3

—— tens = —— ones

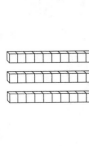

Go to the next side.

Practice on Your Own

Write how many tens. Then write how many ones.

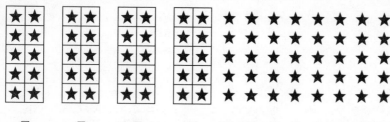

___4___ tens = ___40___ ones

Write how many tens. Then write how many ones.

1

___8___ tens = ___80___ ones

2

___ tens = ___ ones

3

___ tens = ___ ones

4

___ tens = ___ ones

▶ Quiz

Write how many tens. Then write how many ones.

5

___ tens = ___ ones

6

___ tens = ___ ones

Using Skill 7

OBJECTIVE Identify tens and ones three different ways

Distribute the materials.

Say: **I am thinking of three different ways to describe the same group of tens and ones. First, take 4 tens rods and put them on your workmat.** Ask: **Where will you put them?** (under the tens) **Why?** (each rod stands for 1 ten)

Say: **Now take 8 ones blocks and place them on your workmat.** Ask: **Where will you put them?** (under the ones) **Why?** (Each block stands for a one.) **How many tens and ones are there?** (4 tens 8 ones) **How many are there in all?** (48)

Write *4 tens 8 ones = 48* on the board. Say: **Here's one way to describe the number: 4 tens 8 ones equal 48.**

Say: **Look at your workmat again. Count by tens.** Ask: **What number did you get?** (40)

Say: **Now, count the ones.** Ask: **How many did you count?** (8) **How many in all?** (48)

Write *40 + 8 = 48* on the board and say: **Here's another way to describe the number: 40 + 8 = 48.**

Say: **Look at your workmat once more. How many cubes in all?** (48) Write 48 on the board and say: **Here's another way to describe the number: 48.**

Then direct children's attention to the model at the top of the page and discuss what they see. (Three workmats; all with 2 tens and 3 ones; below each workmat is a different way to write the number 23.) You might have children model the number on their own workmats.

TRY THESE Exercises 1–3 give children practice writing how many tens and ones in three different ways.

MATERIALS Workmat 3 and base-ten blocks (4 tens, 8 ones) for each child

- **Exercise 1** Write the model as 3 tens 6 ones, 30 + 6, and 36.

- **Exercise 2** Write the model as 5 tens 7 ones, 50 + 7, and 57.

- **Exercise 3** Write the model as 4 tens 5 ones, 40 + 5, and 45.

PRACTICE ON YOUR OWN Review the examples at the top of the page. Children should recognize that all three models show the same number of tens and ones—they are just described differently. Exercises 1–2 provide practice in identifying the same number of tens and ones three different ways.

QUIZ Determine if children can write how many tens and ones three different ways. Success is indicated by 2 out of 2 correct responses.

Children who successfully complete **Practice on Your Own** and **Quiz** are ready to move to the next skill.

COMMON ERRORS

- Children may reverse the digits in the tens and ones place when writing two-digit numbers.

- Children may have difficulty counting by tens and ones and recording the tens and ones in numbers greater than 50.

If a child makes an error in the **Practice on Your Own**, or was not successful in the **Quiz** section, you may wish to have the child model the problems with you using base-ten blocks. Encourage the child to model the tens first, before modeling the ones. The child may also benefit from the **Alternative Teaching Strategy** on the next page.

Alternative Teaching Strategy

20 Minutes

OBJECTIVE Model and write two-digit numbers in different ways

MATERIALS for each pair: a container of 98 connecting cubes; number cards for 21, 32, 43, 54, 65, 76, 87, and 98

Distribute materials to partners.

Say: **You will use the connecting cubes to model the numbers on the cards.**

Display a number card, such as 21, and have children read aloud the number. Say: **Count out 21 cubes.**

Say: **Make as many groups of ten as you can by connecting the cubes. Ask: How many groups of ten are there?** (2) **How many ones?** (1)

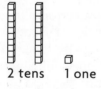

2 tens   1 one

Say: **Another way you can say 2 tens and 1 one is 20 + 1. Look at the model you made.** Ask: **What is 20 + 1?** (20 + 1 = 21)

Repeat the procedure with 65. Have children count out the cubes and make as many groups of ten as they can. Ask: **How many groups of ten are there?** (6) **How many ones?** (5). **What is another way of saying 6 tens and 5 ones?** (60 + 5)

Say: **Look at your model.** Ask: **What is 60 + 5?** (60 + 5 = 65)

Now, have partners take turns picking number cards, modeling the numbers with cubes, and recording the numbers in different ways on their paper.

Grade 2
Skill 7

Tens and Ones to 100

You can write the number of tens and ones in three different ways.

tens	ones
▭▭▭▭▭▭▭▭▭▭ ▭▭▭▭▭▭▭▭▭▭	▢ ▢ ▢

2 tens 3 ones = 23

tens	ones
▭▭▭▭▭▭▭▭▭▭ ▭▭▭▭▭▭▭▭▭▭	▢ ▢ ▢

20 + 3 = 23

tens	ones
▭▭▭▭▭▭▭▭▭▭ ▭▭▭▭▭▭▭▭▭▭	▢ ▢ ▢

2   3

Try These

Write how many tens and ones three different ways.

1

tens	ones
▭▭▭▭▭▭▭▭▭▭ ▭▭▭▭▭▭▭▭▭▭ ▭▭▭▭▭▭▭▭▭▭	▢ ▢ ▢ ▢ ▢ ▢

3 tens 6 ones = 36

30 + 6 = 36

          36

2

tens	ones
▭▭▭▭▭▭▭▭▭▭ ▭▭▭▭▭▭▭▭▭▭ ▭▭▭▭▭▭▭▭▭▭ ▭▭▭▭▭▭▭▭▭▭	▢ ▢ ▢ ▢ ▢ ▢

____ tens ____ ones = ____

____ + ____ = ____

          ____

3

tens	ones
▭▭▭▭▭▭▭▭▭▭ ▭▭▭▭▭▭▭▭▭▭ ▭▭▭▭▭▭▭▭▭▭	▢ ▢ ▢ ▢

____ tens ____ ones = ____

____ + ____ = ____

          ____

Go to the next side.

Practice on Your Own

Skill 7

Write how many tens and ones in three different ways.

tens	ones

tens	ones

tens	ones

__6__ tens __2__ ones = __62__   __60__ + __2__ = __62__   __62__

Write how many tens and ones in three different ways.

1

tens	ones

__4__ tens __8__ ones = __48__

__ + __ = ___

___

2

tens	ones

___ tens ___ ones = ___

__ + __ = ___

___

▶ **Quiz**

Write how many tens and ones in three different ways.

3

tens	ones

___ tens ___ ones = ___

__ + __ = ___

___

4

tens	ones

___ tens ___ ones = ___

__ + __ = ___

___

Skill 8

Understand Place Value

Using Skill 8

OBJECTIVE Recognize and understand the value of a digit in a 2-digit number

Example

Distribute 3 tens rods, 5 ones cubes, and a place-value mat to each child.

In Step 1, review modeling 35 using base-ten blocks. On the overhead, color the 3 in red and the 5 in blue to differentiate the tens from the ones. Have the children do the same on their worksheets or place-value mats.

Proceed to Step 2 and say: **In this step we find the value of the digit 3 in 35.** Have children count the tens rods by tens. Ask: **How many ones are there in 3 tens rods?** (30)

Encourage the children to count the ones in the rod. Say: **So, the digit 3 in 35 has a value of 30.** Remind the children of the definition of the word digit.

Proceed to Step 3 and say: **In this step we find the value of the digit 5 in 35.** Have the children point to the ones column on their workmat. Ask: **How many ones blocks are there?** (5) Say: **So, the digit 5 in 35 has a value of 5.**

TRY THESE Exercises 1–2 give the children practice in recognizing and understanding the value of a particular digit.

- **Exercises 1–2** Circle the value of the underlined digit.

MATERIALS base-ten blocks, place-value mats for children, overhead place-value mat

PRACTICE ON YOUR OWN Review the examples at the top of the page. Exercise 1 provides practice in recognizing the value of digits using models. Exercises 2–6 provide practice in recognizing the value of digits without models.

QUIZ Determine if children can recognize the value of a particular digit without using a model. Success is indicated by 2 out of 3 correct responses.

Children who successfully complete **Practice on Your Own** and **Quiz** are ready to move to the next skill.

COMMON ERRORS

- Children may not understand that 1 tens rod is equal to 10 ones.

- Children may transpose the tens and ones digits when giving the value of the digit.

If a child makes an error in more than 2 exercises, have the child redo the exercise using base-ten blocks as you observe. Determine if the child has not understood the concept of the value of the tens rod or if he or she is confusing the digits. The child may also benefit from the **Alternative Teaching Strategy** on the next page.

Alternative Teaching Strategy

15 Minutes

OBJECTIVE Use models to recognize and understand place value in 2-digit numbers

You may wish to have children work in pairs.

Explain to children that they will use connecting cubes to model the 2-digit numbers on the card.

Display a number card with the number 12. Have the children count out 12 cubes.

12

Prompt children to make a train of ten by connecting 10 cubes. Ask: **How many groups of ten are there?** (1) **How many ones?** (2)

1 ten   2 ones

Point to the 1 in the 12 on the number card. Say: **This 1 means there is 1 ten.** Ask: **How many ones are in 1 ten?** (10) Have children count the cubes in their train of ten. Say: **So, the value of the digit 1 in 12 is 10.**

Have the children count the remaining 2 cubes. Point to the 2 on the number card. Say: **This 2 means there are 2 ones.** Say: **So, the value of the digit 2 in 12 is 2.**

MATERIALS 75 connecting cubes, number cards, paper, pencil for each pair of students

Guide the children through modeling another 2-digit number. Display a number card with the number 27. Have the children count out 27 cubes. Prompt children to make 2 trains of ten.

Ask: **How many groups of ten are there? (2) How many ones?** (7)

Point to the 2 in the 27 on the number card. Say: **This 2 means there are 2 tens.** Ask: **How many ones are in 2 tens?** (20) Have children count the cubes in their trains of ten. Ask: **So, what is the value of the digit 2 in 27?** (20)

Point to the 7 on the number card. Say: **This 7 means there are 7 ones.** Ask: **So, what is the value of the digit 7 in 27?** (7)

Encourage pairs to choose a number, model it with cubes, and record the value of the digits. As children develop greater proficiency, decrease your guidance and have children model and write numbers independently.

© Harcourt

Understand Place Value

0, 1, 2, 3, 4, 5, 6, 7, 8, and 9 are **digits**.

> A **digit** is a symbol used to write numbers.

Step 1

35

Step 2

Find the value of the digit 3.
Count by tens.

10 20 30

3<u>5</u>

The digit 3 has a value of 30.

Step 3

Find the value of the digit 5.
Count by ones.

① ② ③ ④ ⑤

3<u>5</u>

The digit 5 has a value of 5.

Go to the next side.

▲ Try These

Circle the value of the underlined digit.

1   2<u>3</u>

2 or 20

2   4<u>7</u>

7 or 70

Practice on Your Own

Circle the value of the underlined digit.

3<u>6</u>

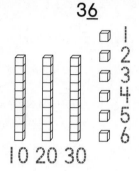

10 20 30

(6) or 60

Circle the value of the underlined digit.

1

5<u>8</u>

(8) or 80

2

<u>7</u>1

7 or 70

3

<u>1</u>4

1 or 10

4

<u>2</u>5

2 or 20

5

2<u>1</u>

1 or 10

6

4<u>0</u>

0 or 10

▶ Quiz

Circle the value of the underlined digit.

7

<u>4</u>5

4 or 40

8

<u>8</u>7

8 or 80

9

6<u>2</u>

2 or 20

Skill 9

Order Numbers to 100

Using Skill 9

OBJECTIVE Identify missing numbers in order to 100

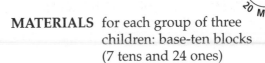

MATERIALS for each group of three children: base-ten blocks (7 tens and 24 ones)

Distribute the base-ten blocks to groups of three children. Draw a number line from 24 to 30 on the board to model the example. Have children say the numbers as you point to each one in order.

Then point to 25 on the number line. Ask: **25 is between what two numbers?** (24 and 26) **What number is just before 25?** (24) **What number is just after?** (26)

Say: **Use base-ten blocks to model 24, 25, and 26.** Have each child in a group model one of the three numbers.

Ask: **Look at the models. How many tens does each one have?** (2) **Which has the fewest ones?** (24) **Which has 1 more than 24?** (25)
Say: **That's why 25 is to the right of 24 on the number line.**
Ask **Which has 1 more than 25?** (26)
Say: **That's why 26 is to the right of 25 on the number line.**

Have children model other consecutive numbers on the number line. Have them tell how they are alike and different, and how they know the numbers are in the correct order.

Then, erase 24 and 26.
Say: **Look at the number line.**
Ask: **Which numbers are missing?** (24 and 26) **Where does 24 belong?** (to the left of 25) **Why?** (25 is 1 more than 24; 24 is 1 less than 25) **Where does 26 belong?** (to the right of 25) Why? (26 is 1 more than 25; 25 is one less than 26.)
Write the missing numbers.

Summarize by saying: **On the number line the numbers are arranged from left to right in order from least to greatest.**

TRY THESE Exercises 1–3 give children practice in identifying and writing missing numbers to prepare them for exercises in the **Practice on Your Own Section**.

- **Exercise 1** Write the number that is 1 more.

- **Exercise 2** Write the number that is 1 less.

- **Exercise 3** Write the number that is 1 more or 1 less.

PRACTICE ON YOUR OWN Review the example at the top of the page. In Exercises 1–5, children identify and write missing numbers in a sequence.

QUIZ Determine if children can correctly identify and write missing numbers in a sequence. Success is indicated by 2 out of 3 correct responses.

Children who successfully complete **Practice on Your Own** and **Quiz** are ready to move to the next skill.

COMMON ERRORS

- Children may write a number that is 1 more instead of 1 less when the numbers in a sequence are in order from greatest to least.

- Children may have difficulty counting backwards or counting beyond 50.

If a child makes more than 1 error in **Practice on Your Own**, or was not successful in the **Quiz** section, work through an exercise together. Have the child use a number line and base-ten blocks to model numbers to determine 1 more or 1 less than the given number. The child may also benefit from the **Alternative Teaching Strategy** on the next page.

Alternative Teaching Strategy

20 Minutes

OBJECTIVE Order numbers and match models to numbers

MATERIALS for each pair: a set of number cards for 6 consecutive numbers such as 24 to 29 or 39 to 44 and a set of cards illustrating the numbers as tens and ones

Distribute a set of number cards to one partner and the corresponding set of cards illustrating the numbers as tens and ones to the other partner. Mix up the cards in each set beforehand.

Have one partner arrange the number cards in counting order as the other partner matches the tens and ones cards to the corresponding number cards.

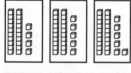

| 24 | 25 | 26 | 27 | 28 | 29 |

As children are working, discuss their decisions. Say, for example: **I see that you put 24 first and 29 last.**
Ask: **Both have the same number of tens, so how did you decide that 24 is the least of all 6 numbers?** (24 has the fewest ones)
How did you know that 29 is the greatest of all 6 numbers? (29 has the most ones)

Say: **I see that you put 25 to the right of 24. That's correct!**
Ask: **Both 24 and 25 have 2 tens, so how did you decide that 25 goes just to the right of 24?** (25 has 5 ones. That's 1 more than 24, so 25 goes just to the right of 24.)

Say: **I also see that you put 28 between 27 and 29.**
Ask: **How did you decide to put 28 between these two numbers?** (28 is 1 more one than 27 and 1 less than 29) Encourage children to use the tens and ones cards to explain.

Repeat with other sets of cards. You may also wish to have children arrange the cards in descending order such as 29 to 24 or 44 to 39. Remind children that when they order numbers from greatest to least, place the greater number to the left and the lesser number to the right.

Children should always compare tens first when ordering numbers. They should also understand the concept of 1 more than and 1 less than when discussing the order of numbers.

© Harcourt

Grade 2

Skill 9

Order Numbers to 100

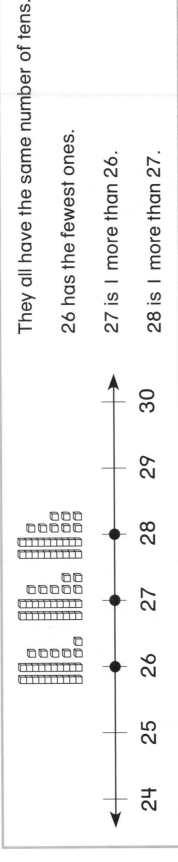

They all have the same number of tens.

26 has the fewest ones.

27 is 1 more than 26.

28 is 1 more than 27.

24 25 26 27 28 29 30

▲ Try These

Write the missing number.

1.

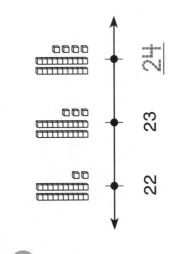

22 23 24

2.

___ 66 67

3.

19 ___ 21

Go to the next side.

Practice on Your Own

Skill 9

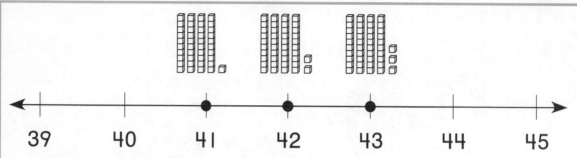

39   40   41   42   43   44   45

They all have the same number of tens.

41 has the fewest ones.

42 is 1 more than 41.

43 is 1 more than 42.

Write the missing numbers.

1 __39__, 40, 41, 42, 43, __44__, __45__, 46

2 28, 27, 26, _____, _____, 23, 22, _____, _____, 19

3 57, _____, 59, _____, 61, 62, _____, 64, _____

4 94, _____, _____, _____, 90, 89, _____, 87, _____

5 92, _____, 94, _____, 96, 97, _____, _____, 100

▶ Quiz

Write the missing numbers.

6 76, _____, 78, _____, _____, 81, _____, 83, _____

7 40, _____, 38, 37, _____, _____, _____, 33, _____

8 _____, 19, _____, 21, 22, _____, _____, 25, _____

Number Sense, Concepts, and Operations

Whole Number Addition

15 Minutes

Using Skill 10

OBJECTIVE Use the addition strategy counting on to add 1, 2, and 3

MATERIALS number line marked 0–12 on transparency; 12 counters for each child

You may wish to have the children model the example with their counters.

Example

Read the first addition problem: $6 + 1 =$
Ask: **Which number is greater?** (6)

Say: **Since 6 is greater, we start at 6 on the number line.** Point to the 6 on the number line transparency.

As you draw a jump from 6 to 7, say: **Six, then count on one to seven; six...seven.**

Ask: **How many spaces to the right did I move?** (1)

Have children model $5 + 2$ and $4 + 3$ in a similar way. Emphasize that when they count on, they begin with the greater number, and count on the amount shown by the other number.

You may wish to provide additional examples in which the second addend is the greater number. Have students identify the greater number and then complete the addition.

For example:

$1 + 7$ (8) $2 + 4$ (6) $3 + 7$ (10) $2 + 9$ (11)

TRY THESE Exercises 1–3 give children practice in counting on 1, 2, and 3.

- **Exercise 1** Count on 1
- **Exercise 2** Count on 2
- **Exercise 3** Count on 3

Encourage children to use the number line to count on.

PRACTICE ON YOUR OWN Review the example at the top of the page. Exercises 1–12 provide practice in counting on 1, 2, and 3, varying the order of the greater addend.

QUIZ Determine if children can count on 1, 2, and 3 to find sums. Success is indicated by 4 out of 6 correct responses.

Children who successfully complete **Practice on Your Own** and **Quiz** are ready to move to the next skill.

COMMON ERRORS

- Children may begin counting from the lesser number.

- Children may count the number they count on from, making their answers 1 less than they should be.

Children who made more than 3 errors in the **Practice on Your Own**, or who were not successful in the **Quiz** section, may benefit from the **Alternative Teaching Strategy** on the next page.

Alternative Teaching Strategy

15 Minutes

OBJECTIVE Use the addition strategy counting on 1, 2, and 3

MATERIALS overhead projector, 10 counters, blank transparencies, construction paper

Prepare several transparencies by turning the page in a horizontal position and drawing lines as shown below.

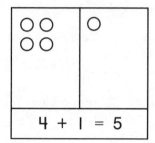

4 + 1 = 5

Continue with several more examples for counting on 1. Vary the position of the greater addend.

Display 4 counters on the left side of the transparency. Ask children to count them, as you record this first addend.

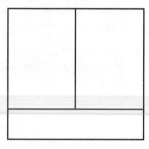

4 + ___ = ___

Then repeat the activity for counting on 2 and 3. First show the greater addend in the left position on the transparency, then show the lesser addend on the right of the transparency.

After children have had several opportunities to count on 1, 2, and 3 with counters, display a transparency with only a number sentence. Have children count on to add.

Then, cover the counters with the construction paper, and display 1 counter on the right side of the transparency. Have children tell you how many counters are on the right. Then point to the 4, have the children say 4 aloud and count on 1 to find the sum. Complete the recording of the addition below the counters. Ask children to verify the answer by counting what they see.

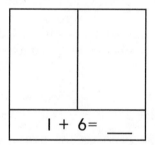

1 + 6 = ___

Have children work with guidance until you feel confident they can count on 1, 2, and 3. Then have children try several examples independently using paper and pencil.

© Harcourt

Grade 2
Skill 10

© Harcourt

Count on to Add

Circle the greater number.
Use the number line. Count on to add.

Count on 1

(6) + 1 = ___

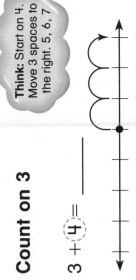

Think: Start on 6. Move 1 space to the right. 7

0 1 2 3 4 5 6 7

6 + 1 = 7

Count on 2

(5) + 2 = ___

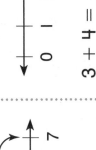

Think: Start on 5. Move 2 spaces to the right. 6, 7

0 1 2 3 4 5 6 7

5 + 2 = 7

Count on 3

3 + (4) = ___

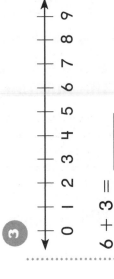

Think: Start on 4. Move 3 spaces to the right. 5, 6, 7

0 1 2 3 4 5 6 7

3 + 4 = 7

Try These

Circle the greater number.
Use the number line. Count on to add.

1

0 1 2 3 4 5 6

(5) + 1 = 6

2

0 1 2 3 4 5 6 7 8 9 10

2 + 8 = ___

3

0 1 2 3 4 5 6 7 8 9

6 + 3 = ___

Go to the next side.

Practice on Your Own

Skill **10**

Circle the greater number.
Use the number line. Count on to add.

Think: Start on 10. Move 2 spaces to the right. 11, 12

2 + ⟨10⟩ = _____

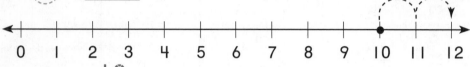

0   1   2   3   4   5   6   7   8   9   10   11   12

2 + 10 = __12__

Circle the greater number.
Use the number line. Count on to add.

0   1   2   3   4   5   6   7   8   9   10   11   12

1 ⟨6⟩ + 1 = __7__   2 4 + 3 = _____   3 8 + 1 = _____

4 6 + 2 = _____   5 1 + 10 = _____   6 2 + 4 = _____

7 11 + 1 = _____   8 3 + 8 = _____   9 9 + 3 = _____

10 1 + 7 = _____   11 9 + 2 = _____   12 8 + 2 = _____

▶ **Quiz**

Circle the greater number.
Use the number line. Count on to add.

13 4 + 1 = _____   14 5 + 3 = _____   15 2 + 10 = _____

16 7 + 2 = _____   17 3 + 8 = _____   18 9 + 1 = _____

© Harcourt

Using Skill 11

OBJECTIVE Add doubles and doubles plus one

MATERIALS 7 connecting cubes for each child

Example

Give 6 connecting cubes to each child. Direct children to make two 3-cube trains to model 3 + 3 in the first column of the example.
Ask: **How much is 3 plus 3?** (6)
Have children trace 6 in the example.
Ask: **Why is 3 + 3 = 6 called a doubles fact?** (It shows double the number 3.)

Give each child one more cube. Have children add the connecting cube to one of their trains to model 3 + 4 in the second column of the example.

Remind children of the doubles fact they modeled, 3 + 3 = 6.
Ask: **What is the sum now that you have added one cube?** (7)
Have children trace the 7.
Ask: **Why is 3 + 4 = 7 called a doubles plus one fact?** (The doubles fact is 3 + 3, and 3 + 4 is 1 more.)

Have children compare the numbers in the last column of the example to those in the second column.
Say: **Explain how you know that both columns show doubles plus one.** (The numbers are the same, but they are in a different order.)
Have children trace 7 in the last column.

Guide children as they use their cubes to model a different doubles and doubles plus 1 fact, such as 2 + 2 and 2 + 3 or 3 + 2.

TRY THESE Exercises 1–3 provide practice adding doubles and doubles plus one.

- **Exercises 1–3** Identify doubles, and write sums for doubles and doubles plus 1.

PRACTICE ON YOUR OWN Review the example at the top of the page. Point out the cube trains illustrated above Exercise 1. Remind children that knowing the doubles sum makes it easy to find the sum for doubles plus 1 by counting on 1. Tell children that in Exercises 1–5, they should begin by writing the doubles sum. Then it will be easy to find the sum for doubles plus 1.

QUIZ Determine if children can write sums for doubles facts and for doubles plus one. Success is indicated by 2 out of 2 correct responses.

Children who successfully complete **Practice on Your Own** and **Quiz** are ready to move to the next skill.

COMMON ERRORS

- Children may not recognize a number sentence as one that represents doubles plus 1.

- Children may forget to add the doubles first, or may only add the doubles and forget to add 1 more.

If a child makes more than 1 error in the **Practice on Your Own**, or in the **Quiz** section, the child may benefit from the **Alternative Teaching Strategy** on the next page.

© Harcourt

Alternative Teaching Strategy

15 Minutes

OBJECTIVE Model and add doubles and doubles plus one

MATERIALS number cube with the numbers 0–5, connecting cubes, paper, and pencils for each pair

Have children work in pairs. Distribute the materials.

Have one partner roll the number cube and arrange connecting cubes in two rows to show the corresponding doubles fact.

Direct the other partner to write the doubles number sentence.

Then, have the first partner add a connecting cube to one of the rows to model doubles plus one. Have the other partner write the doubles plus one number sentence.

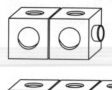

2 + 2 = 4
2 + 3 = 5

Have partners switch roles. Continue guiding children until you are confident they can work independently.

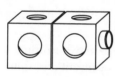

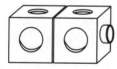

2 + 2 = 4

© Harcourt

Doubles and Doubles Plus One

Write the sum.

$$\begin{array}{r} 3 \\ +3 \\ \hline 6 \end{array}$$

$3 + 3 = 6$ is a
doubles fact.

$$\begin{array}{r} 3 \\ +4 \\ \hline 7 \end{array}$$

$3 + 4 = 7$ is a
doubles plus one fact.

$$\begin{array}{r} 4 \\ +3 \\ \hline 7 \end{array}$$

$4 + 3 = 7$ is a
doubles plus one fact, too.

Try These

Circle the doubles. Then write the sums.

1.
$$\begin{array}{r} 5 \\ +5 \\ \hline 0 \end{array}$$

$$\begin{array}{r} 5 \\ +6 \\ \hline \end{array}$$

$$\begin{array}{r} 6 \\ +5 \\ \hline \end{array}$$

2.
$$\begin{array}{r} 4 \\ +4 \\ \hline \end{array}$$

$$\begin{array}{r} 5 \\ +4 \\ \hline \end{array}$$

$$\begin{array}{r} 4 \\ +5 \\ \hline \end{array}$$

3.
$$\begin{array}{r} 2 \\ +2 \\ \hline \end{array}$$

$$\begin{array}{r} 3 \\ +2 \\ \hline \end{array}$$

$$\begin{array}{r} 2 \\ +3 \\ \hline \end{array}$$

Go to the next side.

Name _____ Skill _____

Practice on Your Own

Skill 11

Write the sum.

5
+5
10

$5 + 5 = 10$ is a
doubles fact.

5
+6
11

$5 + 6 = 11$ is a
doubles plus one
fact.

6
+5
11

$6 + 5 = 11$ is a
doubles plus one
fact, too.

Write the sum.

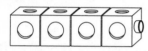   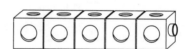

1. $2 + 2 =$ __4__,   so $2 + 3 =$ __5__

2. $0 + 0 =$ ____,   so $1 + 0 =$ ____

3. $1 + 1 =$ ____,   so $1 + 2 =$ ____

4. $4 + 4 =$ ____,   so $5 + 4 =$ ____

5. $5 + 5 =$ ____,   so $5 + 6 =$ ____

▶ Quiz

Write the sum.

6. $3 + 3 =$ ____,   so $4 + 3 =$ ____

7. $6 + 6 =$ ____,   so $6 + 7 =$ ____

© Harcourt

IN86 Intervention • Skills

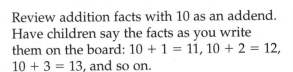
Using Skill 12

OBJECTIVE Make a ten to find sums to 18

MATERIALS 1 overhead ten frame, 14 counters for teacher demonstration

Review addition facts with 10 as an addend. Have children say the facts as you write them on the board: 10 + 1 = 11, 10 + 2 = 12, 10 + 3 = 13, and so on.

Then work through the example with children, modeling it on the overhead.
Say: **Look at the first box at the top of the page.** Ask: **What are the two addends in the problem?** (7 and 5)
Write 7 + 5 = on the board.

As you demonstrate, say: **You can find the sum of 7 and 5 by first making a 10.**
Ask: **How many counters did I put in the ten-frame?** (7)
Say: **Notice that 7 is the greater addend.**

Ask: **How many counters must I move to make a ten?** (3) **How can you tell?** (There are 3 empty squares in the ten-frame.)

Fill the empty squares with counters.
Ask: **How many counters are inside the ten frame now?** (10) **How many are outside?** (2)
Say: **The counters in the ten-frame and outside stand for 10 + 2. Look at the addition sentences on the board.**
Ask: **What is the sum of 10 + 2?** (12)
What is the sum of 7 + 5? (12)

TRY THESE These exercises provide practice finding sums to 18 by making a ten and prepare children for the exercises they will encounter in the **Practice on Your Own** section.

- **Exercises 1–4** Use counters and a ten-frame to find the sum.

PRACTICE ON YOUR OWN Review the example at the top of the page. In Exercises 1–9, children use ten-frames and counters to find the sum.

QUIZ Determine if children can use the addition strategy *make a ten* to find sums to 18. Success is indicated by 4 out of 5 correct responses.

Children who successfully complete **Practice on Your Own** and **Quiz** are ready to move to the next skill.

COMMON ERRORS

- Children may add an incorrect number to make a ten.

- Children may correctly add to make 10, but forget to add the remaining number to find the correct sum.

Children who made more than 2 errors in **Practice on Your Own**, or who were not successful in the **Quiz** section, may benefit from the **Alternative Teaching Strategy** on the next page.

15 Minutes

© Harcourt

Alternative Teaching Strategy

 15 Minutes

OBJECTIVE Model the strategy *make a ten* to find sums to 18

MATERIALS 10-section egg cartons, 18 two-color counters, addition fact cards

Cut 2 sections from the end of each 12-egg carton. Give each child one egg carton and 18 counters.

Display the addition fact cards and have children choose one, such as 8 + 6.

Ask: **What are the addends?** (8 and 6) **Which addend is greater?** (8)

Say: **Choose 8 counters of one color and put them in your ten-frame to represent 8, the greater addend. Then choose 6 counters of a different color to represent 6, the other addend.**

Ask: **How can you make a ten?** (by putting 2 counters in the egg carton) Model placing 2 counters in the egg carton. Then have children do the same.

Ask: **How many counters are in the ten-frame?** (10) **How many are outside?** (4) **How many counters are there in all?** (14)

Call attention to the addition fact card that children chose at the beginning of the activity, 8 + 6, and review what they did.

Say: **You made a 10. Then you added 4 more to find a sum of 14: 10 + 4 = 14. So, 8 + 6 = 14.**

Repeat with different facts. Guide children to work through the process. Gradually reduce the amount of guidance until all children are working independently.

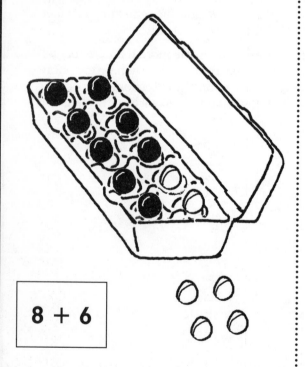

8 + 6

Grade 2
Skill 12

Make a Ten

What is 7 + 5?

Use a ten frame.
Put in 7 counters.
Put 5 counters outside.

Then make a ten.
Move 3 counters to fill the ten frame.

Now you have 10 and 2.
10 + 2 = 12,
so 7 + 5 = 12.

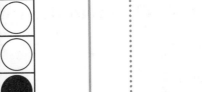

$$10$$
$$+2$$
$$\overline{12}$$

$$7$$
$$+5$$
$$\overline{12}$$

▲ **Try These**

Use a ten frame and ● to make a ten.
Find the sum.

1
$$9$$
$$+5$$
$$\overline{14}$$

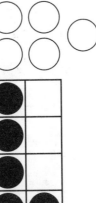

2
$$6$$
$$+7$$
$$\overline{}$$

3
$$4$$
$$+8$$
$$\overline{}$$

4
$$8$$
$$+8$$
$$\overline{}$$

Go to the next side.

Practice on Your Own

Use a ten frame and ● to find the sum.
What is 8 + 6?

Use a ten frame.
Put in 8 counters.
Put 6 counters
outside.

Think: Start with the greater addend. Borrow from the other addend to make a ten.

$$\begin{array}{r} 10 \\ +4 \\ \hline 14 \end{array} \qquad \begin{array}{r} 8 \\ +6 \\ \hline 14 \end{array}$$

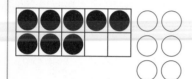

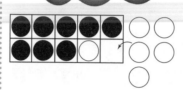

Use a ten frame and ● to find the sum.

1 $\begin{array}{r} 4 \\ +9 \\ \hline 13 \end{array}$ **Think:** $\begin{array}{r} 10 \\ +3 \\ \hline 13 \end{array}$ **2** $\begin{array}{r} 7 \\ +9 \\ \hline \end{array}$ **3** $\begin{array}{r} 8 \\ +9 \\ \hline \end{array}$ **4** $\begin{array}{r} 6 \\ +4 \\ \hline \end{array}$

5 $\begin{array}{r} 3 \\ +9 \\ \hline \end{array}$ **6** $\begin{array}{r} 4 \\ +7 \\ \hline \end{array}$ **7** $\begin{array}{r} 7 \\ +8 \\ \hline \end{array}$ **8** $\begin{array}{r} 9 \\ +9 \\ \hline \end{array}$ **9** $\begin{array}{r} 6 \\ +8 \\ \hline \end{array}$

▶ Quiz

Use a ten frame and ● to find the sum.

10 $\begin{array}{r} 6 \\ +9 \\ \hline \end{array}$ **11** $\begin{array}{r} 7 \\ +7 \\ \hline \end{array}$ **12** $\begin{array}{r} 9 \\ +7 \\ \hline \end{array}$ **13** $\begin{array}{r} 5 \\ +8 \\ \hline \end{array}$ **14** $\begin{array}{r} 8 \\ +3 \\ \hline \end{array}$

Skill 13

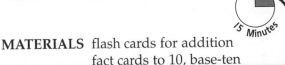

Mental Math to Add Tens

Using Skill 13

OBJECTIVE Use mental math to add tens

MATERIALS flash cards for addition fact cards to 10, base-ten blocks (4 tens)

Using the flash cards, review addition facts to 10 with children.

Then work through the example at the top of the page. Begin by reading the word problem.

Ask: **What are you asked to find out?** (how many points Sam scores in all)

Ask: **Will you add or subtract? Explain.** (add; the words 10 more and in all are clues to add)

Ask: **What numbers will you add?** (30 and 10) Write 30 + 10 in vertical form on the board.

Say: **When you add tens such as 30 and 10, you can use mental math.**

Ask: **How many tens are in 30?** (3 tens) Display 3 ten rods.

Ask: **How many ten rods show 10?** (1). Display 1 ten rod.

Say: **So when you add 30 plus 10, just think 3 tens plus 1 ten.**

Display the 4 ten rods together and have children count aloud by tens: 1, 2, 3, 4.

Ask: **What is the sum?** (4 tens or 40)

Write the sum on the board. Then guide children to complete the example in their books.

TRY THESE Exercises 1–3 give children practice using mental math to add tens.

• **Exercises 1–3** Use mental math to add tens by first writing the number of tens for each addend and then finding a sum for the tens. Record the number of tens in standard form.

PRACTICE ON YOUR OWN Review the example at the top of the page. Remind children to think of 20 + 30 as 2 tens + 3 tens. Encourage children to think of familiar addition facts and use mental math as they work through the exercises.

QUIZ Determine that children can add tens using mental math. Success is indicated by 6 out of 8 correct responses.

Children who successfully complete **Practice on Your Own** and **Quiz** are ready to move to the next skill.

COMMON ERRORS

• Children may forget to record a zero in the ones place after adding the tens column.

• Children may forget basic addition facts.

Children who made more than 3 errors in **Practice on Your Own**, or who were not successful in the **Quiz** section, may benefit from the **Alternative Teaching Strategy** on the next page.

Alternative Teaching Strategy

15 Minutes

OBJECTIVE Use base-ten rods to add tens and build mental math

MATERIALS for each pair: base-ten blocks (9 tens); 10 cards with two-digit tens addition facts; pair of scissors

Prepare a set of 10 addition cards for each pair of children as follows: fold index cards in half. On the left half show the problem such as 20 + 30 in vertical format and leave the right side blank.

Direct Child A to choose a card, say 20 + 30, and model the problem using ten rods. Have Child B record the problem as tens. Guide the children through the process with the following example.

Say: **Show your partner how many tens there are in 20 using ten rods.** (2 ten rods)

Say: **Write the number of tens on the card to the right of the first addend. In this example, you would write 2 tens across from the 20.**

Say: **Show your partner how many tens there are in 30 using ten rods.** (3 tens)

Say: **Write the number of tens on the card to the right of the second addend. In this example, you would write 3 tens across from the 30.**

Say: **Show how many tens there are in all using ten rods.** (5 ten rods)

Say: **Write the number of tens on the card to the right of the blank where the sum will go. In this example, you would write 5 tens across from the sum's place.**

Ask: **What is another name for 5 tens?** (50) Count the 5 ten rods by tens aloud. Guide the children to record the sum of 50 on the card.

Have partners reverse roles and continue modeling and recording the addition of tens using ten rods. Then have the pairs cut their cards in half along the fold line, mix them up, place them face down in 5 rows of 4, and encourage them to match the halves as you would in the concentration game.

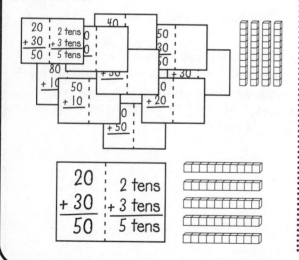

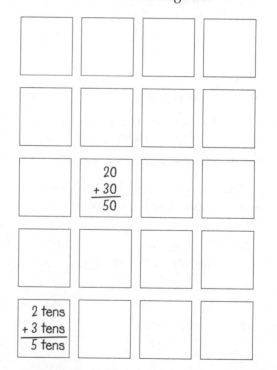

© Harcourt

Mental Math to Add Tens

Sam scores 30 points.
Then he scores 10 more points.
How many points does Sam score in all?

Think: I start with 3 tens and add 1 more ten.

$$\begin{array}{r} 30 \\ +10 \\ \hline 40 \end{array}$$

$$\begin{array}{r} 3 \text{ tens} \\ +1 \text{ ten} \\ \hline 4 \text{ tens} \end{array}$$

Sam scores __40__ points in all.

Try These

Write the tens. Add.

Think:

1
$$\begin{array}{r} 20 \\ +10 \\ \hline 30 \end{array}$$

$\boxed{2}$ tens
$+ \boxed{1}$ tens
$\overline{\boxed{3}}$ tens

2
$$\begin{array}{r} 50 \\ +40 \\ \hline \end{array}$$

$\boxed{}$ tens
$+ \boxed{}$ tens
$\overline{\boxed{}}$ tens

3
$$\begin{array}{r} 30 \\ +20 \\ \hline \end{array}$$

$\boxed{}$ tens
$+ \boxed{}$ tens
$\overline{\boxed{}}$ tens

Go to the next side.

Practice on Your Own

Skill 13

Missy reads 20 books.
Then she reads 30 more books.
How many books does Missy read in all?

$$\begin{array}{r} 20 \\ +30 \\ \hline 50 \end{array}$$

$$\begin{array}{r} 2 \text{ tens} \\ + 3 \text{ tens} \\ \hline 5 \text{ tens} \end{array}$$

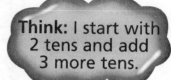

Think: I start with 2 tens and add 3 more tens.

Missy reads __50__ books in all.

Add.

1 $\begin{array}{r} 40 \\ +30 \\ \hline 70 \end{array}$ **Think: 4 tens + 3 tens 7 tens**

2 $\begin{array}{r} 50 \\ +20 \end{array}$

3 $\begin{array}{r} 30 \\ +60 \end{array}$

4 $\begin{array}{r} 20 \\ +20 \end{array}$

5 $\begin{array}{r} 10 \\ +40 \end{array}$

6 $\begin{array}{r} 60 \\ +20 \end{array}$

7 $\begin{array}{r} 40 \\ +50 \end{array}$

8 $\begin{array}{r} 10 \\ +10 \end{array}$

9 $\begin{array}{r} 20 \\ +10 \end{array}$

10 $\begin{array}{r} 40 \\ +40 \end{array}$

11 $\begin{array}{r} 30 \\ +20 \end{array}$

12 $\begin{array}{r} 10 \\ +50 \end{array}$

▶ Quiz

Add.

13 $\begin{array}{r} 20 \\ +70 \end{array}$

14 $\begin{array}{r} 40 \\ +20 \end{array}$

15 $\begin{array}{r} 10 \\ +60 \end{array}$

16 $\begin{array}{r} 30 \\ +50 \end{array}$

17 $\begin{array}{r} 80 \\ +10 \end{array}$

18 $\begin{array}{r} 40 \\ +10 \end{array}$

19 $\begin{array}{r} 30 \\ +30 \end{array}$

20 $\begin{array}{r} 10 \\ +30 \end{array}$

Skill 14

Grade 2

Add Tens and Ones

Using Skill 14

OBJECTIVE Model adding 2-digit numbers without regrouping

MATERIALS base-ten blocks (5 tens, 4 ones); flip chart

⏱ 15 Minutes

Example

Use base-ten blocks to model the example for children.

Demonstrate how to model the numbers 31 and 23 with base-ten blocks.

Help children see how the base-ten blocks are related to the numbers in the place value table. Help children say how many tens and ones are in each number. Guide them to say:

31 is 3 tens 1 one
23 is 2 tens 3 ones

Then, ask: **What are the ones digits?** (1 and 3) **What is the sum of 1 and 3?** (4) Show on the flip chart how to write 4 in the ones place of the sum. Continue with the tens digits. Ask: **What are the tens digits?** (3 and 2) Ask: **What is 3 tens plus 2 tens?** (5 tens)

Show how to write 5 in the tens place of the sum on the flip chart. Emphasize that the sum of 31 and 23 is 54, or 5 tens 4 ones.

TRY THESE Exercises 1–3 give children practice in adding tens and ones without regrouping and prepare children for the work they will encounter in the **Practice on Your Own** section.

PRACTICE ON YOUR OWN Review the example at the top of the page. Exercises 1–6 provide practice in adding tens and ones with place value charts to reinforce place value position of digits. Exercises 7–10 provide practice in adding tens and ones without place value charts. Alert children to align the tens and ones in the correct places in exercises 7–10. As children work through the exercises remind them to always add the ones digits first.

QUIZ Determine if children can add tens and ones without regrouping. Success is indicated by 3 out of 4 correct responses.

Children who successfully complete **Practice on Your Own** and **Quiz** are ready to move to the next skill.

COMMON ERRORS

- Children may add the tens digits before adding the ones. Although their answers may be correct, they may use this process later when they add with regrouping, setting up an error pattern.

- Children may not know basic addition facts.

Children who made more than 3 errors in the **Practice on Your Own**, or who were not successful in the **Quiz** section, may benefit from the **Alternative Teaching Strategy** on the next page.

Alternative Teaching Strategy

15 Minutes

OBJECTIVE Model adding 2-digit numbers without regrouping

MATERIALS connecting cubes (40 of one color, 40 of another color) for each child; addition sentence cards

Write addition sentences on index cards that show a two-digit addend and a one-digit addend, for example 33 and 2, and others with two addends.

Begin with adding a two-digit and a one-digit number.

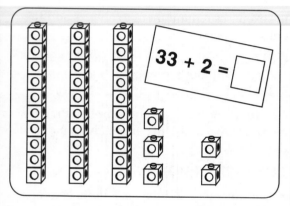

Demonstrate how to model each of the addends with connecting cubes. Then, demonstrate how to combine the connecting cubes to find the sum.

Have children repeat the process with a different exercise as you observe. Provide guidance as needed.

For additional practice, you may wish to have children work in pairs, with each partner writing and modeling one of the addends. Remind children to add the ones first and then the tens. Have partners take turns writing the sum.

When all children appear to be working successfully, repeat the process with problems in which both addends are 2-digit numbers. You may wish to do this in another session.

Grade 2
Skill
14

Add Tens and Ones

Find 31 + 23 = ☐.

Step 1
Show 31 and 23.

Tens	Ones
3	1
+2	3

Step 2
Add the ones. Write 4.

Tens	Ones
3	1
+2	3
	4

Step 3
Add the tens. Write 5.

Tens	Ones
3	1
+2	3
5	4

So, 31 + 23 = 54.

Try These

Add.

1

Tens	Ones
3	1
+1	4
4	5

2

Tens	Ones
2	5
+3	4

3

Tens	Ones
4	6
+2	0

Go to the next side.

Practice on Your Own

Add the ones and tens.

Tens	Ones
2	4
+1	5
3	9

Add.

1

Tens	Ones
1	7
+4	2
5	9

2

Tens	Ones
2	6
+5	0

3

Tens	Ones
3	1
+3	5

4

Tens	Ones
2	3
+2	4

5

Tens	Ones
5	7
+2	2

6

Tens	Ones
6	0
+3	9

7
18
+20

8
35
+42

9
51
+47

10
82
+15

| ▶ **Quiz** |

Add.

11
31
+24

12
50
+37

13
46
+32

14
81
+17

© Harcourt

Skill 14

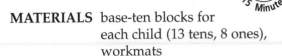

Using Skill 15

OBJECTIVE Model adding a two-digit and a one-digit numbers with regrouping

MATERIALS base-ten blocks for each child (13 tens, 8 ones), workmats

Example

You may wish to model Steps 1–3 with children using base-ten blocks.

Remind them that they always begin by adding the ones digits. Ask: **What are the ones digits?** (3 and 8) Guide children to add 3 + 8 to find a sum of 11.

Go to Step 2 and ask: **Are there ten or more ones?** (yes)
Guide the children to regroup the 10 ones as 1 ten.

In Step 3, guide children to count the tens rods and the ones blocks. Have them trace the totals on the student page.

Ask: **What would you do if there were no ones left?** (We would write a zero in the ones space.)

Ask: **What number do you get when you add 2 tens and 1 one?** (21) Have children count their blocks if necessary. Ask: **So what is the sum of 13 and 8?** (21)

TRY THESE In Exercises 1–2 children practice adding a two-digit and one-digit number with regrouping, to prepare for the work they will encounter in the **Practice on Your Own** section.

- **Exercises 1–2** Add the ones. Regroup the ones if needed. Write how many tens and ones.

PRACTICE ON YOUR OWN Review the example at the top of the page. Encourage children to ask themselves, "Are there ten or more ones? Can I make a ten?" as they work through each exercise. Remind them that if the answer is *yes*, they regroup the ten ones as 1 ten.

QUIZ Determine if children can add a two-digit and a one-digit number with and without regrouping. Success is indicated by 2 out of 2 correct responses.

Children who successfully complete **Practice on Your Own** and **Quiz** are ready to move to the next skill.

COMMON ERRORS

- Children may forget to regroup the ones and write an answer with ten or more in the ones place.

- Children may forget to add the regrouped ten to the tens column.

Children who made more than 1 error in the **Practice on Your Own**, or who were not successful in the **Quiz** section, may benefit from the **Alternative Teaching Strategy** on the next page.

Alternative Teaching Strategy

15 Minutes

OBJECTIVE Model adding a two-digit and a one-digit number with regrouping

MATERIALS connecting cubes, overhead projector, transparency, paper

Write 16 + 7 = _____ on the transparency. Guide children to model the first addend with connecting cubes. Point out that 16 can be shown with a group of 10 connected cubes and 6 single cubes.

Have children fold their paper in half to make a workmat. Then guide children to connect ten cubes to show the tens digit. Tell them to put 1 ten on the left side of the paper. Then, guide them to put 6 single cubes on the right side of the paper to represent the ones digit, 6.

Guide children to model the second addend, 7, with the cubes. Tell them to put 7 single cubes on the right side of the paper, just below the 6 cubes.

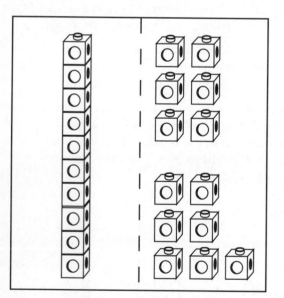

Have children combine the ones to find the sum. Ask: **How many ones do you have?** (13) **Can you make a ten?** (yes)

Guide children to connect a group of 10 cubes to form 1 ten. Then have children place this ten with the other ten on the left side of the workmat.

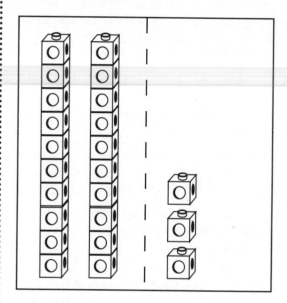

Point out that there are now 3 cubes on the right side of the workmat. Remind children these are the ones. Have children count the tens and ones and say the sum. Check to be sure that all children understand the relationship between connecting cubes, addends, and the sum. Record the sum in the sentence on transparency: 16 + 7 = 23.

Write a new addition sentence on the transparency. Have children model the addends and find the sum. Encourage children to work independently. Offer guidance when necessary.

© Harcourt

© Harcourt

Regroup Ones as Tens

Use Workmat 3 and ▱.

Step 1
Show 13 + 8.

Add the ones.
3 + 8 = 11

tens	ones
▭▭▭ (10-rod)	▯▯▯ ▯▯▯▯▯▯▯▯

Step 2
Are there 10 or more ones?

(Yes) No

If yes, regroup 10 ones as 1 ten.

tens	ones
▭▭▭▭▭ (▭▭▭▭▭)	(▯▯) ▯▯▯▯▯▯▯

Step 3
Write how many tens and ones.

2 tens ___ ones

tens	ones
▭▭▭▭▭ ▭▭▭▭▭	▯

▲ **Try These**

Use Workmat 3 and ▱.
Show.
Add the ones.

Are there 10 or more ones?
Circle Yes or No. If yes,
regroup 10 ones as 1 ten.

(Yes) No

Yes   No

Write how many tens and ones.

2 tens 3 ones

___ tens ___ ones

1 17 + 6

Think: 7 + 6 = 13

2 19 + 7

Think: 9 + 7 = 16

Go to the next side. →

Practice on Your Own

Use Workmat 3 and ⬚⬚⬚⬚⬚⬚⬚⬚ ▢.

Show. Add the ones.	Are there 10 or more ones? Circle Yes or No. If yes, regroup 10 ones as 1 ten.	Write how many tens and ones.
22 + 9 2 + 9 = 11	(Yes) No	_3_ tens _1_ ones

Use Workmat 3 and ⬚⬚⬚⬚⬚⬚⬚⬚ ▢.

Show. Add the ones.	Are there 10 or more ones? Circle Yes or No. If yes, regroup 10 ones as 1 ten.	Write how many tens and ones.
1 38 + 5	Yes No	____ tens ____ ones
2 35 + 4	Yes No	____ tens ____ ones
3 45 + 6	Yes No	____ tens ____ ones

▶ **Quiz**

Use Workmat 3 and ⬚⬚⬚⬚⬚⬚⬚⬚ ▢.

Show. Add the ones.	Are there 10 or more ones? Circle Yes or No. If yes, regroup 10 ones as 1 ten.	Write how many tens and ones.
4 49 + 8	Yes No	____ tens ____ ones
5 32 + 7	Yes No	____ tens ____ ones

Skill 16

Model 2-Digit Addition

Using Skill 16

OBJECTIVE Model adding two-digit numbers with regrouping

Write 17 + 15 on the board. Have children model Steps 1–3 of the example using base-ten blocks and Workmat 3.

Say: **Show 17 + 15 on your workmat.**
Ask: **How many tens will you show for 17?** (1) **How many ones?** (7) **How many tens for 15?** (1) **How many ones?** (5)
Check children's models.

Ask: **When you add two-digit numbers, what do you add first?** (ones)
Emphasize that children should always begin by adding ones.

Ask: **How many ones are there?** (12) **Do you have enough ones to make a group of ten?** (yes) **How many groups of ten can you make?** (1)

Say: **Exchange 10 ones for 1 ten.**
Ask: **How many tens and ones are there now?** (3 tens 2 ones)
Write 3 tens 2 ones on the board.
Ask: **How else can we write 3 tens 2 ones?** (32)

Write = 32 to complete the number sentence. Say: **So, 17 + 15 = 32.**

TRY THESE In Exercises 1–3 children practice adding two-digit numbers.

- **Exercise 1** Add two-digit numbers without regrouping.

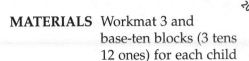

MATERIALS Workmat 3 and base-ten blocks (3 tens 12 ones) for each child

- **Exercises 2–3** Add two-digit numbers with regrouping.

PRACTICE ON YOUR OWN Review the example with children. As children work through Exercises 1–3, remind them to always add ones first. Watch for children who forget to move the ten to the tens column when they regroup.

QUIZ Determine if children can add two-digit numbers with regrouping. Success is indicated by 2 out of 2 correct responses.

Children who successfully complete **Practice on Your Own** and **Quiz** are ready to move to the next skill.

COMMON ERRORS

- Children may not align the digits, causing them to add a tens digit as a ones digit or the reverse.

- Children may not regroup and record a sum of 10 or more in the ones place.

If a child makes 1 or more errors in **Practice on Your Own**, have the child redo the exercises while you observe. The child may also benefit from the **Alternative Teaching Strategy** on the next page.

© Harcourt

Alternative Teaching Strategy

15 Minutes

OBJECTIVE Model adding two-digit numbers with regrouping

MATERIALS 75 connecting cubes and Workmat 3 for each pair; two-digit addition cards

Prepare a set of cards with two-digit addition requiring regrouping. The sums should not exceed 75.

Have children work in pairs. Distribute connecting cubes and a workmat to each pair.

Display an addition card, such as 19 + 24. Have each partner choose an addend and then count out that many connecting cubes.

Say: **Use the connecting cubes you counted out to model your addends. Make a ten train to show each ten. Then put your models on the workmat.**

19 + 24

tens	ones

Check to see that children place the cubes correctly.

Ask: **How many tens are in 19?** (1) **How many ones?** (9) **How many tens are in 24?** (2) **How many ones?** (4)

Say: **Now let's add. Begin with the ones. Count the ones.**

Ask: **What is the sum?** (13) **Can you make a ten-cube train?** (yes)
Give children time to make the ten-cube train.

Say: **Now move the ten-cube train to the tens column.**

Ask: **How many single cubes are there now?** (3)

Say: **They represent the ones.**

Ask: **How many tens and ones do you see?** (4 tens 3 ones) **What is another way of saying 4 tens 3 ones?** (43)

Repeat with the other addition cards. Have children continue modeling the addends, adding ones, regrouping, and then telling how many tens and ones until they become proficient. Gradually decrease the amount of guidance you provide.

© Harcourt

Grade 2
Skill 16

Model 2-Digit Addition

Step 1
Show 17 + 15.

tens	ones

Step 2
Add the ones. If there are 10 or more ones, regroup 10 ones as 1 ten.

tens	ones

Step 3
Write how many tens and ones.

$\underline{3}$ tens

$\underline{2}$ ones

tens	ones

▲ **Try These**

Use Workmat 3 and [rod] .

Show the expression.
Add the ones.

Are there 10 or more ones?
Circle Yes or No.
If yes, regroup 10 ones as 1 ten.

Write how many tens and ones.

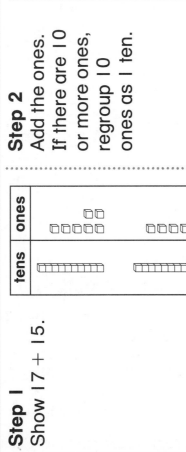

1 14 + 25   Yes (No) $\underline{3}$ tens $\underline{9}$ ones

2 26 + 16   Yes No   ___ tens ___ ones

3 37 + 49   Yes No   ___ tens ___ ones

Go to the next side.

© Harcourt

Practice on Your Own

Use Workmat 3 and ▭▭▭▭ ▫ **.**

Step 1	**Step 2**	**Step 3**
Show 29 + 12.	Add the ones. If there are 10 or more ones, regroup 10 ones as 1 ten.	Write how many tens and ones.
		_4_ tens
		_1_ one

Use Workmat 3 and ▭▭▭▭ ▫ **.**

Show the expression. Add the ones.	Are there 10 or more ones? Circle Yes or No. If yes, regroup 10 ones as 1 ten.	Write how many tens and ones.
1 18 + 39	(Yes) No	_5_ tens _7_ ones
2 53 + 27	Yes No	___ tens ___ ones
3 33 + 66	Yes No	___ tens ___ ones

▶ Quiz

Use Workmat 3 and ▭▭▭▭ ▫ **.**

Show the expression. Add the ones.	Are there 10 or more ones? Circle Yes or No. If yes, regroup 10 ones as 1 ten.	Write how many tens and ones.
4 48 + 24	Yes No	___ tens ___ ones
5 36 + 57	Yes No	___ tens ___ ones

© Harcourt

Using Skill 17

OBJECTIVE Model and record two-digit addition with regrouping

Distribute the materials. Read the example aloud. Draw a place-value chart on the board and write 24 + 27. Have children record on their charts.

tens	ones
☐	
2	4
+ 2	7

Ask: **What does the 24 represent?** (The length of the woolly monkey's body.) **What does the 27 represent?** (The length of the woolly monkey's tail.)

Say: **Use the blocks to model 24 and 27.** Ask: **How many tens and ones are in 24?** (2 tens 4 ones) **How many tens and ones are in 27?** (2 tens 7 ones) Check children's models.

Remind children to add the ones first. Ask: **How many ones do you have in all?** (11) **Can you regroup?** (yes) Say: **Exchange 10 ones for 1 ten.** Ask: **How many ones are there?** (1)

Demonstrate how to record the digits on the place-value chart. Have children record on their charts. Emphasize the placement of the regrouped ten. Say: **Now add the tens.** Ask: **How many tens are there?** (5 tens) Record the tens as children do the same. Ask: **What is the sum?** (51) Say: **The spider monkey is 51 inches.**

TRY THESE In Exercises 1–4, children practice recording two-digit addition with and without regrouping.

MATERIALS base-ten blocks (5 tens, 11 ones), place-value chart for each child

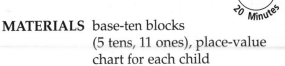
20 Minutes

- **Exercises 1, 3** Add two-digit numbers with regrouping.

- **Exercises 2, 4** Add two-digit numbers without regrouping.

PRACTICE ON YOUR OWN Review the example at the top of the page with children. Exercises 1–4 provide practice in adding two-digit numbers using place-value charts. Exercises 5–8 provide practice on a modified place-value chart. Remind children to record any regrouped tens in the tens column.

QUIZ Determine if children can add two-digit numbers with regrouping. Success is indicated by 3 out of 4 correct responses.

Children who successfully complete **Practice on Your Own** and **Quiz** are ready to move to the next skill.

COMMON ERRORS

- Children may add the tens digits first, writing, for example, 24 + 27 = 411.

- Children may not write a regrouped 1 ten in the tens column.

If a child makes more than 2 errors in the **Practice on Your Own** section, have the child redo the incorrect exercises using base-ten blocks while you observe. The child may also benefit from the **Alternative Teaching Strategy** on the next page.

© Harcourt

Alternative Teaching Strategy

20 Minutes

OBJECTIVE Model adding two-digit numbers with regrouping

MATERIALS 9 trains of 10 connecting cubes, 19 single cubes, lined paper for each child; index cards

Prepare a set of two-digit addition cards that require regrouping. Distribute the materials.

Have a child select an index card with a problem such as 29 + 34.

$$29 + 34$$

Guide children to turn their lined paper sideways and record the problem in vertical form. Then have them model each addend. Check children's models.

Ask: **How many ten-cube trains and ones do you need to model 29?** (2 ten-cube trains and 9 ones) **How many ten-cube trains and ones do you need to model 34?** (3 ten-cube trains and 4 ones)

Ask: **What should you add first?** (the single cubes, or ones) **How many ones are there in all?** (13 ones) **When you have ten or more ones, what can you do?** (Regroup 10 ones as 1 ten.)

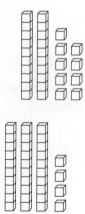
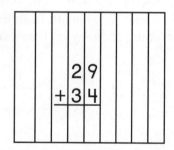

Have children connect 10 single cubes to make a ten-cube train and put it with the other ten trains.

Ask: **How can you show that you regrouped 10 ones as 1 ten?** (Write 1 at the top of the tens column.) **What should you write in the ones place of the sum?** (3) **Why?** (There are a total of 3 ones now.)

Have children record the regrouped 1 ten in the tens column and 3 in the ones place of the sum.

Ask: **What will you add now?** (the tens) Remind children to count the regrouped 10-cube train. **How many ten-cube trains are there in all?** (6) **Where will you write the 6?** (in the tens place)

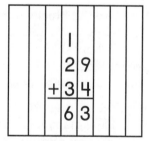
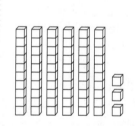

After correctly adding and recording the sum, have children choose another addition card. Repeat the process, gradually decreasing the amount of guidance you provide until you observe children working independently.

© Harcourt

Grade 2
Skill
17

Add 2-Digit Numbers

About how long is the woolly monkey?

Woolly Monkey Measurement	
body	about 24 inches
tail	about 27 inches

tens	ones
▨	
2	4
+ 2	7
5	▬

The woolly monkey is about

5 ▬ inches long.

▶ **Try These**

Add. Regroup if you need to.

1

tens	ones
▨	
2	3
+ 1	8
4	▬

2

tens	ones
▨	
4	5
+ 1	4

3

tens	ones
▨	
2	9
+ 3	3

4

tens	ones
▨	
4	2
+ 3	5

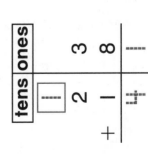 Go to the next side.

© Harcourt

Practice on Your Own

Skill 17

Add. Regroup if you need to.

About how long is the spider monkey?

Spider Monkey Measurement	
body	about 25 inches
tail	about 29 inches

	tens	ones
	1	
	2	5
+	2	9
	5	4

The spider monkey is about __54__ inches long.

Add. Regroup if you need to.

1
tens	ones
1	
5	8
+ 2	4
8	2

2
tens	ones
4	2
+ 1	7

3
tens	ones
3	8
+ 5	6

4
tens	ones
2	3
+ 4	5

5
2	5
+ 3	9

6
1	7
+ 2	4

7
3	6
+ 6	3

8
4	9
+ 3	2

▶ **Quiz**

Add. Regroup if you need to.

9
2	5
+ 2	6

10
5	2
+ 3	4

11
3	8
+ 2	2

12
3	5
+ 3	7

© Harcourt

Skill 18

Alegbra: Add 3 Numbers

Using Skill 18

OBJECTIVE Add 3 numbers by choosing 2 to add first

MATERIALS 20 counters per child

Write the example from the Skill sheet on the board: $8 + 2 + 3 = \square$

Have children form each of the numbers with their counters.

Ask: **What different pairs can these numbers make?** (8 and 2; 8 and 3; 2 and 3)

Say: **To find this sum, start by choosing two numbers to add first.**

Have a volunteer name a pair of numbers and use counters to find their sum. Say: **Then add the third number to that sum.** Have the class use counters to find the sum.

Repeat starting with a different pair. Repeat for the final pair. Ask: **What do you know about all the answers?** (They are the same.)

Point out that children can add the three numbers in any order to get the same answer.

Find other sums. Have children check their answers by adding in a different order. When choosing two numbers to add first, encourage children to look for two numbers that give an easy or familiar sum.

TRY THESE In Exercise 1, children practice adding three numbers to prepare for the exercises they will encounter in the **Practice on Your Own** section.

- **Exercise 1**   Add $3 + 5 + 2$.
- **Exercise 2**   Add $4 + 5 + 6$.

PRACTICE ON YOUR OWN Review the examples at the top of the page. Exercises 1–10 provide practice in finding the sum of three numbers.

QUIZ Determine if children can add three numbers. Success is indicated by 4 out of 5 correct responses.

Children who successfully complete **Practice on Your Own** and **Quiz** are ready to move to the next skill.

COMMON ERRORS

- Children may have difficulty with certain addition facts.

- Children may not understand why adding in a different order gives the same result.

Children who made more than 3 errors in the **Practice on Your Own,** or who were not successful in the **Quiz** section, may benefit from the **Alternative Teaching Strategy** on the next page.

Alternative Teaching Strategy

15 Minutes

OBJECTIVE Use basic facts to add 3 numbers

MATERIALS overhead projector; transparencies with place-value tables; worksheets with place-value tables

Write a basic addition fact on the transparency: $3 + 4 =$

Have a volunteer give the answer.

Next, have children model three numbers with their counters: 3, 4, and 6.

Ask: **If we want to find the total number of counters, what can we write?** $(3 + 4 + 6)$

Write the addition on the transparency.

Ask: **How can you use the counters, to model how to find $3 + 4$?** Point to the basic fact. Have children group the 7 counters to one side.

Ask: **To find the total number of counters, what else do we need to do?** (Add the other 6 counters to the group of 7.)

Have children add the 6 remaining counters to the group of 7. Record the total (13).

Direct children's attention to the 3-addend problem on the transparency: $3 + 4 + 6 = 13$. Ask: **What other basic facts can you model?** $3 + 6$ or $4 + 6$

Continue with other sums until children understand how to combine basic facts to find the sum of three numbers.

© Harcourt

© Harcourt

Grade 2
Skill 18

Algebra: Add 3 Numbers

You can group three addends in different ways. The sum stays the same.

$8 + 2 + 3 =$ _____

Choose two numbers to add first. Look for facts you know.

Think: I know
8 + 2 is 10.

(8)+(2)+ 3 =

10
+ 3 = 13

Think: I know
8 + 3 is 11.

8 +(2)+(3)=

11
+ 2 = 13

Think: I know
2 + 3 is 5.

8 +(2)+(3)=

5
+ 8 = 13

▲ **Try These**

Circle the addends you add first. Add the third number. Write the sum.

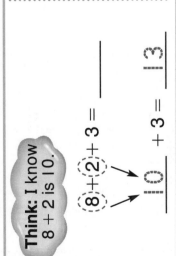

1

Think: I know
3 + 5

(3)+(5)+ 2 = 10

Think: I know
3 + 2

(3)+ 5 +(2)= 10

Think: I know
5 + 2

3 +(5)+(2)= 10

2

Think: I know
4 + 5

4 + 5 + 6 =

Think: I know
4 + 6

4 + 5 + 6 =

Think: I know
5 + 6

4 + 5 + 6 =

Go to the next side.

Practice on Your Own

Skill 18

Write the sum.

$$8 \quad 4 \rightarrow \boxed{12}$$
$$+7$$
$$+7$$
$$\boxed{19}$$

$$8 \quad 4 \rightarrow \boxed{15}$$
$$+7$$
$$+4$$
$$\boxed{19}$$

$$8 \quad 4 \rightarrow \boxed{11}$$
$$+7$$
$$+8$$
$$\boxed{19}$$

Write the sum.

1. 3 9 +2
2. 5 4 +3
3. 6 1 +4
4. 7 8 +2
5. 4 9 +6

6. 3 4 +6
7. 9 1 +8
8. 6 5 +3
9. 2 9 +5
10. 8 5 +2

▶ Quiz

Write the sum.

11. 9 4 +5
12. 3 6 +7
13. 3 2 +7
14. 4 8 +1
15. 6 3 +8

Skill **19**

Practice 2-Digit Addition

20 Minutes

Using Skill 19

OBJECTIVE Review and practice two-digit addition with and without regrouping

Distribute the base-ten blocks. Write $25 + 10$ and $25 + 19$ in vertical form on the board. Have children model the addends in the first problem.

Ask: **When adding 2-digit numbers, what do you add first?** (ones) **How many ones are there?** (5) **Must you regroup?** (no) **Why not?** (There aren't enough ones to make 1 ten.)

Write 5 in the ones place of the sum. Then guide children to combine the tens.
Ask: **How many tens are there?** (3)
Write 3 in the tens places.
Ask: **What is the sum of 25 + 10?** (35)

Model $25 + 19$ in a similar manner.
Ask: **Must you regroup this time?** (yes) **Why?** (There are 14 ones, and that's more than 10 ones.) Have children exchange 10 ones for 1 ten.
Ask: **How many ones are there?** (4) Say: **I'll write 4 in the ones place of the sum and 1 in the tens column to show that we regrouped.**

Have children add the tens.
Ask: **How many tens are there?** (4)
Write 4 in the tens place of the sum.
Ask: **What is the sum of 25 + 19?** (44)

Direct children to the example at the top of the page. Discuss the problem and guide children to solve the problem.

TRY THESE In Exercises 1–5, children practice two-digit addition.

MATERIALS base-ten blocks (4 tens, 15 ones) for each child

- **Exercises 1, 3, 5** Add two-digit numbers with regrouping.

- **Exercises 2, 4** Add two-digit numbers without regrouping.

PRACTICE ON YOUR OWN Review the example at the top of the page. Ask children whether they must regroup (no) and why. (There aren't 10 or more ones.) Exercises 1–10 provide practice in adding two-digit numbers with and without regrouping.

QUIZ Determine if children can add two-digit numbers with and without regrouping. Success is indicated by 4 out of 5 correct responses.

Children who successfully complete **Practice on Your Own** and **Quiz** are ready to move to the next skill.

COMMON ERRORS

- Children may not regroup and record a sum of 10 or more in the ones place.

- Children may forget to record the regrouped ones as 1 ten.

If a child makes more than 3 errors in the **Practice on Your Own** section, have the child redo the exercises while you observe. The child may also benefit from the **Alternative Teaching Strategy** on the next page.

© Harcourt

Alternative Teaching Strategy

20 Minutes

OBJECTIVE Model basic facts to help determine when to regroup and practice two-digit addition

MATERIALS connecting cubes, paper and pencils for each child; index cards

Prepare 6 to 8 cards of basic facts with sums from 10 to 18, such as 5 + 5, 6 + 5, 7 + 5, 9 + 4, 7 + 8, 8 + 8, and 9 + 8.

Have a child choose a card, for example, 6 + 5. Read aloud the problem, and write it on the board in vertical form.

Have children use connecting cubes to model each addend and then count to find the sum. Have a child come to the board and record the sum.

Remind children that they can use the cubes to show the sum another way. Have children make a ten-cube train. Ask: **How many tens do you have?** (1) **How many ones?** (1) Reiterate that the sum of 6 plus 5 is 11, or 1 ten 1 one.

Repeat with other addition fact cards, having children use single cubes to model addends, combine and count them to find sums, and then regroup to show sums as 1 ten and ones. Emphasize that knowing when and how to regroup is an important skill in two-digit addition.

As children gain proficiency regrouping, arrange them in pairs to play a regrouping game.

Give each pair a set of number cards 1–9 and have them place the cards facedown in a pile between them.

One partner chooses two cards and records the numbers to write a 2-digit number on his or her paper. Then he or she places the cards at the bottom of the pile.

The other partner does the same.

Children take turns until they each have written 2 two-digit addends.

Each partner adds the numbers he or she created, regrouping if necessary. Then they compare their sums. The "winner" is the player with the greater sum.

Partners can then shuffle the cards and play again.

© Harcourt

© Harcourt

Practice 2-Digit Addition

How many letters and numbers are there in all?

Telephone Pushbuttons

Letters	26
Numbers	10

Do you need to regroup?

$$\begin{array}{r} 26 \\ +10 \\ \hline 36 \end{array}$$

There are __36__ letters and numbers in all.

Try These

Add.

1 $$\begin{array}{r} 37 \\ +16 \\ \hline 53 \end{array}$$

2 $$\begin{array}{r} 25 \\ +60 \\ \hline \end{array}$$

3 $$\begin{array}{r} 19 \\ +49 \\ \hline \end{array}$$

4 $$\begin{array}{r} 52 \\ +27 \\ \hline \end{array}$$

5 $$\begin{array}{r} 36 \\ +25 \\ \hline \end{array}$$

Go to the next side.

Intervention • Skills IN117

Practice on Your Own

Skill 19

Add.

How many letter keys and symbol keys are there in all?

Keys on a Computer Keyboard	
Letter Keys	26
Symbol Keys	21

$$\begin{array}{r} 26 \\ +21 \\ \hline 47 \end{array}$$

 Do you need to regroup?

There are __47__ letters and numbers in all.

Add.

1.
$$\begin{array}{r} 33 \\ +27 \\ \hline 60 \end{array}$$

2.
$$\begin{array}{r} 15 \\ +33 \\ \hline \end{array}$$

3.
$$\begin{array}{r} 42 \\ +49 \\ \hline \end{array}$$

4.
$$\begin{array}{r} 57 \\ +22 \\ \hline \end{array}$$

5.
$$\begin{array}{r} 28 \\ +35 \\ \hline \end{array}$$

6.
$$\begin{array}{r} 28 \\ + 3 \\ \hline \end{array}$$

7.
$$\begin{array}{r} 31 \\ +39 \\ \hline \end{array}$$

8.
$$\begin{array}{r} 43 \\ +19 \\ \hline \end{array}$$

9.
$$\begin{array}{r} 37 \\ +46 \\ \hline \end{array}$$

10.
$$\begin{array}{r} 28 \\ +31 \\ \hline \end{array}$$

 Quiz

Add.

11.
$$\begin{array}{r} 17 \\ +34 \\ \hline \end{array}$$

12.
$$\begin{array}{r} 68 \\ +25 \\ \hline \end{array}$$

13.
$$\begin{array}{r} 28 \\ +16 \\ \hline \end{array}$$

14.
$$\begin{array}{r} 14 \\ +53 \\ \hline \end{array}$$

15.
$$\begin{array}{r} 29 \\ +49 \\ \hline \end{array}$$

Number Sense, Concepts, and Operations

Whole Number Subtraction

Using Skill 20

OBJECTIVE Count back 1, 2, or 3 to subtract

MATERIALS desktop number line for each child, or masking tape

20 Minutes

Display a number line from 0 to 12 or draw one on the board. Provide children with similar number lines or help children make them on their desks using wide masking tape.

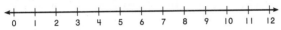

Review how to count backwards from 12 to 0 by having children count aloud in unison as you point to each number. Then have children use their number lines to model the example.

Example

Say: **Read the example: 10 − 2 = __. You can count back on your number line to subtract.** Ask: **Which number will you subtract?** (2) **From which number will you subtract 2?** (10)

Say: **Put your finger on 0 and move it along the number line. When you get to 10, stop. Now you are ready to count back. Move your finger back 2 numbers. Count out loud: 9, 8.**

As children count, draw the "hops" from 10 to 9 and 9 to 8 on the board.
Ask: **On what number did you stop?** (8)
Say: **You used the number line to count back to subtract. So, what is 10 − 2?** (8)
Have children trace the 8 in the example.

Guide children to use their number lines to model different subtraction problems, such as 9 − 1 or 8 − 3.

TRY THESE Exercises 1–4 provide practice in using a number line to count back 1, 2, or 3.

- **Exercise 1** Count back 2 to subtract.
- **Exercises 2–3** Count back 3 to subtract.
- **Exercise 4** Count back 1 to subtract.

PRACTICE ON YOUR OWN Review the example at the top of the page. In Exercises 1–15, children count back 1, 2, or 3. Tell children they will use the same number line to complete all the exercises on this page. Remind children to start on the number line at the greater number. Suggest they use their fingers to trace the "hops" as they work.

QUIZ Determine if children can count back 1, 2, or 3 to subtract. Success is indicated by 4 out of 5 correct responses.

Children who successfully complete **Practice on Your Own** and **Quiz** are ready to move to the next skill.

COMMON ERRORS

- Children may begin counting back with the starting number, resulting in an answer that is 1 more than the correct answer.

- Children may add instead of subtract.

Children who made more than 4 errors in the **Practice on Your Own,** or who were not successful in the **Quiz** section, may benefit from the **Alternative Teaching Strategy** on the next page.

© Harcourt

Alternative Teaching Strategy

OBJECTIVE Use a number line to model counting back

MATERIALS masking tape, marker, index cards, number cube marked 1 to 3, container to hold the numeral cards

Prepare a number line from 0 to 12 on the floor with masking tape and numeral cards. Prepare a separate set of numeral cards 4–12 and place them face down in a pile or in a container.

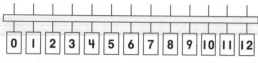

Have child A select a numeral card from the pile—11, for example. Ask the child to find the number on the number line and stand on it.

Then have child B roll the number cube and call out the number that appears on top, 3, for example.

Instruct child A to jump back 3 numbers on the number line, as the other children call out each number, 10, 9, 8.

Ask: **On what number did (name of child) start?** (11) **How many numbers did he/she jump back?** (3) **On what number did he/she stop on?** (8) Say: **You just used a number line to count back to subtract. So, what is 11 − 3?** (8)

Write 11 − 3 = 8 on the board, and have children read the subtraction sentence aloud.

Continue in this way with volunteers using different numeral cards.

© Harcourt

Count Back to Subtract

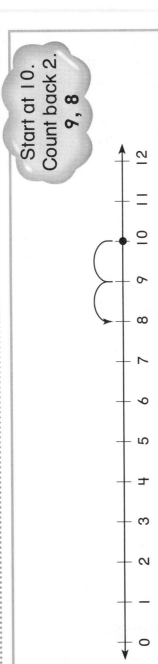

```
  10
 - 2
 ----
   8
```

Start at 10.
Count back 2.
9, 8

▲ Try These

**Count back to subtract. Write the difference.
You can use the number line to help.**

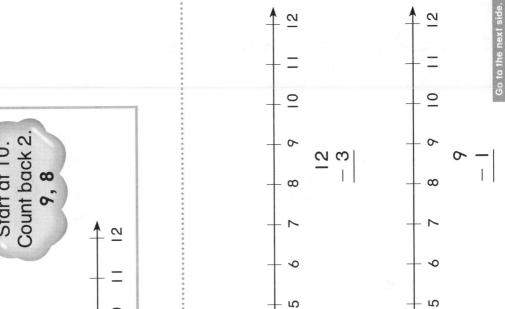

1

```
  11
 - 2
 ----
   9
```

2

```
  12
 - 3
 ----
```

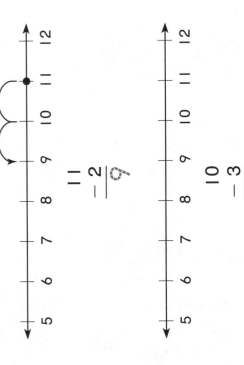

3

```
  10
 - 3
 ----
```

4

```
   9
 - 1
 ----
```

Go to the next side. ⬆

Practice on Your Own

Count back to subtract. Write the difference.
You can use the number line to help.

$$\begin{array}{r} 11 \\ -\ 3 \\ \hline 8 \end{array}$$

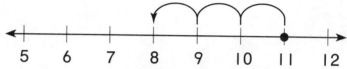

Start at 11.
Then count back 3.
10, 9, 8

Skill 20

Count back to subtract. Write the difference.
You can use the number line to help.

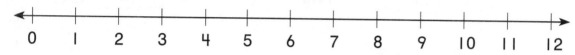

1. $\begin{array}{r} 8 \\ -\ 3 \\ \hline 5 \end{array}$ **2.** $\begin{array}{r} 9 \\ -\ 1 \\ \hline \end{array}$ **3.** $\begin{array}{r} 6 \\ -\ 2 \\ \hline \end{array}$ **4.** $\begin{array}{r} 10 \\ -\ 3 \\ \hline \end{array}$ **5.** $\begin{array}{r} 7 \\ -\ 1 \\ \hline \end{array}$

6. $\begin{array}{r} 11 \\ -\ 3 \\ \hline \end{array}$ **7.** $\begin{array}{r} 8 \\ -\ 2 \\ \hline \end{array}$ **8.** $\begin{array}{r} 7 \\ -\ 3 \\ \hline \end{array}$ **9.** $\begin{array}{r} 9 \\ -\ 2 \\ \hline \end{array}$ **10.** $\begin{array}{r} 6 \\ -\ 1 \\ \hline \end{array}$

11. $\begin{array}{r} 12 \\ -\ 3 \\ \hline \end{array}$ **12.** $\begin{array}{r} 9 \\ -\ 3 \\ \hline \end{array}$ **13.** $\begin{array}{r} 11 \\ -\ 2 \\ \hline \end{array}$ **14.** $\begin{array}{r} 10 \\ -\ 1 \\ \hline \end{array}$ **15.** $\begin{array}{r} 5 \\ -\ 3 \\ \hline \end{array}$

▶ Quiz

Count back to subtract. Write the difference.
You can use the number line to help.

16. $\begin{array}{r} 10 \\ -\ 2 \\ \hline \end{array}$ **17.** $\begin{array}{r} 8 \\ -\ 1 \\ \hline \end{array}$ **18.** $\begin{array}{r} 8 \\ -\ 3 \\ \hline \end{array}$ **19.** $\begin{array}{r} 6 \\ -\ 3 \\ \hline \end{array}$ **20.** $\begin{array}{r} 12 \\ -\ 2 \\ \hline \end{array}$

© Harcourt

Using Skill 21

OBJECTIVE Model related addition and subtraction facts

MATERIALS 10 black and 10 white connecting cubes for each child

⏱ 20 Minutes

Give each child 10 black cubes and 10 white cubes.
Say: **Use 9 black cubes to make a train. Then add 3 white cubes to the train. How many cubes in all?** (12)

Ask: **What number sentence can you write to show what you did?**
As children say *9 + 3 = 12*, write it on the board.

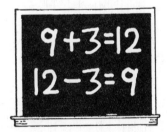

Say: **Use the 12 cubes. Take away 3.**
Ask: **How many cubes are left?** (9)
What number sentence can you write to show what you did?
As children say *12 − 3 = 9*, write it on the board.

$$9 + 3 = 12$$
$$12 - 3 = 9$$

Call children's attention to the two number sentences.
Ask: **What do you notice?** (The numbers are the same but in a different order.)
Say: **That's right. These are related facts. Knowing that 9 + 3 = 12 helps you find the difference, when you subtract 12 − 3, because the numbers are the same and the facts are related.**

Continue by having children model other related facts, such as 6 + 2 = 8 and 8 − 2 = 6. Then call children's attention to the example at the top of the page and have them model the related facts shown.

TRY THESE In Exercises 1–3, children model and find sums and differences of related facts.

- **Exercise 1** Find and write the related subtraction fact for 7 + 2.

- **Exercise 2** Find and write the related subtraction fact for 8 + 3.

- **Exercise 3** Find and write the related subtraction fact for 6 + 4.

PRACTICE ON YOUR OWN Review the example at the top of the page. In Exercises 1–4, children practice writing related addition and subtraction facts. Emphasize that knowing related facts will help children to find and write sums and differences.

QUIZ Determine if children can find sums and differences and write related facts. Success is indicated by 2 out of 2 correct responses.

Children who successfully complete **Practice on Your Own** and **Quiz** are ready to move to the next skill.

COMMON ERRORS

- When writing a related fact, children may record the incorrect sign.

- Children may add instead of subtract or subtract instead of add.

If a child makes more than 1 error in the exercises, the child may benefit from the **Alternative Teaching Strategy** on the next page.

© Harcourt

Alternative Teaching Strategy

20 Minutes

OBJECTIVE Model related addition and subtraction facts

MATERIALS 12 blue counters, 12 red counters, and an egg carton for each pair of children

Provide each pair with a 12–section egg carton, 12 blue counters and 12 red counters. Then tell stories for addition facts, sums 9 to 12, and the related subtraction facts.

For example,
Say: **Maggie picked 8 red flowers and 4 blue flowers.**
Ask: **How many flowers did she pick in all?** (12)

Have one child put the appropriate number of red and blue counters in the sections of the egg carton to model the addition story.
Ask: **What addition sentence tells the story?** (8 + 4 = 12).

Continue with a related subtraction story. For example,
Say: **Maggie had 12 flowers. She gave 4 blue flowers to her friend.**
Ask: **How many flowers does Maggie have left?** (8)

Have the partner take away 4 blue counters to model the subtraction story.
Ask: **What subtraction sentence tells the story?** (12 − 4 = 8)

Write the two facts on the board, and tell children they are called related facts.
Ask: **How can you tell that 8 + 4 = 12 and 12 − 4 = 8 are related facts?** (The numbers are the same.)

Repeat the procedure with similar stories.

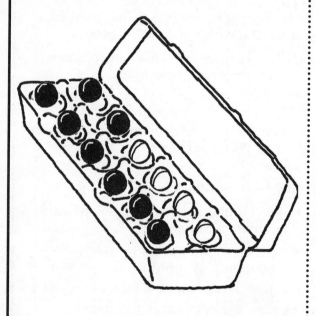

Grade 2
Skill 21

Algebra: Relate Addition and Subtraction

Think: The numbers are the same. $7 + 5 = 12$ and $12 - 5 = 7$ are **related facts.**

$7 + 5 = 12$

$12 - 5 = 7$

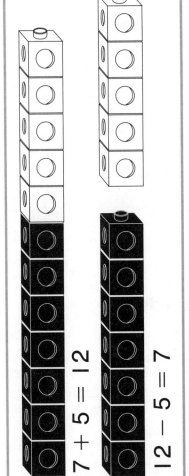

▲ Try These

Use 🎲🎲 to show related facts.
Complete the chart.

	Use 🎲.	Add 🎲.	Write the sum.	Use	Take Away	Write the subtraction sentence.
1	7	2	$7 \oplus 2 = 9$	9	2	$9 \ominus 2 = 7$
2	8	3	$8 \bigcirc 3 \underline{\quad}$	11	3	$\bigcirc \underline{\quad}$
3	6	4	$6 \bigcirc 4 \underline{\quad}$	10	4	$\bigcirc \underline{\quad}$

Go to the next side. →

Practice on Your Own

Write the sum or difference.
Use the same numbers to write a related fact.

_7_ ⊕ _4_ ⊖ _11_   _11_ ⊖ _4_ ⊖ _7_

Think: Related facts use the same numbers.

Write the sum or difference.
Use the same numbers to write a related fact.

1 7 + 3 = 10
_10_ ⊖ _3_ ⊖ _7_

2 11 − 5 = ___
___ ◯ ___ ◯ ___

3 12 − 8 = ___
___ ◯ ___ ◯ ___

4 3 + 6 = ___
___ ◯ ___ ◯ ___

▶ Quiz

Write the sum or difference.
Use the same numbers to write a related fact.

5 9 + 2 = ___
___ ◯ ___ ◯ ___

6 12 − 6 = ___
___ ◯ ___ ◯ ___

Skill 22

Practice the Facts

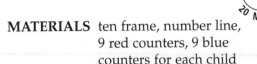

Using Skill 22

OBJECTIVE Review strategies to add and subtract

MATERIALS ten frame, number line, 9 red counters, 9 blue counters for each child

Distribute the materials for children to use to model addition and subtraction strategies.

Write $9 + 3, 7 + 7, 7 + 8, 12 - 3$, on the board.

Point to $9 + 3$.
Ask: **Which strategies could you use to solve this?** (count on, make a ten)
Guide children as they use a number line to count on.
Ask: **At what number on the number line should you start?** (9)
Say: **Put your finger on the 9.**
Ask: **How many numbers will you count on?** (3)
Say: **Move your finger ahead 3 spaces as you count on aloud: 10, 11, 12.**
Ask: **At what number will you stop?** (12)
Say: **So, $9 + 3 = 12$.**

Similarly, guide children to use a ten-frame and counters to find the sum of $9 + 3$ using the *make a ten* strategy.

Point to $7 + 7$ on the board.
Ask: **What strategy could you use to solve this problem?**
Accept all reasonable answers.
Ask: **Why would *using doubles* be a good strategy to use?** (Doubles facts are easy to remember; $7 + 7$ is a doubles fact; $7 + 7 = 14$.)

Point to $7 + 8$ on the board.
Ask: **How can you use *doubles plus 1* to add these numbers?** (I know $7 + 7 = 14$, so $7 + 8$ is one more, or 15.)

Now point to $12 - 3$. Have children follow along as you model using a number line to count back.

Say: **Start on 12. Count back 3: 11, 10, 9. So, $12 - 3 = 9$.**

Then ask: **How can you use a related fact to solve this problem?** (I know that $9 + 3 = 12$, so $12 - 3 = 9$.)

TRY THESE In exercises 1–4, children add and subtract using the strategies they learned.

- **Exercises 1, 3** Add.

- **Exercises 2, 4** Subtract.

PRACTICE ON YOUR OWN Review the strategies at the top of the page with children. Remind children to follow the signs to add or subtract.

QUIZ Determine if children can add and subtract basic facts. Success is indicated by 4 out of 5 correct responses.

Children who successfully complete **Practice on Your Own** and **Quiz** are ready to move on to the next skill.

COMMON ERRORS

- Children may use a strategy incorrectly resulting in an incorrect sum or difference.

- Children may add instead of subtract or subtract instead of add.

If a child makes more than 4 errors in **Practice on Your Own**, or is not successful in the **Quiz** section, work through the problems together. The child may also benefit from the **Alternative Teaching Strategy** on the next page.

Alternative Teaching Strategy

20 Minutes

OBJECTIVE Model and review addition and subtraction strategies

MATERIALS connecting cubes, a ten-frame and a number line for each child; cards on which you have written addition and subtraction problems to 18

Distribute the materials and use them to review the following strategies with children: doubles, doubles plus one, make a ten, counting on, counting back, and related facts.

Write addition and subtraction problems on the board, such as these:

$7 + 7 =$ ___

$7 + 8 =$ ___

$8 + 3 =$ ___

$11 - 3 =$ ___

Ask: **What strategy would you use to add 7 + 7?** (Children may say doubles or make a ten.) Model how to use each strategy to find the sum.

Say: **7 + 7 = 14. Notice that the sum is the same, no matter which strategy is used.**

Ask: **What strategy would you use to add 7 + 8?** (make a ten or doubles plus one). Model for children how to use each strategy to find the sum.

Say: **7 + 8 = 15. Notice that the sum is the same, no matter which strategy is used.**

Ask: **What strategy would you use to add 8 + 3?** (Children may say counting on or make a ten.) Model how to use each strategy to find the sum.

Say: **8 + 3 = 11. Notice that you get the same sum when you count on as when you use related facts.**

Ask: **What strategy would you use to subtract 11 − 3?** (Children may say counting back or related facts.) Model how to use each strategy.

Say: **11 − 3 = 8. Notice that the difference is the same, no matter which strategy is used.**

Have children work in pairs. Give each pair several cards containing addition and subtraction problems. Have children take turns choosing a card and then modeling the strategy they would use to find the sum or difference. Encourage children to tell why they chose a particular strategy.

© Harcourt

Skill
22

Practice the Facts

There are many ways to find sums and differences.
You can count on, make a ten, use doubles, or use doubles plus one to add.

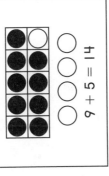

$$\begin{array}{r} 7 \\ +7 \\ \hline 14 \end{array}$$

$9 + 5 = 14$

You can count back or use a related fact to help subtract.

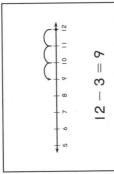

$12 - 3 = 9$

 $8 + 3 = 11$

$11 - 3 = 8$

 **Try These**

Add or subtract.

1
$$\begin{array}{r} 6 \\ +6 \\ \hline 12 \end{array}$$

2
$$\begin{array}{r} 13 \\ -5 \\ \hline \end{array}$$

3
$$\begin{array}{r} 9 \\ +6 \\ \hline \end{array}$$

4
$$\begin{array}{r} 18 \\ -9 \\ \hline \end{array}$$

Go to the next side.

Intervention • Skills IN131

Practice on Your Own

Skill 22

There are many ways to find sums and differences.

Think: You can count on, make a ten, use doubles, or use doubles plus one to add.

Think: You can count back or use a related fact to help subtract.

Add or subtract.

1. 14 − 5 = 9

2. 14 − 7

3. 11 − 3

4. 8 + 9

5. 10 + 10

6. 7 + 8

7. 15 − 6

8. 7 + 3

9. 10 + 6

10. 16 − 8

11. 17 − 9

12. 9 + 9

13. 17 − 8

14. 11 + 4

15. 15 − 8

Quiz

Add or subtract.

16. 10 + 5

17. 15 − 7

18. 7 + 6

19. 16 − 9

20. 8 + 8

15 Minutes

Using Skill 23

OBJECTIVE Use mental math to subtract tens

MATERIALS flash cards for subtraction facts to 10, base-ten blocks: 5 ten rods

Using flash cards, review subtraction facts to 10 with children.

Then work through the example at the top of the page. Begin by reading the word problem.

Ask: **What are you asked to find?** (the number of pennies Alex has left)

Ask: **Will you add or subtract? Explain.** (subtract because Alex ends up with fewer pennies than he started with.)

Ask: **How many pennies does Alex start off with?** (50)

Ask: **How many pennies does he spend?** (30)

Say: **When you subtract tens such as 50 minus 30, you can use mental math.**

Ask: **How many tens are in 50?** (5 tens) Display 5 ten rods.

Ask: **How many tens are in 30?** (3 tens)

Say: **When you take away 30 from 50, think of it as 3 tens taken away from 5 tens.** Have children take 3 ten rods away.

Ask: **How many tens are left?** (2 tens)

Ask: **What is another name for 2 tens?** (20)

Guide children to trace the answers in the first example.

TRY THESE Exercises 1–3 give children practice using mental math to subtract tens.

• **Exercises 1–3** Use mental math to subtract tens by first writing the number of tens for each number and then finding the difference. Record the number of tens in standard form.

PRACTICE ON YOUR OWN Review the example at the top of the page. Remind children to think of 40 − 20 as 4 tens − 2 tens. Encourage children to think of familiar subtraction facts as they work through the exercises.

QUIZ Determine that children can subtract tens using mental math. Success is indicated by 6 out of 8 correct responses.

Children who successfully complete **Practice on Your Own** and **Quiz** are ready to move to the next skill.

COMMON ERRORS

• Children may forget basic subtraction facts.

• Children may forget to record a zero in the ones place after subtracting in the tens column.

Children who made more than 2 errors in the **Practice on Your Own**, or who were not successful in the **Quiz** section, may benefit from the **Alternative Teaching Strategy** on the next page.

Alternative Teaching Strategy

15 Minutes

OBJECTIVE Use base-ten rods to subtract tens and build mental math

MATERIALS for each pair: base-ten blocks—9 ten rods; 5 subtraction sheets

Prepare a set of 5 subtraction sheets for each pair of children. Fold each paper vertically into thirds. On the left two-thirds show a problem written in standard form and then as groups of tens. The third column should be left blank for pairs to model the tens with ten rods and then to make pictorial representations.

Direct Child A to pick a sheet and model the problem using ten rods. For example, 70 − 30.

Ask: **How many tens do you start with?** (7) Have Child A place 7 ten rods in the third column.

Ask: **How many tens do you take away?** (3) Have Child B take 3 of those 7 ten rods off the sheet.

Ask: **How many tens are left?** (4) Have both partners count the number of tens remaining.

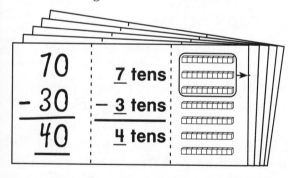

Direct Child B to write the numbers on the sheet. Direct Child A to draw a picture of the 7 ten rods. Then circle 3 tens with an arrow pointing to the right to show they are being taken away.

Ask: **What is another name for 4 tens?** (40) Tell each pair to write the standard number for the difference in the first column.

Have partners reverse roles and repeat using different subtraction sheets.

When partners have completed all of their sheets, have them cut each sheet into 3 parts along the fold-lines, mix them up, and challenge children to put the thirds back together.

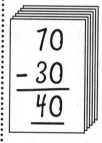 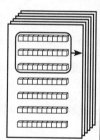

Grade 2
Skill
23

Mental Math to Subtract Tens

Alex has 50 pennies.
He spends 30 pennies on a toy.
How many pennies does Alex have left?

Think: I start with 5 tens and take 3 tens away.

```
  50          5 tens
 -30         -3 tens
 ─────       ───────
  20          2 tens
```

Alex has __20__ pennies left.

Try These

Write the tens. Subtract.

1   Think:
```
  40          4  tens
 -10         -1  tens
 ─────       ───────
  30          3  ten
```

2
```
  30          ☐ tens
 -20         -☐ tens
 ─────       ───────
              ☐ ten
```

3
```
  80          ☐ tens
 -40         -☐ tens
 ─────       ───────
              ☐ tens
```

Go to the next side.

Practice on Your Own

Skill 23

Maggie picks 40 flowers.
She gives 20 flowers away.
How many flowers does Maggie have left?

$$\begin{array}{r} 40 \\ -20 \\ \hline 20 \end{array}$$

$$\begin{array}{r} 4 \text{ tens} \\ -2 \text{ tens} \\ \hline 2 \text{ tens} \end{array}$$

Think: I start with 4 tens and take 2 tens away.

Maggie has __20__ flowers left.

Subtract.

1 $\begin{array}{r} 50 \\ -40 \\ \hline 10 \end{array}$ **Think:** 5 tens − 4 tens 1 ten

2 $\begin{array}{r} 60 \\ -30 \\ \hline \end{array}$

3 $\begin{array}{r} 90 \\ -50 \\ \hline \end{array}$

4 $\begin{array}{r} 20 \\ -20 \\ \hline \end{array}$

5 $\begin{array}{r} 70 \\ -40 \\ \hline \end{array}$

6 $\begin{array}{r} 80 \\ -20 \\ \hline \end{array}$

7 $\begin{array}{r} 40 \\ -30 \\ \hline \end{array}$

8 $\begin{array}{r} 60 \\ -50 \\ \hline \end{array}$

▶ **Quiz**

Subtract.

9 $\begin{array}{r} 50 \\ -10 \\ \hline \end{array}$

10 $\begin{array}{r} 40 \\ -20 \\ \hline \end{array}$

11 $\begin{array}{r} 70 \\ -60 \\ \hline \end{array}$

12 $\begin{array}{r} 90 \\ -20 \\ \hline \end{array}$

13 $\begin{array}{r} 80 \\ -70 \\ \hline \end{array}$

14 $\begin{array}{r} 60 \\ -40 \\ \hline \end{array}$

15 $\begin{array}{r} 80 \\ -50 \\ \hline \end{array}$

16 $\begin{array}{r} 70 \\ -30 \\ \hline \end{array}$

© Harcourt

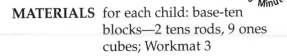
Using Skill 24

OBJECTIVE Subtract one-digit numbers without regrouping

MATERIALS for each child: base-ten blocks—2 tens rods, 9 ones cubes; Workmat 3

Distribute materials to children. Draw a tens and ones frame on the board. Then write 26 − 5 in the frame. Have children read the problem aloud. Guide them through the steps using this example with base-ten blocks and Workmat 3.

Say: **Show 26 on your workmat.**

Ask: **How many tens rods should you put in the tens column? Why?** (2 because there are 2 tens in 26)

Ask: **How many ones cubes will you put in the ones column? Why?** (6 because there are 6 ones in 26) Check children's models.

Say: **Subtract the ones. Slide 5 ones cubes off the workmat.**

Ask: **How many ones are left?** (1) Record 1 in the ones column.

Say: **Now subtract the tens.**

Ask: **What is 2 tens minus 0 tens?** (2 tens) Record 2 in the tens column.

Ask: **So what is 26 minus 5?** (21)

Direct children's attention to the first example in the book. Have them model the steps with their materials as you go through the steps again.

TRY THESE In Exercises 1–3 children model and subtract one digit numbers from two-digit numbers.

- **Exercises 1–3** Use Workmat 3 and base-ten blocks to subtract without regrouping.

PRACTICE ON YOUR OWN Review the example at the top of the page. Exercises 1–4 provide practice in subtracting to find the difference using Workmat 3, tens and ones charts, and base-ten blocks.

QUIZ Determine if children can subtract one-digit numbers from two-digit numbers without regrouping. Success is indicated by 3 out of 4 correct responses.

Children who successfully complete **Practice on Your Own** and **Quiz** are ready to move to the next skill.

COMMON ERRORS

- Children may record ones and then forget to subtract or record tens.

- Children may not remove the correct number of ones cubes.

Have children who made more than 1 error in **Practice on Your Own**, or who were not successful in the **Quiz** section, redo the exercise with you while explaining each step. These children may benefit from the **Alternative Teaching Strategy** on the next page.

Alternative Teaching Strategy

20 Minutes

OBJECTIVE Model subtracting from two-digit numbers without regrouping

MATERIALS for each pair: 9 tens rods and 9 ones cubes; set of 2-digit number cards; Workmat 3; spinner with numbers 1–4; paper

Prepare a set of two-digit number cards. For each number, the digit in the ones place should be from 4–9.

Arrange children in pairs. Give each pair 9 tens rods and 9 ones cubes, a set of two-digit number cards, Workmat 3, and a spinner.

Have Child A pick a number card and record the two-digit number on a sheet of paper. Have Child B spin the pointer and record the one-digit number below Child A's number to make a subtraction problem.

Have Child A use the base-ten blocks to model the two-digit number on Workmat 3. Then have Child B subtract the one-digit number by removing 3 ones. Together, have the pair count the tens and ones and record the difference on their paper.

Have partners switch roles and repeat the activity until they feel comfortable working through these subtraction problems successfully. You may continue play by replacing the spinner with a stack of subtraction equations with two-digit numbers and subtrahends between 5 and 9 that will not require regrouping.

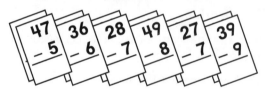

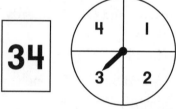

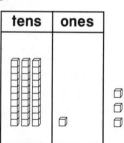

Name _____ Skill _____

© Harcourt

Grade 2 Skill 24

Subtract Tens and Ones

Subtract.

27
−4
―――

Show 27.

27
−4
―――

tens	ones
▭▭▭▭▭▭▭▭▭▭ ▭▭▭▭▭▭▭▭▭▭	▯▯▯▯▯▯▯

Subtract the ones.

27
−4
―――
3

tens	ones
▭▭▭▭▭▭▭▭▭▭ ▭▭▭▭▭▭▭▭▭▭	(▯▯▯▯) ▯▯▯

↑ ▯▯▯▯

Subtract the tens.

27
−4
―――
23

tens	ones
▭▭▭▭▭▭▭▭▭▭ ▭▭▭▭▭▭▭▭▭▭	▯▯▯

Try These

Use Workmat 3 and ▯ to subtract. Write the difference.

1

38
−5
―――
33

tens	ones
▭▭▭▭▭▭▭▭▭▭ ▭▭▭▭▭▭▭▭▭▭ ▭▭▭▭▭▭▭▭▭▭	(▯▯▯▯▯) ▯▯▯

↑ ▯▯▯▯▯

2

17
−2
―――

tens	ones
▭▭▭▭▭▭▭▭▭▭	▯▯▯▯▯ ▯▯

3

29
−7
―――

tens	ones
▭▭▭▭▭▭▭▭▭▭ ▭▭▭▭▭▭▭▭▭▭	▯▯▯▯ ▯▯▯▯

Go to the next side.

Practice on Your Own

Subtract.
$$\begin{array}{r} 35 \\ -4 \\ \hline \end{array}$$

Show 35.

$$\begin{array}{r} 35 \\ -4 \\ \hline \end{array}$$

tens	ones

Subtract the ones.

$$\begin{array}{r} 35 \\ -4 \\ \hline 1 \end{array}$$

tens	ones

Subtract the tens.

$$\begin{array}{r} 35 \\ -4 \\ \hline 31 \end{array}$$

tens	ones

Use Workmat 3 and ▢ to subtract. Write the difference.

1 $\begin{array}{r} 46 \\ -4 \\ \hline 42 \end{array}$

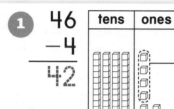

tens	ones

2 $\begin{array}{r} 37 \\ -7 \\ \hline \end{array}$

tens	ones

3 $\begin{array}{r} 18 \\ -6 \\ \hline \end{array}$

tens	ones

4 $\begin{array}{r} 25 \\ -3 \\ \hline \end{array}$

tens	ones

Quiz

Use Workmat 3 and ▢ to subtract. Write the difference.

5 $\begin{array}{r} 36 \\ -3 \\ \hline \end{array}$

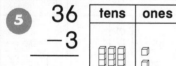

tens	ones

6 $\begin{array}{r} 49 \\ -4 \\ \hline \end{array}$

tens	ones

7 $\begin{array}{r} 19 \\ -5 \\ \hline \end{array}$

tens	ones

8 $\begin{array}{r} 48 \\ -6 \\ \hline \end{array}$

tens	ones

Using Skill 25

OBJECTIVE Subtract from two-digit numbers with regrouping

MATERIALS base-ten blocks (3 tens, 14 ones) and Workmat 3

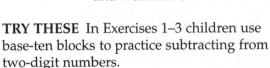

Distribute the materials to each child. Read the example aloud. Write 34 − 6 on the board and have them model it.

Direct children's attention to Step 1.
Say: **Show 34 on your workmat.**
Ask: **How many tens will you put in the tens column?** (3) **Why?** (There are 3 tens, or thirty, in 34.) **How many ones?** (4)

Check children's models.
Ask: **Can you subtract 6 ones from 4 ones?** (no) **Why not?** (6 ones are greater than 4 ones.)

Guide children to look at Step 2.
Say: **When there aren't enough ones to subtract, you can regroup 1 ten as 10 ones. Then there will be enough ones to subtract. To regroup, take 1 ten from your model and exchange it for 10 ones.**

Give children time to complete the step. Then have them look at Step 3.
Ask: **Where should you put the ones?** (in the ones column) **How many ones are there now?** (14) **Can you subtract 6 ones from 14 ones?** (yes)

Have children complete the subtraction.
Ask: **How many tens are there now?** (2 tens) **How many ones are there?** (8 ones)

Write = 2 tens 8 ones on the board to complete the number sentence.
Ask: **How else can we express 2 tens 8 ones?** (as 28)

TRY THESE In Exercises 1–3 children use base-ten blocks to practice subtracting from two-digit numbers.

- **Exercise 1**   Subtract without regrouping.

- **Exercises 2–3**   Subtract with regrouping.

PRACTICE ON YOUR OWN As you review the example at the top of the page, ask whether to regroup (yes) and why (5 is greater than 1). Exercises 1–2 provide practice in subtracting from two-digit numbers with regrouping.

QUIZ Determine if children can subtract from two-digit numbers with regrouping. Success is indicated by 2 out of 2 correct responses.

Children who successfully complete **Practice on Your Own** and **Quiz** are ready to move to the next skill.

COMMON ERRORS

- Children may recognize when to regroup, but may add 10 ones without exchanging a ten.

- Children may not regroup, subtracting the lesser digit from the greater digit.

If a child makes 1 or more errors in the **Practice on Your Own** section or is not successful in the **Quiz** section, have the child redo the exercises. Determine if the child knows how to regroup. The child may benefit from the **Alternative Teaching Strategy** on the next page.

© Harcourt

Alternative Teaching Strategy

20 Minutes

OBJECTIVE Model subtracting from two-digit numbers

MATERIALS 60 connecting cubes and Workmat 3

Distribute 60 connecting cubes and a workmat to each child. Have children make 2 ten-cube trains.

Write 26 − 6 = __tens __ones and 26 − 7 = __ tens __ones on the board. Have children use the cubes to model 26. Then demonstrate how to use the cubes to subtract 26 − 6, giving children time to observe and model the steps after you.

Say: **To model 26, I use 2 ten-cube trains and 6 single cubes. To subtract 6, I take away 6 single cubes. I have 2 ten-cube trains left, so 26 − 6 = 2 tens 0 ones.** Have a child come to the board and write 2 in the tens place and 0 in the ones place to complete the first number sentence.

Continue with the next problem, having children model 26 once again.

Ask: **How many ones do we subtract from 26 this time?** (7) **Can we subtract 7 ones from 6 ones?** (no) **Why not?** (7 ones are greater than 6 ones.)

Say: **That's right. 7 ones are greater than 6 ones. I do not have enough ones to subtract. I have to regroup 1 ten as 10 ones so that I can subtract.**

Demonstrate how to regroup 1 ten-cube train as 10 single cubes.
Say: **Now, I have 16 ones. There are enough ones to subtract. To subtract, I remove 7 cubes from the group of 16. There are 9 cubes left, so 26 − 7 = 1 ten 9 ones.**

Have a child come to the board and write 1 in the tens place and 9 in the ones place to complete the second number sentence.

Provide children with additional subtraction problems, such as 34 − 5, 42 − 7, and 21 − 3. Continue to guide them through the process.

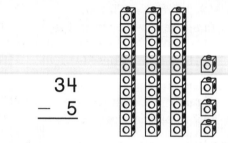

$$\begin{array}{r} 34 \\ -5 \\ \hline \end{array}$$

Once children are able to successfully subtract from two-digit numbers with regrouping, provide them with 3 problems to subtract independently, using the connecting cubes to find the differences.

Observe children as they work, offering assistance as needed. As they complete a problem, have them restate it orally. For example, subtract 5 from 34 equals 2 tens 9 ones.

© Harcourt

Grade 2
Skill 25

Regroup Tens as Ones

Subtract 6 from 34.   34
                      − 6
                      ____

Step 1
Show 34. Are there enough ones to subtract 6 ones?

Step 2
If there are not enough ones, break apart a ten. Regroup 1 ten as 10 ones.

tens	ones

Step 3
Subtract the ones. Write how many tens and ones are left.

tens	ones

_2_ tens _8_ ones

▲ **Try These**

Use Workmat 3 and ▭ ◻.

Subtract.

Do you need to regroup? Circle Yes or No.
If yes, regroup 1 ten as 10 ones.

Subtract. Write how many tens and ones are left.

1 34 − 3   Yes (No)   _3_ tens ____ ones

2 34 − 5   Yes   No   ____ tens ____ ones

3 34 − 7   Yes   No   ____ tens ____ ones

Go to the next side.

Practice on Your Own

Use Workmat 3 and **.**
Subtract 5 from 21.

$$\begin{array}{r} 21 \\ -5 \\ \hline \end{array}$$

Step 1	**Step 2**	**Step 3**
Show 21. Are there enough ones to subtract 5 ones?	If there are not enough ones, break apart a ten. Regroup 1 ten as 10 ones.	Subtract the ones. Write how many tens and ones are left.

Step 3: ___1___ ten ___6___ ones

Use Workmat 3 and **.**

Subtract.	Do you need to regroup? Circle Yes or No. If yes, regroup 1 ten as 10 ones.	Subtract. Write how many tens and ones are left.
1 46 − 7	(Yes) No	___ tens ___ ones
2 50 − 8	Yes No	___ tens ___ ones

▶ **Quiz**

Use Workmat 3 and **.**

Subtract.	Do you need to regroup? Circle Yes or No. If yes, regroup 1 ten as 10 ones.	Subtract. Write how many ones are left.
3 33 − 9	Yes No	___ tens ___ ones
4 40 − 3	Yes No	___ tens ___ ones

Using Skill 26

OBJECTIVE Model subtracting 2-digit numbers with regrouping

MATERIALS base-ten blocks (3 tens,14 ones) and Workmat 3

Distribute the materials so that each child can model the example. Read the problem together.

Direct children's attention to Step 1.
Say: **Show 32 on your workmat.**
Ask: **How many tens will you put in the tens column?** (3) **Why?** (There are 3 tens, or thirty, in 32.) **How many ones?** (2) Check children's models.

Ask: **Can you subtract 7 ones from 2 ones?** (no) **Why not?** (7 is greater than 2.)

Guide children to look at Step 2.
Say: **What do you do when there aren't enough ones to subtract?** (Regroup 1 ten as 10 ones.) **How can you show regrouping using your model?** (Exchange 1 ten for 10 ones.)

Have children look at Step 3.
Ask: **How many ones are in the ones column now?** (12) **Can you subtract 7 ones from 12 ones?** (yes) Have children subtract the ones.
Ask: **What do you do next?** (Subtract the tens.) Say: **Since you regrouped 1 ten as 10 ones, how many tens remain?** (2) **How many tens are you subtracting?** (1) **How do you know?** (There is only 1 ten in 17.)

Have children complete the subtraction.
Ask: **How many tens are there now?** (1) **How many ones are there?** (5) **How do we express 1 ten 5 ones?** (15)

Have children write 15 to complete the number sentence.

PRACTICE ON YOUR OWN In Exercises 1–3 children use base-ten blocks to subtract.

- **Exercises 1, 3** Regroup to subtract.

- **Exercise 2** Subtract without regrouping.

PRACTICE ON YOUR OWN As you review the example at the top of the page, ask children whether they must regroup (yes) and why (6 is greater than 5). Exercises 1–3 provide practice in subtracting two-digit numbers with and without regrouping.

QUIZ Determine if children can subtract two-digit numbers with regrouping. Success is indicated by 2 out of 2 correct responses.

Children who successfully complete **Practice on Your Own** and **Quiz** are ready to move to the next skill.

COMMON ERRORS

- Children may recognize when to regroup, but may add 10 ones without exchanging a ten.

- Children may subtract when there aren't enough ones to subtract.

If a child makes 1 or more errors in the **Practice on Your Own** section, have the child explain the exercises aloud. The child may benefit from the **Alternative Teaching Strategy** on the next page.

Alternative Teaching Strategy

20 Minutes

OBJECTIVE Model subtracting two-digit numbers

MATERIALS 64 connecting cubes and Workmat 3

Distribute 64 connecting cubes and a workmat to each child. Have children make 3 ten-cube trains.

Write 32 − 11 = __ and 32 − 13 = __ on the board. Have children use the cubes to model 32. Then demonstrate how to use the cubes to subtract 11 from 32, allowing time for children to observe and model the steps after you.

Say: **To model 32, I use 3 ten-cube trains and 2 single cubes. I know that 11 is 1 ten and 1 one. I also know that you subtract ones first. To subtract 1 one, I take away 1 single cube. To subtract 1 ten, I take away 1 ten-cube train. I have 2 tens and 1 one left, so 32 − 11 = 21.**

Have a child come to the board and write 21 to complete the first number sentence.

Continue with the next problem, having children model 32 once again.
Ask: **How many tens and ones do we subtract from 32 this time?** (1 ten 3 ones) **Can we subtract 3 ones from 2 ones?** (no) **Why not?** (3 is greater than 2)

Say: **That's right. 3 ones are greater than 2 ones. I don't have enough ones to subtract. I have to regroup 1 ten as 10 ones so that I can subtract.**

Demonstrate how to regroup 1 ten-cube train as 10 single cubes.

Say: **Now, I have 12 ones. There are enough ones to subtract. To subtract, I remove 3 cubes from the group of 12.**

Ask: **How many cubes are left?** (9) Say: **You know that we subtract the tens next. Remember, I used 1 ten-cube train to make 10 ones.**
Ask: **How many ten-trains are left?** (2)

Say: **Remember, 13 has 1 ten. I'm going to take away the 1 ten.**
Complete the step.
Ask: **How many tens are left now?** (1 ten)

Direct children's attention to the remaining tens and ones.
Say: **There is 1 ten and 9 ones left, so 32 − 13 = 19.**

Have a child come to the board and write 19 to complete the second number sentence.

Provide children with additional subtraction problems, such as 44 − 16, 52 − 15, and 30 − 16. Continue to guide them through the process.

Once children are able to successfully subtract two-digit numbers with regrouping, provide them with 3 problems to subtract independently, using the connecting cubes to find the differences. Observe children as they work, offering assistance as needed. As they complete a problem, have them restate it orally. For example, 44 − 16 equals 28.

© Harcourt

Grade 2
Skill 26

Model 2-Digit Subtraction

Subtract 17 from 32.

$$\begin{array}{r} 32 \\ -17 \\ \hline \end{array}$$

Step 1
Show 32. Are there enough ones to subtract 7 ones?

tens	ones

Step 2
When there are not enough ones, break apart a ten. Regroup 1 ten as 10 ones.

tens	ones

Step 3
Subtract the ones. Subtract the tens. Write the difference.

tens	ones

$$32 - 17 = \underline{15}$$

▲ **Try These**

Use Workmat 3 and ▭ **and** ◻ **.**

Subtract.

Do you need to regroup? Circle Yes or No. If yes, regroup 1 ten as 10 ones.

Subtract. Write how many are left.

1 32 − 15   (Yes) No $\underline{7}$

2 32 − 11   Yes No   _____

3 32 − 13   Yes No   _____

Go to the next side.

Name _____ Skill _____

Practice on Your Own

Use Workmat 3 and ⌷⌷⌷⌷⌷⌷ ▱.
Subtract 16 from 35.

$$\begin{array}{r} 35 \\ -16 \\ \hline \end{array}$$

Skill 26

Step 1	Step 2	Step 3
Show 35. Are there enough ones to subtract 6 ones?	When there are not enough ones, break apart a ten. Regroup 1 ten as 10 ones.	Subtract the ones. Subtract the tens. Write the difference.

tens	ones

tens	ones

tens	ones

$$35 - 16 = \underline{19}$$

Use Workmat 3 and ⌷⌷⌷⌷⌷⌷ ▱.

Subtract.	Do you need to regroup? Circle Yes or No. If yes, regroup 1 ten as 10 ones.	Subtract. Write how many are left.
1 46 − 17	(Yes) No	_29_
2 51 − 20	Yes No	___
3 67 − 49	Yes No	___

▶ **Quiz**

Use Workmat 3 and ⌷⌷⌷⌷⌷⌷ ▱.

Subtract.	Do you need to regroup? Circle Yes or No. If yes, regroup 1 ten as 10 ones.	Subtract. Write how many are left.
4 83 − 45	Yes No	___
5 40 − 22	Yes No	___

IN148 Intervention • Skills

Skill **27** Subtract 2-Digit Numbers

Using Skill 27

OBJECTIVE Model and record two-digit subtraction with regrouping

MATERIALS base-ten blocks (5 tens and 12 ones) and Workmat 3

20 Minutes

Distribute the materials to each child. Read the problem together.

Ask: **How can you solve this problem?** (Subtract 27 from 52.) Draw a place-value chart on the board. Write 52 − 27 on the chart.

Say: **Use your blocks to model 52 on your workmat. Use your blocks to model 27.** Check children's models.

Ask: **Will you have to regroup to subtract?** (yes) **Why?** (You can't subtract 7 from 2) Ask: **How will you regroup?** (Exchange 1 ten for 10 ones and add it to the 2 ones.) Check children's models to see that they've regrouped correctly. Ask: **How many ones do you have now?** (12) **How many tens?** (4) **How can you record the regrouping?** (Cross out the 5 in the tens place and write 4. Cross out the 2 in the ones place and write 12.)

Ask: **Now that you've regrouped, what will you do?** (Subtract the ones and then subtract the tens.) Ask: **How much is 52 − 27?** (25) Record the difference on the chart.

TRY THESE In Exercises 1–4 children use a place-value chart to subtract 2-digit numbers.

- **Exercises 1, 3, 4** Subtract with regrouping.

- **Exercise 2** Subtract without regrouping.

PRACTICE ON YOUR OWN Review the example. Have children explain why it is necessary to regroup and how to show regrouping on a place-value chart. Exercises 1–8 provide practice using a place-value chart. Exercises 9–12 provide practice without a chart.

QUIZ Determine if children can subtract two-digit numbers with regrouping. Success is indicated by 3 out of 4 correct responses.

Children who successfully complete **Practice on Your Own** and **Quiz** are ready to move to the next skill.

COMMON ERRORS

- Children may not regroup and subtract the lesser digit from the greater digit.

- Children may not record the regrouping in the tens place.

If a child makes more than 3 errors in **Practice on Your Own**, have the child redo the exercises while you observe. The child may also benefit from the **Alternative Teaching Strategy** on the next page.

Alternative Teaching Strategy

20 Minutes

OBJECTIVE Model and record two-digit subtraction with and without regrouping

MATERIALS 99 connecting cubes, paper for each child; index cards with numbers 10–19 for each pair

Distribute the paper and connecting cubes to children, and have them make 9 ten-cube trains. Guide children to use the cubes to model subtracting two-digit numbers and record the subtraction in vertical form.

As children write the problems, remind them to line up the ones with the ones and the tens with the tens.

Begin by having children model subtracting tens only, such as $30 - 10$, $40 - 20$, and $50 - 30$.

Next, have children model subtracting two-digit numbers without regrouping, such as $49 - 15$, $52 - 11$, and $36 - 23$.
Ask: **What do you subtract first, tens or ones?** (ones)

Finally, have children model subtracting two-digit numbers with regrouping, such as $32 - 18$, $61 - 29$, or $83 - 15$. Guide them through the process of exchanging 10 ones for 1 ten, recording the regrouping, and subtracting.

When children are comfortable subtracting two-digit numbers with and without regrouping, arrange them in pairs to play a subtraction game. Give each pair a set of index cards with numbers 10-19. Have children shuffle the cards and place them face down in a pile.

Direct each child to write the number 99 on his or her paper.

Each partner picks an index card and subtracts that number from 99. Children can use cubes to model the subtraction. Have them record the subtraction on their papers.

Partners take turns picking a card and subtracting the amount from the previous difference.

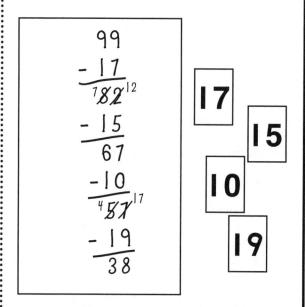

After 4 rounds, have children compare the differences. The partner with the smaller number is the winner.

Children can reshuffle the cards and play again.

Grade 2
Skill
27

Subtract 2-Digit Numbers

Subtract 52 − 27. Regroup if you need to.

Step 1
Are there enough ones to subtract 7?

tens	ones
	5	2
−	2	7

Step 2
Regroup if you need to.
Subtract the ones.

tens	ones
4	5̶	1̶2̶
−	2	7
		5

Step 3
Subtract the tens.
Write how many.

tens	ones
4	5̶	1̶2̶
−	2	7
	2	5

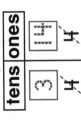

Try These

Subtract. Regroup if you need to.

1

tens	ones
3̶	4̶	4̶
−	1	5
	2	9

2

tens	ones
	7	8
−	2	5

3

tens	ones
	5	0
−	3	3

4

tens	ones
	8	1
−	4	6

Go to the next side.

Practice on Your Own

Subtract 64 − 35. Regroup if you need to.

Step 1	Step 2	Step 3
Are there enough ones to subtract 5?	Regroup if you need to. Subtract the ones.	Subtract the tens. Write how many.
$\begin{array}{r} 64 \\ -35 \\ \hline \end{array}$	$\begin{array}{r} \overset{5\ \ 14}{6\!\!\!/4} \\ -35 \\ \hline 9 \end{array}$	$\begin{array}{r} \overset{5\ \ 14}{6\!\!\!/4} \\ -35 \\ \hline 29 \end{array}$

Subtract. Regroup if you need to.

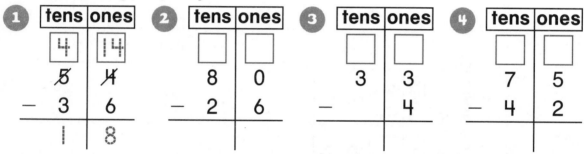

1. tens ones — 4, 14 / 5, 4 / − 3, 6 / 1, 8

2. tens ones — 8, 0 / − 2, 6

3. tens ones — 3, 3 / − , 4

4. tens ones — 7, 5 / − 4, 2

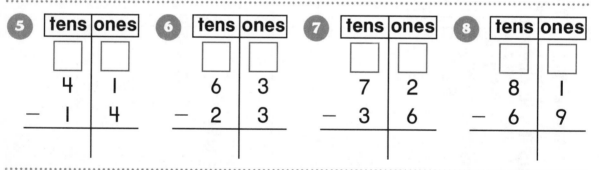

5. tens ones — 4, 1 / − 1, 4

6. tens ones — 6, 3 / − 2, 3

7. tens ones — 7, 2 / − 3, 6

8. tens ones — 8, 1 / − 6, 9

9. $\begin{array}{r} 94 \\ -29 \\ \hline \end{array}$

10. $\begin{array}{r} 85 \\ -48 \\ \hline \end{array}$

11. $\begin{array}{r} 67 \\ -39 \\ \hline \end{array}$

12. $\begin{array}{r} 38 \\ -19 \\ \hline \end{array}$

▶ **Quiz**

Subtract. Regroup if you need to.

13. $\begin{array}{r} 71 \\ -25 \\ \hline \end{array}$

14. $\begin{array}{r} 76 \\ -28 \\ \hline \end{array}$

15. $\begin{array}{r} 23 \\ -\ 6 \\ \hline \end{array}$

16. $\begin{array}{r} 48 \\ -28 \\ \hline \end{array}$

Using Skill 28

OBJECTIVE Subtract two-digit numbers with and without regrouping

MATERIALS base-ten blocks (5 tens and 14 ones) for each child

20 Minutes

Distribute the materials. Have children use them to model the example.

Read the problem aloud.
Ask: **How can you solve this problem?** (subtract 38 from 54)

Write *54 − 38* in vertical form on the board. Say: **Use your blocks to model 54.** Check children's models.

Say: **Look at the problem.**
Ask: **Will you have to regroup?** (yes)
Why? (There aren't enough ones. We can't subtract 8 from 4.)
Ask: **How will you regroup?** (Trade 1 ten for 10 ones and add it to the 4 ones.) Check children's models to see that they've regrouped correctly.

Ask: **How many ones do you have now?** (14) **How many tens?** (4) **How can you record the regrouping?** (Cross out 5 and write 4 above it and cross out 4 and write 14 above it.)
Have children trace the slashes and the numbers in the problem as you record the regrouping on the board.

Ask: **Now that you've regrouped, what will you do?** (Subtract the ones and then subtract the tens.)
Ask: **How much is 54 − 38?** (16)
Record the difference on the board as children trace the numbers in the problem.

Ask: **How many more computers are there at Green Elementary than at Park Elementary?** (16)
Have children trace the number 16 in the sentence.

TRY THESE In Exercises 1–5 children subtract 2-digit numbers with and without regrouping.

- **Exercises 1, 3, 5** Regroup to subtract.
- **Exercises 2, 4** Subtract without regrouping.

PRACTICE ON YOUR OWN As you review the example at the top of the page, have children explain why it is necessary to regroup and tell what the steps are. Point out that Exercises 1–15 provide practice subtracting with and without regrouping.

QUIZ Determine if children can subtract two-digit numbers with regrouping. Success is indicated by 4 out of 5 correct responses.

Children who successfully complete **Practice on Your Own** and **Quiz** are ready to move to the next skill.

COMMON ERRORS

- Children may not regroup, but rather subtract the lesser digit from the greater digit.

- Children may regroup but not record the regrouping in the tens place.

A child who made more than 4 errors in the **Practice on Your Own**, or who was not successful in the **Quiz** section, should be asked to explain a problem aloud to determine if he or she did not regroup or regrouped but forgot to record it in the tens place. The child may benefit from the **Alternative Teaching Strategy** on the next page.

Alternative Teaching Strategy

20 Minutes

OBJECTIVE Model and record two digit subtraction with and without regrouping

MATERIALS for each child: 50 connecting cubes; for each pair set of index cards numbered 4–9; set of index cards numbered 10–20

Distribute paper and connecting cubes to children and have them make 5 ten-cube trains.

Write 37 − 26 in vertical form on the board and have children record the problem on their paper. Remind them to line up the ones with the ones and the tens with the tens.

Ask: **What do you subtract first, tens or ones?** (ones)
Guide children to model the subtraction and record it on their papers.

Then write 46 − 27 in vertical form on the board and have children record the problem on their paper. Have children model subtracting the numbers. Guide them through the process of trading 10 ones for 1 ten, recording the regrouping, and then subtracting.

Say: **Look at the two problems you just solved.**
Ask: **For which problem did you have to regroup?** (46 − 27)
Say: **Circle that problem.**

Group children in pairs and have partners combine their connecting cubes. In addition, provide each pair with sets of index cards. Have partners work together to practice subtracting with and without regrouping.

Child A selects two cards from the 4–9 set, arranges the numbers to create a 2-digit number, then models the number with connecting cubes.

Child B selects a number from the second set and subtracts that number from the first, regrouping if necessary.

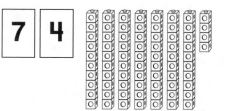

One partner records the problem on paper and circles it if they regrouped. Then partners switch roles and repeat the activity.

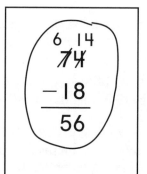

© Harcourt

Name _____

Practice 2-Digit Subtraction

How many more computers are there at
Green Elementary than at Park Elementary?

Number of Computers in Schools	
Green Elementary	54
Westville Elementary	49
Park Elementary	38

Regroup 1 ten
as 10 ones.

$$
\begin{array}{r}
4\,14 \\
5\,\;4 \\
-\,3\,\;8 \\
\hline
1\,\;6
\end{array}
$$

There are __16__ more computers at Green
Elementary than at Park Elementary.

Try These

**Circle the problems in which you will need to regroup.
Then subtract.**

1
$$
\begin{array}{r}
42 \\
-23 \\
\hline
19
\end{array}
$$

2
$$
\begin{array}{r}
38 \\
-14 \\
\hline
\end{array}
$$

3
$$
\begin{array}{r}
73 \\
-37 \\
\hline
\end{array}
$$

4
$$
\begin{array}{r}
56 \\
-16 \\
\hline
\end{array}
$$

5
$$
\begin{array}{r}
86 \\
-27 \\
\hline
\end{array}
$$

Go to the next side.

Name ____________________ Skill ____________________

Practice on Your Own

Skill 28

How many more computers are there at Wilson Elementary than at Pike Elementary?

Number of Computers in Schools	
Wilson Elementary	53
Pike Elementary	36
Lee Elementary	29

$$\begin{array}{r} {}^{4}\,{}^{13} \\ 53 \\ -36 \\ \hline 17 \end{array}$$

Regroup 1 ten as 10 ones.

There are 17 more computers at Wilson Elementary.

Circle the problems in which you will need to regroup. Then subtract.

1. $\begin{array}{r} 71 \\ -55 \\ \hline 16 \end{array}$
2. $\begin{array}{r} 38 \\ -17 \\ \hline \end{array}$
3. $\begin{array}{r} 64 \\ -29 \\ \hline \end{array}$
4. $\begin{array}{r} 83 \\ -56 \\ \hline \end{array}$
5. $\begin{array}{r} 92 \\ -38 \\ \hline \end{array}$
6. $\begin{array}{r} 52 \\ -10 \\ \hline \end{array}$
7. $\begin{array}{r} 43 \\ -24 \\ \hline \end{array}$
8. $\begin{array}{r} 67 \\ -47 \\ \hline \end{array}$
9. $\begin{array}{r} 88 \\ -39 \\ \hline \end{array}$
10. $\begin{array}{r} 30 \\ -14 \\ \hline \end{array}$
11. $\begin{array}{r} 75 \\ -37 \\ \hline \end{array}$
12. $\begin{array}{r} 96 \\ -18 \\ \hline \end{array}$
13. $\begin{array}{r} 51 \\ -19 \\ \hline \end{array}$
14. $\begin{array}{r} 59 \\ -12 \\ \hline \end{array}$
15. $\begin{array}{r} 85 \\ -26 \\ \hline \end{array}$

Quiz

Circle the problems in which you will need to regroup. Then subtract.

16. $\begin{array}{r} 83 \\ -47 \\ \hline \end{array}$
17. $\begin{array}{r} 66 \\ -37 \\ \hline \end{array}$
18. $\begin{array}{r} 41 \\ -26 \\ \hline \end{array}$
19. $\begin{array}{r} 54 \\ -14 \\ \hline \end{array}$
20. $\begin{array}{r} 92 \\ -39 \\ \hline \end{array}$

Number Sense, Concepts, and Operations

Money

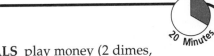

Using Skill 29

OBJECTIVE Count groups of nickels and pennies and dimes and pennies

MATERIALS play money (2 dimes, 2 nickels, 2 pennies) for each child, brown crayon

Distribute play coins and crayons. Have children identify their coins and review the value of each one.

Example

Focus attention on the first example.
Ask: **What coins do you see?** (2 dimes and 2 pennies)
Say: **Match your coins with the coins in the example. Then you can count to find the total amount. You'll start by counting dimes.**
Ask: **Will you count the dimes by tens, fives, or ones?** (tens) **Why?** (A dime is worth 10 cents.) **How will you count the pennies?** (by ones) **Why?** (A penny is worth 1 cent.)
Say: **Remove each coin as you count aloud. 10¢, 20¢, 21¢, 22¢. The total is 22¢.** Have children trace the numbers.

Ask: **When you see dimes, what do you count by?** (tens)
Say: **Circle the dimes.**
Ask: **When you see pennies, what do you count by?** (ones)
Say: **Color the pennies.**

Focus attention on the next example.
Ask: **What coins do you see?** (2 nickels and 2 pennies)
Say: **Match your coins with the coins in the example. Then you can count to find the amount.**
Ask: **What will you count first?** (nickels) **Will you count by tens, fives, or ones?** (fives) **Why?** (A nickel is worth 5 cents.) **How will you count on the pennies?** (by ones) **Why?** (A penny is worth 1 cent.)
Say: **Remove each coin as you count aloud. 5¢, 10¢, 11¢, 12¢. The total is 12¢.**
Have children trace the numbers.

Ask: **When you see nickels, what do you count by?** (fives)
Say: **Draw a box around the nickels.**
Ask: **When you see pennies, what do you count by?** (ones)
Say: **Color the pennies.**

TRY THESE In Exercises 1–2 children practice counting on to find the total amount for a group of coins.

- **Exercise 1**   Count dimes and pennies.
- **Exercise 2**   Count nickels and pennies.

PRACTICE ON YOUR OWN Review the examples at the top of the page. Exercises 1–3 provide children with practice counting dimes, nickels, and pennies.

QUIZ Determine if children can correctly count groups of coins. Success is indicated by 2 out of 2 correct responses.

Children who successfully complete **Practice on Your Own** and **Quiz** are ready to move to the next skill.

COMMON ERRORS

- Children may forget how to count on or which counting pattern to use.

- Children may confuse the values of dimes, nickels, and pennies.

Children who made more than 1 error in the **Practice on Your Own**, or who were not successful in the **Quiz** section, may benefit from the **Alternative Teaching Strategy** on the next page.

© Harcourt

Alternative Teaching Strategy

20 Minutes

OBJECTIVE Count groups of nickels and pennies and dimes and pennies

MATERIALS for each pair, a sheet of paper and a paper bag with play pennies and nickels, or pennies and dimes; pennies, nickels and dimes for display

Display the coins. Then use riddles to help children recall the features and values of each.

Say: **I am silver. I am larger than a penny and a dime, and my edge is smooth. I am worth 5 cents. What coin am I?** (nickel)
Have a volunteer point to the nickel.

Say: **I am copper in color. I have a smooth edge and a picture of Abraham Lincoln is on my face. I am worth 1 cent. What coin am I?** (penny)
Have a volunteer point to the penny.

Say: **I am the smallest silver coin. My edge has ridges. I am worth 10 cents. What coin am I?** (dime)
Have a volunteer point to the dime.

Display several dimes. Review counting by tens to find the total. Similarly, display nickels and count by fives and then display pennies and count by ones.

Arrange for children to work in pairs. Give each pair a paper bag with coins. Direct Child A in each pair to reach into the bag and take a handful of coins.

Direct Child B in the pair to group the coins that are alike together and then count the coins and record the total amount.

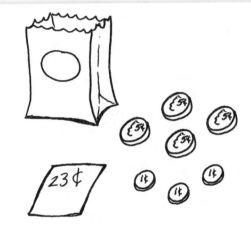

Then have Child A count the coins to check. If partners agree on the total, they return the coins to the bag and switch roles.

After several rounds, direct pairs who have nickels and pennies to trade bags with pairs who have dimes and pennies. Have partners repeat the activity using their new bag of coins.

© Harcourt

Count Groups of Coins

Think:
Count by tens.

___¢, 10 ___¢, 20 ___¢

Think:
Then count
on by ones.

21 ___¢, 22 ___¢

22 ¢

Think:
Count by fives.

5 ___¢, 10 ___¢

Think:
Then count
on by ones.

11 ___¢, 12 ___¢

12 ¢

▲ Try These

**Count by tens or fives. Then count on by ones.
Write the amount.**

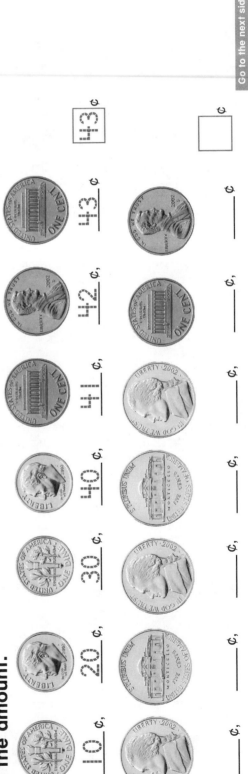

1 ___¢, 10 ___¢, 20 ___¢, 30 ___¢, 40 ___¢, 41 ___¢, 42 ___¢, 43 ___¢

43 ¢

2 ___¢, ___¢, ___¢, ___¢, ___¢, ___¢

___¢

Go to the next side.

Practice on Your Own

Skill 29

Think: Count by tens.

Think: Then count on by ones.

Think: Count by fives.

Think: Then count on by ones.

_10_ ¢, _20_ ¢, _30_ ¢, _31_ ¢ [31]¢

_5_ ¢, _10_ ¢, _15_ ¢, _16_ ¢ [16]¢

Count. Write the amount.

1

_10_ ¢, _20_ ¢, _30_ ¢, _31_ ¢, _32_ ¢, _33_ ¢, _34_ ¢ [34]¢

2

____ ¢, ____ ¢, ____ ¢, ____ ¢, ____ ¢, ____ ¢, ____ ¢ [ ]¢

3

____ ¢, ____ ¢, ____ ¢, ____ ¢, ____ ¢, ____ ¢ [ ]¢

▶ Quiz

4

____ ¢, ____ ¢, ____ ¢, ____ ¢, ____ ¢, ____ ¢, ____ ¢ [ ]¢

5

____ ¢, ____ ¢, ____ ¢, ____ ¢, ____ ¢, ____ ¢ [ ]¢

Skill 30

Count Collections

Using Skill 30

OBJECTIVE Count dimes, nickels, and pennies

MATERIALS play coins (5 dimes, 5 nickels, and 5 pennies)

Example

Distribute play coins. Have children begin by identifying the 3 types of coins and naming the value of each.

Ask: **What coin is worth 1 cent?** (a penny) Say: **Match a penny with each penny in the example.** Ask: **How many pennies will you use?** (2)

Ask: **What coin is worth 5 cents?** (a nickel) Say: **Match a nickel with each nickel in the example.** Ask: **How many nickels will you use?** (3)

Ask: **What coin is worth 10 cents?** (a dime) Say: **Match a dime with each dime in the example.** Ask: **How many dimes will you use?** (1)

Now look at the row of coins.

Ask: **How are the coins arranged?** (from greatest in value to least in value)

Say: **That's right. Now we will count the total amount. When counting a collection of coins, begin with the coins of greatest value.**

Ask: **Which coins should we count first?** (dimes) **What will you count by?** (tens) **Why?** (Dimes are worth 10 cents.)

Ask: **Which coins should we count next?** (nickels) **What number will you count on by?** (fives) **Why?** (Nickels are worth 5 cents.)

Ask: **Which coins should we count last?** (pennies) **What number will you count on by?** (ones) **Why?** (Pennies are worth 1 cent.)

Say: **Touch each coin as we count aloud together. 10¢, 15¢, 20¢, 25¢, 26¢, 27¢. So, the total amount is 27¢.**

TRY THESE Exercises 1–3 give children practice counting on to find the total amount for a collection of mixed coins.

- **Exercise 1** Count 2 dimes, 2 nickels, and 1 penny.

- **Exercise 2** Count 3 dimes, 1 nickel, and 3 pennies.

- **Exercise 3** Count 1 dime, 2 nickels, and 4 pennies.

PRACTICE ON YOUR OWN Review the example at the top of the page. Ask children to explain the order in which to count a collection of coins. Exercises 1–4 provide practice counting collections of dimes, nickels, and pennies.

QUIZ Determine if children can correctly count collections of dimes, nickels, and pennies. Success is indicated by 2 out of 2 correct responses.

Children who successfully complete **Practice on Your Own** and **Quiz** are ready to move to the next skill.

COMMON ERRORS

- Children may forget how to count on or which counting pattern to use.

- Children may forget to begin counting with coins of the greatest value.

Children who made errors in the **Practice on Your Own**, or who were not successful in the **Quiz** section may benefit from the **Alternative Teaching Strategy** on the next page.

Alternative Teaching Strategy

20 Minutes

OBJECTIVE Count and record collections of dimes, nickels, and pennies

MATERIALS play dimes, nickels, and pennies (6 of each coin), spinner, paper and pencil for each pair

Prepare a 3-part spinner which displays a penny, a nickel, and a dime. Review the value of each coin.

Arrange children in pairs and distribute materials. Direct partners to take turns spinning the spinner and selecting the coins indicated. After each child has had 2 spins, have partners arrange the 4 coins on a piece of paper beginning with the coins of greatest value.

For instance, let's say one child spins a dime and a nickel and the other child spins a nickel and a penny. Have them line the coins up on the paper starting with the dime, followed by the 2 nickels and ending with the penny. Then direct Child A to draw circles on the paper to represent the coins and have them indicate what each coin is by inserting the value inside each circle. Then have Child A place a write-on line below each coin to show the counting on process, the last line should be followed by a cent sign.

Monitor the pairs to be sure that children are arranging their coins correctly, as well as counting on correctly.

Discuss how the value of each coin tells what number to use when you skip count to find the total amount. Then have Child B count the coins beginning with the coin of greatest value and recording each amount on the write-on lines below each coin. Then have Child B circle the total amount at the end of the row.

Have partners reverse roles and repeat the activity. As children become more comfortable grouping the coins and counting on to find the amount, have them increase the number of spins to 3 each, which will result in collections of 6 coins.

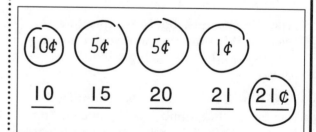

© Harcourt

Grade 2
Skill
30

Count Collections

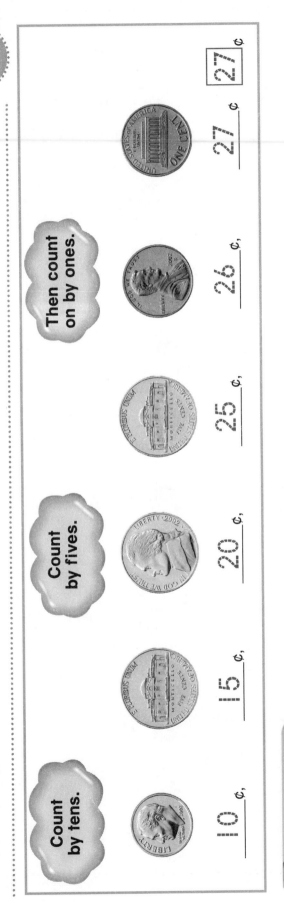

Count by tens.

10 ¢,

15 ¢,

Count by fives.

20 ¢,

25 ¢,

Then count on by ones.

26 ¢,

27 ¢

27 ¢

Try These

Count. Write the amount.

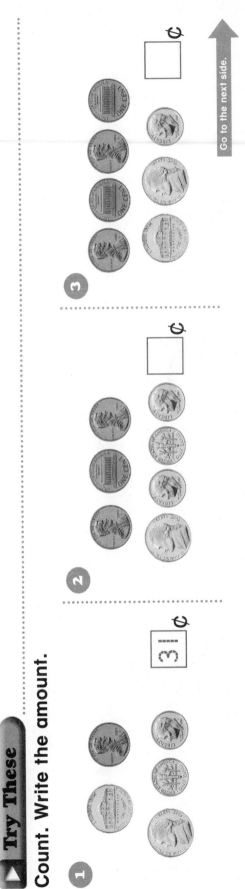

1   3 ---- ¢

2   □ ¢

3   □ ¢

Go to the next side.

Practice on Your Own

Skill 30

Count by tens. Count by fives. Then count on by ones.

__10__ ¢, __20__ ¢, __30__ ¢, __35__ ¢, __36__ ¢, __37__ ¢ [37] ¢

Count. Write the amount.

1   □ ¢

2   □ ¢

3   □ ¢

4   □ ¢

 **Quiz**

Count. Write the amount.

5   □ ¢

6   □ ¢

Skill **31**

Value of a Quarter

Using Skill 31

⏱ 20 Minutes

OBJECTIVE Identify groups of coins equal in amount to a quarter

MATERIALS play money (quarters, dimes, nickels, and pennies)

Provide each child with an envelope containing play coins—1 quarter, 2 dimes, 5 nickels, and 25 pennies. Have children sort the coins.

Ask: **How many kinds of coins do you have?** (4) **What are they?** (pennies, nickels, dimes, quarter)

Have children point to each kind of coin as they identify them.
Ask: **Which coin is worth 1 cent?** (penny) **5 cents?** (nickel) **10 cents?** (dime) **25 cents?** (quarter)

Invite children to count the pennies.
Ask: **Will you count by ones, fives, or tens?** (by ones)
Ask: **How many pennies do you have?** (25) **What are 25 pennies worth?** (25 cents) **Which coin is worth the same amount as 25 pennies?** (quarter)

Example

Focus attention on the model at the top of the page.

Say: **We just showed 2 ways to make 25 cents but there are still more combinations you can use. For example, you could use just nickels to make 25 cents or you could use nickels and dimes to make 25 cents. There are several possibilities.**

Ask: **How do you count dimes?** (by tens) **nickels?** (by fives)

Say: **When you count a group of mixed coins, remember to start with the coin of greatest value.**

TRY THESE In Exercises 1–2 children practice ways to make 25 cents.

• **Exercises 1–2** Show 2 ways to make 25 cents using nickels and pennies.

PRACTICE ON YOUR OWN Review the example at the top of the page. Exercises 1–2 provide practice showing 2 ways to make 25 cents using dimes and nickels.

QUIZ Determine if children can correctly show ways to make 25 cents using dimes, nickels, and pennies. Success is indicated by 2 out of 2 correct responses.

Children who successfully complete **Practice on Your Own** and **Quiz** are ready to move to the next skill.

COMMON ERRORS

• Children may forget the values of the coins.

• Children may forget how to count on.

If a child makes 1 error or more in **Practice on Your Own**, work through the exercises together. Have the child explain the exercises aloud to determine if he or she knows the values of the different coins and how to count on beginning with coins of the greatest value. The child may also benefit from the **Alternative Teaching Strategy** on the next page.

© Harcourt

Alternative Teaching Strategy

20 Minutes

OBJECTIVE Identify collections of coins that show 25 cents

MATERIALS index cards, play coins (1 quarter, 25 pennies, 2 dimes, 5 nickels)

Have children form pairs. Provide each pair with play coins, a set of 12 cards with a variety of combinations of coins showing 25 cents and some showing less than 25 cents, and 2 sheets of paper—one labeled Group 1 25¢, the other labeled Group 2 Not 25¢.

Tell children that they will work together with partners to determine the combinations of coins that show 25 cents.

Guide partners to take turns choosing a card from the deck. For each card they choose, children should:

- model the coins with a one-to-one correspondence

- count aloud to find the total amount

- record the amount on the back of the card

Remind children that when they count a group of mixed coins, they should start with the coins of greatest value.

After each pair works through their set of cards, have them sort the cards into two groups on the handouts labeled Group 1 25¢ and Group 2 Not 25¢.

For more practice, encourage the groups to use their cards as flash cards. For example, one partner might hold up the coin side of a card and have the other partner name the amount.

Another way to use them might be to use the other side showing a number amount say, 25¢, where the card holder provides the number of coins shown on the other side. Let's say 5 coins were used. The guesser would have to choose 5 coins to equal this amount. Encourage the pairs to help each other when needed.

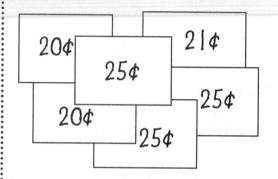

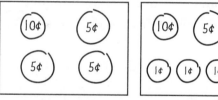

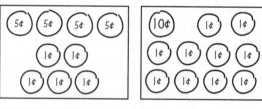

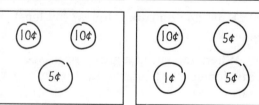

Grade 2
Skill 31

Value of a Quarter

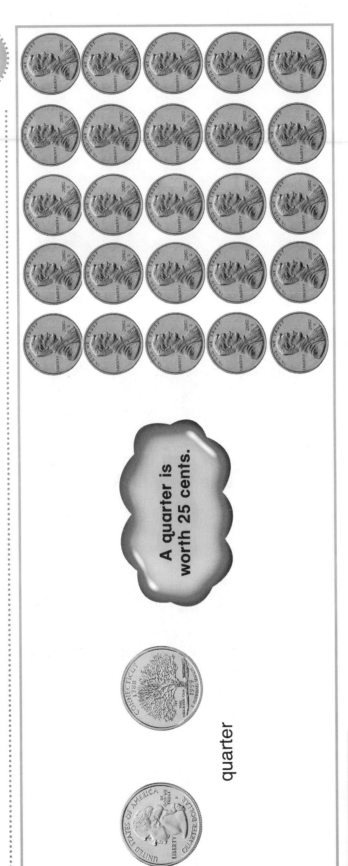

A quarter is worth 25 cents.

quarter

Go to the next side.

Try These

Show ways to make 25 cents. Draw the coins. Use nickels and pennies.

1

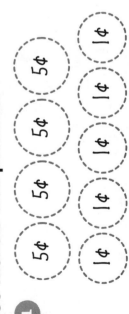

| 5¢ | 5¢ | 5¢ | 5¢ |
| 1¢ | 1¢ | 1¢ | 1¢ | 1¢ |

2

Practice on Your Own

Skill 31

quarter

A quarter is worth 25 cents.

Show ways to make 25 cents. Draw and label the coins.
Use dimes and nickels.   **Use only nickels.**

1   10¢   10¢   5¢   2

▶ Quiz

Show ways to make 25 cents. Draw and label the coins.
Use dimes, nickels, and pennies.

3   4

Skill 32

Grade 2

Using Skill 32

OBJECTIVE Recognize and identify the value of a half dollar and a dollar

Provide each child with an envelope containing 50¢ in play money (pennies, nickels, dimes, or quarters). Review the value of each. Have children examine the contents of their envelopes.

Ask: **What type of coin is in your envelope? How many?** (Answers will vary.) **What is the value?** (50¢)
Say: **50¢ has the same value as a half dollar.**
Write 50¢ on the board, and point out the cent symbol. Show children a half dollar coin, and identify it as a half dollar.
Ask: **How many pennies have the same value as a half dollar?** (50) **How many nickels have the same value as a half dollar?** (10) **How many dimes?** (5) **How many quarters?** (2)

Pair children who have the same kind of coins. Have pairs combine their coins and count by ones, fives, tens, or twenty-fives to find their value.
Ask: **What is the value of your combined coins?** (100¢)
Say: **100¢ has the same value as a dollar.**
Write $1 on the board, and point out the symbol for dollar. Show children a one dollar bill, and identify it as a dollar.
Ask: **How many pennies have the same value as a dollar?** (100) **How many nickels?** (20) **How many dimes?** (10) **How many quarters?** (4) **How many half dollars?** (2)

TRY THESE Exercises 1–2 uses coins to make a half dollar and a dollar.

MATERIALS envelopes, play money (coins and dollar bills)

- **Exercise 1**   Use dimes to make a half dollar.

- **Exercise 2**   Use quarters to make a dollar.

PRACTICE ON YOUR OWN Review the example at the top of the page. Exercises 1–3 provide practice using nickels, dimes, and quarters to make half dollars or dollars.

QUIZ Determine if children can draw and write the correct number of coins it takes to make a dollar. Success is indicated by 2 out of 2 correct responses.

Children who successfully complete **Practice on Your Own** and **Quiz** are ready to move to the next skill.

COMMON ERRORS

- Children may count the value of the coins rather than the number of coins.

- Children may confuse the values of nickels, dimes, and quarters.

- Children may be unable to count by fives, tens, twenty-fives, or fifties.

If a child makes 1 or more errors in **Practice on Your Own**, have the child model the amounts in the exercises while you observe. The child may also benefit from the **Alternative Teaching Strategy** on the next page.

Alternative Teaching Strategy

20 Minutes

OBJECTIVE Use nickels, dimes, and quarters to model the value of half dollars and dollars

MATERIALS play money (20 nickels, 10 dimes, 4 quarters) for each child

Display a half dollar and a dollar bill and review the value of each.

Distribute the play money (nickels, dimes, and quarters) and have children sort them into three groups. Then review the value of each coin.
Ask: **What is the value of a nickel?** (5¢)
What is the value of a dime? (10¢) **What is the value of a quarter?** (25¢)

Say: **We are going to pretend to go shopping.**
Display a classroom item, such as a book, with a price tag of 50¢.
Ask: **How much does this book cost?** (50¢)
Say: **Using only one kind of coin, show the coins that you could use to pay for this book.**
Check to see that children have arranged the correct number of nickels, dimes, or quarters to make 50¢.

Begin a chart on the board like the one below to record the groups of coins as children describe them.

	nickels	dimes	quarters
half dollar	(10)	(5)	(2)
1 dollar	(20)	(10)	(4)

Say: **Let's see how many nickels make 50¢. For those who used nickels, touch each nickel and count aloud by fives to check that you have 50¢.**
Ask: **How many nickels did it take to make 50¢, or the value of a half dollar?** (10 nickels)

Say: **Let's see how many dimes make 50¢. For those who used dimes, touch each dime and count aloud by tens to check that you have 50¢.**
Ask: **How many dimes did it take to make 50¢, or the value of a half dollar?** (5 dimes)

Say: **Let's see how many quarters make 50¢. For those who used quarters, touch each quarter and count aloud by 25's to check that you have 50¢.**
Ask: **How many quarters did it take to make 50¢, or the value of a half dollar?** (2 quarters)

Display a different item with a price tag of $1. Ask children to use one kind of coin to show how to pay for the item.

Have children count by fives to 100 to determine how many nickels it takes to equal the value of a dollar, by tens to determine how many dimes, and by 25 to determine how many quarters.

Record each grouping on the chart. Point out that it takes 2 half dollars to make 100¢ or 1 dollar.

© Harcourt

Value of Half Dollars and Dollars

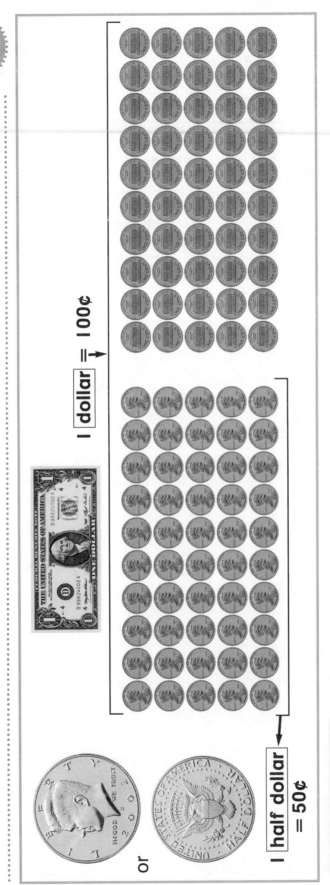

I dollar = 100¢

I half dollar
= 50¢

Go to the next side.

Try These

Show ways to make a half dollar or a dollar. Draw the coins. Write how many.

1 Use only dimes.

5 ___ dimes = I half dollar

2 Use only quarters.

___ quarters = I dollar

Practice on Your Own

Skill 32

| I half dollar | I dollar | I dollar |

2 half dollars

Show ways to make a half dollar or a dollar.
Draw the coins. Write how many.

1 Use only nickels.

_____ nickels = I half dollar

2 Use only dimes.

_____ dimes = I dollar

3 Use only quarters.

_____ quarters = I half dollar

▶ Quiz

Show ways to make a dollar.
Draw the coins. Write how many.

4 Use only nickels.

_____ nickels = I dollar

5 Use only half dollars.

_____ half dollars = I dollar

Using Skill 33

OBJECTIVE Compare amounts of money

MATERIALS play money in coins

Write pairs of numbers on the board such as 32 and 38, 50 and 49, and 64 and 58. Have children identify the greater number in each pair. Then distribute the play money (coins) to pairs of children.

Say: **Make 2 groups of coins. Put 1 quarter, 1 dime, 2 nickels, and 3 pennies in a group on the left side of your desk.**
Give children time to complete the task.
Say: **Put 1 quarter, 2 dimes, 1 nickel, and 4 pennies in a group on the right side of your desk.**
Check that children have selected the correct combination of coins.

Remind children to begin counting the coins with the greatest value first.
Ask: **What is the value of the coins in the group on the left side?** (48¢)
Write 48¢ on the board.
Ask: **What is the value of the coins in the group on the right side?** (54¢)
Write 54¢ on the board.
Ask: **Which is the greater amount?** (54¢) **How do you know?** (54 is greater than 48, so 54¢ is greater than 48¢.)

Repeat the procedure using other groups of coins.

Direct children's attention to the example at the top of the page.
Ask: **What is the value of the coins on the left?** (40¢) **What is the value of the coins on the right?** (45¢)
Have children trace the numbers.
Ask: **Which is the greater value?** (45¢)
Have children trace the circle around the amount with the greater value.

TRY THESE These exercises provide practice in counting groups of coins and comparing values.

- **Exercises 1–2** Count 2 groups of coins and circle the greater amount.

PRACTICE ON YOUR OWN Review the example at the top of the page. Encourage children to explain how they know which amount is greater. Exercises 1–2 provide practice counting groups of coins and identifying the greater amount in each pair.

QUIZ Determine if children can determine the greater value of two groups of coins. Success is indicated by 2 out of 2 correct responses.

Children who successfully complete **Practice on Your Own** and **Quiz** are ready to move to the next skill.

COMMON ERRORS

- Children may count the number of coins rather than their value.

- Children may confuse the values of pennies, nickels, dimes, quarters, and half dollars.

If a child makes 1 error in **Practice on Your Own**, have the child use coins to model the exercises while you observe. The child may benefit from the **Alternative Teaching Strategy** on the next page.

Alternative Teaching Strategy

20 Minutes

OBJECTIVE Count groups of coins and compare amounts

MATERIALS play money in coins, paper for each child; spinner showing quarters, dimes, nickels and pennies for each pair

Prepare spinners like the one shown below.

Distribute coins to children and review the value of pennies, nickels, dimes, quarters, and half dollars.

Have children form pairs and combine their coins into one collection. Give each pair a spinner.

One partner spins the spinner and selects the coin or coins shown. Then the other partner does the same. Partners continue taking turns until they have each had 4 turns to spin.

Say: **Now, count your coins and write the value. Remember to count on from the coins with the greatest value to the coins with the least value.**

Ask: **What coins will you count first?** (quarters) **Second?** (dimes) **Third?** (nickels) **Last?** (pennies)

Have partners count their coins. Offer help as needed, modeling counting on, if necessary.

Say: **Now, compare the two amounts.** Ask: **Which amount is greater?** (Answers will vary.) Say: **The partner with the greater amount scores 1 point.**

Have partners play again. After 4 turns have them count their coins, record the amount, and compare to see who has the greater amount. The partner with the greater amount scores a point. Suggest that children continue playing until one partner scores 3 points.

© Harcourt

Compare Values of Coins

Count each group of coins. Circle the amount that is greater.

40 ¢   (45) ¢

▲ **Try These**

Count each group of coins. Circle the amount that is greater.

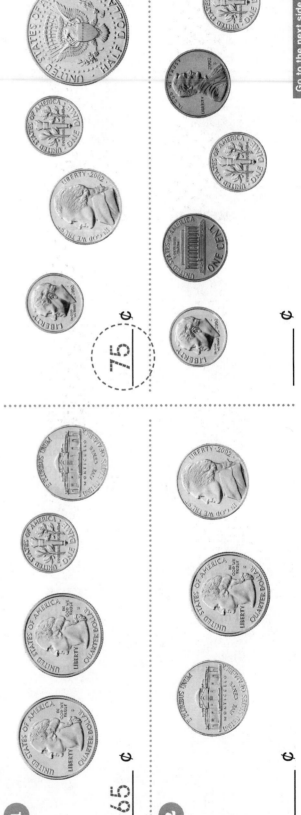

①   65 ¢   (75) ¢

②   _____ ¢   _____ ¢

Go to the next side.

Practice on Your Own

Count each group of coins. Circle the amount that is greater.

50 ¢   49 ¢

Count each group of coins. Circle the amount that is greater.

1   85 ¢   90 ¢

2   _____ ¢   _____ ¢

Quiz

Count each group of coins. Circle the amount that is greater.

3   _____ ¢   _____ ¢

4   _____ ¢   _____ ¢

Skill 34

Grade 2

Using Skill 34

OBJECTIVE Make different combinations of coins to show equal amounts of money

Example

Distribute the coins. Focus attention on the example at the top of the page. Discuss the amount of the pen. Have the children find and hold up the 2 coins used in the first example.

Ask: **What are these coins called?** (quarters) **How much is 1 quarter worth?** (25¢) **So what is the value of 2 quarters?** (50¢) Draw two circles on the board. Write 25¢ in each circle to represent the quarters.

Say: **Two quarters do make 50¢ but you can also show 50¢ in other ways. Look at the next example. Find the coin they used to make 50¢ and hold it up.**

Ask: **What is this coin called?** (half-dollar) **How much is 1 half-dollar worth?** (50¢) Draw 1 large circle on the board. Write 50¢ inside of it to represent the half-dollar.

Ask: **What is the greatest number of coins used to make 50¢ in this example?** (2)

Ask: **What is the fewest number of coins used to make 50¢ in this example?** (1)

Ask: **Why is the picture of 1 coin circled instead of the one with 2 coins?** (The directions say to circle the way that uses the fewest number of coins and one half-dollar is fewer coins than 2 quarters.)

Before continuing, you may want to ask the children to show a few more ways to show 50¢ other than the 2 ways already described. Then have them compare the number of coins used in each grouping to determine which used the least amount of coins.

MATERIALS play coins per child: 1 half-dollar; 3 quarters; 9 dimes; 19 nickels

TRY THESE In Exercises 1–2 children draw different variations of coins to show equal amounts of money.

Exercises 1–2 Use coins to model 2 ways of showing a given amount, draw the coins, and circle the way that uses fewer coins.

PRACTICE ON YOUR OWN Review the example at the top of the page. Encourage children to explain why the combination of 4 coins is circled. Exercises 1–2 provide practice in modeling and drawing two different combinations of coins to show an amount and then identifying the combination that uses fewer coins.

QUIZ Determine if children can make and compare two combinations of coins for equal amounts and determine which one used the fewest number of coins. Success is indicated by 2 out of 2 correct responses.

Children who successfully complete **Practice on Your Own** and **Quiz** are ready to move to the next skill.

COMMON ERRORS

- Children may forget the value of coins.

- Children may draw too few or too many circles for coins.

If a child makes an error on the **Practice on Your Own**, or is not successful on the **Quiz**, work through an exercise with the child. Have the child explain the exercise aloud to determine if he or she knows the value of the coins. This child may also benefit from the **Alternative Teaching Strategy** on the next page.

© Harcourt

Alternative Teaching Strategy

OBJECTIVE Use play coins to show equal amounts of money

MATERIALS play coins per child: 19 nickels, 9 dimes, 3 quarters, and 1 half-dollar; paper, pencil

Review the names for each coin: *nickel*, *dime*, *quarter*, and *half-dollar* and discuss their values. Provide each child with a set of play coins.

Say: **You will use your coins to show different ways to make equal amounts of money.**

Work through an example or two together as a class. Write 45¢ on the board.

Say: **Name one way to show 45¢.** Give children time to think about an answer using their coins to help them come up with a combination. Choose one volunteer to share his or her combination but encourage the others to leave their combinations in front of them for later use. Let's say the first volunteer chose 4 dimes and 1 nickel. Draw 5 circles on the board to represent each of the coins, the coins' value should be written inside.

Ask: **Which of these coins are worth the most?** (dimes) **How much are they worth?** (10¢ each) Say: **So we can count the dimes by tens.**

Ask: **How much is the nickel worth?** (5¢) Say: **So we can count on by 5's after we count the dimes.**

Say: **Let's count together: 10, 20, 30, 40, 45¢.** Emphasize the counting pattern by pointing to each coin value as you count on.

Say: **Now draw 5 circles on your paper. Write the amounts inside. Under each circle, show the counting on process and circle the total amount.**
Observe children's work.

Say: **Now I need someone to share a different combination of coins to show the same amount.** Once again, give children some time to work this out. While some children may already have a different combination from their first try, others may want some time to think of a new combination. Let's say the next volunteer chooses 1 quarter and 2 dimes. Draw 3 circles on the board to represent each of the coins with their value written inside.

Ask: **Which of these coins is worth the most?** (quarter) **How much is it worth?** (25¢) Say: **We already know to count the dimes by tens. So let's count these coins together: 25, 35, 45¢.** Emphasize the counting pattern by pointing to each coin as you count aloud.

Say: **Let's look at the two groups of coins we used to show 45¢. Remember, both groups show equal amounts even though they don't use the same number of coins.**

Ask: **Which group uses fewer coins?** (the group with 1 quarter and 2 dimes) **Why?** (this combination only used 3 coins to make 45¢, the other group used 5.)

Repeat this activity with different amounts such as 75¢, 40¢, 85¢, and 60¢. Encourage children to work independently and then review possible answers together.

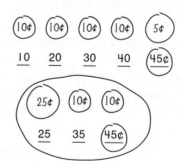

Make Equal Amounts

Grade 2
Skill
34

Use coins. Show the amount in two ways.
Draw the coins. Circle the way that uses fewer coins.

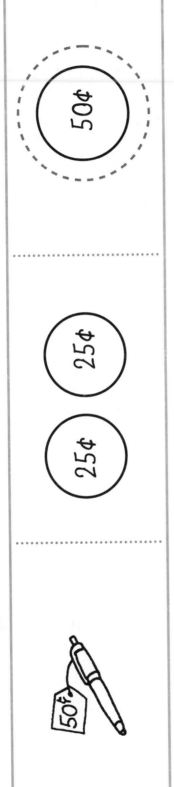

Try These

Use coins. Show the amount in two ways.
Draw the coins. Circle the way that uses fewer coins.

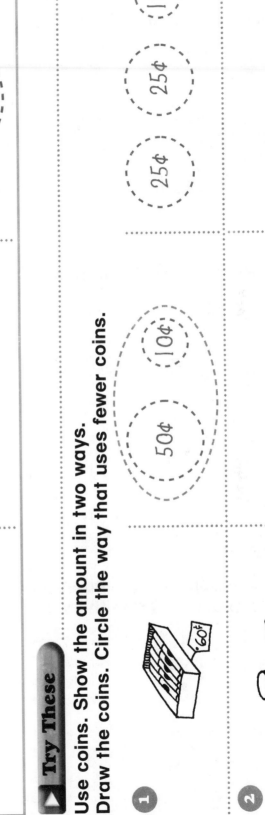

Go to the next side.

© Harcourt

Practice on Your Own

Skill 34

Use coins. Show the amount in two ways.
Draw the coins. Circle the way that uses fewer coins.

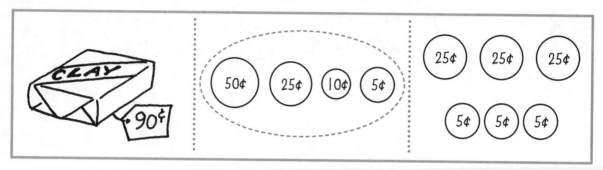

Use coins. Show the amount in two ways.
Draw the coins. Circle the way that uses fewer coins.

1

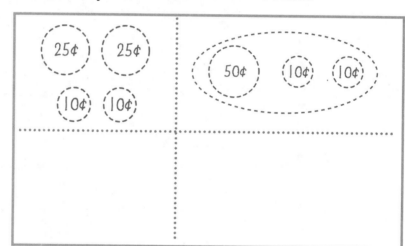

2

▶ Quiz

Use coins. Show the amount in two ways.
Draw the coins. Circle the way that uses fewer coins.

3

4

Number Sense, Concepts, and Operations

Whole Number Multiplication

Using Skill 35

OBJECTIVE Act out making and counting equal amounts

MATERIALS class set of color tiles

Call on eight children and invite them to come to the front of the classroom. Then ask the children to form pairs. Have each pair stand in a different spot.

Ask: **How many groups are there?** (4) **Are the groups equal?** (yes) **How can you tell?** (There are 2 children in each group and no one left over.) **How many children are there in all?** (8) **How do you know?** (Possible answers: I counted each child; I counted by 2's because there are 2 children in each of the 4 groups.) You may wish to have the children in the 4 groups count off by ones and then again by 2's.

Repeat the procedure with other groups of children, such as 2 groups of 5; 4 groups of 4; and 5 groups of 3.

Example

Distribute color tiles. Focus children's attention on the example at the top of the page. Have children model the example.

Ask: **How many groups of tiles are there?** (2) **How many tiles are in each group?** (4) **How many tiles are there in all?** (8)

TRY THESE In Exercises 1–3, children practice making equal groups and count how many in all to prepare them for the work they will encounter in the **Practice on Your Own.**

- **Exercise 1** Make 2 groups of 3.
- **Exercise 2** Make 4 groups of 3.
- **Exercise 3** Make 3 groups of 5.

PRACTICE ON YOUR OWN Review the example at the top of the page with children. Exercises 1–3 provide practice making equal groups and counting how many in all. As children work, remind them that there should be no tiles left over when groups have equal amounts. When finding the total, encourage children to count by the number of tiles in each group.

QUIZ Determine if children can make equal groups of a given number and count how many in all. Success is indicated by 2 out of 2 correct responses.

Children who successfully complete **Practice on Your Own** and **Quiz** are ready to move to the next skill.

COMMON ERRORS

- Children may reverse the number of groups with the number of tiles in each group.

- Children may only count the number of groups or only the number of tiles in one group instead of counting the number of tiles in all.

Children who made more than 1 error in **Practice On Your Own** or who were not successful in the **Quiz** section may benefit from the **Alternative Teaching Strategy** on the next page.

Alternative Teaching Strategy

20 Minutes

OBJECTIVE Make and count equal groups

MATERIALS for each pair of children: 20 connecting cubes; 2 sets of number cards from 2–5 (color code sets; red & blue)

In advance, prepare two sets of number cards for each pair of children. Use red paper (or red marker) for one set of numbers and blue paper (or blue marker) for the other set.

Arrange children in pairs. Give each pair 20 connecting cubes and 2 sets of number cards.

Say: **Use the connecting cubes to make equal groups. Choose 1 number card from each set. The red cards tell you how many groups to make. The blue cards tell you how many cubes to put in each group. Then count to find how many cubes there are in all.**

Model the process. Have one child select a red card, 5, for example.

Ask: **How many groups will you make?** (5)

Have the partner pick a blue number card, 3, for example, from the other set.

Ask: **How many connecting cubes will you put in each group?** (3)

Have the pairs work together to model the groups and tell how many in all. First, have them count each cube individually and then have them count by the number in each group to check their work.

Ask: **How do you know there are 15 cubes in all?** (Possible answers: We counted by 1's; we counted by 3's.)

Have pairs continue play by selecting a new number card from each set until all cards have been used. Observe children as they work. Encourage them to verbalize how many groups, how many in each group, and how many cubes in all by counting by 2's, 3's, 4's, or 5's.

5	3

© Harcourt

Grade 2
Skill
35

© Harcourt

Counting Equal Groups

Use ■ **. Draw them. Write how many in all.**

There are 2 equal groups.
Each group has 4 tiles.
There are 8 tiles in all.

■ ■ ■ ■   ■ ■ ■ ■

▶ Try These

Use ■ **. Draw them. Write how many in all.**

1 Make 2 groups.
Put 3 ■ in each group.

■ ■ ■   ■ ■ ■

How many in all? _____

2 Make 4 groups.
Put 3 ■ in each group.

How many in all? _____

3 Make 3 groups.
Put 5 ■ in each group.

How many in all? _____

Go to the next side.

Practice on Your Own

Skill 35

There are 3 equal groups.
Each group has 3 tiles.
There are 9 tiles in all.

Use ■. Draw them. Write how many in all.

1 Make 4 groups. Put 4 ■ in each group.

How many in all? __16__

2 Make 3 groups. Put 4 ■ in each group.

How many in all? _____

3 Make 5 groups. Put 2 ■ in each group.

How many in all? _____

▶ Quiz

Use ■. Draw them. Write how many in all.

4 Make 2 groups. Put 6 ■ in each group.

How many in all? _____

5 Make 4 groups. Put 2 ■ in each group.

How many in all? _____

© Harcourt

Number Sense, Concepts, and Operations

Fractions

Using Skill 36

OBJECTIVE Identify two equal parts, or halves

MATERIALS construction paper, scissors

Make two large circles from construction paper. Display one circle. Then cut it into two unequal parts. Allow time for children to examine the two parts.

Ask: **Are these two parts equal?** (no) **How can you tell?** (The 2 parts do not match; one part is larger than the other.) Display the two parts again with the smaller section on top of the larger one. Then put them together to form a circle. Say: **You are right. They are two unequal parts of a whole.**

Display the other circle. Have children observe as you cut the circle into two equal parts. Allow time for children to examine the two parts.

Ask: **Are these two parts equal?** (yes) **How can you tell?** (The 2 parts are exactly the same size and shape.) Display the two parts one on top of the other. Then put them together to form a circle. Say: **They are two equal parts of a whole. They are halves. Two halves make one whole. To be called** *halves*, **there must be two equal parts.**

Repeat the procedure with triangles, squares, and rectangles.

Example

Direct children's attention to the example at the top of the page. Read the example together. Have children put a finger on the shaded half of the circle, and then on the other half.

Say: **These are 2 equal parts. Each part is called one half. Together they make one whole.**

TRY THESE These exercises prepare children for the exercises they will encounter in **Practice on Your Own.**

- **Exercises 1–2** Identify shapes that show halves.

PRACTICE ON YOUR OWN As you review the example at the top of the page, have children explain how they know the two parts are halves. Exercises 1–3 provide practice identifying two equal parts, or halves.

QUIZ Determine if children can identify halves. Success is indicated by 2 out of 2 correct responses.

Children who successfully complete **Practice on Your Own** and **Quiz** are ready to move to the next skill.

COMMON ERRORS

- Children may identify a shape with two unequal parts as a shape that shows halves.

- Children may color both halves of a shape instead of one half.

If a child makes 1 or more errors in the **Practice on Your Own,** have the child explain the exercises aloud. Determine whether he or she understands the concept that 2 equal parts, or halves, make one whole. The child may also benefit from the **Alternative Teaching Strategy** on the next page.

Alternative Teaching Strategy

20 Minutes

OBJECTIVE Identify and show equal parts, or halves

MATERIALS scissors; pairs of identical construction paper circles, triangles, rectangles, or squares of two different colors; and one large paper circle, triangle, rectangle or square

For each pair of shapes, draw a line to divide one shape into equal halves, and the other shape into 2 unequal parts.

Distribute the materials to each child. Instruct children to set aside the large paper shapes until later and look at the two same-sized construction paper shapes.

Say: **Cut along the line that divides each shape.** Ask: **How many parts does each shape have?** (2 parts)

Say: **One of the shapes you cut apart has 2 equal parts called halves. The other has 2 unequal parts.** Ask: **How can you tell which shape has two unequal parts?** (The two parts do not match; one part is smaller than the other part.) **How can you tell which shape has two equal parts, or halves?** (Both parts are exactly the same size and shape; both parts match.)

Say: **Now, put together the two parts of each shape to make a whole. Point to the shape that shows halves. Point to the shape that does *not* show halves.** (Check children's responses.)

Have children display the large paper shape they set aside earlier. Ask: **How can you divide your shape into two equal parts?** (Fold the shape in half and then cut along the fold line.)

Have children fold their shapes, cut along the lines, and then trade the parts with one another. Say: **Look at the two parts. Put one part on top of the other.** Ask: **Are they halves?** (yes) **How can you be sure?** (They match exactly.) Say: **Now put the two parts together to make a whole.** (Check children's responses.)

© Harcourt

Grade 2 Skill

Halves

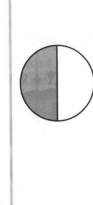

1 out of 2 equal parts is $\frac{1}{2}$ or **one half**.
Two halves make one whole.

whole

Try These

Circle the shapes that show halves. Color $\frac{1}{2}$.

1.

2.

Go to the next side.

Practice on Your Own

whole

1 out of 2 equal parts is $\frac{1}{2}$ or **one half**. Two halves make one whole.

Circle the shapes that show halves. Color $\frac{1}{2}$.

1

2

3

▶ Quiz

Circle the shapes that show halves. Color $\frac{1}{2}$.

4

5

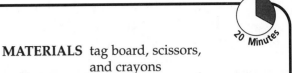

Using Skill 37

OBJECTIVE Identify fourths

MATERIALS tag board, scissors, and crayons

Make two large circles from white tag board. Display one of the circles and have children identify the shape. Have children observe as you fold the circle in half and then in half again. Cut along the folds. Display the 4 fourths, one on top of the other.

Ask: **Are the four parts of this circle equal?** (yes) **How can you tell?** (Each part is exactly the same size and shape.)

Ask a volunteer to color one of the fourths. Say: **1 out of 4 equal parts is called $\frac{1}{4}$. Four fourths make one whole.** Put the fourths back together to form the original circle. Write $\frac{1}{4}$ on the board.

Focus children's attention on the models at the top of the page. Encourage them to describe the shapes and how they're divided. Have them look at the second figure and tell the fraction of the whole that is shaded.

TRY THESE In Exercises 1–2 children identify shapes that show fourths. This will prepare children for the exercises they will encounter in **Practice On Your Own**.

- **Exercises 1–2** Find the shapes that show fourths. Color $\frac{1}{4}$.

PRACTICE ON YOUR OWN Review the example at the top of the page. Display the other whole circle. Have children observe as you fold the circle in half. Cut along the fold. Display the halves, one on top of the other and repeat the questions used for reviewing fourths. Exercises 1–6 provide practice coloring one part of a whole and circling the fraction that matches.

QUIZ Determine if children can color one part of a whole and correctly identify the fraction that names the shaded part. Success is indicated by 2 out of 3 correct responses.

Children who successfully complete **Practice on Your Own** and **Quiz** are ready to move to the next skill.

COMMON ERRORS

- Children may forget how to identify parts of a whole.

- Children may count or color all the parts of the whole.

Children who made more than 2 errors in **Practice on Your Own**, or who were not successful in the **Quiz** section, may benefit from the **Alternative Teaching Strategy** on the next page.

Alternative Teaching Strategy

20 Minutes

OBJECTIVE Identify and write fractions for one fourth and one half

MATERIALS for each group of 4 children: 12 labeled envelopes with either circle, rectangle or square tag board parts to equal the whole (for each shape type: divide into 4 equal parts and 2 equal parts; and 4 unequal parts and 2 unequal parts); crayons; 2 recording sheets

Divide the class into groups of 4 and pass out the materials. Have each group place the four envelopes that say *square* in front of them. Begin by modeling the activity on the board.

Draw four large squares on the board. Divide one square into four equal parts, one into four unequal parts, one into two equal parts and one into two unequal parts. As you point to each square, have the children count the number of parts each square has been divided into. Have each group assemble their 4 squares and identify the same patterns.

Guide groups to compare the 2 squares that have been divided into four parts. Ask: **What makes these squares different?** (One square has four parts that are the same size and shape; the other square has four parts that are not.)

Direct each group to sort the squares with four equal parts from the ones that are not equal. Then compare the ones with two parts in the same way. Have each group continue to sort the remaining shapes in the same manner. Observe the groups and offer feedback as needed.

Once the shapes have been correctly sorted, instruct groups to place the unequal part shapes aside. Explain how fractions use equal parts to make up a whole.

Say: **Look at the squares.** Ask: **How many equal parts does each square have?** (1 has four equal parts and 1 has 2 equal parts.) Color one equal part from each square and then put them back in place.

Ask: **How many equal parts are colored in each?** (1 out of 4 equal parts and 1 out of 2 equal parts)

Say: **That's right. So, we can say one fourth of this square is colored and one half of that square is colored.** Write $\frac{1}{4}$ and $\frac{1}{2}$ on the board. Show children how to read the fractions. Next to the ones write *part colored* and next to the 4 and 2 write *equal parts in the whole.* Repeat this process with the remaining 5 equal part shapes. Offer guidance as needed.

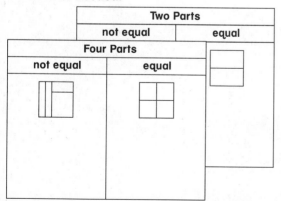

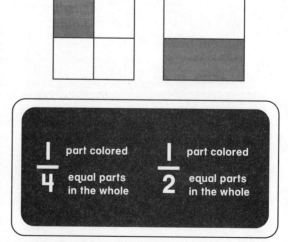

© Harcourt

Grade 2
Skill 37

Fourths

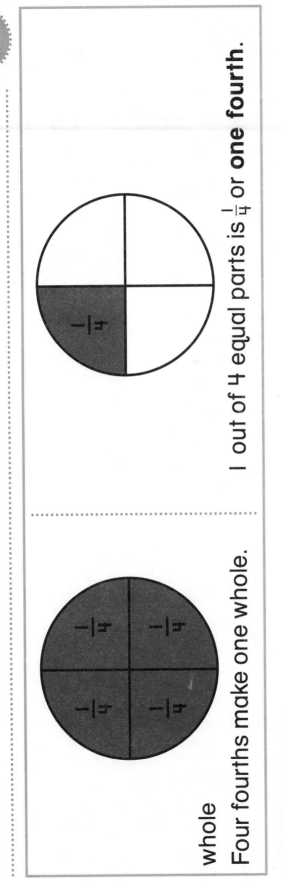

whole
Four fourths make one whole.

1 out of 4 equal parts is $\frac{1}{4}$ or **one fourth**.

Try These

Find the shapes that show fourths. Color $\frac{1}{4}$.

1.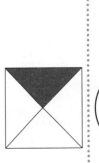

2.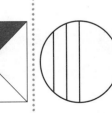

Go to the next side.

Name _____   Skill _____

Practice on Your Own

Skill **37**

 whole

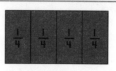 $\frac{1}{2}$

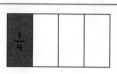 whole

$\frac{1}{4}$

I out of 2 equal parts is $\frac{1}{2}$ or **one half**.

I out of 4 equal parts is $\frac{1}{4}$ or **one fourth**.

Color one part. Circle the fraction.

1
$\frac{1}{2}$ $\frac{1}{4}$

2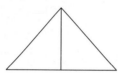
$\frac{1}{2}$ $\frac{1}{4}$

3
$\frac{1}{2}$ $\frac{1}{4}$

4
$\frac{1}{2}$ $\frac{1}{4}$

5
$\frac{1}{2}$ $\frac{1}{4}$

6
$\frac{1}{2}$ $\frac{1}{4}$

▶ **Quiz**

Color one part. Circle the fraction.

7
$\frac{1}{2}$ $\frac{1}{4}$

8
$\frac{1}{2}$ $\frac{1}{4}$

9
$\frac{1}{2}$ $\frac{1}{4}$

© Harcourt

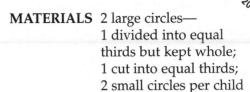

Using Skill 38

OBJECTIVE Identify one third

MATERIALS 2 large circles—
1 divided into equal
thirds but kept whole;
1 cut into equal thirds;
2 small circles per child

Display the large circles divided in thirds. Have children identify the number of parts in the whole. Pass out 2 circle patterns per child. Instruct children to cut along the lines of one of the circle patterns to make 3 parts. Place the 3 parts on top of one another.

Ask: **Are the 3 parts of the circle equal?** (yes) **How can you tell?** (Each part is exactly the same size and shape.) Place the 3 equal parts together to make a circle and place it next to the whole circle. Remove one part, color it and put it back in place.

Ask: **How many parts are colored?** (1) Say: **One out of three equal parts is called one third. So, we can say one third of the circle is colored.** Write $\frac{1}{3}$ on the board. Call on a few volunteers to explain the fraction in their own words.

Look at the whole.
Ask: **How many parts make up the whole?** (3) Say: **So, we can say three thirds make up one whole.**

Example

Focus attention on the models at the top of the page.

Ask: **How many parts are in the whole?** (3) **Are the parts equal?** (yes) **How many parts of the whole are shaded in the first square?** (3 out of 3 parts) **Are the equal parts halves, fourths, or thirds?** (thirds)

TRY THESE In exercises 1–2 children identify shapes that show thirds. This will prepare children for the exercises they will encounter on the **Practice On Your Own.**

- **Exercises 1–2** Find the shapes that show thirds. Color $\frac{1}{3}$.

PRACTICE ON YOUR OWN Review the example at the top of the page. Exercises 1–6 provide practice coloring one part of a whole and circling the fraction it matches.

QUIZ Determine if children can color one part of a whole and correctly identify the fraction that names the shaded part. Success is indicated by 2 out 3 correct responses.

Children who successfully complete **Practice on Your Own** and **Quiz** are ready to move to the next skill.

COMMON ERRORS

- Children may forget how to identify parts of a whole and may incorrectly identify a fraction in doing so.

- Children may count or color all the parts of each shape.

Children who made more than 2 errors in the **Practice on Your Own**, or who were not successful in the **Quiz** section, may benefit from the **Alternative Teaching Strategy** on the next page.

Alternative Teaching Strategy

20 Minutes

OBJECTIVE Identify and read $\frac{1}{3}$, $\frac{1}{4}$, and $\frac{1}{2}$ of wholes

MATERIALS drawing paper, marker, circles cut in thirds, fourths, and halves, paste, red crayon

Before cutting the circles into their fractional parts, use a marker to trace over the division lines so each part of the whole is clearly marked.

Have children form pairs. Distribute the circles that have been cut in thirds.

Say: **Look at the parts and put them together to make a circle.**

Ask: **How many parts make up the whole?** (3) **Are all three parts equal?** (yes) **How can you tell?** (When I place them on top of each other, they are the same size and shape.)

Say: **Pick up one part of the circle and color it red.**

Give children time to complete the task. Write one third as a fraction on the board. Across from the 1 write *part colored red* and across from the 3 write *parts make up the whole*.

Say: **Fractions name parts of a whole. The part you colored red can be explained by saying one third of the circle is colored red.**

Have the children paste the three parts on to a piece of paper to make a circle and write the fraction $\frac{1}{3}$ below it.

Continue this procedure to review fourths and halves.

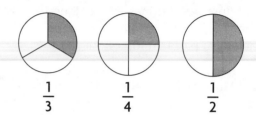

$\frac{1}{3}$ $\frac{1}{4}$ $\frac{1}{2}$

Grade 2
Skill 38

© Harcourt

Thirds

| $\frac{1}{3}$ | $\frac{1}{3}$ | $\frac{1}{3}$ |

whole

Three thirds make one whole.

| $\frac{1}{3}$ | | |

1 out of 3 equal parts is $\frac{1}{3}$ or **one third**.

Try These

Find the shapes that show thirds. Color $\frac{1}{3}$.

1.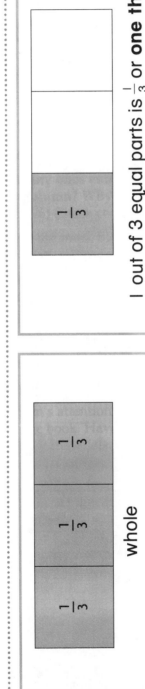

2.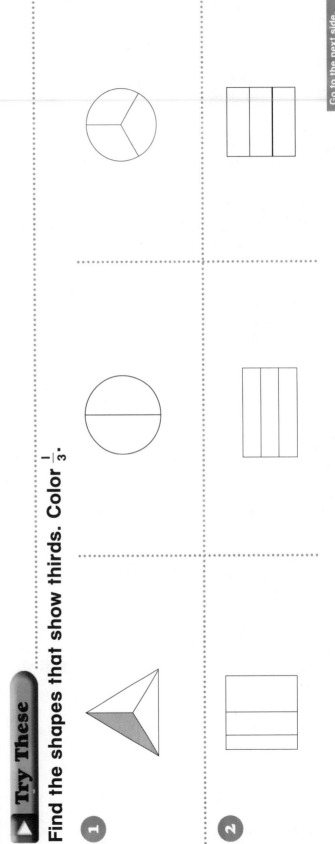

Go to the next side.

Practice on Your Own

I out of 2
equal parts is $\frac{1}{2}$.

I out of 3
equal parts is $\frac{1}{3}$.

I out of 4
equal parts is $\frac{1}{4}$.

Color one part. Circle the fraction.

1

$\frac{1}{3}$ $\frac{1}{2}$ $\frac{1}{4}$

2

$\frac{1}{3}$ $\frac{1}{2}$ $\frac{1}{4}$

3

$\frac{1}{3}$ $\frac{1}{2}$ $\frac{1}{4}$

4

$\frac{1}{3}$ $\frac{1}{2}$ $\frac{1}{4}$

5

$\frac{1}{3}$ $\frac{1}{2}$ $\frac{1}{4}$

6

$\frac{1}{3}$ $\frac{1}{2}$ $\frac{1}{4}$

▶ Quiz

Color one part. Circle the fraction.

7

$\frac{1}{3}$ $\frac{1}{2}$ $\frac{1}{4}$

8

$\frac{1}{3}$ $\frac{1}{2}$ $\frac{1}{4}$

9

$\frac{1}{3}$ $\frac{1}{2}$ $\frac{1}{4}$

Using Skill 39

OBJECTIVE Model and identify $\frac{1}{2}$, $\frac{1}{3}$, and $\frac{1}{4}$ of a group

MATERIALS for each child: large square stencil; ruler; drawing paper; red and blue crayons; scissors

Distribute materials to children.
Say: **Trace a square on your paper and cut it out.**

Show children how to fold the square into two equal parts.
Say: **Color one part of the square blue. Color the other part red.**
Ask: **How many equal parts are there?** (2) **How many parts are blue?** (1 part) **What part of the square is blue?** ($\frac{1}{2}$)
Say: **That's right. One out of two equal parts is one half, and two halves make one whole.**

Say: **Cut the parts of the square apart to make a group.**
Ask: **Is each part of the group the same?** (yes) **How many equal parts are in the group?** (2 equal parts) **How many are blue?** (1) **What part of the group is blue?** ($\frac{1}{2}$)
Say: **That's right. One half is one out of two equal parts.**

Repeat the activity, having children divide and cut a square into thirds and another square into fourths.

Example

Direct children's attention to the model at the top of the page. Discuss each set and the fractions represented.

TRY THESE In Exercises 1–3 children practice coloring the part of a group that shows a fraction of the group.

- **Exercise 1** Color to show $\frac{1}{3}$.

- **Exercise 2** Color to show $\frac{1}{2}$.

- **Exercise 3** Color to show $\frac{1}{4}$.

PRACTICE ON YOUR OWN Review the example at the top of the page. Exercises 1–4 provide practice in coloring one part of a group to model the fraction.

QUIZ Determine if children can correctly model each fraction by coloring the correct number of parts. Success is indicated by 2 out of 2 correct responses.

Children who successfully complete **Practice on Your Own** and **Quiz** are ready to move to the next skill.

COMMON ERRORS

- Children may simply color in all the parts of the group instead of one part of the group to model a fraction.

- Children may forget that in the fraction $\frac{1}{4}$, for example, 4 represents the number of equal parts in all, and 1 represents 1 of the 4 equal parts.

If a child makes more than 1 error in the **Practice on Your Own** or was not successful in the **Quiz**, work through an exercise together. Determine if the child understands what each number of the fraction means and what part of the whole the fraction represents. The child may also benefit from the **Alternative Teaching Strategy** on the next page.

Alternative Teaching Strategy

OBJECTIVE Model and record $\frac{1}{2}$, $\frac{1}{3}$, and $\frac{1}{4}$ of a group

MATERIALS paper plate, paper, red crayon, large sheet of drawing paper folded in thirds, 1 red counter, and 3 blue counters for each child

Distribute the materials.

Write $\frac{1}{2}$, $\frac{1}{3}$, and $\frac{1}{4}$ on the board. Have children name each fraction as you point to it and explain what it means. For example, $\frac{1}{2}$ means 1 out of 2 equal parts, $\frac{1}{3}$ means 1 out of 3 equal parts, and so on.

Say: **Put one red counter and one blue counter on your paper plate.**
Ask: **How many counters make up the group?** (2) **Are they equal parts?** (yes) **How many parts are red?** (1 part)
Say: **One red counter represents $\frac{1}{2}$ of the group.**
Point to the fraction on the board.

Say: **Write $\frac{1}{2}$ at the top of your paper. Draw a large circle. Then draw 2 triangles inside the circle.**
Ask: **How many out of the 2 triangles will you color red to show $\frac{1}{2}$?** (1 out of 2)
Have children color 1 triangle to model $\frac{1}{2}$.

$$\frac{1}{2}$$

Say: **Now put one more blue counter on your paper plate.**
Ask: **How many counters make up the group now?** (3) **Are they equal parts?** (yes) **How many parts are red?** (1 part) **One red counter represents what part of the group?** ($\frac{1}{3}$) Point to the fraction on the board.

Say: **Write $\frac{1}{3}$ in the middle of your paper. Draw a large circle. Inside the circle draw 3 squares.**
Ask: **How many out of the 3 squares will you color red to show $\frac{1}{3}$?** (1 out of 3) Have

$$\frac{1}{3}$$

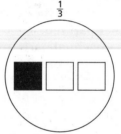

children color one of the 3 squares to model $\frac{1}{3}$.

Say: **Put one more blue counter on your plate.**
Ask: **How many counters make up the group now?** (4) **Are they equal parts?** (yes) **How many parts of the group are red?** (1 part) **One red counter represents what part of the group?** ($\frac{1}{4}$) Point to the fraction on the board.

Say: **Write $\frac{1}{4}$ at the bottom of your paper. Draw a large circle. Inside the circle draw 4 rectangles.**
Ask: **How many out of the 4 rectangles will you color red to show $\frac{1}{4}$?** (1 out of 4) Have children color one of the 4 rectangles to model $\frac{1}{4}$.

$$\frac{1}{4}$$

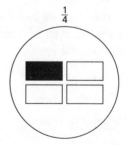

Grade 2
Skill
39

Parts of a Group

I out of 2 is black.
$\frac{1}{2}$ are black.

I out of 3 is black.
$\frac{1}{3}$ are black.

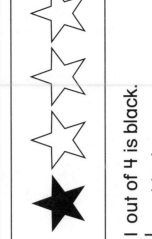

I out of 4 is black.
$\frac{1}{4}$ are black.

Go to the next side.

Try These

Color to show each fraction.

1 $\frac{1}{3}$

2 $\frac{1}{2}$

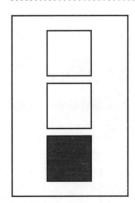

3 $\frac{1}{4}$

Practice on Your Own

Skill  39

		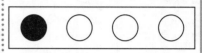
I out of 2 is black.	I out of 3 is black.	I out of 4 is black.
$\frac{1}{2}$ are black.	$\frac{1}{3}$ are black.	$\frac{1}{4}$ are black.

Color to show each fraction.

1 $\frac{1}{4}$

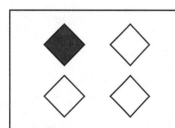

2 $\frac{1}{2}$

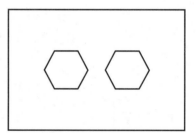

3 $\frac{1}{3}$

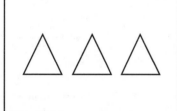

4 $\frac{1}{4}$

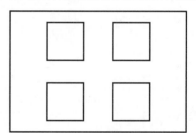

▶ **Quiz**

Color to show each fraction.

5 $\frac{1}{3}$

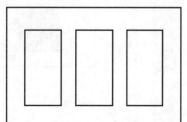

6 $\frac{1}{4}$

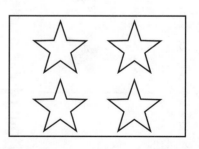

© Harcourt

Measurement

Skill 40

Grade 2

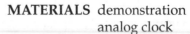

20 Minutes

Using Skill 40

OBJECTIVE Tell time to the hour

MATERIALS demonstration analog clock

Display the demonstration clock. Have children say the numbers as you point to them.

Say: **Look at the hands of the clock. One hand is called the hour hand. The other hand is called the minute hand.**

Ask: **How are the hands different?** (Possible answer: One hand is longer than the other.) **Which one is the hour hand?** (short hand) **Which one is the minute hand?** (long hand)

Example

Next, show how the minute hand moves around the clock every 60 minutes as the hour hand moves from one number to the next. Then set the hands to show 5 o'clock, the time shown in the example, and review how to tell time to the hour.

Say: **The hour hand points to the number on the clock that tells the hour. The minute hand tells how many minutes past the hour it is.**

Ask: **At what number is the hour hand pointing?** (5) **At what number is the minute hand pointing?** (12)

Say: **Whenever the minute hand points to the 12, it shows the time to the hour.**

Ask: **So, what time does the clock show?** (5 o'clock) Repeat with several other examples.

TRY THESE In Exercises 1–3 children practice modeling and recording time to the hour.

• **Exercises 1–3** Use a clock to show each time. Trace the hour hand and write the time.

PRACTICE ON YOUR OWN Review the example at the top of the page. Encourage children to explain how to read the clock. Exercises 1–6 provide practice modeling, reading, and recording time to the hour.

QUIZ Determine if children can tell time to the hour. Success is indicated by 2 out of 3 correct responses.

Children who successfully complete **Practice on Your Own** and **Quiz** are ready to move to the next skill.

COMMON ERRORS

• Children may confuse the minute hand and the hour hand.

• Children may record the incorrect number.

If a child makes more than 2 errors in the **Practice on Your Own** or was not successful in the **Quiz**, have the child redo the incorrect exercises while you observe. Determine if he or she is confused about the hour and minute hands. The child may also benefit from the **Alternative Teaching Strategy** on the next page.

© Harcourt

Alternative Teaching Strategy

OBJECTIVE Model and read times to the hour

MATERIALS for each child: demonstration analog clock; tagboard hour and minute hands; paper fastener; paper plate; and marker

Use the demonstration clock to point to the parts of a clock.

Ask: **What numbers do you see?** (1–12) **What do the numbers stand for?** (Possible answer: the 12 hours we use to tell time) **Which parts move to show the time?** (the hour hand and the minute hand)

Move the hands to show 8 o'clock. Discuss the minute and hour hands.

Ask: **Which hand is longer, the minute hand or the hour hand?** (minute hand) **Which hand is pointing to the 8?** (hour hand). **Which hand is pointing to the 12?** (minute hand)

Emphasize that the minute hand points to the 12 when it shows the time to the hour.

Ask: **What time does the clock show?** (8 o'clock) Call on volunteers to model other times to the hour.

Distribute materials to children, and help them assemble clock faces. You may need to assist as children push the fastener through the center of the clock face.

Once the clocks have been made, help children move the hands around to show different times.

Say: **Show 1 o'clock.**

Ask: **Where will you point the minute hand?** (at the 12) **Where will you point the hour hand?** (at the 1)

Repeat until children have mastered modeling times to the hour. Then have children work in pairs. Have partners take turns modeling times to the hour and reading the time on their partner's clock. Guide children as they practice, gradually reducing the amount of support until they are able to work independently.

© Harcourt

Grade 2
Skill
40

Read a Clock

The time is 5 o'clock.

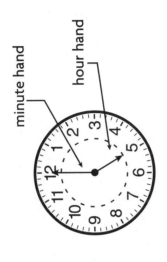

minute hand

hour hand

Try These

Use a 🕐 . Show each time.
Draw the hour hand. Write the time.

1

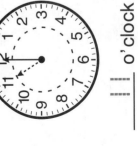

_____ o'clock

2

_____ o'clock

3

_____ o'clock

Go to the next side.

Practice on Your Own

Skill 40

The time is 8 o'clock.

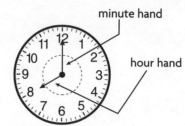
minute hand
hour hand

Use a . Show each time.
Draw the hour hand. Write the time.

1

___2___ o'clock

2

_____ o'clock

3

_____ o'clock

4

_____ o'clock

5

_____ o'clock

6

_____ o'clock

▶ Quiz

Use a . Show each time.
Draw the hour hand. Write the time.

7

_____ o'clock

8

_____ o'clock

9

_____ o'clock

Using Skill 41

OBJECTIVE Tell time to the hour

Example 1

Remind children that the clock in the first picture has an hour hand and a minute hand that move to show the time. Ask:

How are the hour and minute hands different? (Possible answer: One hand is longer than the other hand.)
Which is the hour hand? (short hand)
Which is the minute hand? (long hand)

Explain that the hour hand points to the number on the clock that tells the hour. The minute hand tells how many minutes past the hour it is. Ask: **At what number is the hour hand pointing?** (3) **At what number is the minute hand pointing?** (12)

Explain that when the minute hand points to the 12, it shows time to the hour. Ask:
What time does the clock show? (3 o'clock)

Example 2

Discuss the digital clock. Explain that there are different ways to show the same time. Point out the time written with a colon. Tell the children that the two zeros to the right of the colon mean there are no minutes past the hour.

TRY THESE In Exercises 1–3 children read a clock and write the time two ways to prepare for the time exercises that they will encounter in the **Practice On Your Own** section:

- **Exercise 1** Read clocks that show 5 o'clock.

- **Exercise 2** Read a clock that shows 9 o'clock.

- **Exercise 3** Read a clock that shows 11 o'clock.

PRACTICE ON YOUR OWN Review the example at the top of the page. Exercises 1–3 provide practice in reading analog and digital clocks and writing times in two ways. Exercises 4–6 provide practice in writing times shown on an analog or a digital clock.

QUIZ Determine if children can read and write time to the hour. Success is indicated by 2 out of 3 correct responses.

Children who successfully complete **Practice on Your Own** and **Quiz** are ready to move to the next skill.

COMMON ERRORS

- Children may confuse the minute hand and hour hand.

- Children may forget how to write times with a colon separating the hour and minutes.

Have children who made more than 2 errors in the **Practice on Your Own**, or who were not successful in the **Quiz** section, explain the example aloud to determine if they are confused about the hour and minute hands. These children may also benefit from the **Alternative Teaching Strategy** on the next page.

Alternative Teaching Strategy

20 Minutes

OBJECTIVE Tell time to the hour

MATERIALS analog clock model, clock hands, fasteners, and scissors for each child

Begin the activity by displaying an analog clock model. Point out the parts of the clock. Ask: **What numbers do you see?** (1–12) **What do you think they stand for?** (Possible answer: The 12 hours we use to tell time.) **Which parts move to show the time?** (the hour and minute hands)

Move the hands to show 2 o'clock. Talk about the minute and hour hands. Point out the difference in their lengths. Remind children that the hour hand points to the hour, or 2. Emphasize that the minute hand points to the 12 when it is exactly 2 o'clock. Invite volunteers to model other times to the hour.

Distribute materials to children and assist them in assembling clock faces. You may need to offer help as children push the fastener through the center of the clock face.

Help children move the hands to show different times. For example, 3 o'clock.

Give children practice in showing times on their clocks, by saying times to the hour. Have children show the times on their clocks.

Once children have mastered modeling and reading times to the hour, repeat the process, introducing two ways to write the times. (2 o'clock, and 2:00)

Guide children in practicing reading and writing times to the hour. Gradually reduce the amount of support you provide until children are working independently.

2 o'clock
2:00

Grade 2
Skill 41

Tell Time to the Hour

Both clocks show time to the hour.

Read the clock.

Write the time.

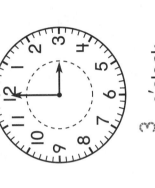

minute hand

hour hand

3 ___ o'clock

Read each clock.

Write the time
two ways.

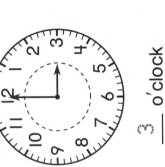

3 ___ o'clock

Think: Both clocks show 3 o'clock.

3:00

3:00

▲ **Try These**

Read the clock. Write the time two ways.

1

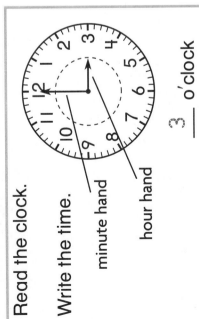

5 ___ o'clock

5:00

2

5:00

___ : ___ o'clock

3

9:00

___ : ___ o'clock

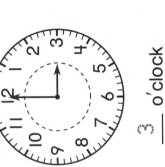

___ : ___ o'clock

Go to the next side.

Practice on Your Own

Think: The hour hand is shorter than the minute hand.

Both clocks show 2 o'clock.

   2:00

_2_ o'clock   2:00

Read the clock. Write the time.

1    6:00

_6_ o'clock   6:00

2    8:00

___ o'clock _____:_____

3    12:00

___ o'clock _____:_____

4

_____:_____

5 2:00

_____:_____

6

_____:_____

▶ **Quiz**

Read the clock. Write the time.

7 3:00

_____:_____

8

_____:_____

9

_____:_____

Skill 42

Make Reasonable Estimates: One Minute

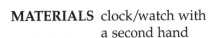

20 Minutes

Using Skill 42

OBJECTIVE Estimate one minute

MATERIALS clock/watch with a second hand

Invite children to tell how long they think a minute is.

Say: **Name some things that take about a minute to do.**
Record children's suggestions on the board.

Ask: **How long is a minute?** (60 seconds)

Say: **Let's see if you can tell when a minute has passed. Stand on one foot at my signal. Put your foot down when you think a minute has passed. I will say, "Time," when the minute is up.** Time a minute.

Ask: **Was your estimate close?** (Answers will vary.)

Note any children whose estimates are very far off. To help children develop a benchmark, suggest that they repeat a simple activity, such as writing their name, while you time a minute. Then discuss how many times they were able to write their name in a minute.

You may also wish to have children observe the second hand of a watch or clock for 1 minute.

Conclude by reviewing the list of activities children generated earlier. Time children as they attempt some of the activities to determine if they take more than a minute, less than a minute, or about a minute to complete. Record the results on the board.

TRY THESE In Exercises 1–3 children estimate and check whether an activity takes more than a minute or less than a minute.

- **Exercises 1–3** Estimate about how long each activity would take. Circle your estimate and then act it out to check.

PRACTICE ON YOUR OWN Repeat a similar timing activity to reinforce the sense of how long a minute is. Exercises 1–6 provide practice estimating and then checking whether an activity takes more than a minute or less than a minute to complete.

QUIZ Determine if children can correctly estimate whether an activity takes more than a minute or less than a minute to complete. Success is indicated by 2 out of 3 correct responses.

Children who successfully complete **Practice on Your Own** and **Quiz** are ready to move to the next skill.

COMMON ERRORS

- Children may be unable to sense or understand how long a minute is and give an incorrect estimate.

- Children may confuse *more than* and *less than*.

Children who made more than 2 errors in the **Practice on Your Own**, or who were not successful in the **Quiz** section, may benefit from the **Alternative Teaching Strategy**.

Alternative Teaching Strategy

20 Minutes

OBJECTIVE Understand and estimate one minute

MATERIALS demonstration clock with a second hand

Display a clock with a second hand.

Ask: **How long is a minute?** (60 seconds) **Watch the second hand. Each time it travels around the clock once, 60 seconds pass, or 1 minute.** Point out how the minute hand moves as each minute passes.

One way to time a minute would be to count to 60. To make sure you count at the correct pace of a second, use this counting trick—1 one thousand, 2 one thousand, 3 one thousand until you reach 60 one thousand. Model the counting trick, having children count along with you.

Then ask children to stand in order to participate in a timed activity.

Say: **When I say "Begin!" raise both arms above your head. Try to stand this way for 1 minute. I will time you. When you think a minute has passed put your arms down.** Have children discuss the results.

Say: **Sometimes a minute may seem like a long time. Other times it seems to pass very quickly. Now that you have a better idea about how long a minute is, think about the time it takes you to write your name, your address, or your telephone number.**

Ask: **Do you think these things will take more than a minute or less than a minute to complete?** (Answers will vary.) Say: **Let's find out.**

Have several volunteers come to the board as other children work at their desks. At your signal, have them begin by writing their first and last name followed by their address and telephone number. If they finish under a minute, have them put their pencils down or stop when they hear you say, "Time."

Ask: **Did you finish writing your name, address, and telephone number in a minute or less, or do you still need more time?** (Answers will vary.)

Repeat with other activities to give children additional practice estimating a minute.

Grade 2
Skill
42

Make Reasonable Estimates: One Minute

A minute is 60 seconds.

Stand on one foot.

Estimate when 1 minute has passed.
Put your foot down.

Try These

About how long would it take? Circle your estimate.
Then act it out to check.

1 say your address

17 East Street

more than a minute
less than a minute

2 write the alphabet

A B C D

more than a minute
less than a minute

3 count to 150

...6, 7, 8

more than a minute
less than a minute

Go to the next side.

Practice on Your Own

Skill 42

 Run in place.

 Estimate when 1 minute has passed. Stop running.

A minute is 60 seconds.

About how long would it take? Circle your estimate.
Then act it out to check.

1 read a story

(more than a minute)
less than a minute

2 draw a tree

more than a minute
less than a minute

3 trace your hand

more than a minute
less than a minute

4 write 1 to 10

more than a minute
less than a minute

5 spin 10 times

more than a minute
less than a minute

6 sing a song

more than a minute
less than a minute

▶ **Quiz**

About how long would it take? Circle your estimate.
Then act it out to check.

7 write a poem

more than a minute
less than a minute

8 tie your shoelace

more than a minute
less than a minute

9 jump rope 25 times

more than a minute
less than a minute

Skill 43

Grade 2

Using Skill 43

OBJECTIVE Read a calendar

Example

Use the example to review the features of a calendar.

Start by reviewing the names of the months of the year. Have children say them in order beginning with January. Ask: **What month begins every new year?** (January) **What month is just before March?** (February) **What month is just after March?** (April) **What is the last month of the year?** (December)

Call attention to the calendar in the example. Remind children that a calendar shows the month, the days of the week, and the date for each day. Ask: **What month does this calendar show?** (March) **In what order are the seven days of the week on a calendar?** (Sunday, Monday, Tuesday, Wednesday, Thursday, Friday, Saturday) **How many days are in the month of March?** (31) **How can you tell?** (31 is the last number on the calendar)

Demonstrate how to use the calendar. Write *March 23* on the board.
Say: **To tell what day March twenty-third is, find 23 on the calendar. Then look for the day of the week at the top of that column. March twenty-third is on what day?** (Tuesday)

Ask: **What other dates fall on a Tuesday in March?** (March 2nd, 9th, 16th, and 30th) **How can you tell?** (Look at the dates in the column under Tuesday.)

TRY THESE In exercises 1–3 children practice using a calendar.

- **Exercises 1–3** Identify specific days of the week.

PRACTICE ON YOUR OWN Have children read the calendar at the top of the page to identify the month and then name the month that comes just before and the month that comes just after. For the first part of the exercises, children fill in the calendar for the month of August. Then, children answer the questions according to the calendar.

QUIZ Determine if children can use a calendar. Success is indicated by 2 out of 3 correct responses.

Children who successfully complete **Practice on Your Own** and **Quiz** are ready to move to the next skill.

COMMON ERRORS

- Children may confuse the order of the days of the week or months.

- Children may forget how to find the day of the week or the date on the calendar.

Children who made more than 1 error in the **Practice On Your Own**, or who were not successful in the **Quiz** section, may benefit from the **Alternative Teaching Strategy** on the next page.

Alternative Teaching Strategy

15 Minutes

OBJECTIVE Read a calendar

MATERIALS index cards, old calendars, scissors, envelopes, glue, and construction paper

Write the names of the days of the week and the months of the year on index cards—one name per card. Prepare a set of cards for each pair of children.

Review the order of the days of the week.

Then distribute the days of the week cards. Direct partners to place the cards face down in a pile. Have them take turns drawing a card and arranging the cards in order to show a week.

Ask: **How many days are in a week?** (7) **What day comes before Wednesday?** (Tuesday) **What day comes after Saturday?** (Sunday)

Follow a similar procedure with the months of the year.

Then give each partner an old calendar page and scissors. Direct children to cut apart the calendar page into strips to show the month, the names of the days of the week, and each week. Have partners put the strips into an envelope and exchange envelopes.

Instruct partners to reconstruct a calendar on a sheet of construction paper.

Provide guidance as children work. Ask questions such as:

What month is your calendar?
How many days are in the month?
On what day of the week does the month begin?
What is the day and date of the last day of the month?
How many Wednesdays are there in the month?
What is the date of the last Monday?
The fifteenth is on what day of the week?

April 2004						
Sunday	Monday	Tuesday	Wednesday	Thursday	Friday	Saturday
				1	2	3
4	5	6	7	8	9	10
11	12	13	14	15	16	17
18	19	20	21	22	23	24
25	26	27	28	29	30	

© Harcourt

© Harcourt

Use a Calendar

Grade 2
Skill
43

			March 2004			
Sunday	Monday	Tuesday	Wednesday	Thursday	Friday	Saturday
	1	2	3	4	5	6
7	8	9	10	11	12	13
14	15	16	17	18	19	20
21	22	23	24	25	26	27
28	29	30	31			

January
February
March
April
May
June

July
August
September
October
November
December

▲ Try These

Use the calendar to answer the questions.

1. On what day of the week does March begin?

   Monday

2. What day of the week is March 17?

   _____

3. What is the date of the first Friday?

   _____

Go to the next side.

Practice on Your Own

Skill **43**

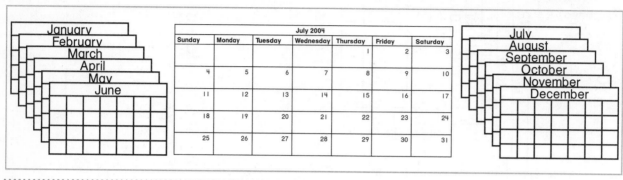

....

Fill in the calendar for the month after July.
Use the calendar to answer the questions.

Sunday	Monday	Tuesday	Wednesday	Thursday	Friday	Saturday

1 What day of the week is the twentieth? _____

2 What is the date of the last Monday? _____

▶ **Quiz**

Use the calendar to answer the questions.

3 What day is the last day of the month? _____

4 What is the date of the first Wednesday? _____

5 How many Mondays are in August? _____

Using Skill 44

OBJECTIVE Compare lengths

15 Minutes

MATERIALS 3 sets of 20 connecting cubes (each set a different color); 3 different color pieces of yarn

Draw two line segments of different lengths horizontally across the board. Show directional lines at both ends of each line to show length.

Ask: **Do you think these lines are the same length?** (answers will vary) **How could we find out?** (We could measure the 2 lines.)

Call on children to help you measure the lines by making connecting cube trains to match the length of each line. Make each train a different color. Help children align each cube train to make sure it is the same length as the line on the board.

Ask: **How can we use the cube trains to see whether or not the lines are the same lengths?** (Count the cubes in each train and compare the totals.)

Help children complete the task. Ask: **Which train is longer? Which is shorter?** (answers will vary)

Draw a third line on the board that is a different length than the other two. Have children make a third color cube train to measure and compare the length of the third line. Guide children to conclude that the three lines are all different lengths.

Ask: **Which line is the longest? Which line is the shortest? How can you use the cube trains to find out?** (answers will vary determining the longest and shortest; compare the lengths of the cube trains and rank them from shortest to longest.)

Help children determine which is the longest, which is the shortest and which line falls in between the two. Then focus their attention on the example at the top of the page. Point out that instead of connecting cubes, they will be using string of different colors to compare length.

TRY THESE In Exercises 1–3 children will be given three pieces of string that they will put in order from shortest to longest and then they will draw them.

PRACTICE ON YOUR OWN After reviewing the example, have children explain how to measure an item. Exercises 1–4 provide practice in comparing the lengths of objects.

QUIZ Determine if children can compare lengths. Success is indicated by 2 out of 2 correct responses.

Children who successfully complete **Practice on Your Own** and **Quiz** are ready to move on to the next skill.

COMMON ERRORS

- Children may confuse the terms *shortest* and *longest*.

- Children may have difficulty comparing the lengths.

Children who made more than 1 error in the **Practice on Your Own,** or who were not successful in the **Quiz** section may benefit from the **Alternative Teaching Strategy** on the next page.

Alternative Teaching Strategy

15 Minutes

OBJECTIVE Compare lengths

MATERIALS for each child: 3 paper strips of different lengths; construction paper; glue; and a pencil; assortment of 3 objects to sort by lengths

Write the terms *shorter*, *shortest*, *longer*, and *longest* on the board. Encourage children to describe real objects using these terms. To help children get started, suggest that a ruler is longer than an eraser, or a piece of chalk is shorter than a new pencil.

Next, tell children that they will be given 3 paper strips to arrange in order from shortest to longest.

Distribute 3 paper strips of different lengths, construction paper, glue, and a pencil to each child. Explain that the shortest strip should be glued near the top of the paper and the longest strip should be glued near the bottom. Be sure to tell children to align the strips on the left.

Check the order of children's strips. Say: **Point to the longest strip. Label it longest. Point to the shortest strip. Label it shortest.**

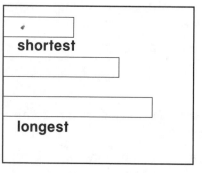

Provide additional practice by having children compare and arrange sets of 3 different lengths in order from shortest to longest and from longest to shortest. Sets may include such items as pencils, crayons, straws, cube trains, paper clip chains, and pieces of string.

As children arrange the objects, prompt them with a variety of comparison questions such as:

Ask: **Which is longer, the red crayon or the blue crayon?**

Ask: **Which is shorter, the yellow cube train or the blue cube train?**

Ask: **Which of the three pencils is the longest?**

Ask: **Which of the 3 paper clip chains is the shortest?**

© Harcourt

Compare Lengths

Grade 2
Skill
44

These pieces of string are in order from **shortest** to **longest**.

shortest

longest

Try These

Put three pieces of string in order from shortest to longest. Draw them.

1 shortest

2 ....

3 longest

Go to the next side.

Name _____ Skill _____

Practice on Your Own

Skill 44

Use real objects.
Cut pieces of ribbon to show each length.
Then compare the pieces of ribbon.
Tell which is longest or shortest.

Circle the object to answer the question.

1 Which is shorter?

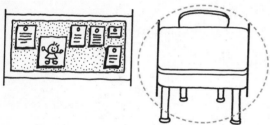

2 Which is longer?

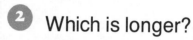 

3 Which is longer?

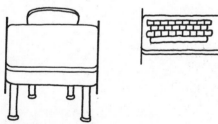

4 Which is shortest?

▶ **Quiz**

Circle the object to answer the question.

5 Which is shorter?

6 Which is longest?

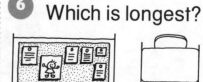

© Harcourt

IN228 Intervention • Skills

Using Skill 45

OBJECTIVE Estimate and measure length using nonstandard units

MATERIALS for each group: four 8-inch paper strips, 14 large paper clips, 6-inch piece of string, 24-inch piece of string, tape

20 Minutes

Divide the class into small groups. Distribute materials to each group. Have children tape both ends of each piece of string to the floor.

Explain to children that they will be learning how to use nonstandard units to measure length. Emphasize that when they measure length in nonstandard units, they should always use units that are the same size, like paper clips, for example.

Ask: **What do you notice about these paper clips?** (They are all the same size.)

Say: **Place a paper clip at the left end of the shorter piece of string.**

Ask: **Does 1 paper clip measure the length?** (no) **About how many more paper clips do you think it will take?** (answers will vary) Record estimates.

Demonstrate how to line the paper clips up to measure the length of the string.

Ask: **About how many paper clips long is it?** (about 3 paper clips) Have children compare and discuss estimates and actual measurements. Then repeat the procedure, having children estimate and measure the longer string.

Say: **Now let's use a different nonstandard unit to measure the longer string. Place a paper strip under the left end.**

Ask: **How many strips long do you think this string is?** (answers will vary) Record the estimates. Then have children measure the string.

Ask: **Was it easier to measure with paper clips or paper strips? Why?** (It was easier to use the paper strips because it took fewer strips to measure the length.)

TRY THESE In Exercises 1–2 children practice estimating and measuring two objects of different lengths using nonstandard units.

PRACTICE ON YOUR OWN After reviewing the example, have children explain how to measure an item. Exercises 1–3 provide practice using paper clips to estimate and measure the lengths of different objects.

QUIZ Determine if children can estimate and measure lengths using nonstandard units. Success is indicated by 2 out of 2 correct responses.

Children who successfully complete **Practice on Your Own** and **Quiz** are ready to move on to the next skill.

COMMON ERRORS

- Children may miscount the number of nonstandard units used.

- Children may not align the units of measure correctly.

Children who make more than 1 error in the **Practice on Your Own,** or who were not successful in the **Quiz** section may also benefit from the **Alternative Teaching Strategy** on the next page.

Alternative Teaching Strategy

20 Minutes

OBJECTIVE Estimate and measure length using non-standard units

MATERIALS units of measure such as connecting cubes, jumbo paper clips, large paper clips, 4-inch paper strips, counters, drawing paper

Have children form pairs. Assign each pair a different unit of measure. Then distribute drawing paper and the set of nonstandard units each pair will need to measure 3 classroom objects.

Call attention to a child's desk. Review how to measure the length of the desk using large paper clips. As you begin placing them end to end across the desktop, encourage children to estimate how many paper clips long the desktop is. Then have children count the paper clips aloud to check.

Say: **Now it is your turn to estimate and measure your desktop. You and your partner will use the unit of measure you were given. Decide on an estimate together. Then measure to check.**

Observe as partners work. Offer help as necessary. Prompt with questions.

Ask: **How did you decide on your estimate?** (Answers will vary.)

Ask: **How will you check your estimate?** (by measuring)

Ask: **How will you measure using round counters?** (Place the counters so that each one touches the next, across the desk, from edge to edge.)

Then invite partners to choose 2 other classroom objects to estimate and measure using their given unit of measure

Say: **Draw each object on your paper. Record your estimates. Measure to check. Record your results.**

Encourage partners to take turns drawing, measuring, and recording estimates and results.

Object	Estimate.	Measure.
	about <u>8</u> counters	about <u>10</u> counters

Invite partners to use their charts to summarize the results. Encourage them to explain how they measured.

© Harcourt

© Harcourt

Grade 2
Skill 45

Use Nonstandard Units

Use  to measure
short things.

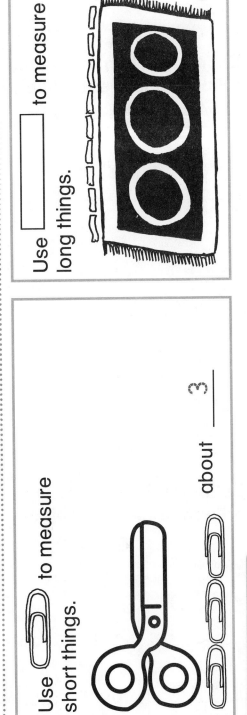

about _____ 3

Use ☐ to measure
long things.

about _____ 9

▲ Try These

Choose the unit you would use to measure.

Circle 📎 **or** ☐ **. Then measure.**

Unit. _____

Measure.

about _____ 4

about _____

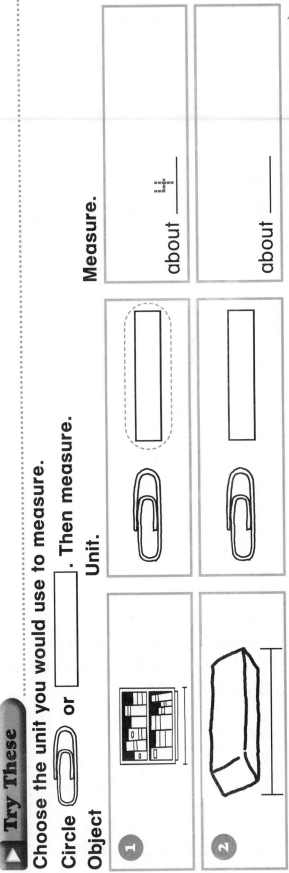

1

2

Go to the next side.

Practice on Your Own

Skill 45

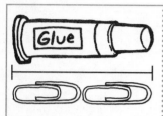
Use ⌷ to measure. Estimate. about _____ ⌷ | Measure. about __2__ ⌷

Use real objects and ⌷. Estimate. Then measure.
Circle the shortest object. Underline the longest object.

Object	Estimate.	Measure.
1 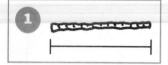	about __4__ ⌷	about __5__ ⌷
2 	about _____ ⌷	about _____ ⌷
3 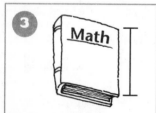	about _____ ⌷	about _____ ⌷

▶ Quiz

Use real objects and ⌷. Estimate. Then measure.
Circle the shortest object. Underline the longest object.

Object	Estimate.	Measure.
4 	about _____ ⌷	about _____ ⌷
5 	about _____ ⌷	about _____ ⌷

20 Minutes

Using Skill 46

OBJECTIVE Estimate and measure weight using nonstandard units

MATERIALS balance, wooden blocks, paper clips, classroom objects

Provide small groups of children with a balance, wooden blocks, and paper clips. Set up a table with classroom objects such as markers, rolls of tape, notepads, balls of clay, and containers of glue.

Review how a balance works. Place an object, such as a ball, on one side and enough blocks, 2 for example, on the other side to balance the ball.

Say: **Notice that one side is *not* higher or lower than the other. The two sides are level or even. This means the sides are balanced. You can see that it takes 2 blocks to balance the ball.**

Guide children to estimate and measure the number of wooden blocks or paper clips it takes to balance another object.

Say: **Choose an object and put it on one side of the balance. Estimate the number of blocks it will take to balance your object. Then put that many blocks on the other side.**

Ask: **How can you tell if you estimated accurately?** (Both sides are level.)

Ask: **What does it mean if the sides are not even?** (If the side with the blocks is higher, then the object is heavier and I need to add blocks. If the side with the blocks is lower, then the object is lighter and I need to take away blocks.)

Have groups complete the task and share the results with the class by naming the object they chose, the number of blocks they estimated, and the number of blocks it took to balance the object.

Repeat the activity. This time have children estimate the number of paper clips they think it will take to balance the object and then measure to check.

Ask: **Do you think it will take more paper clips than blocks to balance your object?** (yes) **Why?** (Paper clips are lighter than blocks.)
Have children share their results.

TRY THESE In Exercises 1–3 children choose whether to use paper clips or blocks to measure an object.

- **Exercises 1–3** Choose the best unit and measure the objects.

PRACTICE ON YOUR OWN Review the example at the top of the page. Exercises 1–2 provide practice estimating and measuring the number of paper clips it takes to balance objects and then identify the heaviest and lightest objects.

QUIZ Determine if children can estimate and measure the number of nonstandard units that it takes to balance objects. Success is indicated by 2 out of 3 correct responses.

Children who successfully complete **Practice on Your Own** and **Quiz** are ready to move on to the next skill.

COMMON ERRORS

- Children may not understand how to use a balance correctly.

- Children may confuse the terms *heaviest* and *lightest*.

Children who make more than 1 error in the **Practice on Your Own,** or who were not successful in the **Quiz** section may also benefit from the **Alternative Teaching Strategy** on the next page.

Alternative Teaching Strategy

20 Minutes

OBJECTIVE Use a balance scale

MATERIALS 2 identical student books, 2 chalkboard erasers, balance scale, connecting cubes

Display a balance scale. Place a book in one pan and a chalkboard eraser in the other pan.

Say: **The balance scale can help us compare the weight of the book and the eraser.**
Ask: **Which is heavier, the book or the eraser?** (book)

Say: **That's right. The side of the balance with the book is lower than the side with the eraser. It shows us that the book is heavier than the eraser.**

Ask: **What can you tell about the eraser?** (It is lighter than the book.) **How can you tell?** (The side with the eraser is higher than the side with the book.)

Next, replace the eraser with a book that is identical to the one in the opposite pan to demonstrate *balance*.

Ask: **What can you tell about the height of the 2 pans?** (They are even.) **Why do you think they are even?** (The two books are the same weight.)

Say: **That's right. The book on one side *balances* the book on the other side.**

Remove one book.
Ask: **How can we use connecting cubes to make the scale balance again?** (Put cubes in the other pan.)

Ask: **How many cubes do you think it will take?** Record children's estimates on the board.

Distribute several cubes to each child.
Say: **Take turns putting your cubes in the pan.**
Encourage children to comment on what happens to the pans as they add cubes.

Ask: **How will we know when there are enough cubes to balance the book?** (Both sides of the scale will be level, or at the same height.)

When both sides are level, have children count the cubes and tell how many it took to balance the book. Then compare the actual number to the estimates listed on the board.

Repeat the activity using the eraser.

Ask: **How many cubes did it take to balance the book? How many cubes did it take to balance the eraser? Which is heavier? How do you know?** (It took more cubes.) **Which is lighter? How do you know?** (It took fewer cubes.)

You may wish to continue by having pairs of children work together to practice estimating and measuring connecting cubes and other classroom objects with a balance.

Grade 2
Skill
46

Use a Balance

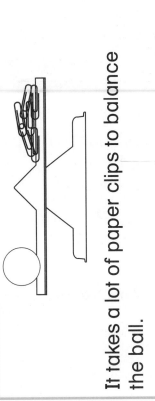

It takes 2 blocks to balance the ball.

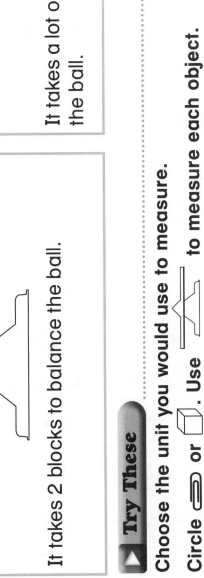

It takes a lot of paper clips to balance the ball.

▶ Try These

Choose the unit you would use to measure.

Circle ⊂⊃ or ▱ . Use ▱ to measure each object.

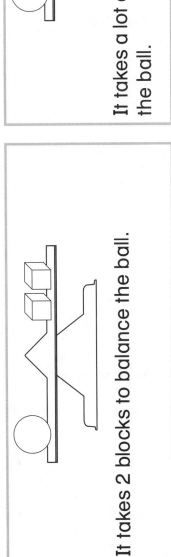

Think: It is easier to measure heavy objects using blocks.

Object	Unit		Measure.
1	⊂⊃	▱	about ____
2	⊂⊃	▱	about ____
3	⊂⊃	▱	about ____

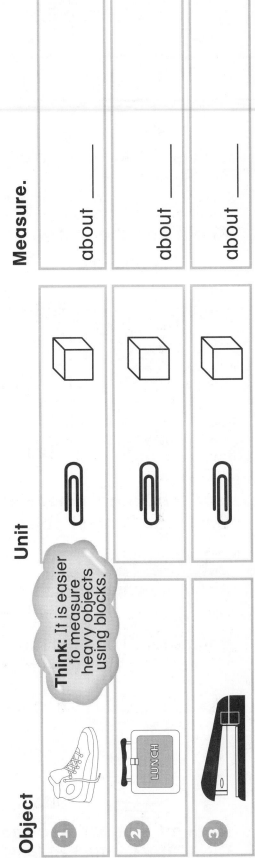

Go to the next side.

Intervention • Skills IN235

Practice on Your Own

Skill 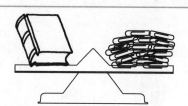 46

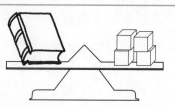

It takes 4 blocks to balance the book.

It takes a lot of paper clips to balance the book.

About how many ⌷ does it take to balance?

Use real objects, a ⟋△⟍ , and ⌷.
Estimate. Then measure.

Object	Estimate.	Measure.
1	about _____ ⌷	about _____ ⌷
2 	about _____ ⌷	about _____ ⌷

Mark an X on the heaviest object.
Circle the lightest object.

▶ **Quiz**

About how many ⌷ does it take to balance?

Use real objects, a ⟋△⟍ , and ⌷.
Estimate. Then measure.

Object	Estimate.	Measure.
3 	about _____ ⌷	about _____ ⌷
4 	about _____ ⌷	about _____ ⌷
5 	about _____ ⌷	about _____ ⌷

Mark an X on the heaviest object.
Circle the lightest object.

© Harcourt

20 Minutes

Using Skill 47

OBJECTIVE Estimate and measure the weight of objects in pounds

MATERIALS 1-pound weights, balance scale, classroom objects

Pass around 1-pound weights.
Say: **A pound is a unit we use to measure how heavy something is. You are holding a weight that measures 1 pound.**

Pass around a book that weighs one pound. Have children hold the book and estimate its weight compared to the 1-pound weight.

Ask: **Do you think the book weighs about 1-pound, more than 1-pound, or less than 1-pound?** Allow children to respond. Then display a balance scale. Tell children they will use it to measure the weight of the book in pounds.

Have a child place a 1-pound weight in one pan and the book in the other pan.

Ask: **What do you notice?** (The pans are even, or level.)

Say: **That's right. The scale is balanced. The book weighs about 1 pound.**
Record *book = 1 pound* on the board.

Pass around another object that weighs more than a pound. Have children estimate if the object weighs more than 1-pound, less than 1-pound or about 1-pound. Then place the object on the scale with the 1-pound weight.

Ask: **What do you notice this time?** (The pans are not level; the side with the object is lower than the side with the weight. The object is heavier than the 1-pound weight.)

Ask: **How can you find out how much the object weighs?** (Add 1-pound weights until the sides balance. Then count the 1-pound weights.)

Have children add weights to find the weight of the object. Then record the object and its weight on the board.

Repeat the procedure with a third object. Have children review the results and then identify the heaviest object and the lightest object.

TRY THESE In Exercises 1–3 children decide which estimate is closer to an object's actual weight.

- **Exercises 1–3** Circle the better estimate for the object's weight.

PRACTICE ON YOUR OWN Review the example at the top of the page and how to determine the weight of each object. Exercises 1–2 provide practice estimating, measuring, and comparing the weight of items in pounds using a balance scale and 1-pound weights.

QUIZ Determine if children can estimate, measure, and compare the weight of items in pounds using a balance scale and 1-pound weights. Success is indicated by 2 out of 2 correct responses.

Children who successfully complete **Practice on Your Own** and **Quiz** are ready to move to the next skill.

COMMON ERRORS

- Children may not understand how to use a balance correctly.

- Children may confuse the terms *heaviest* and *lightest*.

Children who make an error in the **Practice on Your Own**, or who are not successful in the **Quiz** section may benefit from the **Alternative Teaching Strategy** on the next page.

© Harcourt

Alternative Teaching Strategy

OBJECTIVE Weigh items in pounds using a balance scale and 1-pound weights

MATERIALS balance scale, index cards, 1-pound weights

Prepare a set of 9 cards for each group. On each of 3 cards, draw a picture of a classroom item children can weigh. With another set of 3 cards, write the corresponding weight of the items on each. On the remaining 3 cards, draw 1-pound weights per card to show the weight of the items. Each item should be a different weight between 1 and 10 pounds. Display the items on a table.

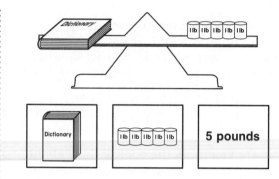

Arrange children in pairs or small groups. Distribute a set of cards, balance scale, and ten 1-pound weights to partners or groups. Have children sort the cards.

Say: **Look at the items pictured on your cards. Find those items on the table. Then place one of the items on one side of your balance scale.**

Ask: **How can you use the weights to find out how much the item weighs?** (Place enough weights in the pan until both sides of the scale balance.)

Give children time to complete the task. Ask: **How many 1-pound weights did it take to balance your item? So, how much does your item weigh?** Give children time to count the weights and respond.

Say: **Now, find and match the cards that show how many weights and how many pounds your item weighs.**

Have children repeat the procedure for the remaining 2 items, using the 1-pound weights and balance scale to weigh the items and then match the cards. Offer guidance as necessary. Then, have children return the items to the table and trade cards with another group.

Say: **Look at the items on your cards and find them on the table. This time, estimate how much each object will weigh. Match the picture card of each item with the cards that show how many weights you think it will take to balance each item and how many pounds each one will weigh. Then measure to see if your estimates are correct.**

Observe as children work through the process. Encourage them to explain why they think their estimates are accurate.

© Harcourt

Pounds

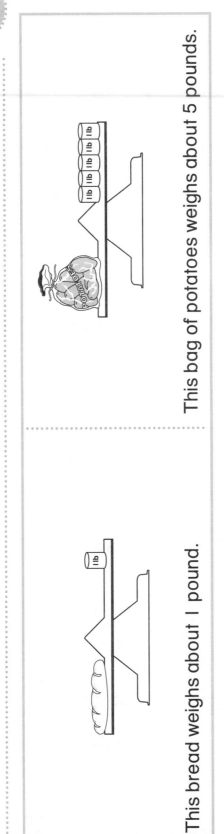

This bread weighs about 1 pound.

This bag of potatoes weighs about 5 pounds.

▲ **Try These**

Look at each object. Circle the better estimate.

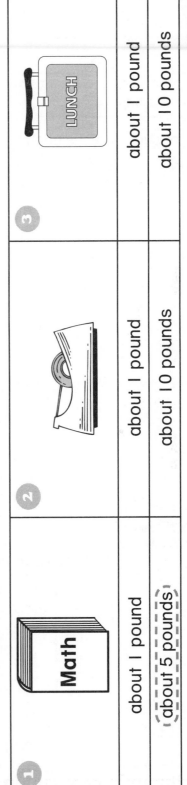

1	2	3
Math		LUNCH
about 1 pound	about 1 pound	about 1 pound
about 5 pounds	about 10 pounds	about 10 pounds

Go to the next side.

Practice on Your Own

Skill 47

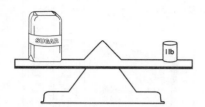

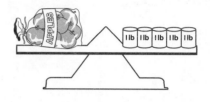

This bag of sugar weighs about
1 pound.

This bag of apples weighs about
5 pounds.

**Find four items to weigh. Draw them.
Estimate how much each object will weigh.
Then measure.**

Object	Estimate.	Measure.
1	about _____ pounds	about _____ pounds
2	about _____ pounds	about _____ pounds

Circle the heaviest item in blue. Circle the lightest item in red.

▶ Quiz

Object	Estimate.	Measure.
3	about _____ pounds	about _____ pounds
4	about _____ pounds	about _____ pounds

Circle the heaviest item in blue. Circle the lightest item in red.

Skill 48

Use Nonstandard Units to Measure Capacity

20 Minutes

Using Skill 48

OBJECTIVE Estimate and measure capacity using nonstandard units

MATERIALS plastic coffee scoop, plastic mug, rice, a 4-ounce container, and a 24-ounce container

Pass around the coffee scoop and plastic mug. Then display the small and large containers along with a bowl of rice.

Say: **We can use the scoop and the mug to measure *capacity*, which is how much each container will hold.**

Ask: **Which is larger, the mug or the scoop?** (the mug) **Which would you rather use to measure how much the large container will hold?** (the mug) **Why?** (Possible answer: It would be faster. Since the mug is bigger, it would take fewer mugs to fill the container.)

Ask: **Which unit would you use to measure how much the small container will hold?** (the scoop) **Why?** (Possible answer: I could get a more accurate measurement using the scoop because it's smaller.) Display the scoop and the small container.

Say: **Estimate how many scoops of rice you think it will take to fill this container.**

Record children's estimates on the board. Then have children count as a volunteer pours scoops of rice into the small container to measure its capacity. Compare the measured results to the estimates recorded on the board.

Repeat the process for the mug and large container. Then review the example at the top of the page.

TRY THESE In Exercises 1–3 children choose between two nonstandard units of measure to determine the capacity of three containers.

PRACTICE ON YOUR OWN Review the example of how to estimate and measure how much a container will hold. Exercises 1–3 provide practice using a coffee scoop as a nonstandard unit to estimate and measure the capacity of 3 containers.

QUIZ Determine if children can estimate and measure the capacity of 2 containers using a coffee mug. Success is indicated by 2 out of 2 correct responses.

Children who successfully complete **Practice on Your Own** and **Quiz** are ready to move to the next skill.

COMMON ERRORS

- Children may have difficulty estimating how many scoops, or mugs, of rice a container will hold.

- Children may miscount the number of scoops or mugs used to fill a container.

Children who made more than 1 error in **Practice on Your Own**, or who were not successful in the **Quiz** section, may benefit from the **Alternative Teaching Strategy** on the next page.

© Harcourt

Alternative Teaching Strategy

20 Minutes

OBJECTIVE Estimate and measure capacity using nonstandard units

MATERIALS assorted nonstandard units to measure capacity (scoops, small jars, shampoo bottle cap, small paper cups, empty vitamin containers); beans; a variety of containers; funnel; paper and pencil

Have children form pairs. Provide each pair with an empty container, a bag of beans, a funnel, 3 nonstandard units of measure, along with paper and pencil for recording the data.

To make the recording chart, guide children to fold their papers into 3 vertical columns with the headings, *Container, Estimate* and *Measure*.

Review the process for making estimates and measuring capacity. Display a container, a mug, and a bag of beans. As you scoop beans into the mug, encourage children to estimate how many mugs of beans they think it will take to fill the container. Then have children count aloud as you pour each mug of beans into the container to check.

Say: **Now it is your turn to estimate and measure. You and your partner will use the units of measure you were given. Choose one to start. Write or draw a picture of the container in the first column. Next, decide on an estimate together and include a picture, or the name, for your unit of measure. Record this in the second column. Then measure to check. Record the measurement in the third column.**

Encourage partners to take turns drawing, measuring, and recording estimates and results. Observe as they work, offering help as necessary. Prompt with questions.

Ask: **How did you decide on your estimate?** (Answers will vary.)

Ask: **How will you check your estimate?** (by measuring)

Ask: **How will you measure using the paper cup?** (Possible answer: Count each time we pour a cup of beans into the container.)

Invite pairs to share their results with the class. Encourage them to explain how they estimated and then measured.

Container	Estimate	Measure
cereal bowl	about 10 paper cups	about 18 paper cups

Use Nonstandard Units to Measure Capacity

Example 1

It took 2 of these scoops to fill the container.

Example 2

It took 4 of these mugs to fill the container.

▶ **Try These**

Choose the unit you would use to measure. Circle  or  .
Measure.

Container	Unit.		Measure.
1			about ____
2			about ____
3			about ____

Go to the next side.

Practice on Your Own

It took 3 of these scoops to fill the container.

It took 8 of these mugs to fill the container.

Use real containers and a 🥄.

Container	Estimate.	Measure.
1 MARGARINE	about _____ 🥄	about _____ 🥄
2 PEANUT BUTTER	about _____ 🥄	about _____ 🥄
3 YOGURT	about _____ 🥄	about _____ 🥄

▶ Quiz

Use real containers and a ☕.

Container	Estimate.	Measure.
4 Cookies	about _____ ☕	about _____ ☕
5 MILK	about _____ ☕	about _____ ☕

20 Minutes

Using Skill 49

OBJECTIVE Estimate and measure length in centimeters

MATERIALS centimeter rulers, paper

Distribute centimeter rulers for children to examine.

Ask: **What do you call this tool?** (a ruler) **Why do you use a ruler?** (to measure how long, wide, or high something is)

Say: **This ruler measures in units called centimeters. The space between one number mark and the next is 1 centimeter. Place your thumb on the ruler like this.** (demonstrate.)

Say: **A centimeter is about the width of your thumb.**

Draw a line segment about 10 centimeters long on the board. Have children observe as you demonstrate how to correctly align the ruler on the left to measure the line segment. Then invite a volunteer to tell how many centimeters long the line segment is.

Draw another line segment about 6 centimeters long.

Ask: **About how long do you think this line segment is?** Record children's estimates on the board.

Invite a volunteer to come up and measure it. Compare the actual answer with the estimates.

Next, distribute paper.

Say: **Draw a line between 1 and 15 centimeters long. Then trade papers with a partner. Estimate the length of the line. Then measure to check your estimate.**

TRY THESE In Exercises 1–2 children practice measuring length in centimeters.

• **Exercises 1–2** Children will use a centimeter ruler to measure the length of a new pencil and a child's index finger.

PRACTICE ON YOUR OWN Review the example at the top of the page. Exercises 1–3 provide practice estimating and measuring the length of objects using a centimeter ruler.

QUIZ Determine if children can estimate and measure the length of objects in centimeters using a ruler. Success is indicated by 2 out of 2 correct responses.

Children who successfully complete **Practice on Your Own** and **Quiz** are ready to move to the next skill.

COMMON ERRORS

• Children may forget to align the ruler with the end of the object they are measuring.

• Children may have difficulty visualizing about how many centimeters long an object is when giving an estimate.

Children who make more than 1 error in the **Practice on Your Own**, or who are not successful in the **Quiz** section may benefit from the **Alternative Teaching Strategy** on the next page.

Alternative Teaching Strategy

20 Minutes

OBJECTIVE Measure length in centimeters

MATERIALS for each child: centimeter ruler; plastic drinking straws cut in varying lengths from 1–15 centimeters

Write *centimeter* on the board. Remind children that a centimeter is another type of unit used to measure length.

Say: **Look at your thumb. It is about 1 centimeter wide.**

Distribute a centimeter ruler and a straw segment that is 6 centimeters long to each child.

Ask: **If you know that your thumb is about 1 centimeter wide, about how long do you think your straw segment is?** (Answers will vary.Give children time to estimate. Then record their estimates on the board.)

Ask: **How can we determine which estimate is correct?** (Measure the straw segment with a centimeter ruler.)

Ask: **When you measure, which end of the ruler will you align one end of the straw segment with?** (The end that starts with 0.)

Observe as children measure the straw segment. Make sure they are aligning correctly.

Ask: **How long is the straw segment?** (6 centimeters)

Have children form pairs. Provide partners with several straw segments. Have partners take turns selecting a straw segment and estimating and measuring its length in centimeters. Observe as children work. Encourage them to explain how they are making their estimates and how they are measuring the length of the straw segment.

To extend the activity, partners might arrange the straw segments in order from shortest to longest.

| 1 | 2 | 3 | 4 | 5 | 6 | 7 | 8 | 9 | 10 | 11 | 12 | 13 | 14 | 15 |
centimeters

© Harcourt

Grade 2
Skill 49

Centimeters

Example 1

Your thumb is about 1 **centimeter** wide.

Example 2

This eraser is about 6 **centimeters** long.

▲ Try These

How many centimeters long is the object?
Use a centimeter ruler to measure.

Object

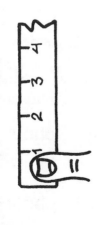

Measure.

1 about __9__ centimeters

2 about _____ centimeters

Go to the next side.

Practice on Your Own

**Use real objects and a centimeter ruler.
Estimate. Then measure.**

Object	Estimate.	Measure.
[ruler 0 1 2 3 4 5 6]	about _____ centimeters	about _____ centimeters

**Use real objects and a centimeter ruler. Estimate.
Then measure.**

Object	Estimate.	Measure.
1	about __3__ centimeters	about __4__ centimeters
2	about _____ centimeters	about _____ centimeters
3	about _____ centimeters	about _____ centimeters

▶ Quiz

**Use real objects and a centimeter ruler. Estimate.
Then measure.**

Object	Estimate.	Measure.
4	about _____ centimeters	about _____ centimeters
5	about _____ centimeters	about _____ centimeters

Using Skill 50

OBJECTIVE Estimate and measure the mass of objects in grams and kilograms

Pass around a 1-kilogram mass.
Say: **A kilogram is a unit of measure used to determine how heavy something is. The mass you were just given measures 1 kilogram.**

Pass around an item such as a book that has the mass of about 1 kilogram. Have children hold the book and compare its mass to the 1-kilogram mass.

Ask: **About how much do you estimate the book's mass to be?** (about a kilogram)

Say: **Let's use a balance scale to check.** Display a balance scale. Have a child place a 1-kilogram mass in one pan and the book across the other pan.

Ask: **What do you see?** (The pans balance. Their mass is the same.)

Say: **That's right. The scale is balanced. The book has the mass of about 1 kilogram.**

Pass around 1-gram masses.

Say: **This mass measures 1 gram. A gram is another unit of measure for mass.** Have children handle and compare the gram and kilogram masses.

Ask: **What do you notice?** (A kilogram is heavier than a gram; a gram is lighter than a kilogram.)

Pass around items measuring about 1 gram. Have children compare them to the gram mass.

TRY THESE In Exercises 1–3 children will determine the best unit of measure to measure each object.

MATERIALS gram and kilogram masses, balance scale, classroom objects

- **Exercises 1–3** Circle the unit, grams or kilograms, you would use to measure each object.

PRACTICE ON YOUR OWN Review the example at the top of the page and discuss how to measure the mass of each object. Exercises 1–3 provide practice estimating and measuring the mass of items in grams and kilograms using a balance scale along with gram and kilogram masses.

QUIZ Determine if children can estimate and measure the mass of items in grams and kilograms using a balance scale with gram and kilogram masses. Success is indicated by 2 out of 2 correct responses.

Children who successfully complete **Practice on Your Own** and **Quiz** are ready to move to the next skill.

COMMON ERRORS

- Children may not understand how to use the balance correctly.

- Children may confuse grams and kilograms.

Children who make more than 1 error in the **Practice on Your Own**, or who are not successful in the **Quiz** may benefit from the **Alternative Teaching Strategy** on the next page.

Alternative Teaching Strategy

OBJECTIVE Measure items using a balance scale with kilogram and gram masses

MATERIALS balance scale; gram and kilogram masses, classroom objects

Review *kilogram* and *gram*. Pass around a 1-kilogram mass and a 1-gram mass. Guide children to conclude that the kilogram mass is heavier than the gram mass. Encourage children to find items in the classroom they think will measure about 1 kilogram or about 1 gram. Then use the balance scale and masses to check children's estimates.

Have children work in small groups. Provide each group with a balance scale, gram and kilogram masses, and a set of 8 cards. Each of four cards in a set should show a different classroom item that can easily be measured in grams or kilograms. Each of the 4 remaining cards should indicate the mass of the corresponding items in grams or kilograms. Display the items for all sets on a table. Have children study them for a minute.

Say: **Which unit of measure will work best for measuring the heavier objects?** (kilograms)

Say: **Which unit of measure will work best for measuring the lighter objects?** (grams)

Say: **Each pair should take a look at the items on your cards and then come get them from the table. Once you have found your 4 items, place a kilogram or gram mass in front of each object to show the best unit of measure.** Demonstrate with an example as you continue to explain the directions.

Say: **Look at the 4 remaining cards. Place each card in front of the object you think shows how many grams or kilograms it measures. Then measure to see if your estimates are correct.**

Say: **Make sure you keep placing the masses you choose in the opposite pan until both sides balance.** Give children time to complete the task.

Have children follow this procedure for all 4 items pictured on their cards. Observe as children work through the process. Encourage them to explain how they know how many grams or kilograms each item measures. Offer guidance as necessary. If time allows, have pairs return the items to the table and trade cards.

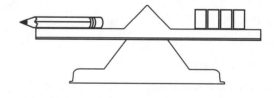

pencil

4 grams

Grade 2
Skill 50

Kilograms

1 kilogram — clay

This box of clay is about 1 **kilogram**.

1 gram

This marble is about 1 **gram**.

 **Try These**

Circle the unit you would use to measure each object.

1

grams

kilograms

2

grams

kilograms

3

grams

kilograms

Go to the next side.

Practice on Your Own

Skill **50**

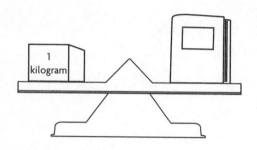
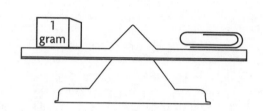

This large book is about
I **kilogram**.

This paper clip is about I **gram**.

**Estimate how much each object will measure.
Use grams or kilograms. Then measure.**

	Object	Estimate.	Measure.
1		about __ kilograms	about __ kilograms
2		about __ grams	about __ grams
3	PHONE BOOK	about __ kilograms	about __ kilograms

▶ **Quiz**

**Estimate how much each object will measure.
Use grams or kilograms. Then measure.**

	Object	Estimate.	Measure.
4		about __ grams	about __ grams
5		about __ kilograms	about __ kilograms

20 Minutes

Using Skill 51

OBJECTIVE Estimate and measure capacity in liters

MATERIALS 1-liter bottle, large bowl, 1-cup measure, quart bottle, 8-ounce milk container, 1-gallon milk jug

Example

Display a 1-liter bottle filled with water.
Say: **This container holds 1 liter. A liter is a unit that we use to measure capacity, or the amount a container will hold.**

Display a 1-cup measure and a large bowl.
Ask: **Which holds more, 1-liter or 1-cup?**
(1-liter)

Say: **Let's see about how many cups are equal to 1-liter.**
Pour water from the 1-liter bottle into the cup and then into the bowl. Have children count the cups as you measure and pour each cup.

Ask: **Does the liter bottle hold a little more or a little less than 4 cups?** (a little more)

Display a quart bottle. Say: **This bottle holds 1 quart which is exactly 4 cups. We just learned that a liter holds a little more than 4 cups, so a liter bottle holds more than a quart.**

Display an 8-ounce milk carton and a 1-gallon jug both filled with water.

Ask: **Now that you have an idea about how much a liter is, which container do you think holds less than a liter, the milk carton or the jug?** (milk carton) **Which container do you think holds more than a liter?** (the gallon jug) **How can we check?** (Pour the water from each container into a 1-liter bottle.)

Using a funnel and a bowl to catch spills, demonstrate that the milk carton holds less than a liter and the jug holds more than a liter.

TRY THESE In Exercises 1–3 children practice estimating and measuring the capacity of containers in liters.

- **Exercises 1–3** Estimate and measure the capacity of a container to determine if it holds less than or more than a liter.

PRACTICE ON YOUR OWN Review the examples at the top of the page. Exercises 1–3 provide practice estimating the capacity of different containers and measuring them to determine if they hold less than or more than 2 liters.

QUIZ Determine if children can estimate and measure the capacity of different containers to determine if they hold less than 2 liters or more than 2 liters. Success is indicated by 2 out of 2 correct responses.

Children who successfully complete **Practice on Your Own** and **Quiz** are ready to move to the next skill.

COMMON ERRORS

- Children may have difficulty visualizing whether a container holds less than or more than a liter or two.

- Children may have difficulty measuring their estimates.

Children who made more than 1 error in the **Practice on Your Own**, or who were not successful in the **Quiz** section, may benefit from the **Alternative Teaching Strategy** on the next page.

Alternative Teaching Strategy

20 Minutes

OBJECTIVE Estimate and measure capacity in liters

MATERIALS for each pair: 2–3 containers of different capacities (1-liter, more than 1 liter, less than 1 liter); funnel; sand or rice; baking tray; paper and pencil

Label and display a 1-liter container. Remind children that a liter is a unit we use to measure capacity, or how much a container will hold. Then display a 1-cup measure and a 1-quart container.

Ask: **Is a liter a little more or a little less than a quart or 4 cups?** (a little more)

Provide pairs of children with 2–3 containers that are less than 1 liter and 2–3 containers that are more than 1 liter. Label the containers. Children will also need a bag of sand (or rice), a funnel, a 1-liter container for measuring, a baking tray, as well as paper and pencil. Instruct children to fold the paper in half and label one column *more than 1 liter* and the other column *less than 1 liter* to make a recording sheet.

Say: **Look at your 1-liter container. Now look at your other containers and arrange them into two groups: containers that you think hold less than 1 liter and containers that you think hold more than 1 liter. Write the letter of each container on your paper in the column where you think it belongs.**

Allow children enough time to sort all of their containers.

Ask: **How can you use the sand, funnel, and 1 liter measuring container to find out if you are right?** (Fill a container with sand. Then pour the sand into the 1-liter container.)

Ask: **How will you know if it holds more or less than 1 liter?** (If it holds less than 1 liter, the sand will not fill the 1-liter container. If it holds more than 1 liter, the 1-liter container will not be able to hold all the sand.)

Say: **Take turns measuring. On your recording sheet, write *yes* next to the letter of the container if you estimated correctly. Write *no* if you did not.**

Observe as children estimate and measure. Discuss the reasons for any differences.

Go to the next side.

Grade 2
Skill 51

Liters

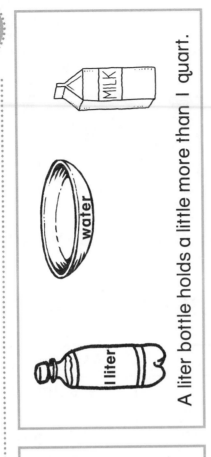

A liter bottle holds a little more than 4 cups.

A liter bottle holds a little more than 1 quart.

▶ Try These

Estimate if each container holds less or more than a liter.
Use a liter to measure each container.

Container	Estimate.	Measure.
1	less than / more than	less than / more than
2	less than / more than	less than / more than
3	less than / more than	less than / more than

Practice on Your Own

A liter bottle holds a little more than 4 cups.

A liter bottle holds a little more than 1 quart.

**Does each container hold less or more than 2 liters?
Estimate. Then measure.**

Container	Estimate.	Measure.
1	less than 2 more than 2	less than 2 more than 2
2	less than 2 more than 2	less than 2 more than 2
3	less than 2 more than 2	less than 2 more than 2

▶ Quiz

**Does each container hold less or more than 2 liters?
Estimate. Then measure.**

Container	Estimate.	Measure.
4	less than 2 more than 2	less than 2 more than 2
5	less than 2 more than 2	less than 2 more than 2

Geometry and Spatial Sense

Using Skill 52

OBJECTIVE Use points on a grid to locate objects

MATERIALS 4 by 4 grid, crayons

Draw a 4 by 4 grid on the board. Mark the 0, 0 coordinate with a star and label it *Start*. Provide each child with a similar grid and crayons.

Begin by reviewing the terms *left*, *right*, *up*, and *down*.

Say: **Listen carefully and follow my directions.**
Use the grid on the board to model the directions as you give them.

Say: **Put your finger on the star. Go right 3. Then go up 2.**

Ask: **Where are you?**

Say: **Draw a red dot to mark the position.**

Repeat, adding a third direction.

Say: **Put your finger on the star. Go right 2. Go up 2. Go left 1.**

Ask: **Where are you?**

Say: **Draw a blue dot to mark the position.**

Repeat, adding a fourth direction.

Say: **Put your finger on the star. Go up 3. Go right 2. Go down 2. Go left 1.**

Ask: **Where are you?**

Say: **Draw a green dot to show the position.**

Example

Direct children's attention to the example at the top of the page. Read the directions together. Have children trace the path with a finger.

TRY THESE Exercise 1 provides practice following directions to find a location on a grid.

• **Exercise 1**   Follow two directions.

PRACTICE ON YOUR OWN Review the example at the top of the page. Exercise 1 provides practice in following directions to locate points on a grid.

QUIZ Determine if children can correctly follow directions to locate a point on a grid. Success is indicated by 1 out of 1 correct responses.

Children who successfully complete **Practice on Your Own** and **Quiz** are ready to move on to the next skill.

COMMON ERRORS

• Children may confuse the directional terms *up* and *down* or *left* and *right* and as a result incorrectly draw the path.

• Children may not follow all the directions in a set, resulting in an incomplete path or the incorrect location on the grid.

Children who made an error in the **Practice on Your Own,** or who were not successful in the **Quiz** section may also benefit from the **Alternative Teaching Strategy** on the next page.

Alternative Teaching Strategy

20 Minutes

OBJECTIVE Follow and give directions using a grid

MATERIALS masking tape, index cards, construction paper shapes of different colors

Use masking tape to make a 4 by 4 grid on the floor. Grid lines should be far enough apart for children to walk on them. Draw a star on an index card and tape it at the bottom left corner, or 0, 0 coordinate.

Prepare a set of construction paper shapes such as a red circle, a blue square, a green triangle to mark coordinates on the grid, and a set of direction cards with 2, 3, and 4 steps.

Start at the ★.
Go right 3.
Go up 2.

Start at the ★.
Go up 3.
Go right 3.
Go down 2.

Start at the ★.
Go right 4. Go
up 3. Go left 1.
Go down 2.

Select a direction card and read it aloud. Call on a volunteer to follow the directions by walking along the floor grid, then marking the position by placing a paper shape on the coordinate.

Continue by having children in turn read and follow the directions and then mark the position with a construction paper shape.

Remove the shapes and distribute them to children. Call on two children at a time.

Say to Child A: **Put your shape on the grid where any two lines meet. Now give directions in order to help Child B get to the shape.**

If necessary, prompt children with questions, such as, Ask: **Where should Child B start?** (on the star) **Does he/she go up, down, right, or left next? Where does Child B go next? Where does he/she go after that?**

When Child B locates the shape, have Child A return to his/her seat and call on Child C. Have Child B place the shape and give directions for Child C to follow. Continue until everyone has had a chance to give and follow directions.

© Harcourt

Grade 2
Skill 52

Give and Follow Directions

From **start**, go right 3. Go up 2.
Where are you?

I'm at the park.

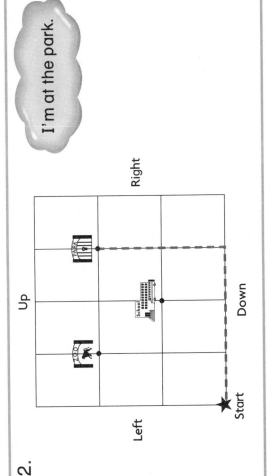

Up

Left

Right

Down

Start

▲ Try These

**Follow the directions in order.
Draw the path. Write the name.**

Start

1 Go left 2.

2 Go down 3.

3 Where are you?

_____

Go to the next side.

Practice on Your Own

Skill 52

From **start**, go right 2. Go up 1.
Where are you?

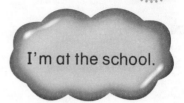

I'm at the school.

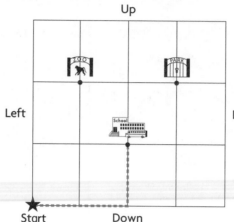

Up

Left   Right

Start   Down

....

Follow the directions in order.
Draw the path. Write the name.

1 Go right 4. Go up 2.
Go left 2. Go down 1.
Where are you?

_____

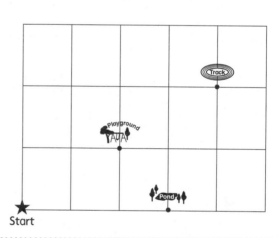

Track

Playground

Pond

Start

....

▶ **Quiz**

Follow the directions in order.
Draw the path. Write the name.

2 Go right 3. Go up 2.
Go left 1. Go down 1.
Where are you?

_____

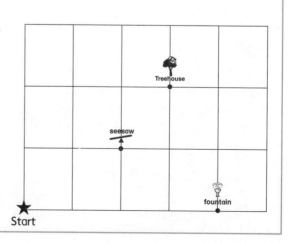

Treehouse

seesaw

fountain

Start

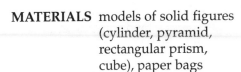

Using Skill 53

OBJECTIVE Identify circles, squares, triangles, and rectangles on solid figures

MATERIALS models of solid figures (cylinder, pyramid, rectangular prism, cube), paper bags

Example

Place a cylinder, a pyramid, a rectangular prism, and a cube in a paper bag. Invite children to reach into the bag, pick up a solid figure, and describe it by touch.

Ask: **Does it have flat sides or round sides? Does it have vertices? What do you think it is?**
(Answers will vary.)

Remove the solid figures from the bags. Display the cylinder. Ask children to name the figure if they know it, or tell them it is called a cylinder. Point to the two circular plane shapes of the cylinder.

Ask: **What plane shapes do you see?**
(2 circles)

Draw and label a circle on the board. Pass around the cylinder for children to examine.

Repeat the procedure for the remaining solid figures, drawing and labeling their plane shapes on the board. Guide children to recognize that the pyramid and the rectangular prism both have two plane shapes—the triangle and the square for the square pyramid, and a rectangle and a square for the rectangular prism.

Conclude by having volunteers identify the solid figure with a plane shape that matches the plane shape on the board.

TRY THESE In exercises 1–3 children practice making and identifying plane shapes from solid figures.

- **Exercises 1–3** Trace the plane shapes of a cylinder, a cube, and a pyramid and name them.

PRACTICE ON YOUR OWN Review the example at the top of the page. Exercises 1–4 provide children with practice making plane shapes by tracing around solid figures and then identifying the shapes by name.

QUIZ Determine if children can trace the plane shapes of 2 solid figures and write the name of the plane shapes. Success is indicated by 2 out of 2 correct responses.

Children who successfully complete **Practice on Your Own** and **Quiz** are ready to move to the next skill.

COMMON ERRORS

- Children may confuse plane shapes that have similar attributes.

- Children may have difficulty with the vocabulary.

Children who made more than 1 error in **Practice On Your Own,** or who were not successful in the **Quiz** section, may benefit from the **Alternative Teaching Strategy** on the next page.

Alternative Teaching Strategy

20 Minutes

OBJECTIVE Identify circles, rectangles, triangles, and squares on solid figures

MATERIALS for each pair: a set of solid figures (cube, pyramid, rectangular prism, cylinder), plane shape cutouts

Prepare sets of cutouts each containing a square, a triangle, a rectangle, and a circle that match the plane shapes of a cube, a pyramid, a rectangular prism, and a cylinder. You may wish to include a square for the bottom of the pyramid and a small square and different size rectangles to show all the different plane shapes of the rectangular prism. Set plane shape cutouts aside.

Begin by reviewing the following plane shapes: triangle, circle, rectangle, and square. Draw the shapes on the board. Label the shapes. Encourage children to identify and describe them.

Ask: **What shapes do you see?** (triangle, circle, rectangle, square)

Ask: **How can you tell which shape is the triangle?** (The one that has 3 sides.)

Ask: **What do you know about circles?** (Circles are round.)

Ask: **How are squares and rectangles alike?** (They both have 4 sides.)

Ask: **How can you tell the difference between a square and a rectangle?** (The sides of a square are all the same length. The sides of a rectangle are not the same length; two parallel sides are long and two parallel sides are short.)

Divide the class into pairs. Distribute a set of solid figures that include the rectangular prism, the cube, the pyramid, and the cylinder for the children to examine. Also provide each pair with a set of plane shape cutouts.

Say: **Trace the lines between the faces of each solid figure with your finger. Then trace the sides of each cutout with your finger. Match the plane shape cutouts to the plane shapes on the solid figures.**

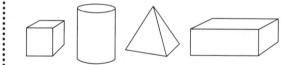

© Harcourt

**Grade 2
Skill 53**

Plane Shapes on Solid Figures

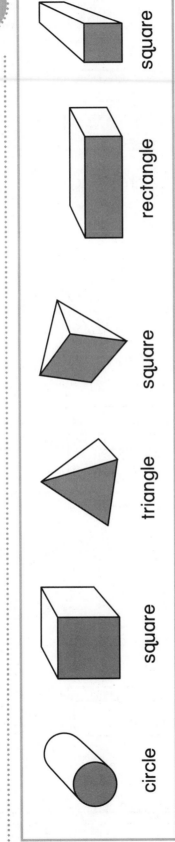

circle | square | triangle | square | rectangle | square

Try These

**Use solids. Trace around each one.
Write the name of the shape you drew.**

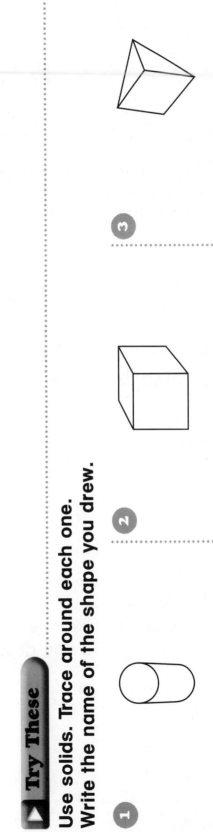

1. circle

2.

3.

Go to the next side.

Practice on Your Own

Skill 53

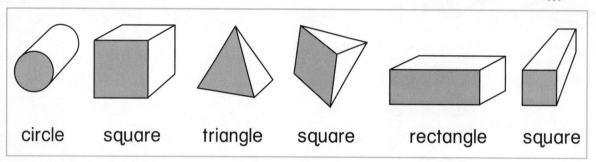

| circle | square | triangle | square | rectangle | square |

Use solids. Trace around each one.
Write the name of the shape you drew.

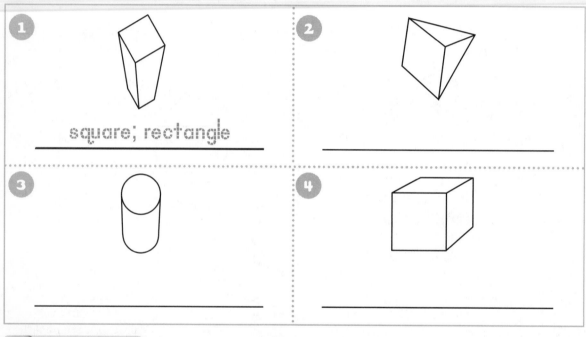

1   square; rectangle
_____

2   _____

3   _____

4   _____

▶ **Quiz**

Use solids. Trace around each one.
Write the name of the shape you drew.

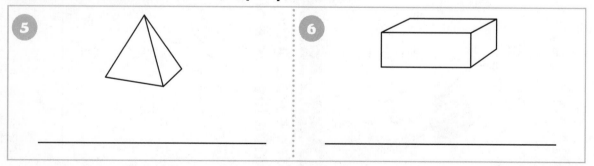

5   _____

6   _____

20 Minutes

Using Skill 54

OBJECTIVE Sort and identify plane shapes by the number of sides and vertices

Example

Review the names of the plane shapes at the top of the page.

Ask: **What shapes are shown?** (rectangle, circle, triangle, and square)

Introduce the terms *sides* and *vertices* and point out examples of each using plane shape models. Focus children's attention on Step 1.

Have children use their fingers to circle the vertices and then trace the sides of the triangle.

Continue with Step 2. Help children count the 3 sides and 3 vertices aloud as each are pointed to.

Ask: **What is the name for a shape with 3 sides and 3 vertices?** (a triangle)

Display a rectangle, a circle, a triangle, and a square on the board or on a chart.

Ask: **Which shape has 0 sides and 0 vertices?** (the circle) Demonstrate by tracing the outer ring of the circle.

Ask: **Which shapes have 4 sides and 4 vertices?** (the square and the rectangle) Demonstrate by tracing the 4 sides and circling the 4 vertices with your finger on each shape.

TRY THESE In Exercises 1–3, children draw the shapes and record the number of sides and vertices each shape has.

MATERIALS cutouts of a rectangle, a triangle, a circle, a square, a hexagon, a parallelogram, a pentagon, and a trapezoid

- **Exercises 1–3** Draw and identify the sides and vertices of a rectangle, a square, and a circle.

PRACTICE ON YOUR OWN Discuss the 4 examples at the top of the page. Exercises 1–2 provide practice identifying and recording the number of sides and vertices of two new plane shapes.

QUIZ Determine if children can recognize the sides and vertices of 4 plane shapes and then record the correct number of sides and vertices for each. Success is indicated by 3 out of 4 correct responses.

Children who successfully complete **Practice on Your Own** and **Quiz** are ready to move to the next skill.

COMMON ERRORS

- Children may have difficulty with the vocabulary.

- Children may miscount the number of sides and vertices.

Children who made an error in **Practice On Your Own,** or who were not successful in the **Quiz** section may benefit from the **Alternative Teaching Strategy** on the next page.

© Harcourt

Alternative Teaching Strategy

15 Minutes

OBJECTIVE Identify the attributes of 8 plane shapes

MATERIALS for each child: set of attribute shapes or punch-out shapes (rectangle, circle, triangle, square, hexagon, parallelogram, pentagon, and trapezoid) and drawing paper

Distribute drawing paper and a set of plane shapes to each child. Ask children to hold up the circle and the rectangle. Encourage them to trace around each shape with their fingers, and then describe how the shapes are different.

Write the terms *side* and *vertex* on the board. Call on children to point out where these are found on the rectangle and why they are not found on the circle.

Ask: **How many sides does the rectangle have?** (4)

Ask: **How many vertices does the rectangle have?** (4)

Ask: **How many sides does the circle have?** (0)

Ask: **How many vertices does the circle have?** (0)

Direct children to trace and label the shapes on drawing paper.

Say: **Record how many sides and vertices a rectangle has. Circle the vertices of the rectangle. Draw arrows that point to each side of the rectangle. Then write how many sides and vertices the circle has.**

Explore the attributes of triangles and squares by having children touch, discuss, trace, and label each shape. Continue pairing up the plane shapes and repeat the process for each pairing.

circle   rectangle

0 sides
0 vertices

4 sides
4 vertices

© Harcourt

Grade 2
Skill
54

Sort and Identify Plane Shapes

**Sort plane shapes by the number
of sides and vertices.**
Find how many sides on a triangle.
Find how many vertices.

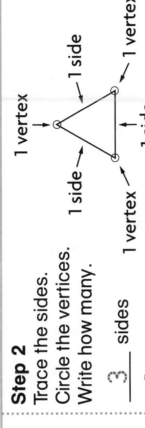

rectangle   circle   triangle   square

Step I
Trace the sides.
Circle the vertices.

1 vertex

1 side

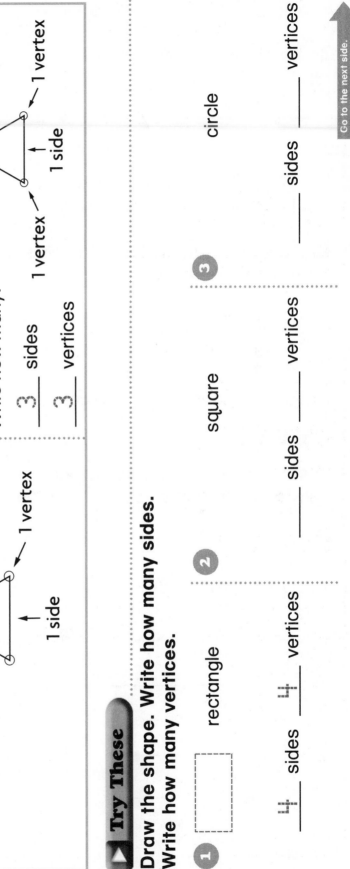

Step 2
Trace the sides.
Circle the vertices.
Write how many.

__3__ sides

__3__ vertices

1 vertex

1 side

1 side

1 side

1 vertex

1 vertex

◢ Try These

**Draw the shape. Write how many sides.
Write how many vertices.**

1   rectangle

____ sides   ____ vertices

2   square

____ sides   ____ vertices

3   circle

____ sides   ____ vertices

Go fo the next side.

Practice on Your Own

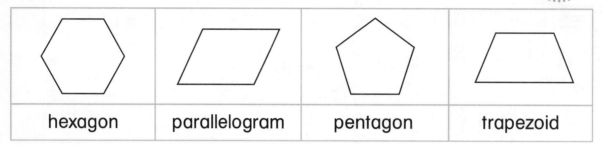

| hexagon | parallelogram | pentagon | trapezoid |

Use a small X to cross out each side. Circle each vertex.
Write how many sides and vertices there are.

1

__4__ sides __4__ vertices

2

____ sides ____ vertices

▶ Quiz

Use a small X to cross out each side. Circle each vertex.
Write how many sides and vertices there are.

3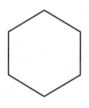

____ sides ____ vertices

4

____ sides ____ vertices

5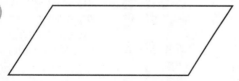

____ sides ____ vertices

6

____ sides ____ vertices

© Harcourt

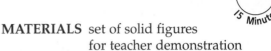

Using Skill 55

OBJECTIVE Identify solid figures

MATERIALS set of solid figures for teacher demonstration

15 Minutes

Example

You may wish to use solid figures to model the examples.

Review the solid figures at the top of the page. Ask: **How are the figures different?** (Possible answer: Some of the figures have flat faces and others have curved surfaces; some have more vertices than others.)

Say the names of the figures aloud. Have children point to each figure as you mention it. Help children pronounce the names. If they still have difficulty, break the names into syllables and demonstrate how to sound them out.

Have children look at the first example. Guide them to find the object that matches. Discuss the attributes of each figure. Explain that children should count the lines between the faces and vertices and check to see if the surfaces are curved or flat to help find the object that matches.

Ask: **What is the first figure called?** (pyramid)

Which object to the right is the same shape? (The picture of a pyramid paperweight.)

TRY THESE In Exercises 1–3 children practice identifying solid figures to prepare them for exercises that they will encounter in the **Practice on Your Own** section:

- **Exercise 1** Circle the object that has the same shape as a cone.

- **Exercise 2** Circle the object that has the same shape as a cylinder.

- **Exercise 3** Circle the object that has the same shape as a pyramid.

PRACTICE ON YOUR OWN Review the example at the top of the page. Exercises 1–2 provide practice in identifying solid figures.

QUIZ Determine if children can identify solid figures. Success is indicated by 2 out of 2 correct responses.

Children who successfully complete **Practice on Your Own** and **Quiz** are ready to move to the next skill.

COMMON ERRORS

- Children may confuse figures that have similar attributes.

- Children may have difficulty with vocabulary.

Have children who made an error in the **Practice on Your Own**, or who were not successful in the **Quiz** section, explain the examples aloud to determine if they are confusing figures that have similar attributes. These children may also benefit from the **Alternative Teaching Strategy** on the next page.

© Harcourt

Alternative Teaching Strategy

15 Minutes

OBJECTIVE Identify solid figures

MATERIALS solid figures, 5 cards labeled with the names of the solid figures: cylinder, sphere, rectangular prism, pyramid, cube, cone (for teacher demonstration), paper bags containing a solid figure for each child

Encourage children to examine each solid figure you display with its corresponding name card. Have children repeat each name in unison.

Encourage children to talk about the attributes of each figure. For example, have children hold the sphere and the cube. Ask: **How is the sphere different from a cube?** (Possible answer: The sphere is all curved and has no vertices. The cube has all flat faces and 8 vertices.)

What objects have you seen at home or at school with the same shape as the sphere? (Possible answer: A baseball and a soccer ball)

Continue comparing the sphere to other solid figures in a similar way.

Draw a 3-column chart on the board. The columns should be labeled as follows: Solid Figure, Drawing, Object.

Give each child a paper bag containing a solid figure. Invite children to open their bags without looking inside and feel the shape of the solid figure. Guide them to think of the attributes of each of the solids they have discussed, and predict which solid is in their bag.

Have children take their solids out of the bags and describe them. Discuss the children's solids. Encourage children to suggest real-world objects with shapes that match their solids. Have children help you complete the table on the board.

Solid Figure	Drawing	Object
sphere		basketball
rectangular prism		
cube		

© Harcourt

© Harcourt

Solid Figures

Look at the solid figures.

  cylinder

 sphere

 rectangular prism

  pyramid

 cube

  cone

Circle the object that has the same shape.

pyramid

soup

Circle the object that has the same shape.

cube

tissue

Try These

Circle the object that has the same shape.

1. cone

2. cylinder

soup

3. pyramid

tissue   Cereal

Go to the next side.

Practice on Your Own

Skill 55

Circle the objects that have the same shape.

rectangular prism

Circle the objects that have the same shape.

1
pyramid

2
cylinder

▶ Quiz

Circle the objects that have the same shape.

3
rectangular prism
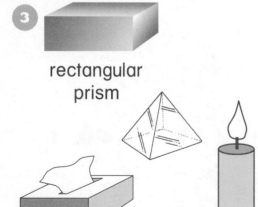

4
cone

© Harcourt

Using Skill 56

15 Minutes

OBJECTIVE Sort solid figures by attributes

MATERIALS sets of solid figures

Example

You may wish to have children use solid figures to model the example.

Review the names of the solid figures.

Have the children find the cube. Then guide children to examine it carefully, holding it flat in the palm of their hands and then placing it flat on the table. Point out that a cube has 6 faces and that all are the same size.

Have children find the sphere. Have children hold the sphere, turn it over, and roll it between their hands. Point out the curved surface.

Continue in a similar way with the other solid figures.

Then, direct children's attention to Step 1. Guide children to recall the faces they examined on the cube.

Continue with Step 2. Have children count the faces of the cube with you. It may be helpful to display the model again.

For Step 3, have children write the number of faces they counted on the cube.

TRY THESE In Exercises 1–3 children practice classifying solids to prepare them for exercises they will encounter in the **Practice on Your Own** section:

- **Exercise 1** Find the cube given the number of faces.

- **Exercise 2** Find the pyramid given the number of faces.

- **Exercise 3** Find the sphere given the number of faces.

PRACTICE ON YOUR OWN Review the example at the top of the page. Encourage children to talk about the faces of solids. Exercises 1–3 provide practice in identifying and classifying solids based on the number of faces they have.

QUIZ Determine if children can classify solid figures. Success is indicated by 2 out of 2 correct responses.

Children who successfully complete **Practice on Your Own** and **Quiz** are ready to move to the next skill.

COMMON ERRORS

- Children may confuse figures that have similar attributes.

- Children may have difficulty with the vocabulary.

Have children who made more than 1 error in the **Practice on Your Own**, or who were not successful in the **Quiz** section, work through the example with you. Provide three-dimensional figures for children to use while working. Children may also benefit from the **Alternative Teaching Strategy** on the next page.

© Harcourt

Alternative Teaching Strategy

15 Minutes

OBJECTIVE Sort solid figures by attributes

MATERIALS solid figures, self-stick notes

Give a rectangular prism to each child. Write *rectangular prism* and *face* on the board. Then say: **This is a solid figure. It is a rectangular prism**. Point to the rectangular prism. Ask: **How many faces do you think a rectangular prism has?**

Distribute self-stick notes and ask children to put one note on each face. Then, have them number the notes beginning with 1. Discuss how many faces the children found.

Then give children a square pyramid. After writing its name on the board, ask children to find the faces. Guide children to use self-stick notes to label the five faces. Ask: **How many faces does a pyramid have?** (5)

Continue with each solid figure. You may wish to have children create a table to record the figures and the number of faces for each.

rectangular prism

Solid Figure	Faces
rectangular prism	6
sphere	0
cube	6
pyramid	5

© Harcourt

Sort Solid Figures by Attributes

cube

pyramid

rectangular prism

sphere

Find how many faces on a cube.

Step 1
Look at the cube.

Step 2
Count the faces.

4 (back)

2

3

1

6 (side)

5 (bottom)

Remember:
You can't see all the faces in the picture.

Step 3
Write how many.

_____ 6 faces

So, a cube has 6 faces.

▶ **Try These**

Circle the object that matches the sentence.

1 The object has 6 faces.

sphere   pyramid   cube

2 The object has 5 faces.

sphere   pyramid   rectangular prism

3 The object has 0 faces.

pyramid   sphere   cube

→ Go to the next side.

Practice on Your Own

  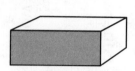

cube   pyramid   rectangular   sphere
                              prism

Circle the object with 5 faces.   **Write the name.**

Think: You can't see all the faces in the picture.

pyramid

1 Circle the object with 6 faces. Write the name.

rectangular

prism

2 Circle the object with 6 faces. Write the name.

_____

3 Circle the object with 0 faces. Write the name.

_____

▶ Quiz

4 Circle the object with 6 faces. Write the name.

_____

5 Circle the object with 0 faces. Write the name.

_____

Using Skill 57

OBJECTIVE Model and identify lines of symmetry

MATERIALS drawing paper, markers, scissors

Example

Distribute drawing paper, a marker, and scissors to each child. Direct children to the model at the top of the page. Guide them to follow each step.

Step 1
Say: **Fold your paper in half as shown in the picture.**

Step 2
Ask: **What will you do next?** (Draw a shape starting at the fold.)

Steps 3 and 4
Ask: **What 2 things will you do next?** (cut along the line and unfold the shape)

Ask: **What do you think your shape will look like when you unfold it?** (Answers may vary.)

Step 5
Say: **Now draw a line along the fold.**

Ask: **How can you tell that the line is down the middle of your shape?** (Both parts of the shape match.)

Say: **This line is called a line of symmetry.**

TRY THESE In Exercises 1–3 children practice drawing a line of symmetry to make two matching parts.

- **Exercise 1** Make 2 matching parts of a square.

- **Exercise 2** Make 2 matching parts of a circle.

- **Exercise 3** Make 2 matching parts of a triangle.

PRACTICE ON YOUR OWN As you review the example at the top of the page, have children explain how they know the shape has a line of symmetry. Exercises 1–6 provide practice in drawing a line of symmetry to make two matching parts.

QUIZ Determine if children can correctly draw a line of symmetry to make two matching parts. Success is indicated by 2 out of 3 correct responses.

Children who successfully complete **Practice on Your Own** and **Quiz** are ready to move to the next skill.

COMMON ERRORS

- Children may have difficulty visualizing and drawing a line of symmetry.

- Children may have difficulty determining if 2 parts of a shape match.

Children who made more than 1 error in **Practice on Your Own**, or who were not successful in the **Quiz** section may also benefit from the **Alternative Teaching Strategy** on the next page.

Alternative Teaching Strategy

OBJECTIVE Identify and create lines of symmetry

MATERIALS construction paper shapes, paper-bag, dot paper, scissors

Fold some of the paper shapes in half. Fold others in two parts that are not equal. Draw a line down each fold. Place the shapes in a paper bag.

Say: **Pick a shape. Then fold it along the line. Look at both parts. If the two parts match, hold up your shape. If the two parts do not match, place your shape on the desk.**

Check children's responses. Repeat several times until children have had opportunities to identify shapes with and without lines of symmetry.

Say: **When you fold a shape into two parts and the two parts match, the line is called a line of symmetry.**

Ask: **How do you know if a shape does not have a line of symmetry?** (When you fold along the line the two parts do not match.)

Provide each child with dot paper and scissors.

Say: **Draw a rectangle on the dot paper.** Then help children draw a line to divide the rectangle in half.

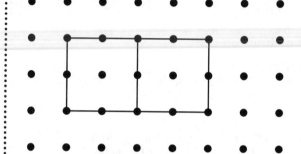

Ask: **What do you see?** (two matching parts)

Say: **The two parts show symmetry because the line divides the shape into two parts that match.**

NOTE: A line of symmetry could also be drawn horizontally through the middle of the rectangle.

Say: **Cut out the rectangle, then cut along the line of symmetry. Now place one part on top of the other.**

Ask: **What do you see?** (The parts match.)

Have children use the dot paper to draw other shapes with lines of symmetry.

© Harcourt

Symmetry

3. Cut along the line.

2. Start at the fold. Draw a shape.

5. Draw a line down the middle.

1. Fold your paper.

4. Open your shape.

The line down the middle is called a **line of symmetry**.
The two parts should match.

Try These

Draw a line of symmetry to make two matching parts.

1

2

3

Go to the next side.

Practice on Your Own

Skill  57

 1. Fold your paper.

 2. Start at the fold. Draw a shape.

 3. Cut along the line.

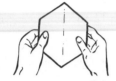 4. Open your shape.

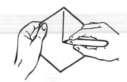 5. Draw a line down the middle.

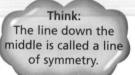 **Think:** The line down the middle is called a line of symmetry.

The two parts match.

Draw a line of symmetry to make two matching parts.

1 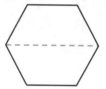   2    3

4 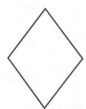   5   6

▶ **Quiz**

Draw a line of symmetry to make two matching parts.

7   8 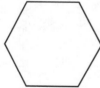   9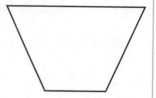

20 Minutes

Using Skill 58

OBJECTIVE Model and identify slides and turns

MATERIALS tagboard rectangles— the same size as in the model

Have children stand up.
Say: **Face me and slide to your right. Next, slide forward. Now, slide to the left. Last, slide back.**
Ask: **What changed with each slide?** (our position) **What did not change?** (our direction)

Say: **Face me. This time, turn to your right. Then turn right again.**
Ask: **What changed with each turn?** (our position and our direction)

Have children take their seats. Give each child a rectangle and direct them to look at the model at the top of the page.
Say: **Place your rectangle above the first rectangle pictured.** Check that children have positioned their rectangles correctly.

Say: **Now slide it to the right.**
Ask: **What do you notice?** (The rectangle's position has changed.)
Say: **Then slide it up. Slide it to the left. Then slide it down.**
Ask: **What changed each time you made a slide?** (the position) **What did not change?** (the direction)

Say: **Flip over your shape and place it above the first rectangle in the next model. Put your shape on top of the first shape.** Check that children have positioned their rectangles correctly.
Say: **Slowly turn your shape until it is on top of the second shape.**
Ask: **What is different about this move?** (The position changed, and the direction of the shape changed.)

TRY THESE In Exercises 1–3 children practice identifying slides and turns to prepare for the exercises they will encounter in **Practice On Your Own**.

- **Exercises 1–3** Identify slides and turns.

PRACTICE ON YOUR OWN Review the example at the top of the page, and have children explain how to tell a slide from a turn. Exercises 1–4 provide practice in identifying slides and turns with triangles.

QUIZ Determine if children can correctly identify slides and turns. Success is indicated by 2 out of 3 correct responses.

Children who successfully complete **Practice on Your Own** and **Quiz** are ready to move to the next skill.

COMMON ERRORS

- Children may have difficulty visualizing and therefore incorrectly distinguishing between slides and turns.

- Children may recognize that the moves are different but identify a slide as a turn or a turn as a slide.

If a child makes more than 1 error in the **Practice on Your Own** section, or was not successful in the **Quiz** section, have the child trace the shape for each exercise, cut the shape out, and then use it to model the move. Encourage the child to explain the move and tell why it is a slide or a turn. The child may also benefit from the **Alternative Teaching Strategy** on the next page.

© Harcourt

Alternative Teaching Strategy

OBJECTIVE Identify and model slides and turns

MATERIALS drawing paper; tagboard rectangle and tagboard triangle for each child; overhead projector

Distribute drawing paper, a rectangle, and a triangle to each child.

Use an overhead projector to model a slide by displaying a vertical rectangle. Trace around the rectangle. Then place the actual rectangle on top of the traced rectangle and slowly slide it diagonally to the right or down. Encourage children to describe the move.

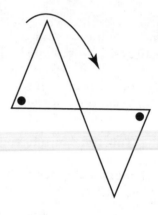

Ask: **Did I model a slide or a turn?** (a slide) **How can you tell?** (The rectangles have the same direction.)

Say: **Now, it's your turn to model a slide. Place the rectangle on your paper and trace around it. Slowly slide it up, down, to the right, or to the left. STOP. Trace the rectangle to show the new place. Now, look at the two shapes.**

Ask: **How are they alike?** (Both have the same direction.) **How are they different?** (The second shape is in a new place.)

Using the overhead again, model a turn by displaying a triangle. Trace around the triangle. Slowly turn it 180 degrees. Encourage children to describe the move.

Ask: **Did I model a slide or a turn?** (a turn) **How can you tell?** (The direction of the triangle has changed.)

Say: **Now you model a turn. Place the triangle on your paper and trace around it. Slowly turn the triangle. STOP. Trace the triangle. Now, look at the two shapes.**

Ask: **What happened to the shape as you made the move?** (The direction changed.) **How can you tell?** (The dot shows how the triangle was turned.)

Have children continue to use the shapes to model and identify slides and turns.

© Harcourt

Grade 2
Skill 58

Slides and Turns

You can move the rectangle.

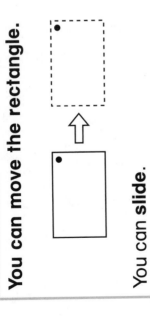

You can slide.

You can turn.

Try These

Circle *slide* or *turn* to name the move.

1.

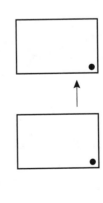

slide   turn

2.

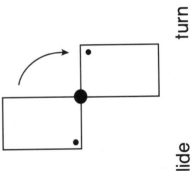

slide   turn

3.

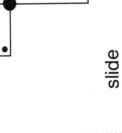

slide   turn

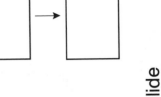
Go to the next slide.

Practice on Your Own

You can move the triangle.

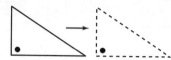   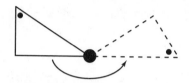

You can **slide**.   You can **turn**.

Circle *slide* or *turn* to name the move.

 1

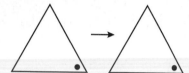

 2

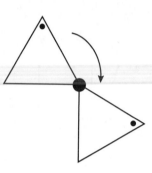

    (slide)   turn   slide   turn

3

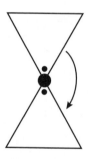

4

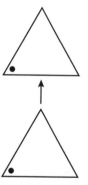

   slide   turn   slide   turn

▶ Quiz

Circle *slide* or *turn* to name the move.

 5

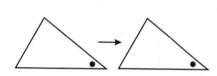

6

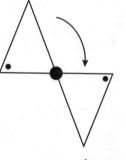

   slide   turn   slide   turn

© Harcourt

Algebraic Thinking, Patterns, and Functions

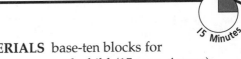

Using Skill 59

OBJECTIVE Identify the greater of two numbers and use the greater than (>) sign

You may wish to model Steps 1–3 using base-ten blocks and workmats.

Example

Review how to count the number of tens blocks and ones blocks that represent a number.

In Step 1, tell children to find how many tens and ones there are in each number. Ask: **How many tens are in 43?** (4) **How many ones?** (3) Say: **So, 43 has 4 tens 3 ones.** Use the same questioning for 39.

In Step 2, ask: **Which number has more tens?** (43)

Help children understand that if 4 tens are greater than 3 tens, then 43 is greater than 39. Point out that it is unnecessary to compare the ones for these numbers. Explain, however, that when the tens are the same, the children should compare the ones. Emphasize that for two-digit numbers, they should always compare tens first.

In Step 3, point to the *greater than* symbol between 43 and 39. Ask the children to read the sentence aloud. Make sure that they are able to say the correct words for the symbol.

TRY THESE Exercises 1–2 prepare children for practice in identifying what makes a number greater than the other, which they will encounter in the **Practice on Your Own** section.

- **Exercise 1** Compare 25 and 34.

- **Exercise 2** Compare 56 and 73.

MATERIALS base-ten blocks for each child (15 tens, 4 ones), workmats

PRACTICE ON YOUR OWN Review the examples at the top of the page to practice identifying the greater number using models. Exercises 1–4 provide practice in identifying the greater number without models. Encourage children to use models to check their work.

QUIZ Determine if children can identify the greater number of two. Success is indicated by 2 out of 2 correct responses.

Children who successfully complete **Practice on Your Own** and **Quiz** are ready to move to the next skill.

COMMON ERRORS

- Children may begin comparing digits in the ones place.

- Children may be confused by the *greater than* symbol.

Have children who made more than one error in the **Practice on Your Own** section, or who were not successful in the **Quiz** section, work through the example with you. Have each child explain the exercise aloud to determine if he or she compares ones first or misreads the *greater than* symbol. The child may also benefit from the **Alternative Teaching Strategy** on the next page.

Alternative Teaching Strategy

OBJECTIVE Identify the greater of two numbers

MATERIALS base-ten blocks (9 tens, 20 ones), overhead projector, transparency

Begin by having the children compare multiples of ten, such as 20 and 30.

Distribute base-ten blocks to each child. Have them model at their desks while you demonstrate on the overhead.

Display base-ten models on the overhead projector, arranging them on a transparency as shown below.

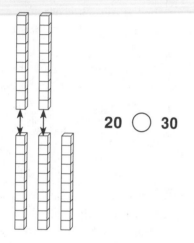

Using one-to-one correspondence, have the children match the tens. On the overhead, draw a line between tens that are matched and point out that there is one unmatched ten. Point out that 30 has one more ten than 20. Also say that 20 has fewer tens than 30.

Ask: **Which number is greater?** (30)

Ask children how to write "30 is greater than 20." You may want to compare the greater than sign to the beak of a bird that always eats bigger numbers.

Repeat other examples until children correctly model and compare numbers that are multiples of 10. Now extend the activity to compare other kinds of numbers.

Compare 37 and 23. Set up the models with multiples of ten, using one-to-one correspondence to compare.

Draw lines to match tens, having children tell you which tens match and which number has more tens. Help children recognize that it is not necessary to compare the ones, since the value of the tens is greater than the value of the ones. Insert the *is greater than* symbol to show that 37 is greater than 23.

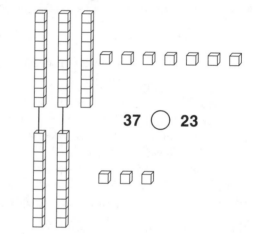

Repeat the activity for other examples such as 17 and 25, and 32 and 41.

Emphasize that when we compare 2-digit numbers we always start by comparing tens.

© Harcourt

Algebra: Greater Than

Use ▭▭▭ ▯ to show each number.

Step 1
Show each number.

tens	ones
▤▤▤▤	▯▯▯

43

tens	ones
▤▤▤	▯▯▯▯ ▯▯▯▯ ▯▯

39

Step 2
Circle the greater number.

(43)   39

Step 3
Write the numbers.

43 is greater than 39 .

43 > 39 .

▶ **Try These**

Circle the greater number. Write the numbers. You can use ▭▭▭ ▯ to help.

1

tens	ones
▤▤	▯▯▯▯▯

25

tens	ones
▤▤▤	▯▯▯▯

34

25   (34)

34 is greater than 25 .

34 > 25 .

2   56   73

_____ is greater than _____ .

_____ > _____ .

Go to the next side.

Practice on Your Own

Circle the greater number. Write the numbers.
You can use 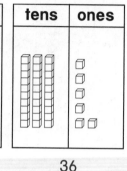 **to help.**

tens	ones	tens	ones

51   36

(51)   36

__51__ is greater than __36__ .

__51__   >   __36__ .

- -

Circle the greater number. Write the numbers.
You can use  **to help.**

1 (39)   36

_____ is greater than _____ .

_____   >   _____ .

2 29   71

_____ is greater than _____ .

_____   >   _____ .

3 60   57

_____ is greater than _____ .

_____   >   _____ .

4 48   63

_____ is greater than _____ .

_____   >   _____ .

▶ Quiz

Circle the greater number. Write the numbers.
You can use **to help.**

5 69   79

_____ is greater than _____ .

_____   >   _____ .

6 57   53

_____ is greater than _____ .

_____   >   _____ .

Using Skill 60

OBJECTIVE Identify the lesser of two numbers

MATERIALS base-ten blocks for each child (7 tens, 4 ones), workmats

15 Minutes

You may wish to model Steps 1–3 using base-ten blocks and workmats.

Example

Review how to use base-ten blocks to make 32 and 42. Ask: **How many tens are in 32?** (3) **How many ones?** (2)

Say: **So, 32 has 3 tens 2 ones.** Use the same questioning for 42.

In Step 2, ask: **Which number has fewer tens?** (32) Help children understand that 3 tens is fewer than 4 tens. So, 32 is less than 42. Point out that it is unnecessary to compare the ones for these numbers. Explain, however, that when the tens are the same, the children should compare the ones. Emphasize that for two-digit numbers, they should always compare tens first.

In Step 3, point to the *less than* symbol between 32 and 42. Ask children to read the sentence aloud, making sure that they are able to say the correct words for the symbol.

TRY THESE Exercises 1–2 prepare children for practice in identifying what makes a number less than the other, which they will encounter in the **Practice on Your Own** section.

- **Exercise 1** Compare 28 and 19.
- **Exercise 2** Compare 37 and 45.

PRACTICE ON YOUR OWN Review the example at the top of the page to practice identifying the lesser number. Exercises 1–4 provide practice in identifying the lesser number without models.

QUIZ Determine if children can identify the lesser of two numbers. Success is indicated by 2 out of 2 correct responses.

Children who successfully complete **Practice on Your Own** and **Quiz** are ready to move to the next skill.

COMMON ERRORS

- Children may first compare digits in the ones place.
- Children may be confused by the *less than* symbol.

Have children who made more than one error in the **Practice on Your Own** section, or who were not successful in the **Quiz** section, work through the first Practice on Your Own problem with you. Have each child explain the exercise aloud to determine if he or she compares ones first or misreads the *less than* symbol. The child may also benefit from the **Alternative Teaching Strategy** on the next page.

Alternative Teaching Strategy

OBJECTIVE Identify the lesser of two numbers

MATERIALS overhead projector; transparencies with place-value tables; for each child: place-value table; base-ten materials;

You may wish to have children model your steps on their worksheets.

Begin by having the children compare multiples of ten, such as 30 and 40.

Distribute place-value charts and base-ten materials. Have children model each example at their seats while you demonstrate on the overhead.

Using the overhead projector and the transparent place-value chart, model 30 using tens. Record a 3 in the tens column and a 0 in the ones column.

Do the same for 40. You may want to have children record the tens in red pen and the ones in blue.

tens	ones
❘❘❘	
❘❘❘❘	

Show that in 30 there are 3 tens, and in 40 there are 4 tens. Point out that 30 has fewer tens than 40. So, 30 is less than 40.

Record the inequality on the transparency: 30 < 40

Continue the exercise with numbers other than multiples of ten, such as 53 and 61.

Model each number with base-ten materials.

tens	ones
❘❘❘❘❘	☐☐☐
❘❘❘❘❘❘	☐

Ask: **Should you compare the tens or the ones first?** (tens) **Which number has fewer tens?** (53)

Help children recognize that it is not necessary to compare the ones, since the tens column expresses greater values than the ones column.

Record the inequality on the transparency: 53 < 61

Repeat the activity for other examples such as 72 and 62, and 43 and 48.

Grade 2
Skill 60

Algebra: Less Than

Use ▭ □ to show each number.

Step 1
Show each number.

tens	ones

tens	ones

Step 2
Circle the number that is less.

(32)   42

Step 3
Write the numbers.

32   is less than   42.

32   <   42.

Go to the next side.

 **Try These**

Circle the number that is less. Write the numbers.
You can use ▭ □ to help.

1   28   (19)

19   is less than   28.

19   <   28.

2   37   45

____ is less than ____.

____   <   ____.

Practice on Your Own

Skill 60

Circle the number that is less. Write the numbers.
You can use to help.

54   (49)

__49__ is less than __54__ .

__49__ < __54__ .

Think: 49 has
fewer tens than 54

Circle the number that is less. Write the numbers.
You can use ▭▭ to help.

1 (53)   65

__53__ is less than __65__ .

__53__ < __65__ .

2 74   47

____ is less than ____ .

____ < ____ .

3 32   37

____ is less than ____ .

____ < ____ .

4 60   54

____ is less than ____ .

____ < ____ .

▶ Quiz

Circle the number that is less. Write the numbers.
You can use ▭▭ to help.

5 53   39

____ is less than ____ .

____ < ____ .

6 68   87

____ is less than ____ .

____ < ____ .

Using Skill 61

OBJECTIVE Compare numbers to 50 using <, > and =

MATERIALS base-ten blocks (5 tens, 7 ones) for each child

Review the meaning of the symbols <, >, and =.

Remind children that the pointed end of the symbol points to the lesser number. Write 4 > 3 on the board. Observe that the *open* end of the symbol points to the greater number.

Example

You may wish to have children model Steps 1–3 using base-ten blocks. Call attention to Step 1. Ask: **How many tens are in the first number?** (3) **How many ones?** (4) **How many tens are in the second number?** (2) **How many ones?** (3)

Continue with Step 2. Remind children that for two-digit numbers, they compare the tens digits first. If the digits are different, decide which digit is greater.

Have children compare the tens of each number. Guide children to see that when the tens digits are different, the greater number is the one with more tens. Emphasize that 34 is the greater number, because 3 tens is greater than 2 tens. Have children read the comparison in Step 2. (34 is greater than 23). Have children write the greater than symbol (>) in Step 3.

TRY THESE In Exercises 1–3 children practice writing > and < to compare numbers.

- **Exercise 1**   Compare 28 and 15.
- **Exercise 2**   Compare 12 and 33.
- **Exercise 3**   Compare 23 and 45.

PRACTICE ON YOUR OWN Review the example at the top of the page. Exercises 1–2 provide practice in comparing numbers using pictured base-ten blocks. Exercises 3–5 provide practice in comparing numbers without models.

QUIZ Determine if children can compare numbers using <, >, or =. Success is indi-cated by 2 out of 3 correct responses.

Children who successfully complete **Practice on Your Own** and **Quiz** are ready to move to the next skill.

COMMON ERRORS

- Children may confuse the symbols < and >.

- Children may begin comparing in the ones place instead of the tens place.

When comparing numbers such as 42 and 26, children may say that 26 is the greater number, because the digit 6 is greater than either of the two digits in 42.

Have children who made more than 1 error in the **Practice on Your Own,** or who were not successful in the **Quiz** section, work through the example with you. Have the child "think aloud" to determine if he or she is confusing the symbols, begins comparing in the ones place, or does not consider the place value of a digit. The child may also benefit from the **Alternative Teaching Strategy** on the next page.

Alternative Teaching Strategy

15 Minutes

OBJECTIVE Compare numbers to 50

MATERIALS blocks (8 tens, 20 ones), pencil, paper for each child, flip chart

On the flip chart, write the numbers 27 and 17. Help children model the numbers using base-ten blocks. Explain that 27 has 2 tens 7 ones and 17 has one ten 7 ones.

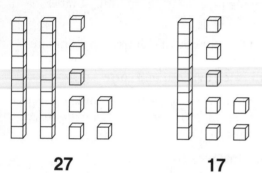

27   17

Guide children to compare the numbers starting with the tens.

Explain that since 2 tens are greater than 1 ten, 27 is greater than 17. Have children use one-to-one correspondence to compare the tens. Then write 27 > 17 on the flip chart.

Have children use base-ten blocks to model and compare other numbers. Increase the tens digits by 1, gradually increasing the dif-ficulty of the comparison. Help children record their work using <, >, and =.

© Harcourt

Algebra: Use Symbols to Compare

> means greater than.
< means less than.

Use <, >, or = to compare 34 and 23.

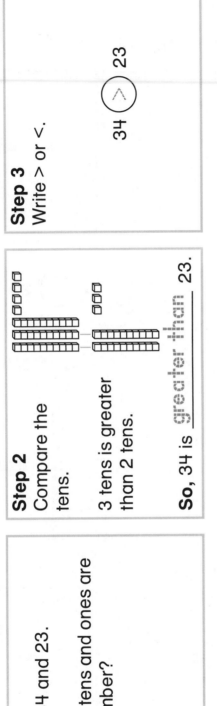

Step 1
Compare 34 and 23.

How many tens and ones are in each number?

Step 2
Compare the tens.

3 tens is greater than 2 tens.

So, 34 is _greater than_ 23.

Step 3
Write > or <.

34 ⬭(>) 23

▲ Try These

Write greater than or less than. Then write > or <.

1

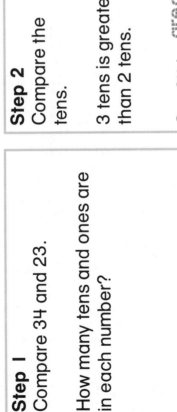

28 is _greater than_ 15.

28 ⬭(>) 15

2

12 is _____ 33.

12 ◯ 33

3

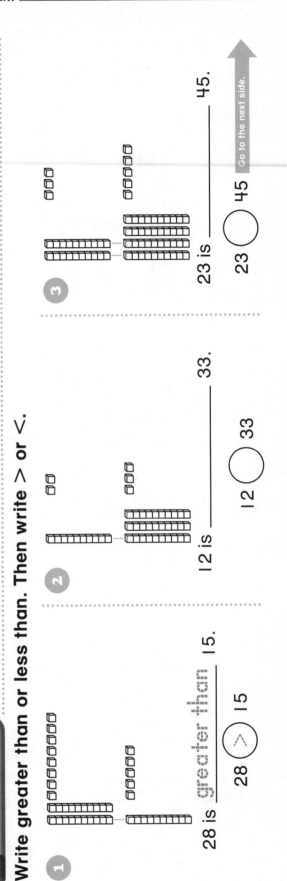

23 is _____ 45.

23 ◯ 45

Go to the next side.

Practice on Your Own

Skill 61

Write greater than or less than. Then write > or <.

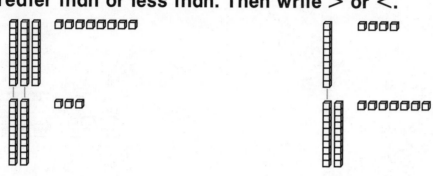

38 is ___greater than___ 23.   14 is ___less than___ 27.

38 (>) 23   14 (<) 27

Write greater than or less than.

36 is ___greater than___ 21.   22 is _____ 47.

Write >, <, or =.

3 17 ( ) 17   4 42 ( ) 26   5 23 ( ) 50

▶ **Quiz**

Write >, <, or =.

6 21 ( ) 21   7 36 ( ) 28   8 19 ( ) 45

Using Skill 62

OBJECTIVE Describe and extend patterns

Draw 6 triangles in a row on the board; shade every other one. Have children describe what they see.

Ask: **What makes this a pattern?** (the same thing repeats over and over) **What comes first in the pattern?** (shaded) **What comes next?** (not shaded) **What part of the pattern repeats?** (shaded/not shaded)

Draw two more triangles.

Ask: **How can you continue the pattern?** (shade in the next triangle)

Point to the triangle after that.

Ask: **Should you shade this triangle?** (no) **Why not?** (The pattern is shaded/ not shaded.)

Example

Focus attention on the model at the top of the page. Invite children to describe the pattern on the ribbon on the left. Point to each heart as children say the pattern aloud.

Ask: **What repeats in the pattern?** (black/white)

Invite children to describe the pattern on the ribbon to the right.

Ask: **What part of the pattern repeats?** (black, white, gray) **If you were to continue this pattern, what would come next?** (black) **How do you know?** (Black always comes after gray in this pattern.)

TRY THESE In exercises 1–2, children practice describing and extending 2 and 3 element patterns.

- **Exercise 1**   Find the pattern. Then color to continue an ABC pattern.

- **Exercise 2**   Find the pattern. Then color to continue an AB pattern.

PRACTICE ON YOUR OWN Review the examples at the top of the page. Encourage children to describe the patterns and tell how they would extend each one. Exercises 1–3 provide practice in describing and extending patterns.

QUIZ Determine if children can identify and extend patterns. Success is indicated by 2 out of 2 correct responses.

Children who successfully complete **Practice on Your Own** and **Quiz** are ready to move to the next skill.

COMMON ERRORS

- Children may have difficulty recognizing what repeats in a pattern and as a result color the shapes incorrectly when extending it.

- Children may recognize a 2 unit pattern, but may have difficulty recognizing a 3 unit pattern.

Children who made more than 1 error in the **Practice On Your Own**, or who were not successful in the Quiz section, may benefit from the **Alternative Teaching Strategy** on the next page.

Alternative Teaching Strategy

15 Minutes

OBJECTIVE Make, identify, and continue patterns

MATERIALS for each child: 8 red, 8 yellow, and 8 blue connecting cubes

Distribute materials to children.

Say: **Listen and follow these directions to make a pattern cube train. First, start with a red cube, then connect a blue cube to the red cube, then connect another red cube after the blue one, followed by a blue cube, followed by a red cube and finally ending the train with a blue cube.**

Ask: **What is the pattern?** (red, blue)

Say: **Add 2 more cubes to continue the pattern.**

Give children time to complete the task.

Ask: **What 2 color cubes did you add to continue the pattern?** (red and blue) **Why?** (They are the 2 colors that are repeated in the pattern.)

Say: **Let's point to the cubes as we read the pattern aloud: red, blue, red, blue, red, blue, red, blue.**

Repeat this procedure with other AB patterns such as red and yellow. Then vary the patterns by including some of the following: an AAB pattern such as red, red, yellow; or an ABB pattern such as blue, yellow, yellow; and an ABC pattern such as red, yellow, blue.

Next have children form pairs. Tell each pair to combine their connecting cubes. Have one partner create a pattern and challenge the other partner to describe it and then extend it. Once the pattern has been revealed, have the children reverse roles.

As children work to make patterns, encourage them to verbalize what colors are repeated in the pattern and in the correct order.

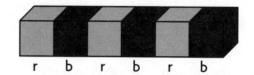

r   b   r   b   r   b

Name _____

Skill _____

Grade 2
Skill
62

© Harcourt

Algebra: Describe and Extend Patterns

The **pattern** on this ribbon is black, white, black, white, black, white.

The **pattern** on this ribbon is black, white, gray, black, white, gray.

 **Try These**

Find the pattern. Then color to continue it.

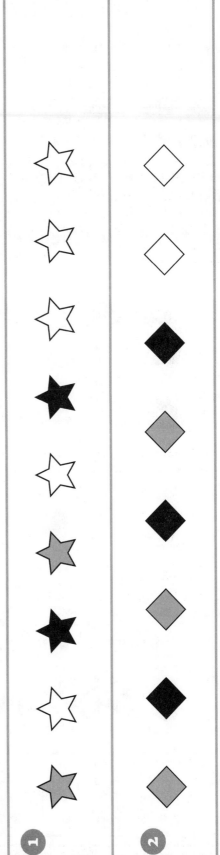

Go to the next side.

Intervention • Skills IN303

Name _____ Skill _____

Practice on Your Own

 **Skill 62**

The **pattern** is white, black, black, white, black, black.

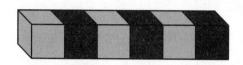

The **pattern** is gray, black, gray, black, gray, black.

Find the pattern. Then color to continue it.

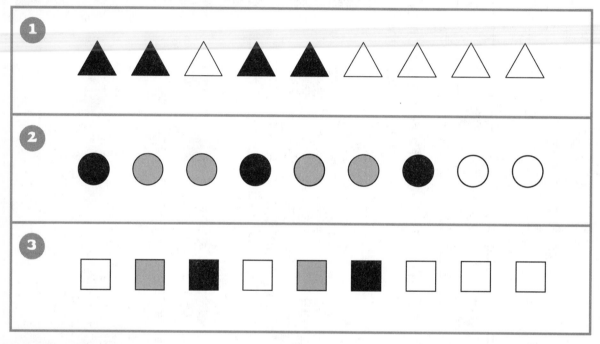

Quiz

Find the pattern. Then color to continue it.

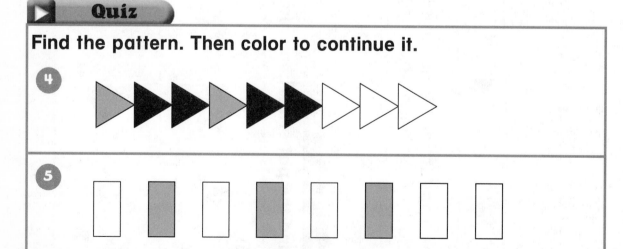

Skill **63**

Algebra: Pattern Units

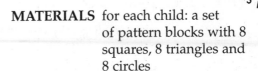

Using Skill 63

OBJECTIVE Identify pattern units

MATERIALS for each child: a set of pattern blocks with 8 squares, 8 triangles and 8 circles

Invite children to listen and join in as soon as they recognize the pattern they hear such as snap, clap, clap; snap, clap, clap. Keep repeating the pattern until all children have joined in.

Ask: **What actions did we repeat over and over?** (snap, clap, clap)

Say: **Snap, clap, clap is called a pattern unit.**

Ask: **How many actions did we repeat in each unit?** (three)

Say: **The part of a pattern that repeats over and over is called the pattern unit. This pattern unit is made up of 3 actions—snap, clap, clap.**

Distribute pattern blocks and have children create their own patterns. Invite children to share their patterns and identify the pattern unit.

Ask: **How many shapes long is the pattern unit?** (Answers will vary.)

Example

Focus attention on the pattern in the example at the top of the page. Invite children to describe the pattern unit.

Ask: **If you could add another pattern unit, what would it be?** (black triangle, gray square)

TRY THESE In exercises 1–3 children practice identifying pattern units to prepare for the exercises they will encounter in **Practice On Your Own.**

- **Exercise 1** Identify an AB pattern unit.
- **Exercise 2** Identify an ABC pattern unit.
- **Exercise 3** Identify an AAB pattern unit.

PRACTICE ON YOUR OWN Review the example at the top of the page. Exercises 1–4 provide practice in identifying pattern units.

QUIZ Determine if children can identify pattern units. Success is indicated by 2 out of 2 correct responses.

Children who successfully complete **Practice on Your Own** and **Quiz** are ready to move to the next skill.

COMMON ERRORS

- Children may have difficulty recognizing a pattern and how it repeats.

- Children may circle too many or too few shapes in each pattern unit.

Children who made errors in **Practice On Your Own**, or who were not successful in the **Quiz** section, may benefit from the **Alternative Teaching Strategy** on the next page.

Alternative Teaching Strategy

15 Minutes

OBJECTIVE Explore pattern units

MATERIALS for each child: construction paper shapes (4–5 inches each)—red triangles, yellow circles, green squares

Give each child either a red triangle, a yellow circle, or a green square. Begin by inviting three children, each with a different shape and color, to come to the front of the classroom.

Say: **Let's make a pattern unit. Arrange yourselves in a row. Then hold up your shapes for everyone to see.**

Ask: **What shape is first?** (yellow circle) **What shape is next?** (green square) **What shape is after that?** (red triangle) (Possible answers are given since they will vary depending on how children arrange themselves.)

Ask: **How many shapes long is your pattern unit?** (3)

Say: **Now, let's repeat the pattern unit.** Invite other children to join the row to continue the pattern by repeating the pattern unit. In this example, children would come up with a yellow circle, a green square and a red triangle.

Repeat with other patterns. Have children include color as another attribute.

Challenge groups of 8–9 children to create a pattern by arranging themselves in front of the class. Have the class identify the pattern unit and then select volunteers to come up and continue the pattern.

yellow   green   red

Grade 2
Skill
63

Algebra: Pattern Units

A pattern unit repeats over and over in the pattern.

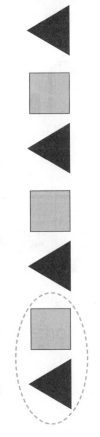

This pattern unit is two shapes long.

Try These

Use shapes to copy the pattern. Then circle the pattern unit.

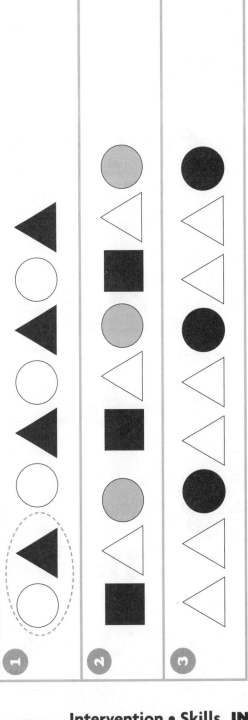

Go to the next side.

Practice on Your Own

A **pattern unit** repeats over and over in the pattern.

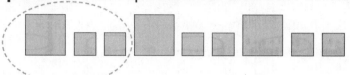

This pattern unit is three shapes long.

Use the pictures. Circle the pattern unit.

1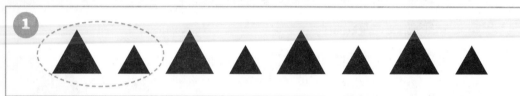

2

3

4

▶ **Quiz**

Use the pictures. Circle the pattern unit.

5

6

Skill 64
Grade 2

Compare Numbers: >, <, and =

15 Minutes

Using Skill 64

OBJECTIVE Use <, >, and = to compare numbers

MATERIALS base-ten blocks (15 tens, 4 ones) for teacher demonstration

Example
You may wish to model Steps 1–3 using base-ten blocks. Review the meaning of the inequality symbols: > (is greater than), < (is less than).

Review how to count the number of tens and ones blocks that represent a number. In Step 1, tell children to find how many tens and ones there are in each number. Ask: **How many tens are in 83?** (8) **How many ones?** (3)

Say: **So, 83 has 8 tens 3 ones.**
Use the same questioning for 71.

Continue with Step 2. Have children compare the tens in each number.

Guide them to look at the models and notice that 83 has one more ten than 71. Help children understand that since 8 tens are more tens than 7 tens, 83 is greater than 71. Point out that it is unnecessary to compare the ones for these numbers. Emphasize that for two-digit numbers, always begin comparing tens first.

In Step 3, point to the *is greater than* symbol between 83 and 71. Ask the children to read the sentence aloud, making sure that they are able to say the correct words for the symbol.

TRY THESE In Exercises 1–3 children practice using <, >, and =, to compare numbers, to prepare them for exercises that they will encounter in the **Practice on Your Own** section:

- **Exercise 1**   Compare 68 and 53 using >.
- **Exercise 2**   Compare 55 and 72 using <.
- **Exercise 3**   Compare 71 and 71 using =.

PRACTICE ON YOUR OWN Review the example at the top of the page. Exercises 1–5 provide practice in comparing numbers with pictured base-ten blocks. Exercises 6–8 provide practice in comparing numbers without models.

QUIZ Determine if children can compare numbers using <, >, and =. Success is indicated by 2 out of 3 correct responses.

Children who successfully complete **Practice on Your Own** and **Quiz** are ready to move to the next skill.

COMMON ERRORS

- Children may begin comparing with the ones place.
- Children may confuse the inequality symbols.

Have children who made more than 1 error in the **Practice on Your Own**, or who were not successful in the **Quiz** section, work through the example with you. Have each child explain the exercise aloud to determine if he or she compares ones first or confuses the inequality symbols. The child may also benefit from the **Alternative Teaching Strategy** on the next page.

Alternative Teaching Strategy

15 Minutes

OBJECTIVE Use <, >, and = to compare numbers

MATERIALS base-ten blocks (9 tens, 20 ones), overhead projector, transparency

Begin by having the children compare multiples of ten, such as 20 and 30.

Display base-ten models on the overhead projector, arranging them on a transparency as shown below. Using one-to-one correspondence, have the children match the tens. Draw a line between tens that are matched and point out that there is one unmatched ten. Point out that 30 has one more ten than 20. Also say that 20 has fewer tens than 30. Ask: **Is 20 less than or greater than 30?** (less than)

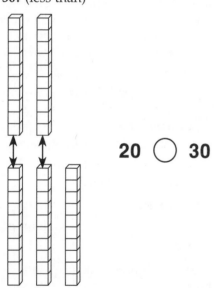

20 ◯ **30**

Ask children which symbol you should insert between the 20 and 30 to compare them. If necessary, review each symbol.

Compare two more sets of numbers, one to review the symbol for *is greater than*, and another to review *is equal to*. Then compare 37 and 23.

Set up the models as with the multiples of ten, using one-to-one correspondence to compare.

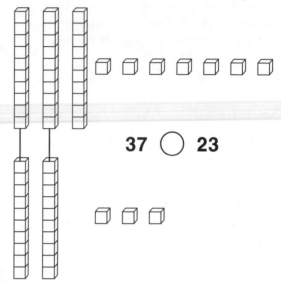

37 ◯ **23**

Draw lines to match tens, having children tell you which tens match and which number has more tens. Help children recognize that it is not necessary to compare the ones, since the value of the tens is greater than the value of the ones. Insert the *is greater than* symbol to show that 37 is greater than 23. Repeat the activity for 17 and 25, and 32 and 32.

In another session, have children use place value tables, rather than base-ten models, to compare numbers.

24 ◯ **31**

tens	ones
2	4
3	1

Link the table to the matching activity, noting that to compare, always begin with the tens.

© Harcourt

© Harcourt

Grade 2
Skill 64

Compare Numbers: >, <, and =

> means greater than.
< means less than.

Use <, >, or = to compare 83 and 71.

Step 1
Compare 83 and 71.
How many tens and ones in each number?

8 tens ___3___ ones
7 tens ___1___ ones

Step 2
Compare the tens.

8 tens is greater than 7 tens.

83 is __greater than__ 71.

Step 3
Write >, <, or =.

83 (>) 71

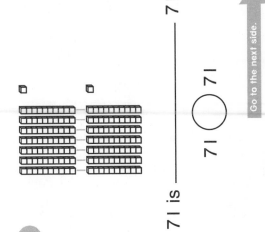

▶ Try These

Write greater than, less than, or equal to. Then write >, <, or =.

1

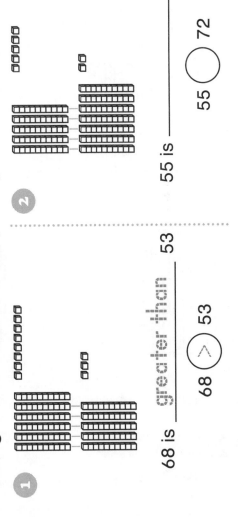

68 is __greater than__ 53

68 (>) 53

2

55 is _____ 72

55 ( ) 72

3

71 is _____ 71

71 ( ) 71

Go to the next side.

Practice on Your Own

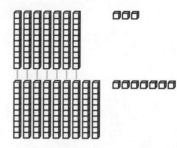

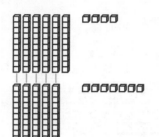

64 is ____greater than____ 57   73 is ____less than____ 97

64 (>) 57   73 (<) 97

Write greater than or less than.

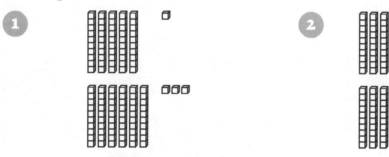

① 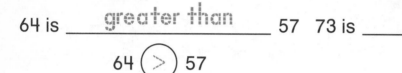   ②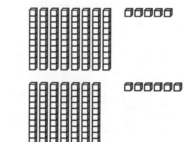

51 is ____less than____ 63   85 is _____ 76

Write >, <, or =.

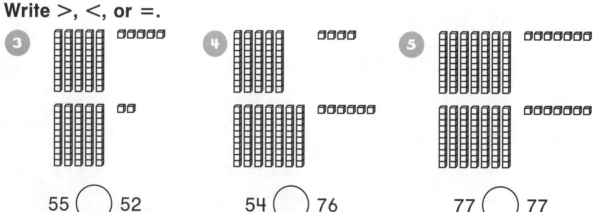

③ 55 ◯ 52   ④ 54 ◯ 76   ⑤ 77 ◯ 77

▶ **Quiz**

Write >, <, or =.

⑥ 75 ◯ 75   ⑦ 64 ◯ 54   ⑧ 89 ◯ 92

© Harcourt

Data Analysis
and Probability

Using Skill 65

OBJECTIVE Represent and interpret data in a tally table

MATERIALS base-ten blocks (1 ten, 1 one) for teacher demonstration

15 Minutes

Example

Focus children's attention on the picture. Review the meaning of survey. Ask: **What question is asked?** (Which pet people like better) **Which pets do you see?** (cats and dogs)

Explain that data from a survey can be shown in a tally table. Review the word data if necessary. Tell children that a tally table helps organize and understand data. Point out a tally mark.

Focus on Step 1. Ask: **What are you asked to do in this step?** (Possible answer: Make a table to show the number of people who like dogs and the number of people who like cats.) Discuss the title and labels of the table. Point out that each pet is shown in a separate row.

Tell children that each tally mark (**I**) stands for one dog or one cat. Draw a tally mark on the board as you explain. Draw the five tally marks on the board and ask: **How many pets do these tally marks stand for?** (5) Count the five tally marks with the children.

Direct the children to Step 2. Ask: **How many tally marks did you write for dogs?** (5) **for cats?** (3) Ask the children to fill out the *total* column for each pet.

Go to Step 3. Have a child read the questions aloud. Guide children to use the table to answer the questions. Help them locate the correct boxes.

TRY THESE In Exercises 1–4, children practice making a table and using the information it provides.

- **Exercise 1** Make a tally table.

- **Exercises 2–4** Use the tally table to answer questions.

PRACTICE ON YOUR OWN Review the example at the top of the page. Exercises 1–4 give practice in filling out tally charts as well as in reading the table to answer questions.

QUIZ Determine if children can fill out a tally table and read it. Success is indicated by 2 out of 3 correct responses.

Children who successfully complete **Practice on Your Own** and **Quiz** are ready to move to the next skill.

COMMON ERRORS

- Children may forget to count the diagonal tally mark.

- Children may record tally marks in the wrong column.

Have the children who made more than 1 error in the **Practice on Your Own,** or who were not successful in the **Quiz** section, work through the example with you. Have the child think aloud as he or she works to determine if he or she understands how to read and write tally marks. Children may also benefit from the **Alternative Teaching Strategy** on the next page.

Alternative Teaching Strategy

15 Minutes

OBJECTIVE Understand the use of a tally table and be able to read the results

MATERIALS blank tally table for each child

Give children the choice between two activities in which they may participate later in the day or the week. For example, the choice may be between reading a story or drawing a picture.

Tell children that the class is going to vote for the activity and make and read a tally table in order to see who won.

Ask the children to write their choice on a piece of paper. (You may want to color-code each choice to make it easier to recognize them.)

After they have all written their choice, collect the papers. Draw a table on the board.

		Total

Ask: **What heading are you going to give to the table?** (Possible answer: What We Want to Do) **to each row?** (Possible answers: Draw a Picture; Read a Story) Have the children copy the headings on their tally tables.

To guide the children, ask: **What information do you want to know?** (Possible answer: Which choice is going to have more votes?)

Then start unfolding the ballots, reading the results as you go. Sort the papers according to each choice.

Have the children draw a tally mark in the appropriate row for each result. Remind children that each ❘ means 1 and each ╫╫ means 5.

Record the marks on the board, after the children have had time to think about where to record the results on their papers.

Once all the results have been recorded, ask the children to count their tally marks and record the count in the total column.

To verify that everyone has counted correctly, have a volunteer count the ballots that have been sorted according to choice.

Check the papers of the children who obtained different results to see whether they have miscounted or misplaced the tally marks in the table.

Then count the votes according to the table on the board.

Ask: **How many people voted for Activity 1? How many voted for Activity 2? Which activity did most people choose?**

Grade 2

Skill 65

Read Tally Tables

Think: Each tally mark l stands for one. Each ||||| stands for 5.

Step 1
Fill in the tally table. Make one tally mark for each dog. Make one tally mark for each cat.

Favorite Pet		Total
Dogs	|||||	5
Cats	|||	3

Step 2
Count the tally marks.

Step 3
Use the tally table to answer these questions.

How many children chose dogs? __5__

How many children chose cats? __3__

Which pet do you like better?

Try These

1) Fill in the tally table. Use the table to answer the questions.

Which shape do you like better?

Favorite Shape		Total
Stars	||||	4

2) How many children chose stars? __4__

3) How many children chose circles? _____

4) Which shape did most children choose? _____

Go to the next side.

Practice on Your Own

Skill 65

Fill in the tally table. Use the table to answer the questions.

Which sport do you like better?
⚾ ⚾ ⚾ ⚽ ⚽ ⚽ ⚽ ⚽ ⚽

Favorite Sports		Total
Baseball	III	3
Soccer	⊞ I	6

How many children chose baseball? _____3_____

Which sport did most children choose? ___soccer___

---

1 Fill in the tally table. Use the table to answer the questions.

Which fruit do you like better?
🍎 🍎 🍎 🍎 🍊 🍊 🍊 🍊 🍊 🍊

Favorite Fruits		Total

2 How many children chose apples? _____

3 How many children chose oranges? _____

4 Did more children choose apples or oranges? _____

▶ Quiz

5 Fill in the tally table. Use the table to answer the questions.

Which lunch do you like better?

Favorite Lunches		Total

6 How many children chose pizza? _____

7 What lunch did most children choose? _____

© Harcourt

Skill **66**

Make Bar Graphs

Using Skill 66

OBJECTIVE Use tally marks to make a bar graph

MATERIALS crayons or markers

Before starting, review the concept of tally marks and how to count them.

Then have the children look at Step 1 and ask: **How many tally marks are there for apples?** (3) **for raisins?** (5) Then ask: **So, how many children chose apples as their favorite snack?** (3) **How many chose raisins?** (5) Have the children trace the answers in the *total* column.

Continue with Step 2. Ask: **How would you show this information on the bar graph?** (Possible answer: Color the bar graph to match the tally marks.)

Review the parts of bar graphs with children. Help children understand that for this graph each box represents 1 child who chose that kind of snack. Guide them to find 1, 2, 3 and so forth on the scale.

Ask: **How many children chose raisins?** (5) Then ask: **So, how many boxes are you going to color next to raisins?** (5) Ask the children to color each shaded box as they count each one aloud. Tell them that they are coloring a bar in the bar graph.

Point out the scale and ask: **Which number should your bar reach on the scale?** (5) Do the same for apples.

Explain that a bar graph makes the data easy to compare. Children can look at the lengths of the bars to tell how many children chose each kind of snack. Emphasize that bar graphs and tally tables can show the same information in different ways.

TRY THESE Exercises 1–2 give children practice in counting tally marks and making a bar graph.

- **Exercise 1**   Count the tally marks.
- **Exercise 2**   Make a bar graph.
- **Exercises 3–4**   Interpret the bar graph.

PRACTICE ON YOUR OWN Review the examples at the top of the page. Exercises 1–4 give practice in counting tally marks, coloring a bar graph to match the tally marks, and answering questions to interpret the graph.

QUIZ Determine if children can count tally marks, color the bar graph to match the tally marks, and interpret the bar graph. Success is indicated by 3 out of 4 correct responses.

Children who successfully complete **Practice on Your Own** and **Quiz** are ready to move to the next skill.

COMMON ERRORS

- Children may count the tally marks incorrectly.
- Children may read the scale incorrectly.

Have the children who made more than 1 error in the **Practice on Your Own,** or who were not successful in the **Quiz** section, explain the example aloud to determine if they understand how to make a bar graph. Children may also benefit from the **Alternative Teaching Strategy** on the next page.

Alternative Teaching Strategy

OBJECTIVE Make a 3-dimensional bar graph and use it to compare data

MATERIALS 1-inch grid paper, crayons, 3 colors of connecting cubes for each child

Before you begin, draw a tally table that shows data about ways children travel to school. Use data from a real or fictitious class.

Tell children they will use the tally table to make a bar graph.

Ways Children Travel to School	Total
Walk IIII	4
Ride Car ‖‖‖‖ ‖‖‖‖ I	11
Ride Bicycle ‖‖‖‖ II	7

Demonstrate how to make a 3-dimensional bar graph using grid paper and connecting cubes. Give each child 1-inch grid paper and red, blue, and yellow connecting cubes. Show them how to draw a stick figure (to stand for walkers), a simple car, and a bicycle as labels for the bottom of the graph. Help children write the scale on the left side of the grid paper.

Help children count the tally marks for *walkers*. Guide them to count and connect blue cubes to show the number of walkers and then place the cubes appropriately on the grid to make one bar of the graph.

Remind children to make sure the number of cubes in the graph matches the number of tally marks. Repeat the process using yellow connecting cubes for *car riders,* and red connecting cubes for *bicycle riders*.

You may wish to have children color squares on the grid to match the connecting cubes.

Then, ask questions that can be answered by comparing data on the bar graph. For example:

- Do more children walk to school or ride the bus to school?
- How do most children travel to school?

Discuss the answers and elicit other questions that can be answered using data in the graph.

© Harcourt

Make Bar Graphs

What is your favorite snack?

Step 1
Write how many tally marks.

Our Favorite Snacks	Total
Raisins	++++	5
Apples	|||	3

Step 2
Color the bar graph to match the tally marks.

How many people chose raisins? 5
So, color 5 boxes next to raisins.

Our Favorite Snacks

Snacks						
Raisins						
Apples						

0   1   2   3   4   5
Number of Children

Color the bar graph to match the tally marks.

② **Favorite Colors**

Colors							
Blue							
Yellow							
Purple							

0   1   2   3   4   5   6   7
Number of Children

Go to the next side.

Try These
Write how many tally marks.

Favorite Colors	Total
Blue	++++		6
Yellow	||||	
Purple	||	

Use the graph to answer the questions.

③ How many chose yellow? _____

④ Which color did most children choose? _____

Practice on Your Own

Skill 66

Make a bar graph by coloring one box for each tally mark.

Favorite Sports		Total
Soccer	IIII	4
Basketball	++++ II	7
Baseball	++++	5

Favorite Sports

Soccer
Basketball
Baseball

0 1 2 3 4 5 6 7 8
Number of Votes

Use the graph to answer questions.

How many children chose soccer? ___4___

How many more children chose basketball than soccer? ___3___

Make a bar graph by coloring one box for each tally mark.

1

Favorite Drinks		Total
Water	II	2
Milk	IIII	
Juice	++++ I	

2

Favorite Drinks

Water
Milk
Juice

0 1 2 3 4 5 6
Number of Votes

Use the graph to answer questions.

3 Which drink did the most children choose? _____

4 How many children chose milk? _____

▶ Quiz

Make a bar graph by coloring one box for each tally mark.

5

Favorite Breakfast		Total
Cereal	++++ I	
Eggs	IIII	
Waffles	++++ III	

6

Favorite Breakfast

Cereal
Eggs
Waffles

0 1 2 3 4 5 6 7 8
Number of Votes

Use the graph to answer questions.

7 How many children chose waffles? _____

8 Which did the fewest children choose? _____

© Harcourt

Using Skill 67

OBJECTIVE Use data from a bar graph

20 Minutes

Example

Focus attention on the bar graph.

Say: **A bar graph makes it easy to see and compare numbers. Let's review the parts of this bar graph.**

Ask: **What is the title?** (Number of Games Won)
Say: **The title tells what kind of data is on the graph. Now, read the label at the left.**
Ask: **How many teams are there?** (5) **What are the names of the teams?** (Lions, Chargers, Jays, Sharks, Rockets)
Ask: **How does the graph show each team?** (with a bar)

Say: **Read the label and the numbers at the bottom.**
Ask: **What do the numbers stand for?** (the number of games won)
How does the graph show each game that a team won? (with a shaded box on the bar)

Review how to read a graph by presenting questions such as these: **How many games did the Jays win? Which team won 8 games?**
Guide children to use the graph to answer the questions.

TRY THESE In Exercises 1–3 children practice using data from a bar graph to solve problems.

- **Exercise 1**   Find how many games a team won.

- **Exercise 2**   Find which team won as many games as another.

- **Exercise 3**   Find which team won the most games.

PRACTICE ON YOUR OWN Review the bar graph at the top of the page and how to read it. Explain that the bars on a graph can be vertical or horizontal. Exercises 1–4 provide practice using data on a bar graph to solve problems.

QUIZ Determine if children can use data on a bar graph to solve problems. Success is indicated by 2 out of 3 correct responses.

Children who successfully complete **Practice on Your Own** and **Quiz** are ready to move to the next skill.

COMMON ERRORS

- Children may incorrectly identify the bar or number.

- Children may transfer from one bar to another while trying to determine the total number.

Children who made more than 1 error in the **Practice On Your Own**, or who were not successful in the **Quiz** section, may benefit from the **Alternative Teaching Strategy** on the next page.

Alternative Teaching Strategy

OBJECTIVE Make a bar graph and use the data to solve problems

MATERIALS chart paper, marker, connecting cubes

Distribute a connecting cube to each child. Then invite children to suggest activities that are fun to do, such as ice skating, playing soccer, skateboarding, biking, playing computer games, swimming, and camping. Choose four or five of the activities and use them to create a bar graph entitled *Favorite Activities*. Draw the graph grid on a large sheet of chart paper and then place it on an easily accessible tabletop.

Favorite Activities

Activities											
Skateboarding											
Ice Skating											
Soccer											
Swimming											
Camping											

0 1 2 3 4 5 6 7 8 9 10
Number of Children

Review the parts of the graph. Have children identify the title at the top and the labels at the left and bottom.

Say: **Let's complete the bar graph and then use the data to solve some problems. First, decide which activity is your favorite. Next, find your favorite activity on the graph and place your cube in that row.**
Offer help as necessary.

When the graph is complete, raise questions such as these:
How many children chose skateboarding as their favorite activity?
Which activity did more/fewer children choose as their favorite activity?

Ask: **How can you find how many children chose skateboarding as their favorite activity using the bar graph?** (Possible answer: Find skateboarding on the graph and count the cubes.)

Have children use the graph to solve the problem. Follow a similar procedure to have them solve the second problem.

Ask: **How can you find which activity, let's say, 5 children chose as their favorite?** (Possible answer: Find the number 5 on the graph and then look to see which bar has 5 cubes in it.)

Once you are sure children can use the data on the bar graph, invite them to write problems of their own. You may wish to suggest the following to help them get started:

- How many more children chose playing soccer than swimming?
- Which activity did the fewest number of children choose?
- How many children chose skateboarding and swimming altogether?

Have children take turns reading and solving the problems using the data on the graph they created.

Grade 2
Skill
67

Use Data From a Bar Graph

Did the Lions win more games than all the other teams?

Ben made a **bar graph** to compare the number of games.
He shaded a box for each game a team won.
Each shaded bar stands for the total number of games a team won.

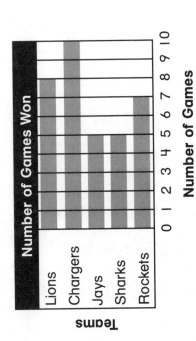

Number of Games Won

Teams: Lions, Chargers, Jays, Sharks, Rockets

0 1 2 3 4 5 6 7 8 9 10

Number of Games

The Lions did not win more games than all the other teams.

Try These

Use the bar graph to answer the questions.

1 How many games did the Lions win? ___8 games___

2 Which team won the same number of games as the Jays? _____

3 Which team won the most games? _____

Go to the next side.

Practice on Your Own

Skill 67

Ben thinks he watched fewer hours of TV than his friends did last week.

He made a **bar graph** to compare the number of hours. Ben shaded a box for each hour of TV watched.

Each bar stands for the number of hours a child watched TV.

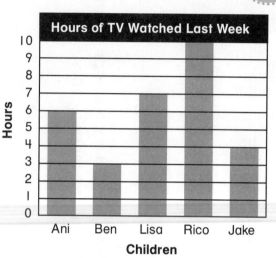

Use the bar graph to answer the questions.

1. Which children watched fewer than 6 hours of TV?

   Ben and Jake

2. Who watched TV 1 hour more than Ben did?

   _____

3. Which child watched 10 hours of TV last week?

   _____

4. How many hours of TV did the children watch in all?

   _____

▶ Quiz

Use the bar graph to answer the questions.

5. How many hours of TV did Ben watch? _____

6. How many more hours of TV did Lisa watch than Jake? _____

7. Which children watched more than 5 hours of TV last week? _____

Using Skill 68

OBJECTIVE Read and interpret data on graphs

Example

Focus attention on the graph in the example.

Say: **You know that a graph shows data, or information. For this graph, children were asked how many hours of TV they watched yesterday. Each number shows a choice from 0 hours to 4 hours.**

Ask: **Which number stands for the least number of hours?** (0) **Which number stands for the greatest number of hours?** (4)

Say: **A graph makes it easy to compare the data. On this graph, each face stands for one child. Put your finger on 0. Now count the number of faces in the column above 0.**
Ask: **How many children watched 0 hours of TV yesterday?** (3)

Say: **Now put your finger on 4.**
Ask: **How many children watched 4 hours of TV yesterday?** (1)

Say: **By comparing the heights of the columns on this graph, you can tell how many hours of TV most children watched yesterday. Point to the tallest column. Then find the number at the bottom of the column.**

Ask: **How many hours of TV did most children watch yesterday?** (1 hour) **How many children watched TV for 1 hour?** (5 children)

TRY THESE In exercises 1–4 children practice reading a graph and interpreting data.

- **Exercises 1–4** Use the graph to answer questions.

PRACTICE ON YOUR OWN Review the example at the top of the page. Encourage children to explain what the graph shows, what the numbers and faces mean, and how to read the graph. Exercises 1–4 provide practice in using a graph to answer questions.

QUIZ Determine if children can use a graph to interpret data. Success is indicated by 3 out of 4 correct responses.

Children who successfully complete **Practice on Your Own** and **Quiz** are ready to move to the next skill.

COMMON ERRORS

- Children may read the graph incorrectly.

- Children may confuse the terms *least* and *greatest*.

Have children who made more than 1 error in the **Practice On Your Own**, or who were not successful in the **Quiz** section, explain the example aloud to determine if they understand how to read a graph and the meaning of the terms *least* and *greatest*. These children may also benefit from the **Alternative Teaching Strategy** on the next page.

© Harcourt

Alternative Teaching Strategy

15 Minutes

OBJECTIVE Make a graph and use it to interpret data

MATERIALS connecting cubes, chart paper

Make a 5-column graph grid on a large sheet of chart paper. Place it on a table along with a container of connecting cubes.

Say: **We will make a tabletop graph to show how many pets each of you have.**
Write *Number of Pets* across the bottom of the graph.

Ask: **What is the least number of pets you can have?** (0) Write 0 at the bottom of the left column.

Ask: **What number should we show next?** (1) **after that?** (2) **then?** (3) **last?** (4) Write the numbers on the graph as children suggest them.

Ask: **What is the greatest number of pets we show on our graph?** (4)

Say: **We will use 4 to stand for 4 or more pets. Now, let's complete the graph. Take a connecting cube and put it in the column that tells how many pets you have.**

Prompt children as needed.
If you don't have a pet, where will you put your cube? (in the 0 column) **If you have 2 cats and a dog, where will you put your cube? Why?**
(2 + 1 = 3) **If you have 5 pets, where will you put your cube?** (in the last column)

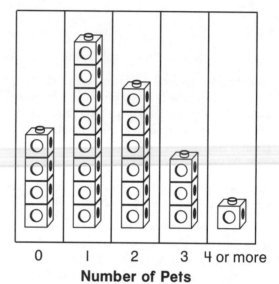

Number of Pets

Then ask questions that children can answer using the graph.
Ask: **How many pets do most of you have? How many pets do the fewest of you have? How many of you have 2 pets? Do more of you have 2 pets than 3 pets?**
(Answers will vary according to data.)

Discuss the answers and elicit other questions that can be answered using data on the graph.

© Harcourt

Grade 2

Skill 68

Interpret Data

Jake's class made a graph to show the number of hours of TV they watched yesterday.

Think: A bar graph uses bars to stand for data. This makes data easy to compare.

Most children watched 1 hour of TV

greatest number of hours

least number of hours

⊙ ⊙ ⊙ ⊙ ⊙
⊙ ⊙ ⊙ ⊙
⊙ ⊙ ⊙ ⊙
⊙ ⊙ ⊙ ⊙
0   1   2   3   4

Number of hours of TV watched

▲ **Try These**

Use the graph to answer the questions.

1 How many books did most children read last week? _____ 3

2 What is the least number of books children read? _____

3 What is the greatest number of books children read? _____

4 What is the difference between the greatest number and the least number of books? ◯ — ◯ — ◯

⊙
⊙ ⊙
⊙ ⊙
⊙ ⊙ ⊙
⊙ ⊙ ⊙ ⊙
0   1   2   3   4

Number of books read last week

Go to the next side.

Intervention • Skills IN329

Practice on Your Own

Skill 68

Ann's class made a graph to show the number of hours they spent doing homework yesterday.

Most children spent 3 hours doing homework.

least number of hours

greatest number of hours

:) :) :) :) :) :) :) :) :) :) :) :) :) :) :) :) :) :) :)
0 1 2 3 4
Number of hours spent doing homework

Use the graph to answer the questions.

:) :) :) :) :) :) :) :) :) :) :) :) :) :) :) :)
0 1 2 3 4
Number of glasses of water

1. How many glasses of water did most children drink? ___3___

2. What is the least number of glasses of water children drank? _____

3. What is the greatest number of glasses of water children drank? _____

4. What is the difference between the greatest number and the least number of glasses of water drank ? __ ◯ __ ◯ __

▶ Quiz

Use the graph to answer the questions.

:) :) :) :) :) :) :) :) :) :) :) :) :) :)
0 1 2 3 4
Number of pets

5. How many pets do most children have? _____

6. What is the least number of pets children have? _____

7. What is the greatest number of pets children have? _____

8. What is the difference between the greatest number and the least number of pets? __ ◯ __ ◯ __

Skill 69

Grade 2

Using Skill 69

OBJECTIVE Explore the probability of selecting an object from a given group of objects

MATERIALS red construction paper squares, paper bag

Display a paper bag. Invite children to observe as you fill it with red paper squares.

Ask: **If you pull a square from the paper bag, what color will it be?** (red) **Are you certain?** (yes) **Why?** (All the squares in the bag are red.) **Is it possible to pull a blue square from the bag?** (no) **Why is it impossible?** (There are no blue squares in the bag.)

Write *certain* and *impossible* on the board and review their meanings.

Ask: **If something is certain to happen, does it mean that it will definitely happen or that it may happen?** (It will definitely happen.) **What is another word for certain?** (sure) **If something is impossible, does it mean that it can happen or that it cannot happen?** (It cannot happen.)

Example

Focus attention on the example.
Ask: **How many bags do you see?** (3) **Are all the marbles in bag A the same color?** (yes) **What color are they?** (black) **What color are the marbles in bag B?** (white) **What color are the marbles in bag C?** (gray)

Ask: **What color marble will Anna pull from bag B?** (white) **Is it certain to be white?** (yes) **Why is it impossible to pull a black marble or a gray marble?** (All the marbles in the bag are white.)

TRY THESE In exercises 1–3 children explore probability.

* **Exercises 1–3** Determine if it is certain or impossible to pull a marble of a particular color from a given bag of marbles.

PRACTICE ON YOUR OWN Review the example at the top of the page. Exercises 1–3 provide practice in determining if it is certain or impossible to pull a marble of a particular color from a given bag of marbles.

QUIZ Determine if children can distinguish between events that are certain or impossible. Success is indicated by 2 out of 2 correct responses.

Children who successfully complete **Practice on Your Own** and **Quiz** are ready to move to the next skill.

COMMON ERRORS

* Children may not understand that all the marbles in one bag are the same color.

* Children may confuse the terms *certain* and *impossible*.

Children who made more than 1 error in the **Practice on Your Own**, or who were not successful in the **Quiz** section, may benefit from the **Alternative Teaching Strategy** on the next page.

Alternative Teaching Strategy

15 Minutes

OBJECTIVE Distinguish between what is certain and what is impossible

MATERIALS red, blue, and yellow connecting cubes; paper bag; 3 clear plastic bowls labeled A, B, and C

Place a bag of red, blue, and yellow cubes on a table. Invite a child to come to the table and take a cube from the bag without revealing it to the class.

Ask: **Do you think (name of child) picked a red cube, a yellow cube, or a blue cube?** (Answers may vary.) **Is it certain that the cube is red?** (no) **Is it certain that the cube is blue?** (no) **Is it certain that the cube is yellow?** (no) **Why not?** (There are cubes of three different colors in the bag. It could be any one of the three colors.)

Have the child then reveal the color of the cube. You may wish to repeat several times to demonstrate that it is not certain which color cube a child will pick when all the cubes are mixed together.

Next, empty the bag of cubes onto the table. Display three bowls, labeled A, B, and C. Have several children sort the cubes, putting red cubes in bowl A, blue cubes in bowl B, and yellow cubes in bowl C. Ask children to close their eyes as a volunteer comes to the table and removes a cube from bowl C and conceals it. Then have children open their eyes.

Say: **(Name of child) took a cube from bowl C.**
Ask: **Do you think (name of child) picked a red cube, a yellow cube, or a blue cube?** (a yellow cube) **Is it certain that the cube is yellow?** (yes) **Is it possible that (name of child) picked a blue cube?** (no) **Why not?** (All the cubes in bowl C are yellow; there are no blue cubes in bowl C.)

Have the child reveal the cube to confirm that it is yellow. Repeat several times with other children. Help children conclude that when all the cubes in a bowl are the same color, it is certain that a cube of that color will be pulled each time and that pulling a different-color cube would be impossible.

Certain or Impossible

Anna is going to pull a marble from bag B.

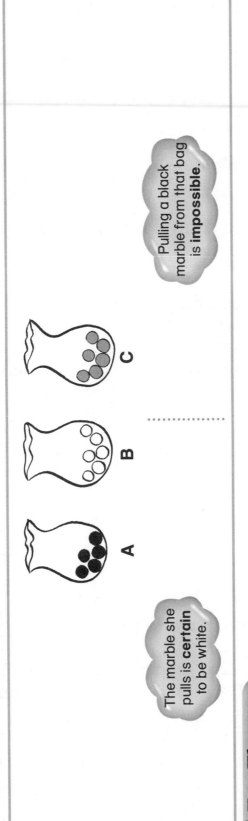

The marble she pulls is **certain** to be white.

Pulling a black marble from that bag is **impossible**.

A   B   C

▲ **Try These**

X to tell if it is certain or impossible to pull that marble from the bag.

	Certain	Impossible
1 Pull a ⬤	X	
2 Pull a ◯		
3 Pull a ◯		

Go to the next side.

Practice on Your Own

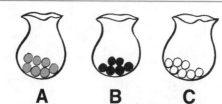

A   **B**   **C**

It is **certain** that a gray marble can be pulled from bag A.

It is **impossible** to pull a white marble from that bag.

X to tell if it is certain or impossible to pull that marble from the bag.

	Certain	Impossible
1 Pull a		X
2 Pull a		
3 Pull a		

▶ Quiz

X to tell if it is certain or impossible to pull that marble from the bag.

	Certain	Impossible
4 Pull a		
5 Pull a		

Exploring Tens

Use 📷 to make tens. Draw the tens. Count by tens. Write the number.

Step 1
Make 2 tens.

Think: 10 ones = 1 ten

Step 2

How many tens are there?

_2_ tens

Step 3
Count by tens.
Write the number.

Think: 2 groups of 10 make tens
2 tens = 20

_2_ tens = _20_
twenty

▶ Try These

Use 📷 to make tens. Count by tens. Write the number.

1. Make 3 tens.
   _3_ tens = _30_
   thirty

2. Make 4 tens.
   _4_ tens = _40_
   forty

Go to the next side. ↑

Practice on Your Own   Skill ①

Use 📷 to make tens. Draw the tens. Count by tens.
Write the number.
Make 5 tens.

_5_ tens = _50_
fifty

Use 📷 to make tens. Draw the tens. Count by tens.
Write the number. Check children's work.

1. Make 6 tens.
   _6_ tens = _60_
   sixty

2. Make 8 tens.
   _8_ tens = _80_
   eighty

3. Make 9 tens.
   _9_ tens = _90_
   ninety

▶ **Quiz**

Use 📷 to make tens. Draw the tens. Count by tens.
Write the number. Check children's work.

4. Make 7 tens.
   _7_ tens = _70_
   seventy

Exploring Tens and Ones to 100

Write how many tens and ones.

Write how many tens.

_2_ tens

Remember: ten ones = 10.

Write how many ones.

_4_ ones

2 tens _4_ ones =

Write the number.

2 tens 4 ones = _24_

▶ Try These

Write how many tens and ones. Write the number.

1. _2_ tens _3_ ones = _23_

2. _3_ tens _1_ ones = _31_

3. _4_ tens _4_ ones = _44_

Go to the next side. ↑

Practice on Your Own   Skill ②

Write how many tens and ones. Write the number.

_5_ tens _4_ ones = _54_

Write how many tens and ones. Write the number.

1. _2_ tens _5_ ones = _25_

2. _3_ tens _6_ ones = _36_

3. _5_ tens _1_ ones = _51_

Write the number.

4. _42_

5. _83_

6. _96_

▶ **Quiz**

Write the number.

7. _63_

8. _74_

9. _100_

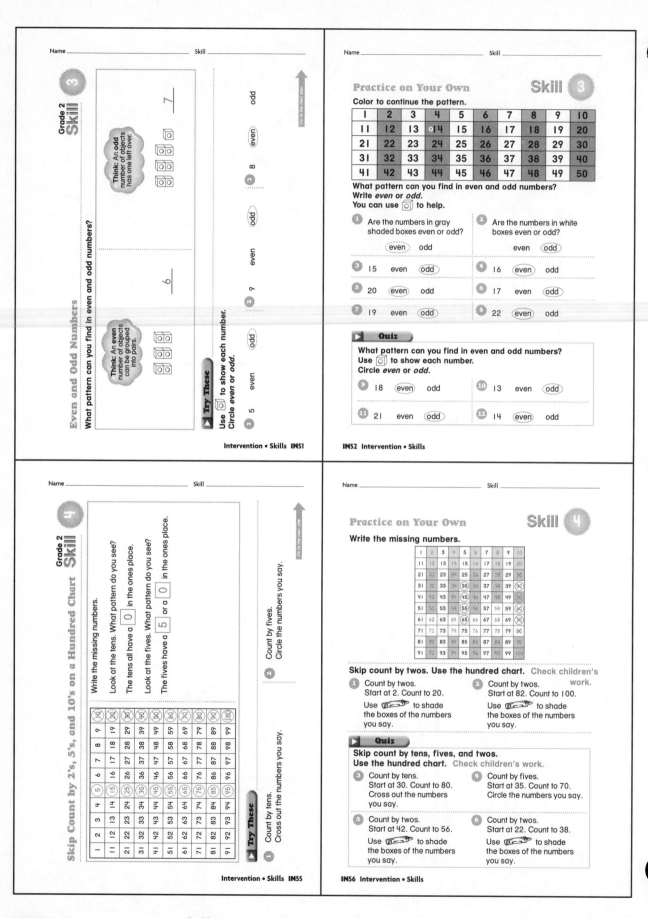

Grade 2

Skill 3

Even and Odd Numbers

What pattern can you find in even and odd numbers?

Think: An **even** number of objects can be grouped into pairs.

Think: An **odd** number of objects has one left over.

6   7

Try These

Use 🎲 to show each number.
Circle *even* or *odd*.

4   5   even   odd

2   9   even   odd

3   8   even   odd

Go to the next side.

Practice on Your Own

Skill 3

Color to continue the pattern.

1	2	3	4	5	6	7	8	9	10
11	12	13	14	15	16	17	18	19	20
21	22	23	24	25	26	27	28	29	30
31	32	33	34	35	36	37	38	39	40
41	42	43	44	45	46	47	48	49	50

What pattern can you find in even and odd numbers?
Write *even* or *odd*.
You can use 🎲 to help.

1. Are the numbers in gray shaded boxes even or odd?
   (even)   odd

2. Are the numbers in white boxes even or odd?
   even   (odd)

3. 15   even   (odd)
4. 16   (even)   odd
5. 20   (even)   odd
6. 17   even   (odd)
7. 19   even   (odd)
8. 22   (even)   odd

▶ **Quiz**

What pattern can you find in even and odd numbers?
Use 🎲 to show each number.
Circle *even* or *odd*.

9. 18   (even)   odd
10. 13   even   (odd)
11. 21   even   (odd)
12. 14   (even)   odd

Grade 2

Skill 4

Skip Count by 2's, 5's, and 10's on a Hundred Chart

Write the missing numbers. What pattern do you see?
Look at the tens. What pattern do you see?
The tens all have a 0 in the ones place.
Look at the fives. What pattern do you see?
The fives have a 5 or a 0 in the ones place.

1	2	3	4	5	6	7	8	9	10
11	12	13	14	15	16	17	18	19	20
21	22	23	24	25	26	27	28	29	30
31	32	33	34	35	36	37	38	39	40
41	42	43	44	45	46	47	48	49	50
51	52	53	54	55	56	57	58	59	60
61	62	63	64	65	66	67	68	69	70
71	72	73	74	75	76	77	78	79	80
81	82	83	84	85	86	87	88	89	90
91	92	93	94	95	96	97	98	99	100

Try These

1. Count by tens.
   Cross out the numbers you say.

2. Count by fives.
   Circle the numbers you say.

Go to the next side.

Practice on Your Own

Skill 4

Write the missing numbers.

1	2	3	4	5	6	7	8	9	10
11	12	13	14	15	16	17	18	19	20
21	22	23	24	25	26	27	28	29	30
31	32	33	35	36	37	38	39	40
41	42	43	44	45	46	47	48	49	50
51	52	53	54	55	56	57	58	59	60
61	62	63	64	65	66	67	68	69	70
71	72	73	74	75	76	77	78	79	80
81	82	83	84	85	86	87	88	89	90
91	92	93	94	95	96	97	98	99	100

Skip count by twos. Use the hundred chart. Check children's work.

1. Count by twos.
   Start at 2. Count to 20.
   Use 🖍 to shade the boxes of the numbers you say.

2. Count by twos.
   Start at 82. Count to 100.
   Use 🖍 to shade the boxes of the numbers you say.

▶ **Quiz**

Skip count by tens, fives, and twos.
Use the hundred chart. Check children's work.

3. Count by tens.
   Start at 30. Count to 80.
   Cross out the numbers you say.

4. Count by fives.
   Start at 35. Count to 70.
   Circle the numbers you say.

5. Count by twos.
   Start at 42. Count to 56.
   Use 🖍 to shade the boxes of the numbers you say.

6. Count by twos.
   Start at 22. Count to 38.
   Use 🖍 to shade the boxes of the numbers you say.

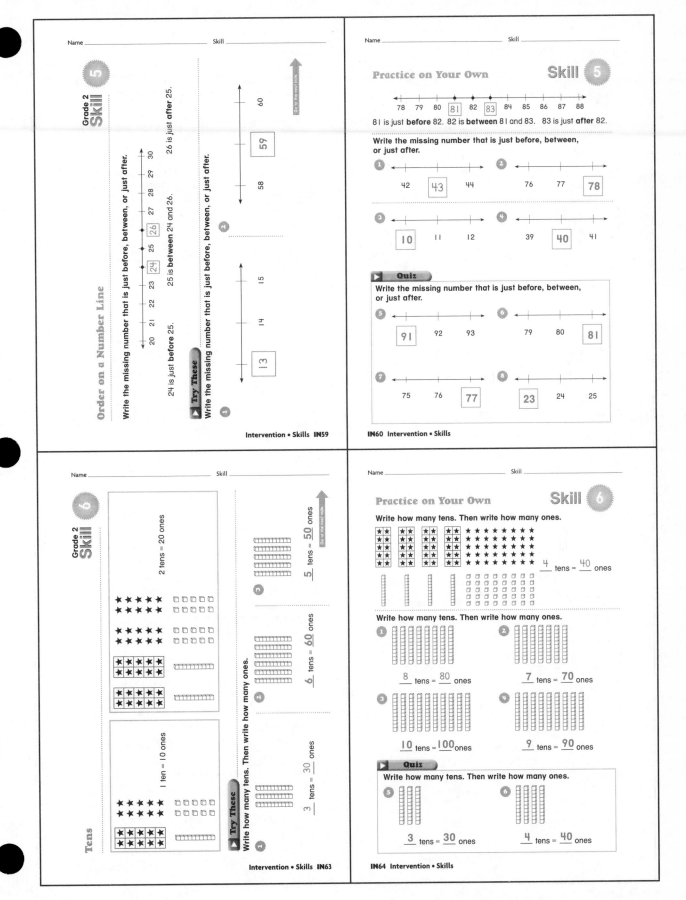

Top-left panel

Name _____ Skill _____

Grade 2
Skill 5

Order on a Number Line

Write the missing number that is just before, between, or just after.

20 21 22 23 24 25 26 27 28 29 30

24 is just **before** 25.
25 is **between** 24 and 26.
26 is just **after** 25.

Try These

Write the missing number that is just before, between, or just after.

1   13   14   15

2   58   59   60

Intervention • Skills **IN59**

Top-right panel

Name _____ Skill _____

Practice on Your Own   **Skill** 5

78 79 80 [81] 82 [83] 84 85 86 87 88

81 is just **before** 82.   82 is **between** 81 and 83.   83 is just **after** 82.

Write the missing number that is just before, between, or just after.

1   42   [43]   44

2   76   77   [78]

3   [10]   11   12

4   39   [40]   41

Quiz

Write the missing number that is just before, between, or just after.

5   [91]   92   93

6   79   80   [81]

7   75   76   [77]

8   [23]   24   25

IN60 Intervention • Skills

Bottom-left panel

Name _____ Skill _____

Grade 2
Skill 6

Tens

1 ten = 10 ones

2 tens = 20 ones

Try These

Write how many tens. Then write how many ones.

1   3 tens = 30 ones

2   6 tens = 60 ones

5 tens = 50 ones

Intervention • Skills **IN63**

Bottom-right panel

Name _____ Skill _____

Practice on Your Own   **Skill** 6

Write how many tens. Then write how many ones.

4 tens = 40 ones

Write how many tens. Then write how many ones.

1   8 tens = 80 ones

2   7 tens = 70 ones

3   10 tens = 100 ones

4   9 tens = 90 ones

Quiz

Write how many tens. Then write how many ones.

5   3 tens = 30 ones

6   4 tens = 40 ones

IN64 Intervention • Skills

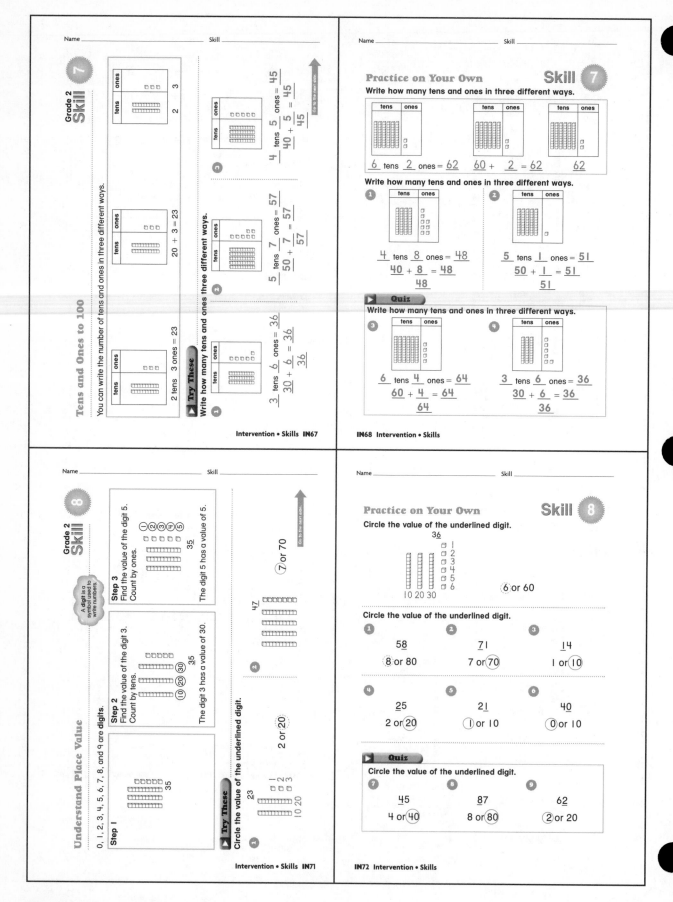

Skill 7 — Grade 2

Tens and Ones to 100

You can write the number of tens and ones in three different ways.

tens	ones

2 tens 3 ones = 23

20 + 3 = 23

45
4 tens 5 ones = 45
40 + 5 = 45
45

57
5 tens 7 ones = 57
50 + 7 = 57
57

Try These

Write how many tens and ones three different ways.

1. 36
3 tens 6 ones = 36
30 + 6 = 36
36

Practice on Your Own — Skill 7

Write how many tens and ones in three different ways.

tens	ones
6 tens 2 ones = 62   60 + 2 = 62   62

Write how many tens and ones in three different ways.

1. 4 tens 8 ones = 48
40 + 8 = 48
48

2. 5 tens 1 ones = 51
50 + 1 = 51
51

Quiz

Write how many tens and ones in three different ways.

3. 6 tens 4 ones = 64
60 + 4 = 64
64

4. 3 tens 6 ones = 36
30 + 6 = 36
36

Intervention • Skills **IN67**

IN68 Intervention • Skills

Skill 8 — Grade 2

Understand Place Value

0, 1, 2, 3, 4, 5, 6, 7, 8, and 9 are digits.

A digit is a symbol used to write numbers.

Step 1
35

Step 2
Find the value of the digit 3.
Count by tens.
10 20 30
35
The digit 3 has a value of 30.

Step 3
Find the value of the digit 5.
Count by ones.
1 2 3 4 5
35
The digit 5 has a value of 5.

Try These

Circle the value of the underlined digit.

1. 2̲3
1 2 3
10 20
2 or 20

2. 4̲7
7 or 70

Practice on Your Own — Skill 8

Circle the value of the underlined digit.

3̲6
1 2 3 4 5 6
10 20 30
6 or 60

Circle the value of the underlined digit.

1. 5̲8   8 or 80
2. 7̲1   7 or (70)
3. 1̲4   1 or (10)

4. 2̲5   2 or (20)
5. 2̲1   (1) or 10
6. 4̲0   (0) or 10

Quiz

Circle the value of the underlined digit.

7. 4̲5   4 or (40)
8. 8̲7   8 or (80)
9. 6̲2   (2) or 20

Intervention • Skills **IN71**

IN72 Intervention • Skills

© Harcourt

IN338 Intervention • Skills

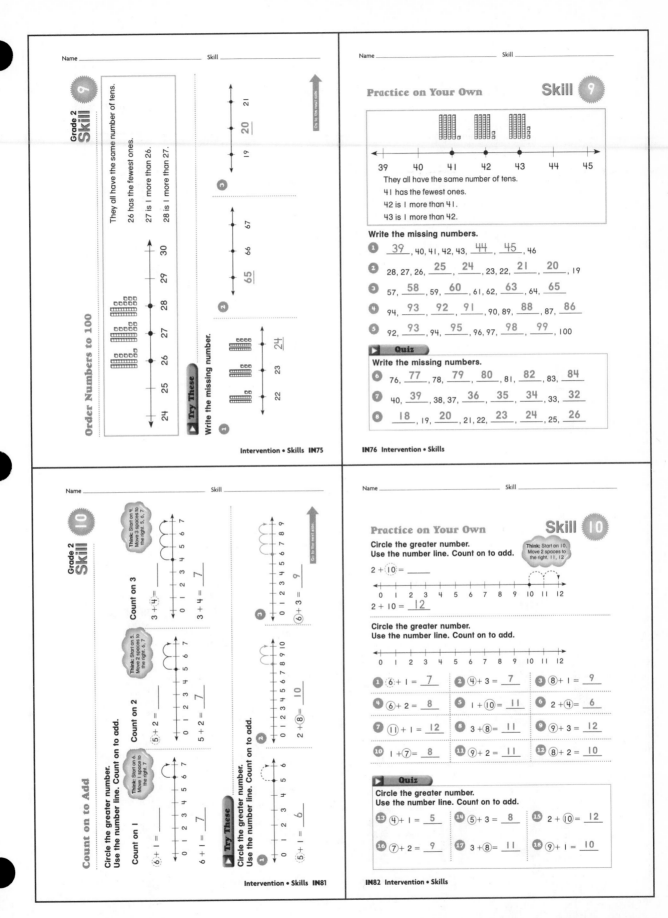

Name _____ **Skill** _____

Order Numbers to 100

They all have the same number of tens.

26 has the fewest ones.

27 is 1 more than 26.

28 is 1 more than 27.

24 25 26 27 28 29 30

Try These

Write the missing number.

1   22   23   24

2   65   66   67

3   19   20   21

Intervention • Skills **IN75**

Name _____ **Skill** _____

←—————————————————————→
39   40   41   42   43   44   45

They all have the same number of tens.

41 has the fewest ones.

42 is 1 more than 41.

43 is 1 more than 42.

Write the missing numbers.

1   _39_, 40, 41, 42, 43, _44_, _45_, 46

2   28, 27, 26, _25_, _24_, 23, 22, _21_, _20_, 19

3   57, _58_, 59, _60_, 61, 62, _63_, 64, _65_

4   94, _93_, _92_, _91_, 90, 89, _88_, 87, _86_

5   92, _93_, 94, _95_, 96, 97, _98_, _99_, 100

► Quiz

Write the missing numbers.

6   76, _77_, 78, _79_, _80_, 81, _82_, 83, _84_

7   40, _39_, 38, 37, _36_, _35_, _34_, 33, _32_

8   _18_, 19, _20_, 21, 22, _23_, _24_, 25, _26_

IN76 Intervention • Skills

Name _____ **Skill** _____

Count on to Add

Circle the greater number.
Use the number line. Count on to add.

Count on 1

6 + 1 =
0 1 2 3 4 5 6 7
6 + 1 = _7_

Count on 2

5 + 2 =
0 1 2 3 4 5 6 7
5 + 2 = _7_

Count on 3

3 + 4 =
0 1 2 3 4 5 6 7
3 + 4 = _7_

Think: Start on 6.
Move 1 space to
the right. 7

Think: Start on 5.
Move 2 spaces to
the right. 6, 7

Think: Start on 4.
Move 3 spaces to
the right. 5, 6, 7

Try These

Circle the greater number.
Use the number line. Count on to add.

1   5 + 1 =
0 1 2 3 4 5 6
5 + 1 = _6_

2   2 + 8 =
0 1 2 3 4 5 6 7 8 9 10
2 + 8 = _10_

3   6 + 3 =
0 1 2 3 4 5 6 7 8 9
6 + 3 = _9_

Intervention • Skills **IN81**

Name _____ **Skill** _____

Circle the greater number.
Use the number line. Count on to add.

2 + 10 =

Think: Start on 10.
Move 2 spaces to
the right. 11, 12

0 1 2 3 4 5 6 7 8 9 10 11 12

2 + 10 = _12_

Circle the greater number.
Use the number line. Count on to add.

0 1 2 3 4 5 6 7 8 9 10 11 12

1   6 + 1 = _7_   2   4 + 3 = _7_   3   8 + 1 = _9_

4   6 + 2 = _8_   5   1 + 10 = _11_   6   2 + 4 = _6_

7   11 + 1 = _12_   8   3 + 8 = _11_   9   9 + 3 = _12_

10   1 + 7 = _8_   11   9 + 2 = _11_   12   8 + 2 = _10_

► Quiz

Circle the greater number.
Use the number line. Count on to add.

13   4 + 1 = _5_   14   5 + 3 = _8_   15   2 + 10 = _12_

16   7 + 2 = _9_   17   3 + 8 = _11_   18   9 + 1 = _10_

IN82 Intervention • Skills

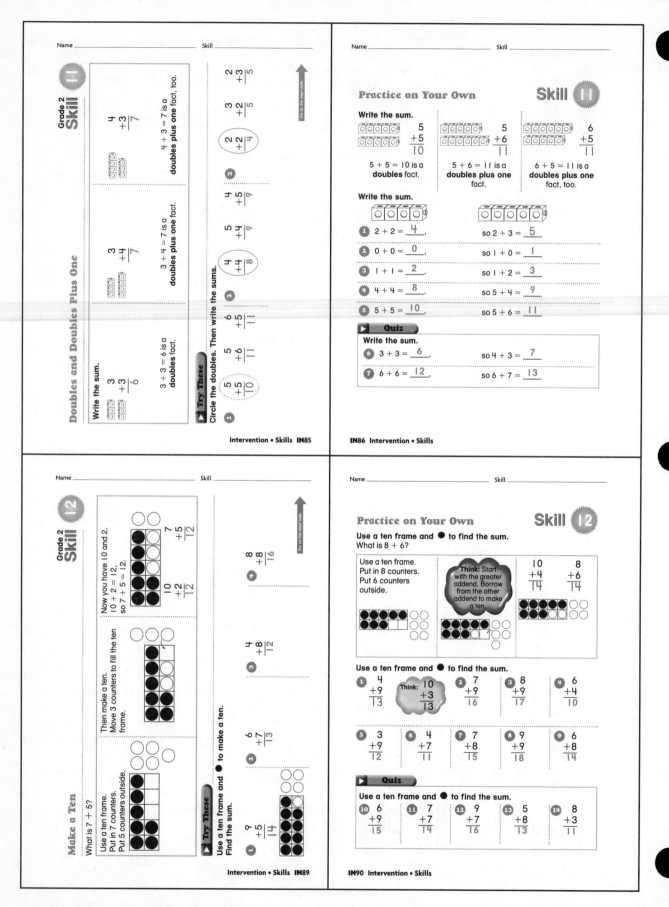

Grade 2 Skill 11

Doubles and Doubles Plus One

Write the sum.

$\begin{array}{r} 3 \\ +3 \\ \hline 6 \end{array}$ 3 + 3 = 6 is a **doubles** fact.

$\begin{array}{r} 3 \\ +4 \\ \hline 7 \end{array}$ 3 + 4 = 7 is a **doubles plus one** fact.

$\begin{array}{r} 4 \\ +3 \\ \hline 7 \end{array}$ 4 + 3 = 7 is a **doubles plus one** fact, too.

Try These
Circle the doubles. Then write the sums.

1. $\begin{array}{r} 5 \\ +5 \\ \hline 10 \end{array}$ (circled) $\begin{array}{r} 5 \\ +6 \\ \hline 11 \end{array}$

2. $\begin{array}{r} 4 \\ +4 \\ \hline 8 \end{array}$ (circled) $\begin{array}{r} 5 \\ +4 \\ \hline 9 \end{array}$

3. $\begin{array}{r} 2 \\ +2 \\ \hline 4 \end{array}$ (circled) $\begin{array}{r} 2 \\ +3 \\ \hline 5 \end{array}$ $\begin{array}{r} 3 \\ +2 \\ \hline 5 \end{array}$

Go to the next skill →

Intervention • Skills IN85

Practice on Your Own Skill 11

Write the sum.

$\begin{array}{r} 5 \\ +5 \\ \hline 10 \end{array}$ 5 + 5 = 10 is a **doubles** fact.

$\begin{array}{r} 5 \\ +6 \\ \hline 11 \end{array}$ 5 + 6 = 11 is a **doubles plus one** fact.

$\begin{array}{r} 6 \\ +5 \\ \hline 11 \end{array}$ 6 + 5 = 11 is a **doubles plus one** fact, too.

Write the sum.

1. 2 + 2 = 4 ,   so 2 + 3 = 5
2. 0 + 0 = 0 ,   so 1 + 0 = 1
3. 1 + 1 = 2 ,   so 1 + 2 = 3
4. 4 + 4 = 8 ,   so 5 + 4 = 9
5. 5 + 5 = 10 ,   so 5 + 6 = 11

Quiz
Write the sum.

6. 3 + 3 = 6 ,   so 4 + 3 = 7
7. 6 + 6 = 12 ,   so 6 + 7 = 13

IN86 Intervention • Skills

Grade 2 Skill 12

Make a Ten

What is 7 + 5?

Use a ten frame.
Put in 7 counters.
Put 5 counters outside.

Then make a ten.
Move 3 counters to fill the ten frame.

Now you have 10 and 2.
10 + 2 = 12,
so 7 + 5 = 12.

$\begin{array}{r} 7 \\ +5 \\ \hline 12 \end{array}$ $\begin{array}{r} 10 \\ +2 \\ \hline 12 \end{array}$

Try These
Use a ten frame and ● to make a ten. Find the sum.

1. $\begin{array}{r} 9 \\ +5 \\ \hline 14 \end{array}$
2. $\begin{array}{r} 6 \\ +7 \\ \hline 13 \end{array}$
3. $\begin{array}{r} 4 \\ +8 \\ \hline 12 \end{array}$
4. $\begin{array}{r} 8 \\ +8 \\ \hline 16 \end{array}$

Go to the next skill →

Intervention • Skills IN89

Practice on Your Own Skill 12

Use a ten frame and ● to find the sum.
What is 8 + 6?

Use a ten frame.
Put in 8 counters.
Put 6 counters outside.

Think: Start with the greater addend. Borrow from the other addend to make a ten.

$\begin{array}{r} 10 \\ +4 \\ \hline 14 \end{array}$ $\begin{array}{r} 8 \\ +6 \\ \hline 14 \end{array}$

Use a ten frame and ● to find the sum.

1. $\begin{array}{r} 4 \\ +9 \\ \hline 13 \end{array}$ Think: $\begin{array}{r} 10 \\ +3 \\ \hline 13 \end{array}$
2. $\begin{array}{r} 7 \\ +9 \\ \hline 16 \end{array}$
3. $\begin{array}{r} 8 \\ +9 \\ \hline 17 \end{array}$
4. $\begin{array}{r} 6 \\ +4 \\ \hline 10 \end{array}$

5. $\begin{array}{r} 3 \\ +9 \\ \hline 12 \end{array}$
6. $\begin{array}{r} 4 \\ +7 \\ \hline 11 \end{array}$
7. $\begin{array}{r} 7 \\ +8 \\ \hline 15 \end{array}$
8. $\begin{array}{r} 9 \\ +9 \\ \hline 18 \end{array}$
9. $\begin{array}{r} 6 \\ +8 \\ \hline 14 \end{array}$

Quiz
Use a ten frame and ● to find the sum.

10. $\begin{array}{r} 6 \\ +9 \\ \hline 15 \end{array}$
11. $\begin{array}{r} 7 \\ +7 \\ \hline 14 \end{array}$
12. $\begin{array}{r} 9 \\ +7 \\ \hline 16 \end{array}$
13. $\begin{array}{r} 5 \\ +8 \\ \hline 13 \end{array}$
14. $\begin{array}{r} 8 \\ +3 \\ \hline 11 \end{array}$

IN90 Intervention • Skills

Top-left panel

Name _____ Skill _____

Grade 2 Skill 13

Mental Math to Add Tens

Sam scores 30 points.
Then he scores 10 more points.
How many points does Sam score in all?

$$\begin{array}{r} 30 \\ +10 \\ \hline 40 \end{array} \qquad \begin{array}{r} 3 \text{ tens} \\ +1 \text{ ten} \\ \hline 4 \text{ tens} \end{array}$$

Think: I start with 3 tens and add 1 more ten.

Sam scores __40__ points in all.

▲ **Try These**

Write the tens. Add.

$$\begin{array}{r} 3 \text{ tens} \\ 2 \text{ tens} \\ +5 \text{ tens} \end{array}$$

Go to the next side →

Think:

1. $\begin{array}{r} 20 \\ +10 \\ \hline 30 \end{array}$ $\begin{array}{r} 2 \text{ tens} \\ +1 \text{ tens} \\ \hline 3 \text{ tens} \end{array}$

2. $\begin{array}{r} 50 \\ +40 \\ \hline 90 \end{array}$ $\begin{array}{r} 5 \text{ tens} \\ +4 \text{ tens} \\ \hline 9 \text{ tens} \end{array}$

3. $\begin{array}{r} 30 \\ +20 \\ \hline 50 \end{array}$ $\begin{array}{r} 3 \text{ tens} \\ 2 \text{ tens} \\ +5 \text{ tens} \end{array}$

Intervention • Skills **IN93**

Top-right panel

Name _____ Skill _____

Practice on Your Own   Skill **13**

Missy reads 20 books.
Then she reads 30 more books.
How many books does Missy read in all?

$$\begin{array}{r} 20 \\ +30 \\ \hline 50 \end{array} \qquad \begin{array}{r} 2 \text{ tens} \\ +3 \text{ tens} \\ \hline 5 \text{ tens} \end{array}$$

Think: I start with 2 tens and add 3 more tens.

Missy reads __50__ books in all.

Add.

Think: 4 tens + 3 tens = 7 tens

1. $\begin{array}{r} 40 \\ +30 \\ \hline 70 \end{array}$
2. $\begin{array}{r} 50 \\ +20 \\ \hline 70 \end{array}$
3. $\begin{array}{r} 30 \\ +60 \\ \hline 90 \end{array}$
4. $\begin{array}{r} 20 \\ +20 \\ \hline 40 \end{array}$

5. $\begin{array}{r} 10 \\ +40 \\ \hline 50 \end{array}$
6. $\begin{array}{r} 60 \\ +20 \\ \hline 80 \end{array}$
7. $\begin{array}{r} 40 \\ +50 \\ \hline 90 \end{array}$
8. $\begin{array}{r} 10 \\ +10 \\ \hline 20 \end{array}$

9. $\begin{array}{r} 20 \\ +10 \\ \hline 30 \end{array}$
10. $\begin{array}{r} 40 \\ +40 \\ \hline 80 \end{array}$
11. $\begin{array}{r} 30 \\ +20 \\ \hline 50 \end{array}$
12. $\begin{array}{r} 10 \\ +50 \\ \hline 60 \end{array}$

▶ **Quiz**

Add.

13. $\begin{array}{r} 20 \\ +70 \\ \hline 90 \end{array}$
14. $\begin{array}{r} 40 \\ +20 \\ \hline 60 \end{array}$
15. $\begin{array}{r} 10 \\ +60 \\ \hline 70 \end{array}$
16. $\begin{array}{r} 30 \\ +50 \\ \hline 80 \end{array}$

17. $\begin{array}{r} 80 \\ +10 \\ \hline 90 \end{array}$
18. $\begin{array}{r} 40 \\ +10 \\ \hline 50 \end{array}$
19. $\begin{array}{r} 30 \\ +30 \\ \hline 60 \end{array}$
20. $\begin{array}{r} 10 \\ +30 \\ \hline 40 \end{array}$

IN94 Intervention • Skills

Bottom-left panel

Name _____ Skill _____

Grade 2 Skill 14

Add Tens and Ones

Find 31 + 23 = ☐.

Step 1
Show 31 and 23.

Tens	Ones
3	1
+2	3

Step 2
Add the ones. Write 4.

Tens	Ones
3	1
+2	3
	4

Step 3
Add the tens. Write 5.

Tens	Ones
3	1
+2	3
5	4

So, 31 + 23 = 54.

Go to the next side →

▲ **Try These**

Add.

1. | Tens | Ones |
   |------|------|
   | 3 | 1 |
   | +1 | 3 |
   | 4 | 4 |

2. | Tens | Ones |
   |------|------|
   | 2 | 5 |
   | +3 | 4 |
   | 5 | 9 |

3. | Tens | Ones |
   |------|------|
   | 4 | 0 |
   | +2 | 6 |
   | 6 | 6 |

Intervention • Skills **IN97**

Bottom-right panel

Name _____ Skill _____

Practice on Your Own   Skill **14**

Add the ones and tens.

Tens	Ones
2	4
+1	5
3	9

Add.

1. | Tens | Ones |
   |------|------|
   | 1 | 7 |
   | +4 | 2 |
   | 5 | 9 |

2. | Tens | Ones |
   |------|------|
   | 2 | 6 |
   | +5 | 0 |
   | 7 | 6 |

3. | Tens | Ones |
   |------|------|
   | 3 | 1 |
   | +3 | 5 |
   | 6 | 6 |

4. | Tens | Ones |
   |------|------|
   | 2 | 3 |
   | +2 | 4 |
   | 4 | 7 |

5. | Tens | Ones |
   |------|------|
   | 5 | 7 |
   | +2 | 2 |
   | 7 | 9 |

6. | Tens | Ones |
   |------|------|
   | 6 | 0 |
   | +3 | 9 |
   | 9 | 9 |

7. $\begin{array}{r} 18 \\ +20 \\ \hline 38 \end{array}$
8. $\begin{array}{r} 35 \\ +42 \\ \hline 77 \end{array}$
9. $\begin{array}{r} 51 \\ +47 \\ \hline 98 \end{array}$
10. $\begin{array}{r} 82 \\ +15 \\ \hline 97 \end{array}$

▶ **Quiz**

Add.

11. $\begin{array}{r} 31 \\ +24 \\ \hline 55 \end{array}$
12. $\begin{array}{r} 50 \\ +37 \\ \hline 87 \end{array}$
13. $\begin{array}{r} 46 \\ +32 \\ \hline 78 \end{array}$
14. $\begin{array}{r} 81 \\ +17 \\ \hline 98 \end{array}$

IN98 Intervention • Skills

© Harcourt

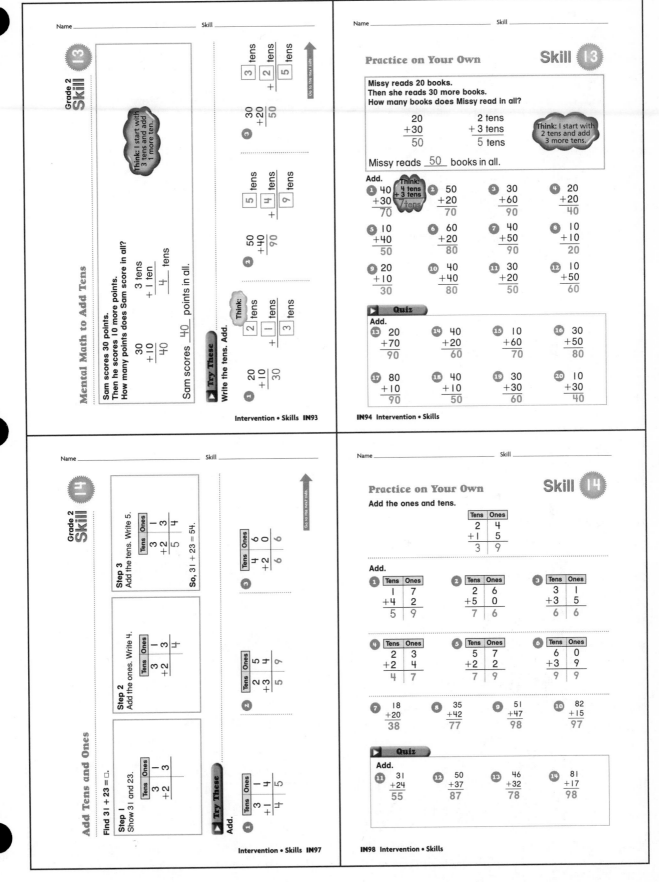

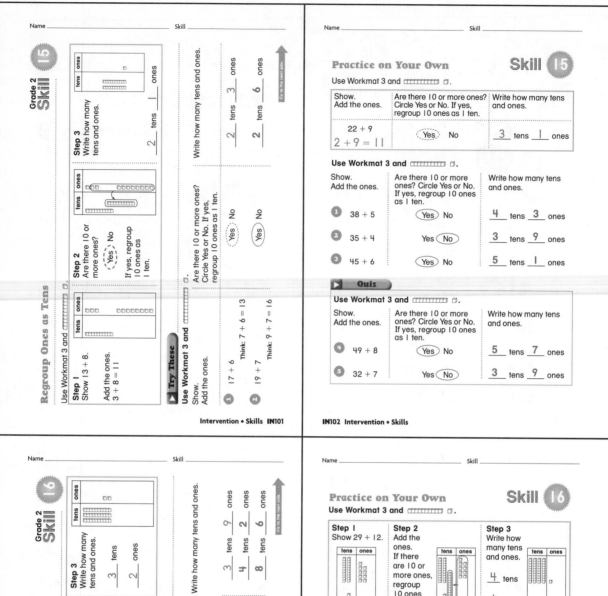

Grade 2 Skill 15

Regroup Ones as Tens

Use Workmat 3 and ▭.

Step 1
Show 13 + 8.
Add the ones.
3 + 8 = 11

Step 2
Are there 10 or more ones?
If yes, regroup 10 ones as 1 ten.

Step 3
Write how many tens and ones.
2 tens

Write how many tens and ones.
2 tens ___ ones

▲ Try These

Use Workmat 3 and ▭.
Show.
Add the ones.

1 17 + 6   Think: 7 + 6 = 13   Yes No   2 tens ___ ones
2 19 + 7   Think: 9 + 7 = 16   Yes No   2 tens 6 ones

Intervention • Skills **IN101**

Name ___ Skill ___

Practice on Your Own

Skill 15

Use Workmat 3 and ▭.

Show. Add the ones.	Are there 10 or more ones? Circle Yes or No. If yes, regroup 10 ones as 1 ten.	Write how many tens and ones.
22 + 9 2 + 9 = 11	(Yes) No	3 tens 1 ones

Use Workmat 3 and ▭.

Show. Add the ones.	Are there 10 or more ones? Circle Yes or No. If yes, regroup 10 ones as 1 ten.	Write how many tens and ones.
1 38 + 5	(Yes) No	4 tens 3 ones
2 35 + 4	Yes (No)	3 tens 9 ones
3 45 + 6	(Yes) No	5 tens 1 ones

▶ **Quiz**

Use Workmat 3 and ▭.

Show. Add the ones.	Are there 10 or more ones? Circle Yes or No. If yes, regroup 10 ones as 1 ten.	Write how many tens and ones.
4 49 + 8	(Yes) No	5 tens 7 ones
5 32 + 7	Yes (No)	3 tens 9 ones

IN102 Intervention • Skills

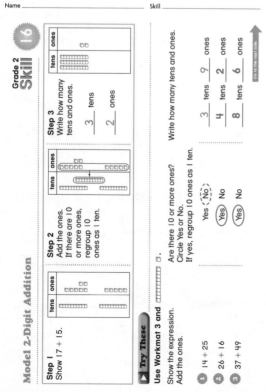

Grade 2 Skill 16

Model 2-Digit Addition

Step 1
Show 17 + 15.

Step 2
Add the ones.
If there are 10 or more ones, regroup 10 ones as 1 ten.

Step 3
Write how many tens and ones.
3 tens 2 ones

Write how many tens and ones.
___ tens ___ ones

▲ Try These

Use Workmat 3 and ▭.
Show the expression.
Add the ones.

1 14 + 25   Yes (No)   3 tens 9 ones
2 26 + 16   (Yes) No   4 tens 2 ones
3 37 + 49   (Yes) No   8 tens 6 ones

Intervention • Skills **IN105**

Name ___ Skill ___

Practice on Your Own

Skill 16

Use Workmat 3 and ▭.

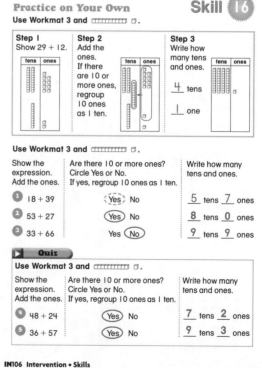

Step 1 Show 29 + 12.

Step 2 Add the ones. If there are 10 or more ones, regroup 10 ones as 1 ten.

Step 3 Write how many tens and ones.
4 tens 1 one

Use Workmat 3 and ▭.

Show the expression. Add the ones.	Are there 10 or more ones? Circle Yes or No. If yes, regroup 10 ones as 1 ten.	Write how many tens and ones.
1 18 + 39	(Yes) No	5 tens 7 ones
2 53 + 27	(Yes) No	8 tens 0 ones
3 33 + 66	Yes (No)	9 tens 9 ones

▶ **Quiz**

Use Workmat 3 and ▭.

Show the expression. Add the ones.	Are there 10 or more ones? Circle Yes or No. If yes, regroup 10 ones as 1 ten.	Write how many tens and ones.
4 48 + 24	(Yes) No	7 tens 2 ones
5 36 + 57	(Yes) No	9 tens 3 ones

IN106 Intervention • Skills

© Harcourt

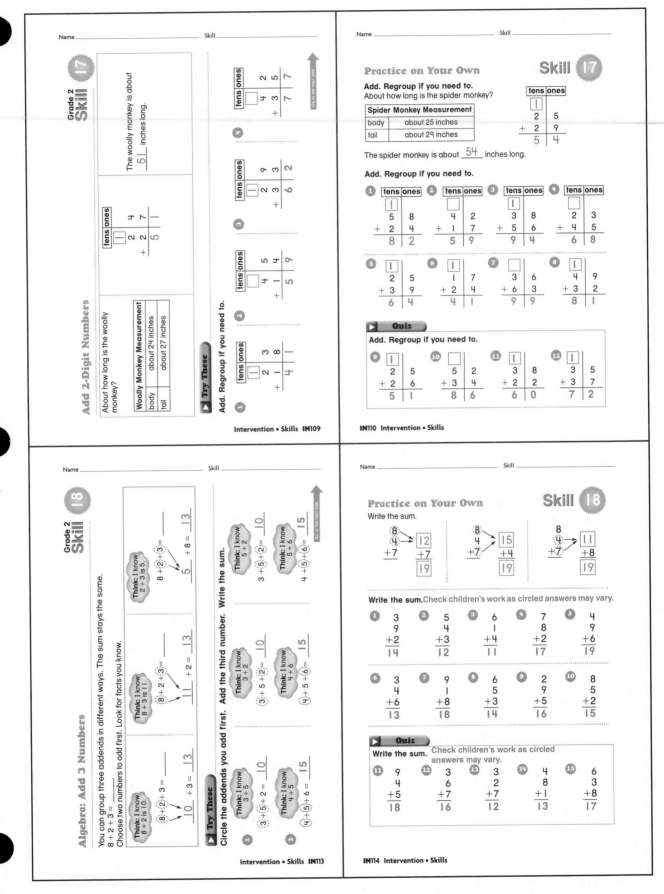

Grade 2 — Skill 17

Add 2-Digit Numbers

About how long is the woolly monkey?

Woolly Monkey Measurement	
body	about 24 inches
tail	about 27 inches

The woolly monkey is about 5⎵ inches long.

	tens	ones
	⎵	2
	4	5
+	2	7
	5	⎵

Try These

Add. Regroup if you need to.

1.

	tens	ones
	⎵	2
+	3	8

2.

	tens	ones
	⎵	4
+	5	9

3.

	tens	ones
	⎵	2
+	3	3
	6	9

4.

	tens	ones
	⎵	5
	4	2
+	3	5
	7	7

Go to the next side.

Intervention • Skills **IN109**

Skill 17

Add. Regroup if you need to.
About how long is the spider monkey?

Spider Monkey Measurement	
body	about 25 inches
tail	about 29 inches

	tens	ones
	1	
	2	5
+	2	9
	5	4

The spider monkey is about __54__ inches long.

Add. Regroup if you need to.

1.

	tens	ones
	⎵	
	5	8
+	2	4
	8	2

2.

	tens	ones
	⎵	
	4	2
+	1	7
	5	9

3.

	tens	ones
	1	
	3	8
+	5	6
	9	4

4.

	tens	ones
	⎵	
	2	3
+	4	5
	6	8

5.

	tens	ones
	1	
	2	5
+	3	9
	6	4

6.

	tens	ones
	1	
	1	7
+	2	4
	4	1

7.

	tens	ones
	3	6
+	6	3
	9	9

8.

	tens	ones
	1	
	4	9
+	3	2
	8	1

▶ Quiz

Add. Regroup if you need to.

9.

	tens	ones
	1	
	2	5
+	2	6
	5	1

10.

	tens	ones
	⎵	
	5	2
+	3	4
	8	6

11.

	tens	ones
	1	
	3	8
+	2	2
	6	0

12.

	tens	ones
	1	
	3	5
+	3	7
	7	2

IN110 Intervention • Skills

Grade 2 — Skill 18

Algebra: Add 3 Numbers

You can group three addends in different ways. The sum stays the same.
$8 + 2 + 3 =$
Choose two numbers to add first. Look for facts you know.

Think: I know 8 + 2 is 10.
$8\!+\!2\!+ 3 =$
$10 + 3 = 13$

Think: I know 2 + 3 is 5.
$8 +\!2\!+\!3\! =$
$5 + 8 = 13$

Think: I know 8 + 3 is 11.
$8\!+ 2\!+\!3\! =$
$11 + 2 = 13$

Try These

Circle the addends you add first. Add the third number. Write the sum.

1.

Think: I know 3 + 5
$3\!+\!5\!+\! 2 = 10$

Think: I know 3 + 2
$3\!+ 5\!+\!2\! = 10$

2.

Think: I know 4 + 6
$4\!+\!5\!+\! 6 = 15$

Think: I know 4 + 5
$4\!+ 5\!+\!6\! = 15$

Go to the next side.

Intervention • Skills **IN113**

Skill 18

Write the sum.

$$\begin{array}{r} \underline{8} \\ 4 \\ +7 \end{array} \rightarrow \begin{array}{r} 12 \\ +7 \\ \hline 19 \end{array}$$

$$\begin{array}{r} \underline{8} \\ 4 \\ +7 \end{array} \rightarrow \begin{array}{r} 15 \\ +4 \\ \hline 19 \end{array}$$

$$\begin{array}{r} 8 \\ \underline{4} \\ +7 \end{array} \rightarrow \begin{array}{r} 11 \\ +8 \\ \hline 19 \end{array}$$

Write the sum. Check children's work as circled answers may vary.

1.

3
9
+2
14

2.

5
4
+3
12

3.

6
1
+4
11

4.

7
8
+2
17

5.

4
9
+6
19

6.

3
4
+6
13

7.

9
1
+8
18

8.

6
5
+3
14

9.

2
9
+5
16

10.

8
5
+2
15

▶ Quiz

Write the sum. Check children's work as circled answers may vary.

11.

9
4
+5
18

12.

3
6
+7
16

13.

3
2
+7
12

14.

4
8
+1
13

15.

6
3
+8
17

IN114 Intervention • Skills

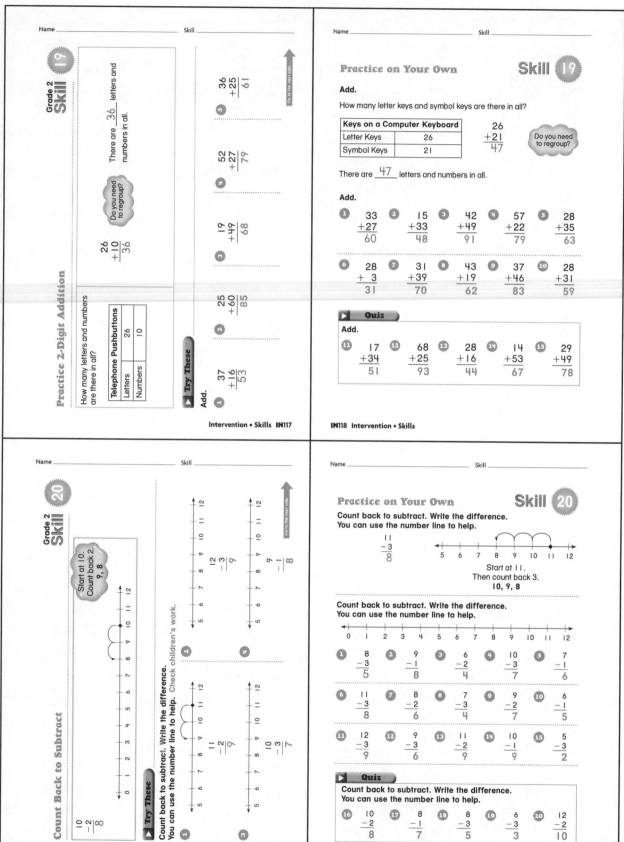

Top-left panel

Grade 2
Skill 19

Practice 2-Digit Addition

How many letters and numbers are there in all?

Telephone Pushbuttons	
Letters	26
Numbers	10

$$\begin{array}{r} 26 \\ +10 \\ \hline 36 \end{array}$$

There are __36__ letters and numbers in all.

Do you need to regroup?

Try These

Add.

1) $\begin{array}{r} 37 \\ +16 \\ \hline 53 \end{array}$ 2) $\begin{array}{r} 25 \\ +60 \\ \hline 85 \end{array}$ 3) $\begin{array}{r} 19 \\ +49 \\ \hline 68 \end{array}$ 4) $\begin{array}{r} 52 \\ +27 \\ \hline 79 \end{array}$ 5) $\begin{array}{r} 36 \\ +25 \\ \hline 61 \end{array}$

Go to the next side.

Top-right panel

Practice on Your Own

Skill 19

Add.

How many letter keys and symbol keys are there in all?

Keys on a Computer Keyboard	
Letter Keys	26
Symbol Keys	21

$$\begin{array}{r} 26 \\ +21 \\ \hline 47 \end{array}$$

Do you need to regroup?

There are __47__ letters and numbers in all.

Add.

1) $\begin{array}{r} 33 \\ +27 \\ \hline 60 \end{array}$ 2) $\begin{array}{r} 15 \\ +33 \\ \hline 48 \end{array}$ 3) $\begin{array}{r} 42 \\ +49 \\ \hline 91 \end{array}$ 4) $\begin{array}{r} 57 \\ +22 \\ \hline 79 \end{array}$ 5) $\begin{array}{r} 28 \\ +35 \\ \hline 63 \end{array}$

6) $\begin{array}{r} 28 \\ +\ 3 \\ \hline 31 \end{array}$ 7) $\begin{array}{r} 31 \\ +39 \\ \hline 70 \end{array}$ 8) $\begin{array}{r} 43 \\ +19 \\ \hline 62 \end{array}$ 9) $\begin{array}{r} 37 \\ +46 \\ \hline 83 \end{array}$ 10) $\begin{array}{r} 28 \\ +31 \\ \hline 59 \end{array}$

▶ Quiz

Add.

11) $\begin{array}{r} 17 \\ +34 \\ \hline 51 \end{array}$ 12) $\begin{array}{r} 68 \\ +25 \\ \hline 93 \end{array}$ 13) $\begin{array}{r} 28 \\ +16 \\ \hline 44 \end{array}$ 14) $\begin{array}{r} 14 \\ +53 \\ \hline 67 \end{array}$ 15) $\begin{array}{r} 29 \\ +49 \\ \hline 78 \end{array}$

Bottom-left panel

Grade 2
Skill 20

Count Back to Subtract

$$\begin{array}{r} 10 \\ -2 \\ \hline 8 \end{array}$$

Start at 10. Count back 2. 9, 8

Try These

Count back to subtract. Write the difference.
You can use the number line to help. *Check children's work.*

1) $\begin{array}{r} 11 \\ -2 \\ \hline 9 \end{array}$ 2) $\begin{array}{r} 12 \\ -3 \\ \hline 9 \end{array}$

3) $\begin{array}{r} 10 \\ -3 \\ \hline 7 \end{array}$ 4) $\begin{array}{r} 9 \\ -1 \\ \hline 8 \end{array}$

Go to the next side.

Bottom-right panel

Practice on Your Own

Skill 20

Count back to subtract. Write the difference.
You can use the number line to help.

$$\begin{array}{r} 11 \\ -3 \\ \hline 8 \end{array}$$

Start at 11.
Then count back 3.
10, 9, 8

Count back to subtract. Write the difference.
You can use the number line to help.

1) $\begin{array}{r} 8 \\ -3 \\ \hline 5 \end{array}$ 2) $\begin{array}{r} 9 \\ -1 \\ \hline 8 \end{array}$ 3) $\begin{array}{r} 6 \\ -2 \\ \hline 4 \end{array}$ 4) $\begin{array}{r} 10 \\ -3 \\ \hline 7 \end{array}$ 5) $\begin{array}{r} 7 \\ -1 \\ \hline 6 \end{array}$

6) $\begin{array}{r} 11 \\ -3 \\ \hline 8 \end{array}$ 7) $\begin{array}{r} 8 \\ -2 \\ \hline 6 \end{array}$ 8) $\begin{array}{r} 7 \\ -3 \\ \hline 4 \end{array}$ 9) $\begin{array}{r} 9 \\ -2 \\ \hline 7 \end{array}$ 10) $\begin{array}{r} 6 \\ -1 \\ \hline 5 \end{array}$

11) $\begin{array}{r} 12 \\ -3 \\ \hline 9 \end{array}$ 12) $\begin{array}{r} 9 \\ -3 \\ \hline 6 \end{array}$ 13) $\begin{array}{r} 11 \\ -2 \\ \hline 9 \end{array}$ 14) $\begin{array}{r} 10 \\ -1 \\ \hline 9 \end{array}$ 15) $\begin{array}{r} 5 \\ -3 \\ \hline 2 \end{array}$

▶ Quiz

Count back to subtract. Write the difference.
You can use the number line to help.

16) $\begin{array}{r} 10 \\ -2 \\ \hline 8 \end{array}$ 17) $\begin{array}{r} 8 \\ -1 \\ \hline 7 \end{array}$ 18) $\begin{array}{r} 8 \\ -3 \\ \hline 5 \end{array}$ 19) $\begin{array}{r} 6 \\ -3 \\ \hline 3 \end{array}$ 20) $\begin{array}{r} 12 \\ -2 \\ \hline 10 \end{array}$

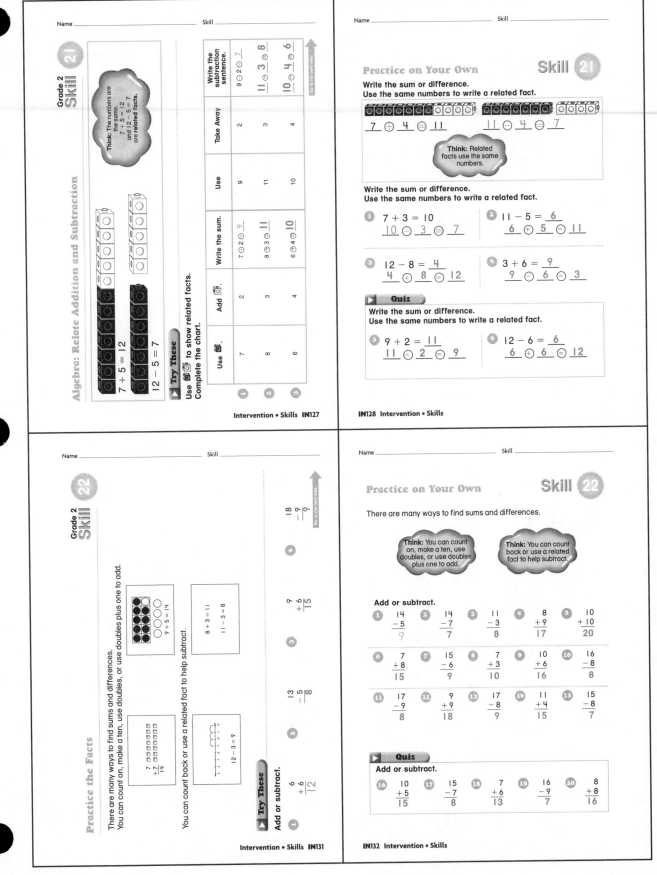

Top-left panel (Skill 21):

Name _____ Skill _____

Grade 2 Skill 21

Algebra: Relate Addition and Subtraction

Think: The numbers are the same, 7 + 5 = 12 and 12 − 5 = 7 are related facts.

7 + 5 = 12

12 − 5 = 7

Try These

Use ☐ to show related facts.
Complete the chart.

Use ☐.	Add ☐.	Write the sum.	Use	Take Away	Write the subtraction sentence.
7	2	7 ⊕ 2 ⊜ 9	9	2	9 ⊖ 2 ⊜ 7
8	3	8 ⊕ 3 ⊜ 11	11	3	11 ⊖ 3 ⊜ 8
6	4	6 ⊕ 4 ⊜ 10	10	4	10 ⊖ 4 ⊜ 6

Intervention • Skills IN127

Top-right panel (Skill 21):

Name _____ Skill _____

Practice on Your Own   Skill 21

Write the sum or difference.
Use the same numbers to write a related fact.

7 ⊕ 4 ⊜ 11   11 ⊖ 4 ⊜ 7

Think: Related facts use the same numbers.

Write the sum or difference.
Use the same numbers to write a related fact.

1. 7 + 3 = 10
   10 ⊖ 3 ⊜ 7

2. 11 − 5 = 6
   6 ⊕ 5 ⊜ 11

3. 12 − 8 = 4
   4 ⊕ 8 ⊜ 12

4. 3 + 6 = 9
   9 ⊖ 6 ⊜ 3

Quiz

Write the sum or difference.
Use the same numbers to write a related fact.

5. 9 + 2 = 11
   11 ⊖ 2 ⊜ 9

6. 12 − 6 = 6
   6 ⊕ 6 ⊜ 12

IN128 Intervention • Skills

Bottom-left panel (Skill 22):

Name _____ Skill _____

Grade 2 Skill 22

Practice the Facts

There are many ways to find sums and differences.
You can count on, make a ten, use doubles, or use doubles plus one to add.

9 + 5 = 14

7
+7
14

You can count back or use a related fact to help subtract.

8 + 3 = 11
11 − 3 = 8

12 − 3 = 9

Try These

Add or subtract.

1. 6
   + 6
   12

2. 13
   − 5
   8

3. 9
   + 6
   15

4. 18
   − 9
   9

Intervention • Skills IN131

Bottom-right panel (Skill 22):

Name _____ Skill _____

Practice on Your Own   Skill 22

There are many ways to find sums and differences.

Think: You can count on, make a ten, use doubles, or use doubles plus one to add.

Think: You can count back or use a related fact to help subtract.

Add or subtract.

1. 14 − 5 = 9
2. 14 − 7 = 7
3. 11 − 3 = 8
4. 8 + 9 = 17
5. 10 + 10 = 20
6. 7 + 8 = 15
7. 15 − 6 = 9
8. 7 + 3 = 10
9. 10 + 6 = 16
10. 16 − 8 = 8
11. 17 − 9 = 8
12. 9 + 9 = 18
13. 17 − 8 = 9
14. 11 + 4 = 15
15. 15 − 8 = 7

Quiz

Add or subtract.

16. 10 + 5 = 15
17. 15 − 7 = 8
18. 7 + 6 = 13
19. 16 − 9 = 7
20. 8 + 8 = 16

IN132 Intervention • Skills

© Harcourt

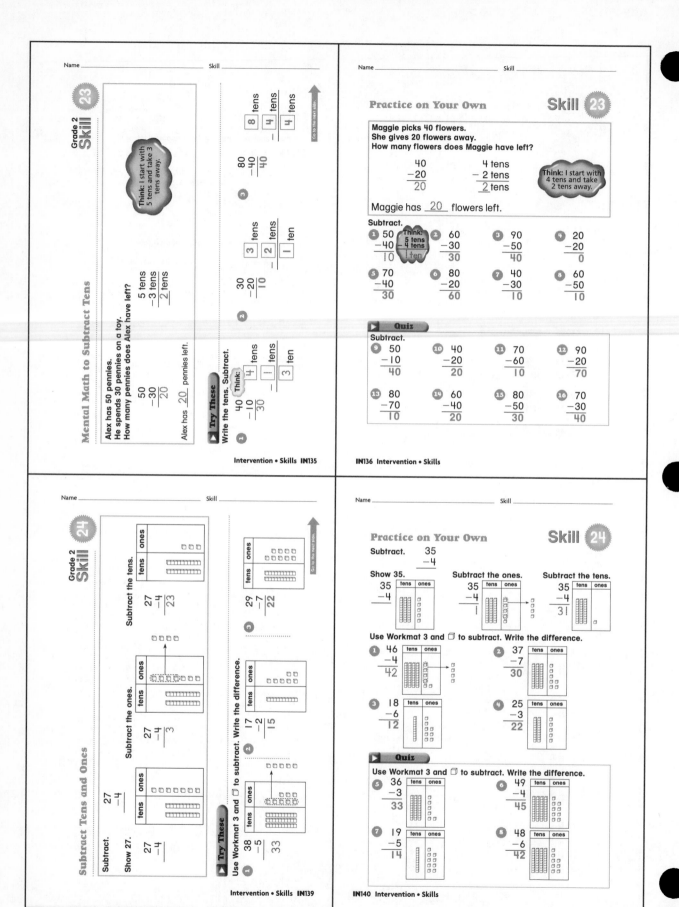

Skill 23 — Mental Math to Subtract Tens

Grade 2 Skill 23

Think: I start with 5 tens and take 3 tens away.

Alex has 50 pennies.
He spends 30 pennies on a toy.
How many pennies does Alex have left?

$$\begin{array}{r} 50 \\ -30 \\ \hline 20 \end{array} \qquad \begin{array}{r} 5 \text{ tens} \\ -3 \text{ tens} \\ \hline 2 \text{ tens} \end{array}$$

Alex has __20__ pennies left.

Try These
Write the tens. Subtract.

1.
$$\begin{array}{r} 40 \\ -10 \\ \hline 30 \end{array} \qquad \begin{array}{r} 4 \text{ tens} \\ -1 \text{ tens} \\ \hline 3 \text{ ten} \end{array}$$
Think:

2.
$$\begin{array}{r} 30 \\ -20 \\ \hline 10 \end{array} \qquad \begin{array}{r} 3 \text{ tens} \\ -2 \text{ tens} \\ \hline 1 \text{ ten} \end{array}$$

3.
$$\begin{array}{r} 80 \\ -40 \\ \hline 40 \end{array} \qquad \begin{array}{r} 8 \text{ tens} \\ -4 \text{ tens} \\ \hline 4 \text{ tens} \end{array}$$

Go to the next side.

Practice on Your Own — Skill 23

Maggie picks 40 flowers.
She gives 20 flowers away.
How many flowers does Maggie have left?

$$\begin{array}{r} 40 \\ -20 \\ \hline 20 \end{array} \qquad \begin{array}{r} 4 \text{ tens} \\ -2 \text{ tens} \\ \hline 2 \text{ tens} \end{array}$$

Think: I start with 4 tens and take 2 tens away.

Maggie has __20__ flowers left.

Subtract.

1.
$$\begin{array}{r} 50 \\ -40 \\ \hline 10 \end{array}$$
Think: 5 tens − 4 tens

2.
$$\begin{array}{r} 60 \\ -30 \\ \hline 30 \end{array}$$

3.
$$\begin{array}{r} 90 \\ -50 \\ \hline 40 \end{array}$$

4.
$$\begin{array}{r} 20 \\ -20 \\ \hline 0 \end{array}$$

5.
$$\begin{array}{r} 70 \\ -40 \\ \hline 30 \end{array}$$

6.
$$\begin{array}{r} 80 \\ -20 \\ \hline 60 \end{array}$$

7.
$$\begin{array}{r} 40 \\ -30 \\ \hline 10 \end{array}$$

8.
$$\begin{array}{r} 60 \\ -50 \\ \hline 10 \end{array}$$

Quiz
Subtract.

9.
$$\begin{array}{r} 50 \\ -10 \\ \hline 40 \end{array}$$

10.
$$\begin{array}{r} 40 \\ -20 \\ \hline 20 \end{array}$$

11.
$$\begin{array}{r} 70 \\ -60 \\ \hline 10 \end{array}$$

12.
$$\begin{array}{r} 90 \\ -20 \\ \hline 70 \end{array}$$

13.
$$\begin{array}{r} 80 \\ -70 \\ \hline 10 \end{array}$$

14.
$$\begin{array}{r} 60 \\ -40 \\ \hline 20 \end{array}$$

15.
$$\begin{array}{r} 80 \\ -50 \\ \hline 30 \end{array}$$

16.
$$\begin{array}{r} 70 \\ -30 \\ \hline 40 \end{array}$$

Skill 24 — Subtract Tens and Ones

Grade 2 Skill 24

Subtract.
$$\begin{array}{r} 27 \\ -4 \end{array}$$

Show 27.
$$\begin{array}{r} 27 \\ -4 \end{array}$$
tens	ones

Subtract the ones.
$$\begin{array}{r} 27 \\ -4 \\ \hline 3 \end{array}$$
tens	ones

Subtract the tens.
$$\begin{array}{r} 27 \\ -4 \\ \hline 23 \end{array}$$
tens	ones

Try These
Use Workmat 3 and ☐ to subtract. Write the difference.

1.
$$\begin{array}{r} 38 \\ -5 \\ \hline 33 \end{array}$$
tens	ones

2.
$$\begin{array}{r} 17 \\ -2 \\ \hline 15 \end{array}$$
tens	ones

3.
$$\begin{array}{r} 29 \\ -7 \\ \hline 22 \end{array}$$
tens	ones

Go to the next side.

Practice on Your Own — Skill 24

Subtract.
$$\begin{array}{r} 35 \\ -4 \end{array}$$

Show 35.
$$\begin{array}{r} 35 \\ -4 \end{array}$$
tens	ones

Subtract the ones.
$$\begin{array}{r} 35 \\ -4 \\ \hline 1 \end{array}$$
tens	ones

Subtract the tens.
$$\begin{array}{r} 35 \\ -4 \\ \hline 31 \end{array}$$
tens	ones

Use Workmat 3 and ☐ to subtract. Write the difference.

1.
$$\begin{array}{r} 46 \\ -4 \\ \hline 42 \end{array}$$
tens	ones

2.
$$\begin{array}{r} 37 \\ -7 \\ \hline 30 \end{array}$$
tens	ones

3.
$$\begin{array}{r} 18 \\ -6 \\ \hline 12 \end{array}$$
tens	ones

4.
$$\begin{array}{r} 25 \\ -3 \\ \hline 22 \end{array}$$
tens	ones

Quiz
Use Workmat 3 and ☐ to subtract. Write the difference.

5.
$$\begin{array}{r} 36 \\ -3 \\ \hline 33 \end{array}$$
tens	ones

6.
$$\begin{array}{r} 49 \\ -4 \\ \hline 45 \end{array}$$
tens	ones

7.
$$\begin{array}{r} 19 \\ -5 \\ \hline 14 \end{array}$$
tens	ones

8.
$$\begin{array}{r} 48 \\ -6 \\ \hline 42 \end{array}$$
tens	ones

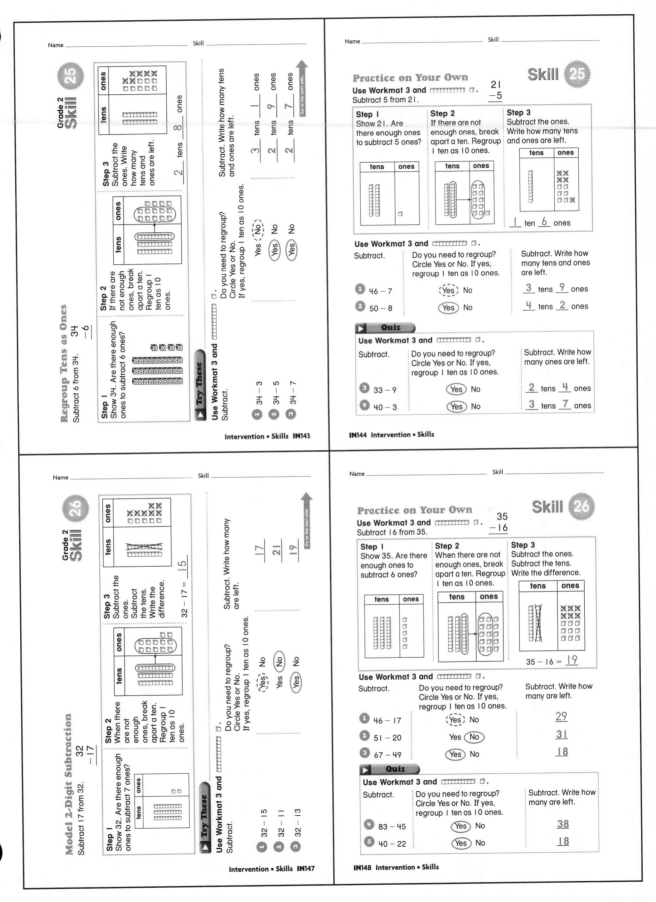

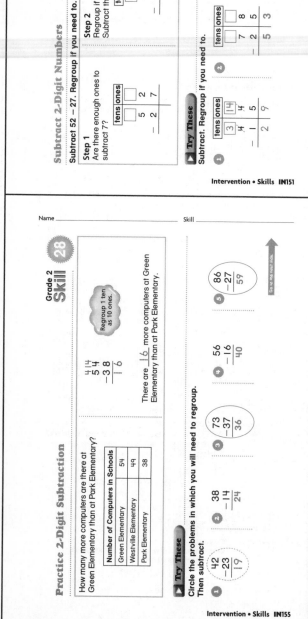

Grade 2 Skill 27

Subtract 2-Digit Numbers

Subtract 52 – 27. Regroup if you need to.

Step 1
Are there enough ones to subtract 7?

tens	ones
5	2
– 2	7

Step 2
Regroup if you need to. Subtract the ones.

tens	ones
4	12
5	2
– 2	7
	5

Step 3
Subtract the tens. Write how many.

tens	ones
4	12
5	2
– 2	7
2	5

▲ **Try These** Subtract. Regroup if you need to.

1.
tens	ones
3	14
4	4
– 1	5
2	9

2.
tens	ones
7	5
– 2	5
5	3

3.
tens	ones
4	10
5	0
– 3	3
1	7

4.
tens	ones
7	11
8	1
– 4	6
3	5

→ Go to the next side.

Subtract 64 – 35. Regroup if you need to.

Step 1	**Step 2**	**Step 3**
Are there enough ones to subtract 5?	Regroup if you need to. Subtract the ones.	Subtract the tens. Write how many.
64 −35	5 14 / 64 −35 / 9	5 14 / 64 −35 / 29

Subtract. Regroup if you need to.

1.
tens	ones
4	14
5	4
− 3	6
1	8

2.
tens	ones
7	10
8	0
− 2	6
5	4

3.
tens	ones
2	13
3	3
−	4
2	9

4.
tens	ones
7	5
− 4	2
3	3

5.
tens	ones
3	11
4	1
− 1	4
2	7

6.
tens	ones
6	3
− 2	3
4	0

7.
tens	ones
6	12
7	2
− 3	6
3	6

8.
tens	ones
7	11
8	1
− 6	9
1	2

9. 94 −29 = 65
10. 85 −48 = 37
11. 67 −39 = 28
12. 38 −19 = 19

▶ **Quiz**

Subtract. Regroup if you need to.

13. 71 −25 = 46
14. 76 −28 = 48
15. 23 − 6 = 17
16. 48 −28 = 20

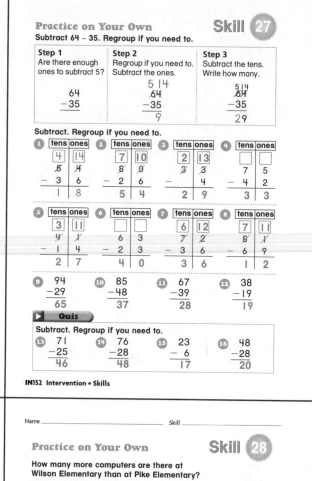

Grade 2 Skill 28

Practice 2-Digit Subtraction

How many more computers are there at Green Elementary than at Park Elementary?

Number of Computers in Schools	
Green Elementary	54
Westville Elementary	49
Park Elementary	38

Regroup 1 ten as 10 ones.

4 14 / 5 4 / − 3 8 / 1 6

There are 16 more computers at Green Elementary than at Park Elementary.

▲ **Try These** Circle the problems in which you will need to regroup. Then subtract.

1. (42 −23 = 19)
2. 38 −14 = 24
3. (73 −37 = 36)
4. 56 −16 = 40
5. (86 −27 = 59)

→ Go to the next side.

How many more computers are there at Wilson Elementary than at Pike Elementary?

Number of Computers in Schools	
Wilson Elementary	53
Pike Elementary	36
Lee Elementary	29

4 13 / 5 3 / − 3 6 / 1 7

Regroup 1 ten as 10 ones.

There are 17 more computers at Wilson Elementary.

Circle the problems in which you will need to regroup. Then subtract.

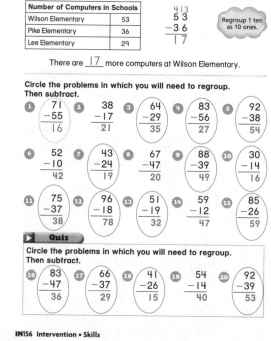

1. (71 −55 = 16)
2. 38 −17 = 21
3. (64 −29 = 35)
4. (83 −56 = 27)
5. (92 −38 = 54)
6. 52 −10 = 42
7. (43 −24 = 19)
8. 67 −47 = 20
9. (88 −39 = 49)
10. (30 −14 = 16)
11. (75 −37 = 38)
12. (96 −18 = 78)
13. (51 −19 = 32)
14. 59 −12 = 47
15. (85 −26 = 59)

▶ **Quiz**

Circle the problems in which you will need to regroup. Then subtract.

16. (83 −47 = 36)
17. (66 −37 = 29)
18. (41 −26 = 15)
19. 54 −14 = 40
20. (92 −39 = 53)

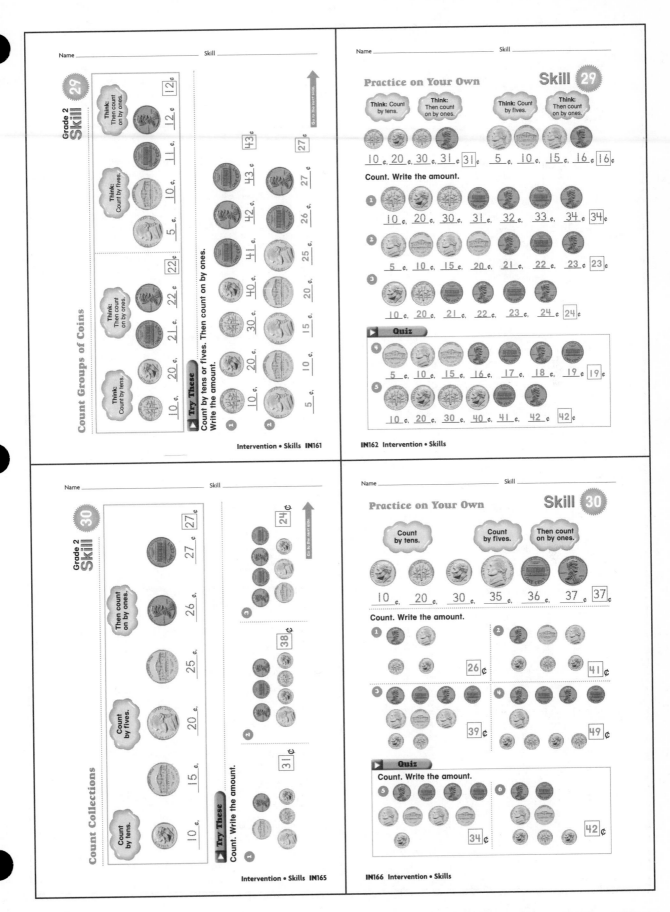

Grade 2 Skill 29

Count Groups of Coins

Think: Count by tens. | Think: Then count on by fives. | Think: Then count on by ones.

10 ¢ 20 ¢ 5 ¢ 10 ¢ 11 ¢ 12 ¢ **12¢**

Think: Count by tens. | Think: Then count on by ones.

10 ¢ 20 ¢ 21 ¢ 22 ¢ **22¢**

Try These

Count by tens or fives. Then count on by ones. Write the amount.

1. 5 ¢ 10 ¢ 15 ¢ 20 ¢ 30 ¢ 40 ¢ 41 ¢ 42 ¢ 43 ¢ **43¢**

2. 5 ¢ 10 ¢ 15 ¢ 20 ¢ 25 ¢ 26 ¢ 27 ¢ **27¢**

Intervention • Skills **IN161**

Practice on Your Own

Skill 29

Think: Count by tens. | Think: Then count on by ones. | Think: Count by fives. | Think: Then count on by ones.

10 ¢ 20 ¢ 30 ¢ 31 ¢ **31**¢   5 ¢ 10 ¢ 15 ¢ 16 ¢ **16**¢

Count. Write the amount.

1. 10 ¢ 20 ¢ 30 ¢ 31 ¢ 32 ¢ 33 ¢ 34 ¢ **34**¢

2. 5 ¢ 10 ¢ 15 ¢ 20 ¢ 21 ¢ 22 ¢ 23 ¢ **23**¢

3. 10 ¢ 20 ¢ 21 ¢ 22 ¢ 23 ¢ 24 ¢ **24**¢

Quiz

4. 5 ¢ 10 ¢ 15 ¢ 16 ¢ 17 ¢ 18 ¢ 19 ¢ **19**¢

5. 10 ¢ 20 ¢ 30 ¢ 40 ¢ 41 ¢ 42 ¢ **42**¢

IN162 Intervention • Skills

Grade 2 Skill 30

Count Collections

Count by tens. | Count by fives. | Then count on by ones.

10 ¢ 15 ¢ 20 ¢ 25 ¢ 26 ¢ 27 ¢ **27¢**

Try These

Count. Write the amount.

1. 3 ¢ **3**¢

2. 38 ¢ **38**¢

3. 24 ¢ **24**¢

Intervention • Skills **IN165**

Practice on Your Own

Skill 30

Count by tens. | Count by fives. | Then count on by ones.

10 ¢ 20 ¢ 30 ¢ 35 ¢ 36 ¢ 37 ¢ **37**¢

Count. Write the amount.

1. **26**¢

2. **41**¢

3. **39**¢

4. **49**¢

Quiz

Count. Write the amount.

5. **34**¢

6. **42**¢

IN166 Intervention • Skills

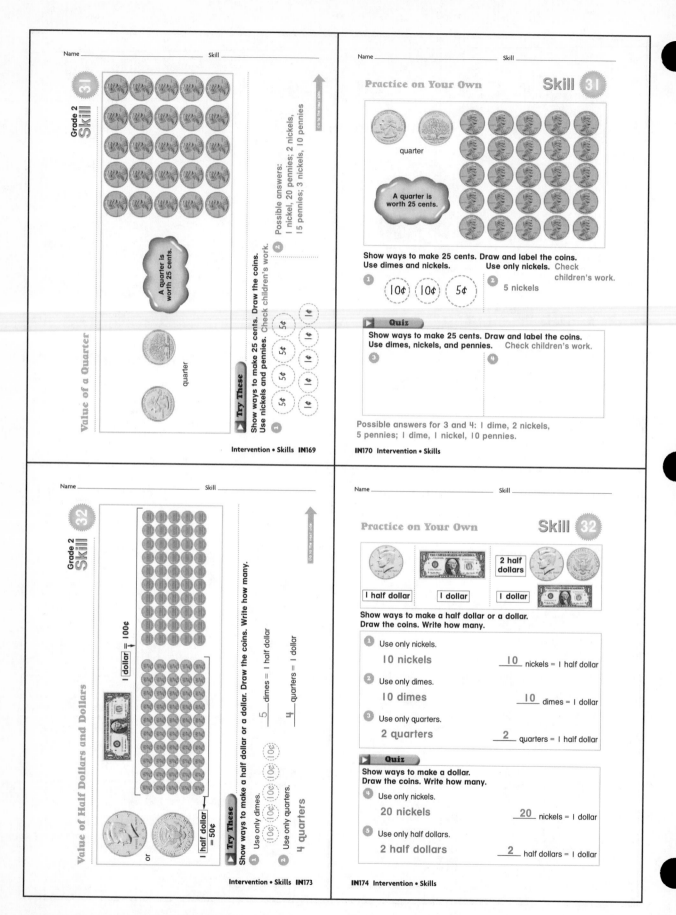

Grade 2 Skill 31

Value of a Quarter

A quarter is worth 25 cents.

quarter

Possible answers:
1 nickel, 20 pennies; 2 nickels,
15 pennies; 3 nickels, 10 pennies

► **Try These**

Show ways to make 25 cents. Draw the coins.
Use nickels and pennies. Check children's work.

5¢ 5¢ 5¢ 5¢ 1¢ 1¢ 1¢ 1¢ 5¢ 1¢

Practice on Your Own **Skill 31**

quarter

A quarter is worth 25 cents.

Show ways to make 25 cents. Draw and label the coins.
Use dimes and nickels.   Use only nickels. Check children's work.

1   10¢ 10¢ 5¢   2   5 nickels

► **Quiz**

Show ways to make 25 cents. Draw and label the coins.
Use dimes, nickels, and pennies.   Check children's work.

3   4

Possible answers for 3 and 4: 1 dime, 2 nickels,
5 pennies; 1 dime, 1 nickel, 10 pennies.

Grade 2 Skill 32

Value of Half Dollars and Dollars

1 dollar = 100¢

1 half dollar = 50¢

or

► **Try These**

Show ways to make a half dollar or a dollar. Draw the coins. Write how many.

1 Use only dimes.
10¢ 10¢ 10¢ 10¢ 10¢
5 dimes = 1 half dollar

2 Use only quarters.
4 quarters = 1 dollar

Practice on Your Own **Skill 32**

1 half dollar | 1 dollar | 1 dollar | 2 half dollars

Show ways to make a half dollar or a dollar.
Draw the coins. Write how many.

1 Use only nickels.
10 nickels   _10_ nickels = 1 half dollar

2 Use only dimes.
10 dimes   _10_ dimes = 1 dollar

3 Use only quarters.
2 quarters   _2_ quarters = 1 half dollar

► **Quiz**

Show ways to make a dollar.
Draw the coins. Write how many.

4 Use only nickels.
20 nickels   _20_ nickels = 1 dollar

5 Use only half dollars.
2 half dollars   _2_ half dollars = 1 dollar

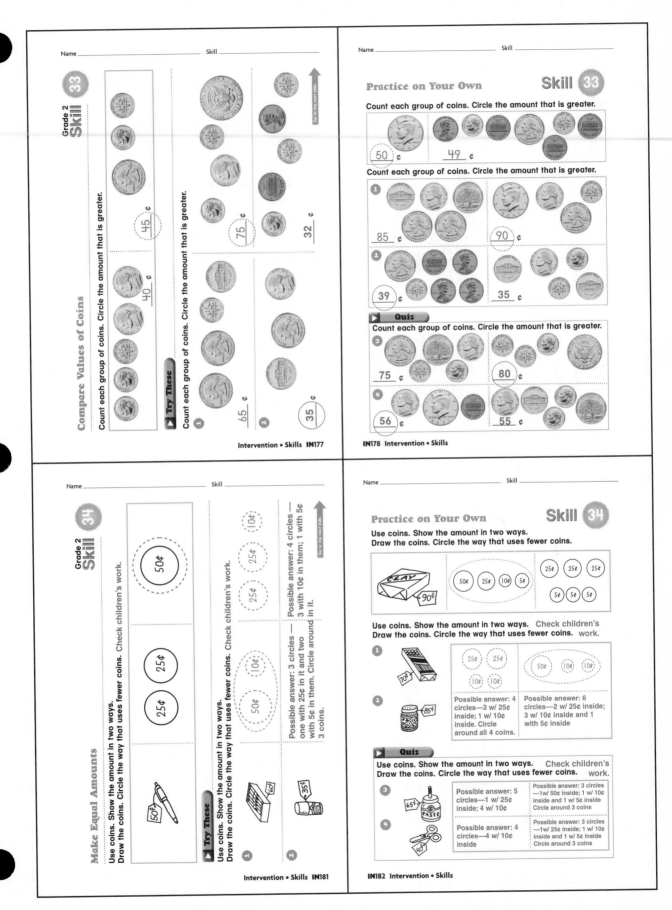

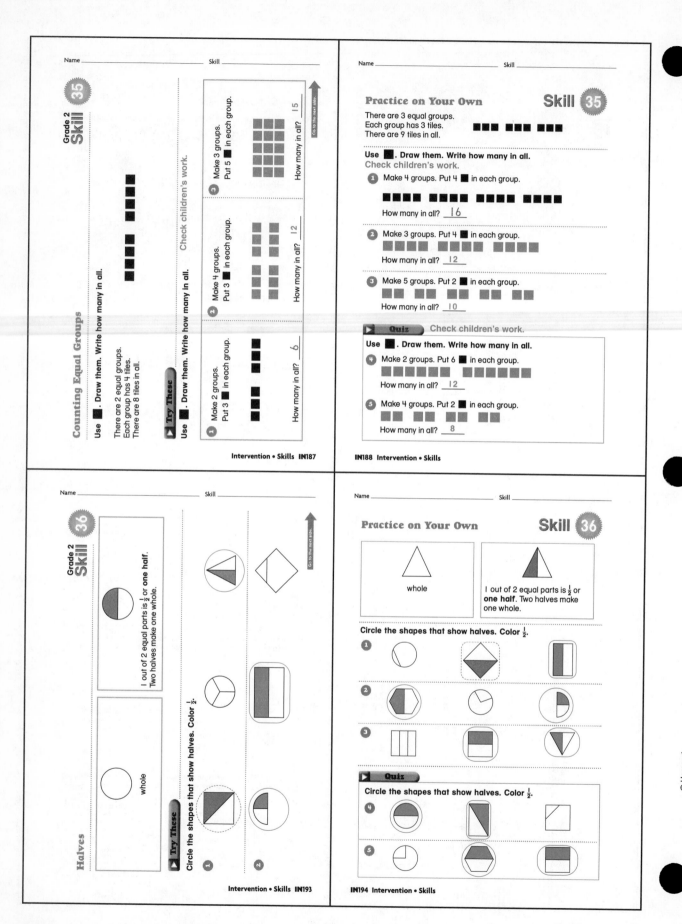

Name _____ Skill _____

Counting Equal Groups

There are 2 equal groups.
Each group has 4 tiles.
There are 8 tiles in all.

Use ■. Draw them. Write how many in all.

▶ **Try These**

Use ■. Draw them. Write how many in all.
Check children's work.

1 Make 2 groups.
Put 3 ■ in each group.

How many in all? 6

2 Make 4 groups.
Put 3 ■ in each group.

How many in all? 12

3 Make 5 groups.
Put 5 ■ in each group.

How many in all? 15

Go to the next side.

Name _____ Skill _____

Practice on Your Own

There are 3 equal groups.
Each group has 3 tiles.
There are 9 tiles in all.

Use ■. Draw them. Write how many in all.
Check children's work.

1 Make 4 groups. Put 4 ■ in each group.

How many in all? 16

2 Make 3 groups. Put 4 ■ in each group.

How many in all? 12

3 Make 5 groups. Put 2 ■ in each group.

How many in all? 10

▶ **Quiz**   Check children's work.

Use ■. Draw them. Write how many in all.

4 Make 2 groups. Put 6 ■ in each group.

How many in all? 12

5 Make 4 groups. Put 2 ■ in each group.

How many in all? 8

Name _____ Skill _____

Halves

whole

1 out of 2 equal parts is $\frac{1}{2}$ or **one half**.
Two halves make one whole.

▶ **Try These**

Circle the shapes that show halves. Color $\frac{1}{2}$.

1

2

Go to the next side.

Name _____ Skill _____

Practice on Your Own

whole

1 out of 2 equal parts is $\frac{1}{2}$ or
one half. Two halves make
one whole.

Circle the shapes that show halves. Color $\frac{1}{2}$.

1

2

3

▶ **Quiz**

Circle the shapes that show halves. Color $\frac{1}{2}$.

4

5

Skill 37 (top left)

Name _____ Skill _____

Grade 2
Skill 37

Fourths

1 out of 4 equal parts is $\frac{1}{4}$ or **one fourth**.

$\frac{1}{4}$

whole

$\frac{1}{4}$ $\frac{1}{4}$
$\frac{1}{4}$ $\frac{1}{4}$

Four fourths make one whole.

▶ **Try These**

Find the shapes that show fourths. Color $\frac{1}{4}$.

1
2

Go to the next side.

Intervention • Skills **IN197**

Skill 37 (top right)

Name _____ Skill _____

Practice on Your Own   **Skill 37**

| whole | $\frac{1}{2}$ | whole | $\frac{1}{4}$ |

1 out of 2 equal parts is $\frac{1}{2}$ or **one half**.

1 out of 4 equal parts is $\frac{1}{4}$ or **one fourth**.

Color one part. Circle the fraction.

1. $\frac{1}{2}$ $\frac{1}{4}$

2. $\frac{1}{2}$ $\frac{1}{4}$

3. $\frac{1}{2}$ $\frac{1}{4}$

4. $\frac{1}{2}$ $\frac{1}{4}$

5. $\frac{1}{2}$ $\frac{1}{4}$

6. $\frac{1}{2}$ $\frac{1}{4}$

▶ **Quiz**

Color one part. Circle the fraction.

7. $\frac{1}{2}$ $\frac{1}{4}$

8. $\frac{1}{2}$ $\frac{1}{4}$

9. $\frac{1}{2}$ $\frac{1}{4}$

IN198 Intervention • Skills

Skill 38 (bottom left)

Name _____ Skill _____

Grade 2
Skill 38

Thirds

1 out of 3 equal parts is $\frac{1}{3}$ or **one third**.

$\frac{1}{3}$

$\frac{1}{3}$
$\frac{1}{3}$
$\frac{1}{3}$

whole

Three thirds make one whole.

▶ **Try These**

Find the shapes that show thirds. Color $\frac{1}{3}$.

1
2

Go to the next side.

Intervention • Skills **IN201**

Skill 38 (bottom right)

Name _____ Skill _____

Practice on Your Own   **Skill 38**

1 out of 2 equal parts is $\frac{1}{2}$.

1 out of 3 equal parts is $\frac{1}{3}$.

1 out of 4 equal parts is $\frac{1}{4}$.

Color one part. Circle the fraction.

1. $\frac{1}{3}$ $\frac{1}{2}$ $\frac{1}{4}$

2. $\frac{1}{3}$ $\frac{1}{2}$ $\frac{1}{4}$

3. $\frac{1}{3}$ $\frac{1}{2}$ $\frac{1}{4}$

4. $\frac{1}{3}$ $\frac{1}{2}$ $\frac{1}{4}$

5. $\frac{1}{3}$ $\frac{1}{2}$ $\frac{1}{4}$

6. $\frac{1}{3}$ $\frac{1}{2}$ $\frac{1}{4}$

▶ **Quiz**

Color one part. Circle the fraction.

7. $\frac{1}{3}$ $\frac{1}{2}$ $\frac{1}{4}$

8. $\frac{1}{3}$ $\frac{1}{2}$ $\frac{1}{4}$

9. $\frac{1}{3}$ $\frac{1}{2}$ $\frac{1}{4}$

IN202 Intervention • Skills

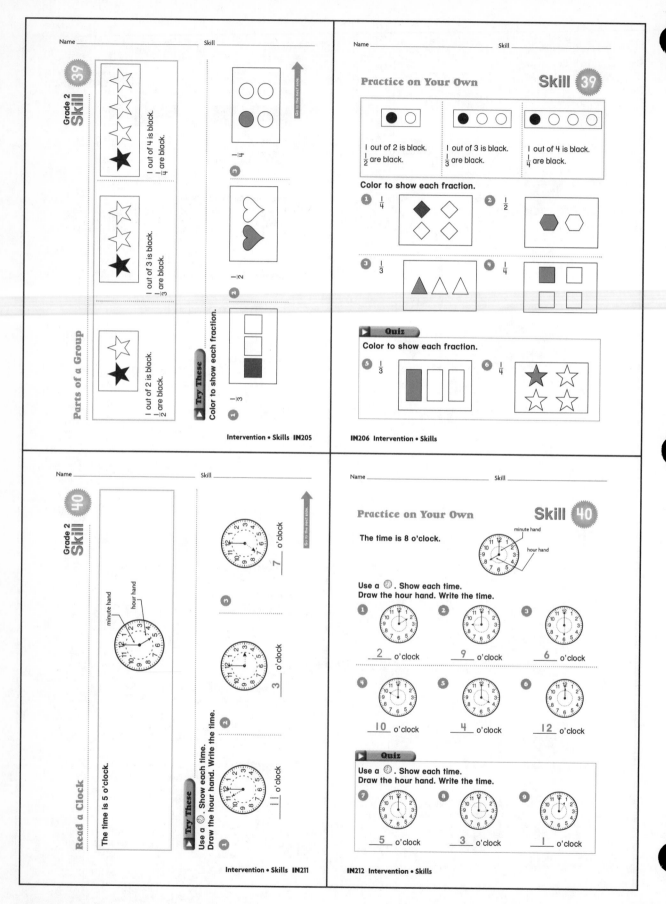

Skill 39 — Parts of a Group (Grade 2)

1 out of 4 is black.
$\frac{1}{4}$ are black.

1 out of 3 is black.
$\frac{1}{3}$ are black.

1 out of 2 is black.
$\frac{1}{2}$ are black.

▶ **Try These**

Color to show each fraction.

1   $\frac{1}{3}$

2   $\frac{1}{2}$

3   $\frac{1}{4}$

Intervention • Skills **IN205**

Practice on Your Own — Skill 39

1 out of 2 is black.
$\frac{1}{2}$ are black.

1 out of 3 is black.
$\frac{1}{3}$ are black.

1 out of 4 is black.
$\frac{1}{4}$ are black.

Color to show each fraction.

1   $\frac{1}{4}$

2   $\frac{1}{2}$

3   $\frac{1}{3}$

4   $\frac{1}{4}$

▶ **Quiz**

Color to show each fraction.

5   $\frac{1}{3}$

6   $\frac{1}{4}$

IN206 Intervention • Skills

Skill 40 — Read a Clock (Grade 2)

The time is 5 o'clock.

minute hand
hour hand

▶ **Try These**

Use a ⊕. Show each time.
Draw the hour hand. Write the time.

1   _____ o'clock

2   3 o'clock

3   7 o'clock

Intervention • Skills **IN211**

Practice on Your Own — Skill 40

The time is 8 o'clock.

minute hand
hour hand

Use a ⊕. Show each time.
Draw the hour hand. Write the time.

1   2 o'clock

2   9 o'clock

3   6 o'clock

4   10 o'clock

5   4 o'clock

6   12 o'clock

▶ **Quiz**

Use a ⊕. Show each time.
Draw the hour hand. Write the time.

7   5 o'clock

8   3 o'clock

9   1 o'clock

IN212 Intervention • Skills

© Harcourt

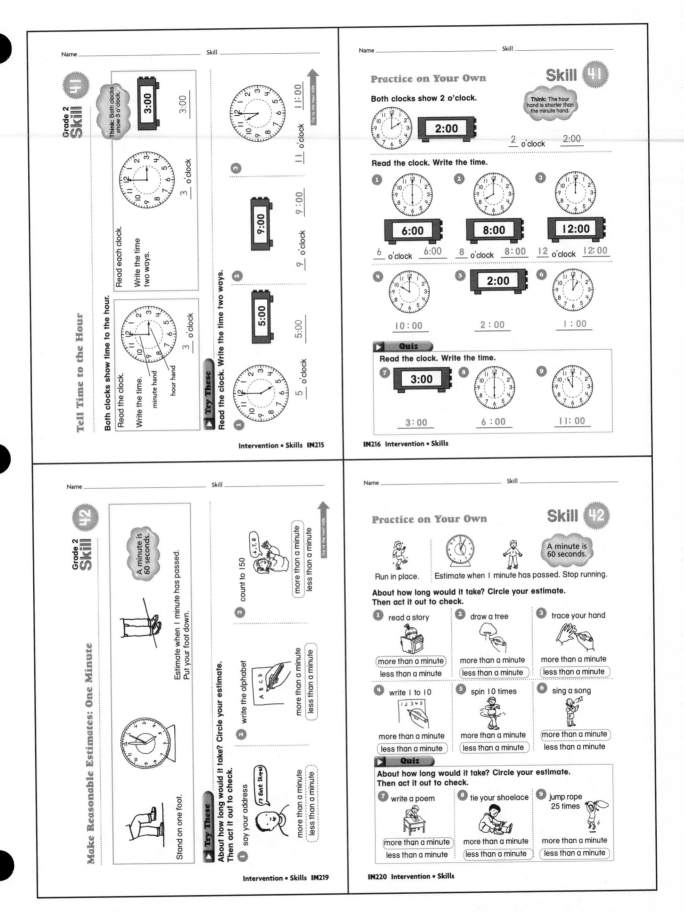

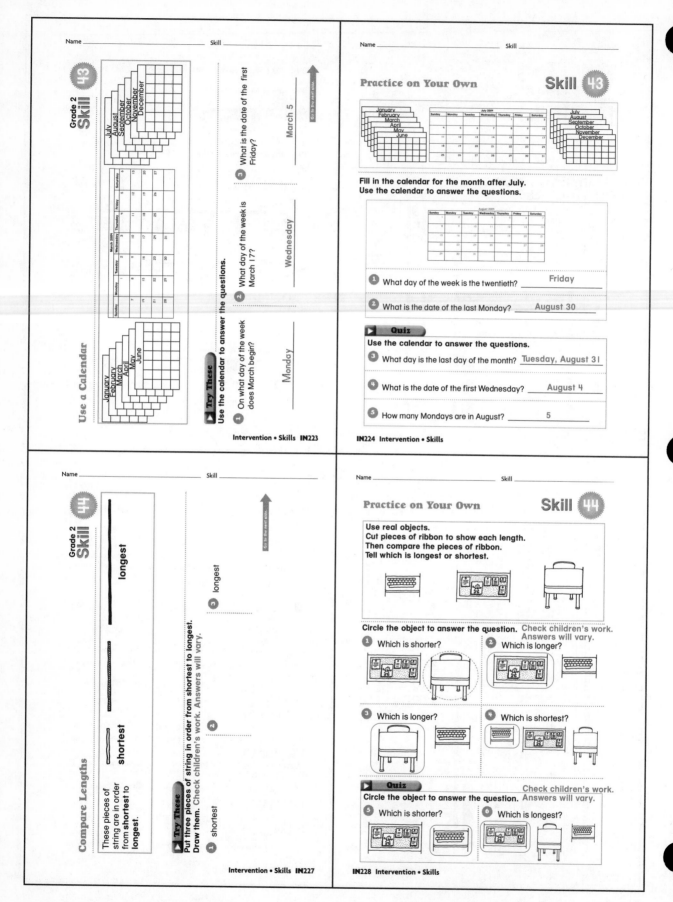

Skill 43 — Grade 2

Use a Calendar

July, August, September, October, November, December

March 2004

January, February, March, April, May, June

Try These
Use the calendar to answer the questions.

1. On what day of the week does March begin? **Monday**

2. What day of the week is March 17? **Wednesday**

3. What is the date of the first Friday? **March 5**

Go to the next side.

Intervention • Skills **IN223**

Practice on Your Own   **Skill 43**

January, February, March, April, May, June   July 2004   July, August, September, October, November, December

Fill in the calendar for the month after July.
Use the calendar to answer the questions.

August 2004

1. What day of the week is the twentieth? **Friday**

2. What is the date of the last Monday? **August 30**

Quiz
Use the calendar to answer the questions.

3. What day is the last day of the month? **Tuesday, August 31**

4. What is the date of the first Wednesday? **August 4**

5. How many Mondays are in August? **5**

IN224 Intervention • Skills

Skill 44 — Grade 2

Compare Lengths

These pieces of string are in order from shortest to longest.

longest

shortest

Try These
Put three pieces of string in order from shortest to longest. Draw them. Check children's work. Answers will vary.

1. shortest

2.

3. longest

Go to the next side.

Intervention • Skills **IN227**

Practice on Your Own   **Skill 44**

Use real objects.
Cut pieces of ribbon to show each length.
Then compare the pieces of ribbon.
Tell which is longest or shortest.

Circle the object to answer the question. Check children's work. Answers will vary.

1. Which is shorter?

2. Which is longer?

3. Which is longer?

4. Which is shortest?

Quiz
Circle the object to answer the question. Check children's work. Answers will vary.

5. Which is shorter?

6. Which is longest?

IN228 Intervention • Skills

© Harcourt

Grade 2 Skill 45
Use Nonstandard Units

Use [ ] to measure long things.

about 9

Use ⊂⊃ to measure short things.

about 3

▲ **Try These**

Choose the unit you would use to measure.
Circle ⊂⊃ or [ ]. Then measure. Check children's work. Answers will vary.

Object | Unit | Measure.

Possible answers

about 4

about 2

Intervention • Skills **IN231**

Practice on Your Own
Skill 45

| Glue | Use ⊂⊃ to measure. Estimate. about _____ ⊂⊃ | Measure. about 2 ⊂⊃ |

Use real objects and ⊂⊃. Estimate. Then measure. Check children's answers. Answers will vary.
Circle the shortest object. Underline the longest object.

Object	Estimate.	Measure.
1	about 4 ⊂⊃	about 5 ⊂⊃
2 Crayons	about _____ ⊂⊃	about _____ ⊂⊃
3 Math	about _____ ⊂⊃	about _____ ⊂⊃

▶ **Quiz** Check children's answers. Answers will vary.
Use real objects and ⊂⊃. Estimate. Then measure.
Circle the shortest object. Underline the longest object.

Object	Estimate.	Measure.
4	about _____ ⊂⊃	about _____ ⊂⊃
5	about _____ ⊂⊃	about _____ ⊂⊃

IN232 Intervention • Skills

Grade 2 Skill 46
Use a Balance

It takes 2 blocks to balance the ball.

It takes a lot of paper clips to balance the ball.

▲ **Try These**

Choose the unit you would use to measure.
Circle ⊂⊃ or ▢. Use _____ to measure each object.
Check children's work. Answers will vary.

Object | Unit | Measure.

Think: It is easier to measure heavy objects using blocks.

about _____

about _____

about _____

Intervention • Skills **IN235**

Practice on Your Own
Skill 46

| It takes 4 blocks to balance the book. | It takes a lot of paper clips to balance the book. |

About how many ⊂⊃ does it take to balance?
Use real objects, a ⟁, and ⊂⊃. Check children's work.
Estimate. Then measure. Answers will vary.

Object	Estimate.	Measure.
1	about _____ ⊂⊃	about _____ ⊂⊃
2	about _____ ⊂⊃	about _____ ⊂⊃

Mark an X on the heaviest object.
Circle the lightest object.

▶ **Quiz**
About how many ⊂⊃ does it take to balance?
Use real objects, a ⟁, and ⊂⊃. Check children's work.
Estimate. Then measure. Answers will vary.

Object	Estimate.	Measure.
3	about _____ ⊂⊃	about _____ ⊂⊃
4	about _____ ⊂⊃	about _____ ⊂⊃
5 ERASER	about _____ ⊂⊃	about _____ ⊂⊃

Mark an X on the heaviest object.
Circle the lightest object.

IN236 Intervention • Skills

© Harcourt

Skill 47

Grade 2

Pounds

This bread weighs about 1 pound.

This bag of potatoes weighs about 5 pounds.

▶ Try These

Look at each object. Circle the better estimate.

Math
1. about 1 pound
   about 5 pounds

2. about 1 pound
   about 10 pounds

3. about 1 pound
   about 10 pounds

Go to the next side.

Practice on Your Own

Skill 47

This bag of sugar weighs about 1 pound.

This bag of apples weighs about 5 pounds.

**Find four items to weigh. Draw them.
Estimate how much each object will weigh.
Then measure.** Check children's work.

Object	Estimate.	Measure.
1	about ____ pounds	about ____ pounds
2	about ____ pounds	about ____ pounds

Circle the heaviest item in blue. Circle the lightest item in red.

▶ Quiz

Object	Estimate.	Measure.
3	about ____ pounds	about ____ pounds
4	about ____ pounds	about ____ pounds

Circle the heaviest item in blue. Circle the lightest item in red.

Skill 48

Grade 2

Use Nonstandard Units to Measure Capacity

Example 1

It took 2 of these scoops to fill the container.

Example 2

It took 4 of these mugs to fill the container.

▶ Try These

Choose the unit you would use to measure. Circle 🥄 or 🍵.
Measure. Check children's work. Answers will vary.

Container	Unit.	Measure.
1		about ____
2		about ____
3		about ____

Go to the next side.

Practice on Your Own

Skill 48

It took 3 of these scoops to fill the container.

It took 8 of these mugs to fill the container.

Use real containers and a 🥄. Check children's work. Answers will vary.

Container	Estimate.	Measure.
1	about ____ 🥄	about ____ 🥄
2	about ____ 🥄	about ____ 🥄
3	about ____ 🥄	about ____ 🥄

▶ Quiz

Use real containers and a 🍵. Check children's work. Answers will vary.

Container	Estimate.	Measure.
4	about ____ 🍵	about ____ 🍵
5	about ____ 🍵	about ____ 🍵

Name ____________ Skill ____________

Grade 2 **Skill 49**

Centimeters

Example 1

Your thumb is about 1 **centimeter** wide.

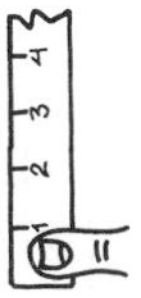

Example 2

This eraser is about 6 **centimeters** long.

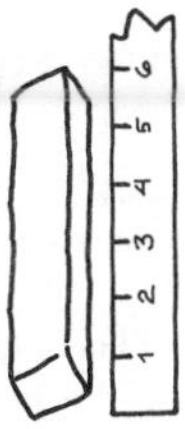

Try These

How many centimeters long is the object? Use a centimeter ruler to measure. Check children's work. Answer will vary.

Object	Measure.
1 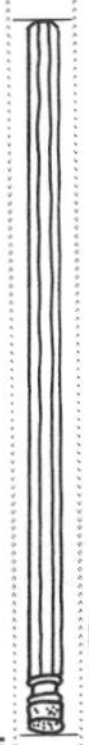	about 19 centimeters
2 	about ___ centimeters

Go to the next side.

Name ____________ Skill ____________

Practice on Your Own — Skill 49

Use real objects and a centimeter ruler. Estimate. Then measure.

Object	Estimate.	Measure.
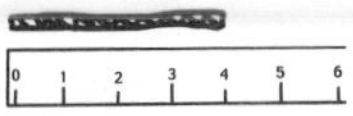	about ___ centimeters	about ___ centimeters

Use real objects and a centimeter ruler. Estimate. Then measure. Check children's work. Answer will vary.

Object	Estimate.	Measure.
1 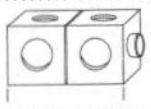	about 3 centimeters	about 4 centimeters
2 	about ___ centimeters	about ___ centimeters
3 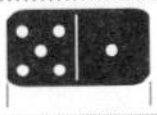	about ___ centimeters	about ___ centimeters

Quiz

Use real objects and a centimeter ruler. Estimate. Then measure. Check children's work. Answer will vary.

Object	Estimate.	Measure.
4 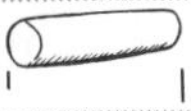	about ___ centimeters	about ___ centimeters
5 	about ___ centimeters	about ___ centimeters

Name ____________ Skill ____________

Grade 2 **Skill 50**

Kilograms

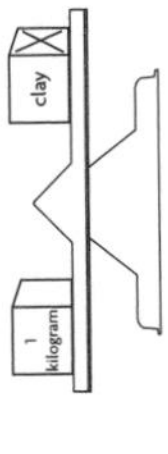

This box of clay is about 1 **kilogram**.

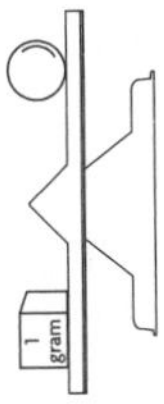

This marble is about 1 **gram**.

Try These

Circle the unit you would use to measure each object. Check children's work.

1 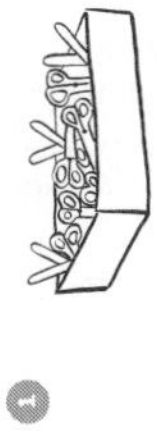 grams / kilograms

2  grams / kilograms

3  grams / kilograms

Go to the next side.

Name ____________ Skill ____________

Practice on Your Own — Skill 50

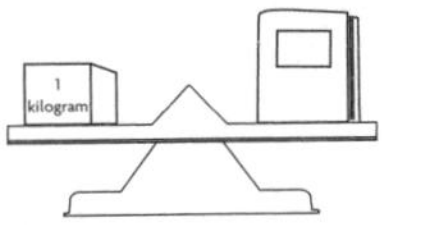

This large book is about 1 **kilogram**.

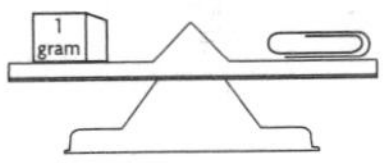

This paper clip is about 1 **gram**.

Estimate how much each object will measure. Use grams or kilograms. Then measure. Check children's work. Answers will vary.

Object	Estimate.	Measure.
1 	about __ kilograms	about __ kilograms
2 	about __ grams	about __ grams
3 	about __ kilograms	about __ kilograms

Quiz Check children's work. Answers will vary.

Estimate how much each object will measure. Use grams or kilograms. Then measure.

Object	Estimate.	Measure.
4 	about __ grams	about __ grams
5 	about __ kilograms	about __ kilograms

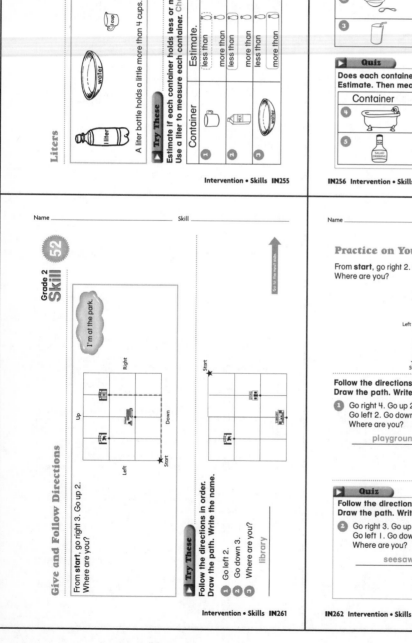

Grade 2
Skill 51

Liters

A liter bottle holds a little more than 4 cups.

A liter bottle holds a little more than 1 quart.

Try These

Estimate if each container holds less or more than a liter. Check children's work.
Use a liter to measure each container.

Container	Estimate.	Measure.
1	less than / more than	less than / more than
2	less than / more than	less than / more than
3	less than / more than	less than / more than

Go to the next side. →

Practice on Your Own
Skill 51

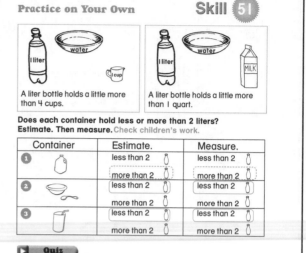

A liter bottle holds a little more than 4 cups.

A liter bottle holds a little more than 1 quart.

Does each container hold less or more than 2 liters?
Estimate. Then measure. Check children's work.

Container	Estimate.	Measure.
1	less than 2 / more than 2	less than 2 / more than 2
2	less than 2 / more than 2	less than 2 / more than 2
3	less than 2 / more than 2	less than 2 / more than 2

Quiz

Does each container hold less or more than 2 liters?
Estimate. Then measure. Check children's work.

Container	Estimate.	Measure.
4	less than 2 / more than 2	less than 2 / more than 2
5	less than 2 / more than 2	less than 2 / more than 2

Grade 2
Skill 52

Give and Follow Directions

From **start**, go right 3. Go up 2.
Where are you?

I'm at the park.

Try These

Follow the directions in order.
Draw the path. Write the name.

1. Go left 2.
2. Go down 3.
   Where are you?

   library

Go to the next side. →

Practice on Your Own
Skill 52

From **start**, go right 2. Go up 1.
Where are you?

I'm at the school.

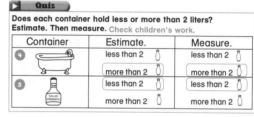

Follow the directions in order.
Draw the path. Write the name.

1. Go right 4. Go up 2.
   Go left 2. Go down 1.
   Where are you?

   playground

Quiz

Follow the directions in order.
Draw the path. Write the name.

2. Go right 3. Go up 2.
   Go left 1. Go down 1.
   Where are you?

   seesaw

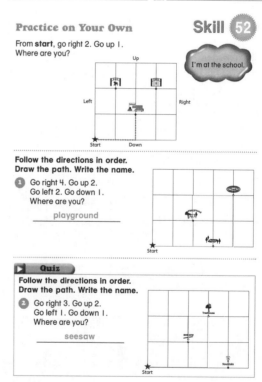

© Harcourt

Grade 2 Skill 53

Plane Shapes on Solid Figures

circle   square   triangle   square   rectangle   square

Try These

Use solids. Trace around each one.
Write the name of the shape you drew. Check children's work.

circle

square

triangle; square

Go to the next side.

Practice on Your Own   Skill 53

circle   square   triangle   square   rectangle   square

Use solids. Trace around each one.
Write the name of the shape you drew. Check children's work.

1. square; rectangle
2. triangle; square
3. circle
4. square

Quiz

Use solids. Trace around each one.
Write the name of the shape you drew. Check children's work.

5. triangle; square
6. rectangle; square

Grade 2 Skill 54

Sort and Identify Plane Shapes

square   triangle   circle   rectangle

Sort plane shapes by the number
of sides and vertices.
Find how many sides on a triangle.
Find how many vertices.

Step 1
Trace the sides.
Circle the vertices.

1 vertex
1 side

Step 2
Trace the sides.
Circle the vertices.
Write how many.

1 vertex   1 side
1 side   1 vertex
1 vertex   1 side

3 sides
3 vertices

Try These   Check children's work.

Draw the shape. Write how many sides.
Write how many vertices.

1. rectangle
   4 sides 4 vertices
2. square
   4 sides 4 vertices
3. circle
   0 sides 0 vertices

Go to the next side.

Practice on Your Own   Skill 54

hexagon   parallelogram   pentagon   trapezoid

Use a small X to cross out each side. Circle each vertex.
Write how many sides and vertices there are. Check children's work.

1. 4 sides 4 vertices
2. 5 sides 5 vertices

Quiz   Check children's work.

Use a small X to cross out each side. Circle each vertex.
Write how many sides and vertices there are.

3. 6 sides 6 vertices
4. 3 sides 3 vertices
5. 4 sides 4 vertices
6. 0 sides 0 vertices

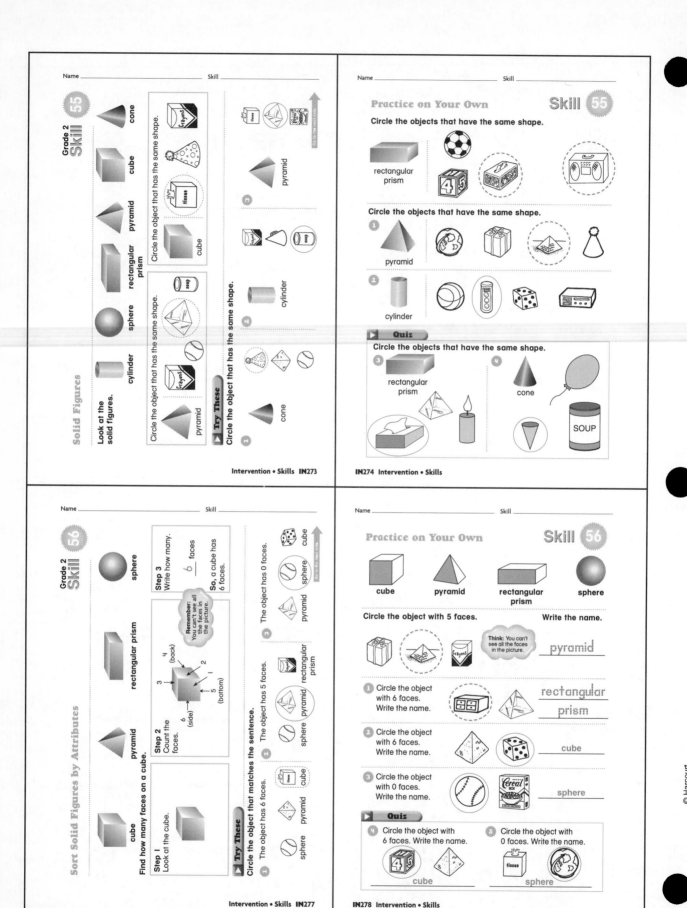

Grade 2
Skill 57

Symmetry

1. Fold your paper.

2. Start at the fold. Draw a shape.

3. Cut along the line.

4. Open your shape.

5. Draw a line down the middle.

The line down the middle is called a **line of symmetry**. The two parts should match.

Try These

Draw a line of symmetry to make two matching parts.
Possible answers are given for Exercises 1–3.

Go to the next skill.

Practice on Your Own
Skill 57

1. Fold your paper.

2. Start at the fold. Draw a shape.

3. Cut along the line.

Think:
The line down the middle is called a line of symmetry.

4. Open your shape.

5. Draw a line down the middle.

The two parts match.

Draw a line of symmetry to make two matching parts.
Possible answers are given.

1   2   3

4   5   6

Quiz   Possible answer is given for Exercise 8.

Draw a line of symmetry to make two matching parts.

7   8   9

Grade 2
Skill 58

Slides and Turns

You can move the rectangle.

You can **slide**.

You can **turn**.

Try These

Circle *slide* **or** *turn* **to name the move.**

1   slide   turn

2   slide   turn

3   slide   turn

Go to the next skill.

Practice on Your Own
Skill 58

You can move the triangle.

You can **slide**.

You can **turn**.

Circle *slide* **or** *turn* **to name the move.**

1   slide   turn

2   slide   turn

3   slide   turn

4   slide   turn

Quiz

Circle *slide* **or** *turn* **to name the move.**

5   slide   turn

6   slide   turn

© Harcourt

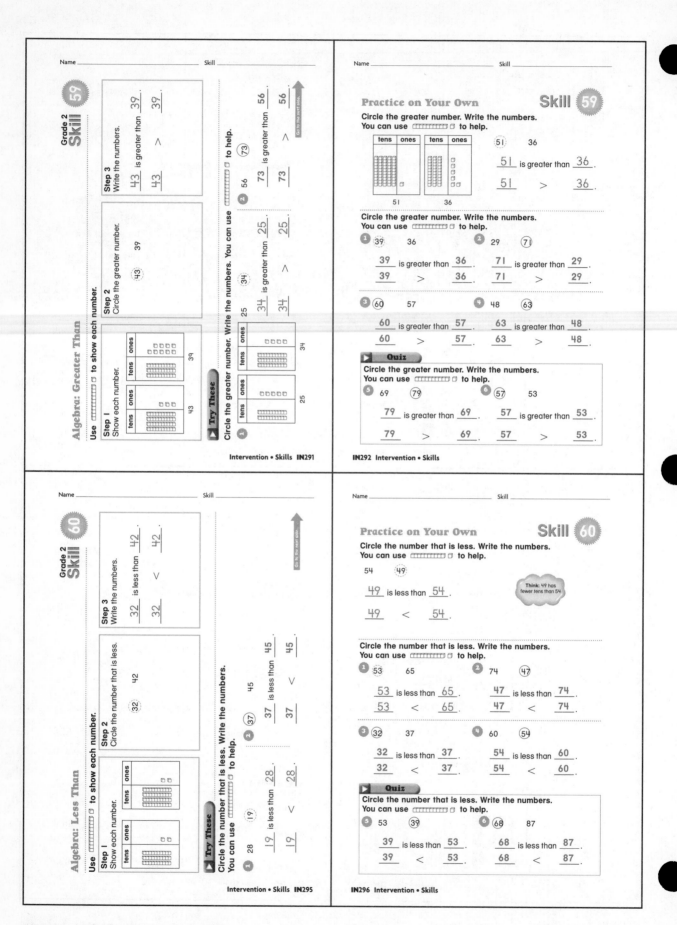

Skill 59

Grade 2

Algebra: Greater Than

Use ▭▭▭▭ ▱ **to show each number.**

Step 1
Show each number.

tens	ones

43

tens	ones

39

Step 2
Circle the greater number.

(43)   39

Step 3
Write the numbers.

43 is greater than 39.

43 > 39

▶ **Try These**

Circle the greater number. Write the numbers. You can use ▭▭▭▭ ▱ to help.

1

tens	ones

34

tens	ones

25

(34)   25

34 is greater than 25.

34 > 25

2 56   (73)

73 is greater than 56.

73 > 56

Go to the next side. ↑

Intervention • Skills **IN291**

Practice on Your Own

Skill 59

Circle the greater number. Write the numbers.
You can use ▭▭▭▭ ▱ to help.

tens	ones

51

tens	ones

36

(51)   36

51 is greater than 36.

51 > 36

Circle the greater number. Write the numbers.
You can use ▭▭▭▭ ▱ to help.

1 (39)   36

39 is greater than 36.

39 > 36

2 29   (71)

71 is greater than 29.

71 > 29

3 (60)   57

60 is greater than 57.

60 > 57

4 48   (63)

63 is greater than 48.

63 > 48

▶ **Quiz**

Circle the greater number. Write the numbers.
You can use ▭▭▭▭ ▱ to help.

5 69   (79)

79 is greater than 69.

79 > 69

6 (57)   53

57 is greater than 53.

57 > 53

IN292 Intervention • Skills

Skill 60

Grade 2

Algebra: Less Than

Use ▭▭▭▭ ▱ **to show each number.**

Step 1
Show each number.

tens	ones

tens	ones

Step 2
Circle the number that is less.

(32)   42

Step 3
Write the numbers.

32 is less than 42.

32 < 42

▶ **Try These**

Circle the number that is less. Write the numbers.
You can use ▭▭▭▭ ▱ to help.

1 28   (19)

19 is less than 28.

19 < 28

2 (37)   45

37 is less than 45.

37 < 45

Go to the next side. ↑

Intervention • Skills **IN295**

Practice on Your Own

Skill 60

Circle the number that is less. Write the numbers.
You can use ▭▭▭▭ ▱ to help.

54   (49)

49 is less than 54.

49 < 54

Think: 49 has fewer tens than 54

Circle the number that is less. Write the numbers.
You can use ▭▭▭▭ ▱ to help.

1 (53)   65

53 is less than 65.

53 < 65

2 74   (47)

47 is less than 74.

47 < 74

3 (32)   37

32 is less than 37.

32 < 37

4 60   (54)

54 is less than 60.

54 < 60

▶ **Quiz**

Circle the number that is less. Write the numbers.
You can use ▭▭▭▭ ▱ to help.

5 53   (39)

39 is less than 53.

39 < 53

6 (68)   87

68 is less than 87.

68 < 87

IN296 Intervention • Skills

© Harcourt

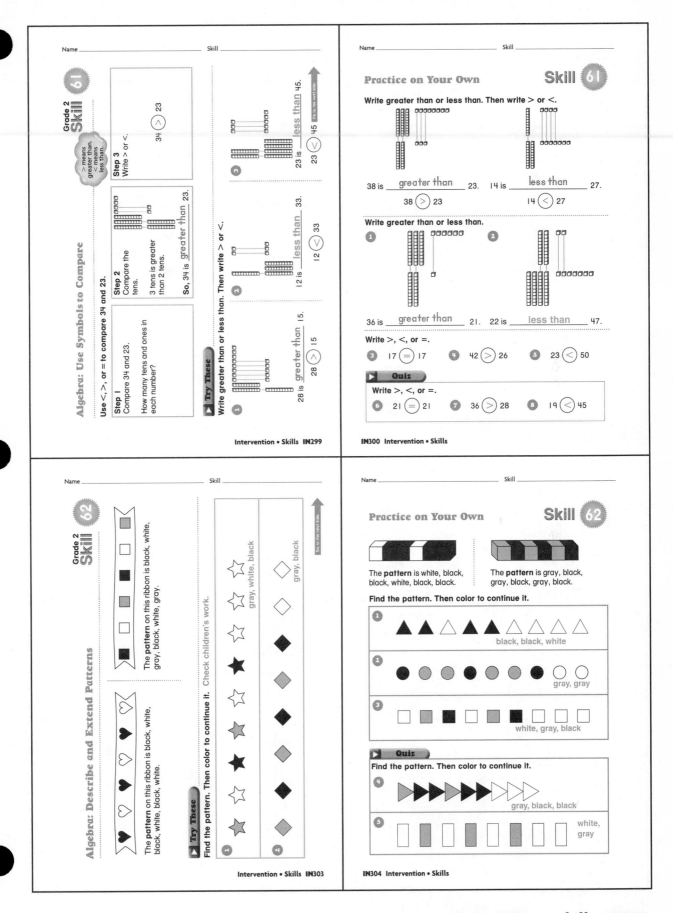

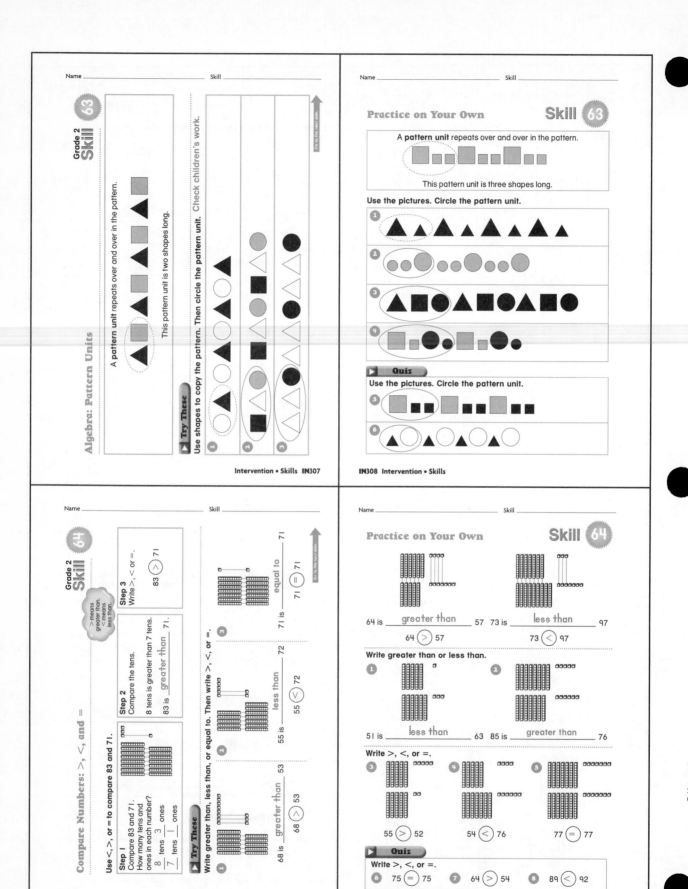

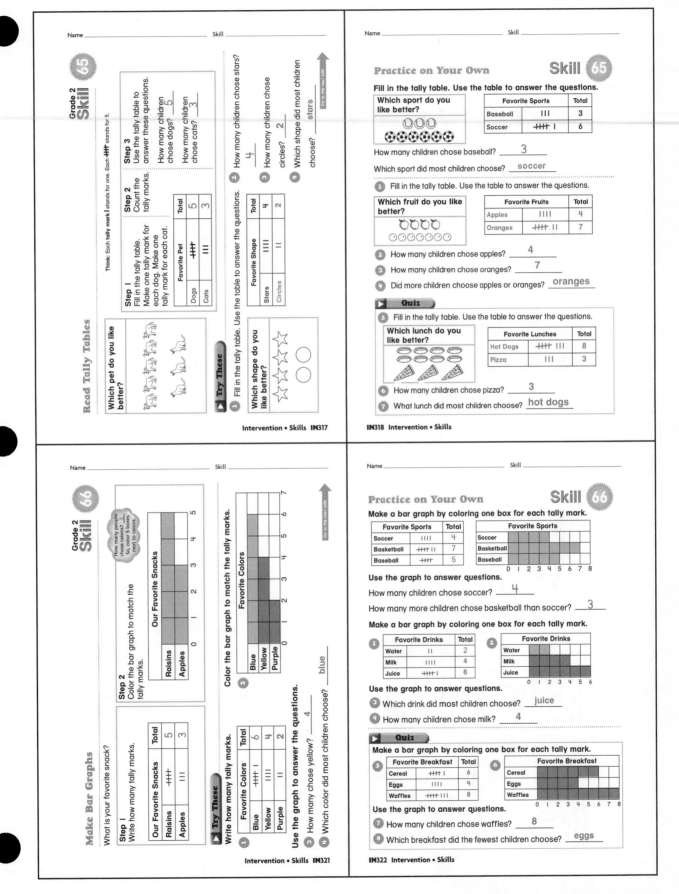

Grade 2 Skill 65 — Read Tally Tables

Think: Each tally mark | stands for one. Each ╫ stands for 5.

Which pet do you like better?

Step 1
Fill in the tally table. Make one tally mark for each dog. Make one tally mark for each cat.

Favorite Pet		Total
Dogs	╫	5
Cats	|||	3

Step 2
Count the tally marks.

Step 3
Use the tally table to answer these questions.

How many children chose dogs? 5

How many children chose cats? 3

Try These

1. Fill in the tally table. Use the table to answer the questions.

Which shape do you like better?
☆ ☆ ☆ ○ ○

Favorite Shape		Total
Stars	||||	4
Circles	||	2

2. How many children chose stars? 4

3. How many children chose circles? 2

4. Which shape did most children choose? stars

Go to the next side.

Intervention • Skills **IN317**

Practice on Your Own — Skill 65

Fill in the tally table. Use the table to answer the questions.

Which sport do you like better?

Favorite Sports		Total
Baseball	|||	3
Soccer	╫		6

How many children chose baseball? 3

Which sport did most children choose? soccer

1. Fill in the tally table. Use the table to answer the questions.

Which fruit do you like better?

Favorite Fruits		Total
Apples	||||	4
Oranges	╫ ||	7

2. How many children chose apples? 4

3. How many children chose oranges? 7

4. Did more children choose apples or oranges? oranges

Quiz

5. Fill in the tally table. Use the table to answer the questions.

Which lunch do you like better?

Favorite Lunches		Total
Hot Dogs	╫ |||	8
Pizza	|||	3

6. How many children chose pizza? 3

7. What lunch did most children choose? hot dogs

IN318 Intervention • Skills

Grade 2 Skill 66 — Make Bar Graphs

What is your favorite snack?

Step 1
Write how many tally marks.

Our Favorite Snacks		Total
Raisins	╫	5
Apples	|||	3

How many people chose raisins? 5 So, color 5 boxes next to raisins.

Step 2
Color the bar graph to match the tally marks.

Our Favorite Snacks

Raisins
Apples
0 1 2 3 4 5

Try These

1. Write how many tally marks.

Favorite Colors		Total
Blue	╫		6
Yellow	||||	4
Purple	||	2

2. Color the bar graph to match the tally marks.

Favorite Colors

Blue
Yellow
Purple
0 1 2 3 4 5 6 7

Use the graph to answer the questions.

3. How many chose yellow? 4

4. Which color did most children choose? blue

Go to the next side.

Intervention • Skills **IN321**

Practice on Your Own — Skill 66

Make a bar graph by coloring one box for each tally mark.

Favorite Sports		Total
Soccer	||||	4
Basketball	╫ ||	7
Baseball	╫	5

Favorite Sports

Soccer
Basketball
Baseball
0 1 2 3 4 5 6 7 8

Use the graph to answer questions.

How many children chose soccer? 4

How many more children chose basketball than soccer? 3

Make a bar graph by coloring one box for each tally mark.

1.
Favorite Drinks		Total
Water	||	2
Milk	||||	4
Juice	╫		6

2. **Favorite Drinks**

Water
Milk
Juice
0 1 2 3 4 5 6

Use the graph to answer questions.

3. Which drink did most children choose? juice

4. How many children chose milk? 4

Quiz

Make a bar graph by coloring one box for each tally mark.

5.
Favorite Breakfast		Total
Cereal	╫		6
Eggs	||||	4
Waffles	╫ |||	8

6. **Favorite Breakfast**

Cereal
Eggs
Waffles
0 1 2 3 4 5 6 7 8

Use the graph to answer questions.

7. How many children chose waffles? 8

8. Which breakfast did the fewest children choose? eggs

IN322 Intervention • Skills

© Harcourt

Grade 2 — Skill 67

Use Data From a Bar Graph

Did the Lions win more games than all the other teams?
Ben made a **bar graph** to compare the number of games.
He shaded a box for each game a team won.
Each shaded bar stands for the total number of games a team won.

The Lions did not win more games than all the other teams.

8 games

Sharks

Chargers

Number of Games Won — Teams: Lions, Chargers, Jays, Sharks, Rockets — 0 1 2 3 4 5 6 7 8 9 10 — Number of Games

▲ Try These

Use the bar graph to answer the questions.

1. How many games did the Lions win?
2. Which team won the same number of games as the Jays?
3. Which team won the most games?

Intervention • Skills IN325

Practice on Your Own — Skill 67

Ben thinks he watched fewer hours of TV than his friends did last week.
He made a **bar graph** to compare the number of hours.
Ben shaded a box for each hour of TV watched.
Each bar stands for the number of hours a child watched TV.

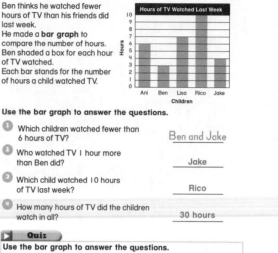

Hours of TV Watched Last Week — Hours 0–10 — Children: Ani, Ben, Lisa, Rico, Jake

Use the bar graph to answer the questions.

1. Which children watched fewer than 6 hours of TV? — Ben and Jake
2. Who watched TV 1 hour more than Ben did? — Jake
3. Which child watched 10 hours of TV last week? — Rico
4. How many hours of TV did the children watch in all? — 30 hours

▶ Quiz

Use the bar graph to answer the questions.

5. How many hours of TV did Ben watch? — 3 hours
6. How many more hours of TV did Lisa watch than Jake? — 3 more hours
7. Which children watched more than 5 hours of TV last week? — Ani, Lisa, Rico

IN326 Intervention • Skills

Grade 2 — Skill 68

Interpret Data

Jake's class made a graph to show the number of hours of TV they watched yesterday.

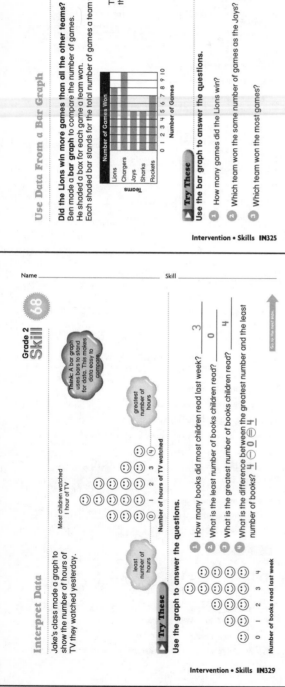

Think: A bar graph uses bars to stand for data. This makes data easy to compare.

Most children watched 1 hour of TV

greatest number of hours

least number of hours

Number of hours of TV watched — 0 1 2 3 4

▲ Try These

Use the graph to answer the questions.

1. How many books did most children read last week? — 3
2. What is the least number of books children read? — 0
3. What is the greatest number of books children read? — 4
4. What is the difference between the greatest number and the least number of books? — $4 \ominus 0 = 4$

Number of books read last week — 0 1 2 3 4

Intervention • Skills IN329

Practice on Your Own — Skill 68

Ann's class made a graph to show the number of hours they spent doing homework yesterday.

Most children spent 3 hours doing homework.

least number of hours

greatest number of hours

Number of hours spent doing homework — 0 1 2 3 4

Use the graph to answer the questions.

1. How many glasses of water did most children drink? — 3
2. What is the least number of glasses of water children drank? — 1
3. What is the greatest number of glasses of water children drank? — 4
4. What is the difference between the greatest number and the least number of glasses of water drank? — $4 \ominus 1 = 3$

Number of glasses of water — 0 1 2 3 4

▶ Quiz

Use the graph to answer the questions.

5. How many pets do most children have? — 2
6. What is the least number of pets children have? — 0
7. What is the greatest number of pets children have? — 4
8. What is the difference between the greatest number and the least number of pets? — $4 \ominus 0 = 4$

Number of pets — 0 1 2 3 4

IN330 Intervention • Skills

© Harcourt

Grade 2 Skill 69

Certain or Impossible

Anna is going to pull a marble from bag B.

The marble she pulls is **certain** to be white.

Pulling a black marble from that bag is **impossible**.

A   B   C

▶ Try These

X to tell if it is certain or impossible to pull that marble from the bag.

	Certain	Impossible
1 Pull a ●	X	
2 Pull a ○		X
3 Pull a ○	X	

Go to the next task.

Practice on Your Own   Skill 69

A   B   C

It is **certain** that a gray marble can be pulled from bag A.   It is **impossible** to pull a white marble from that bag.

X to tell if it is certain or impossible to pull that marble from the bag.

	Certain	Impossible
1 Pull a ●		X
2 Pull a ○	X	
3 Pull a ●		X

▶ Quiz

X to tell if it is certain or impossible to pull that marble from the bag.

	Certain	Impossible
4 Pull a ●		X
5 Pull a ●	X	

Check What You Know

Enrichment

Secret Numbers

Fill in the missing numbers.

1. _3_ , ____, 5, 6, ☐ , 8, ____

2. ____, 17, ____, ____, 20, 21, ☐

3. 51, ____, ____, 54, 55, ☐ , ____

4. ☐ , 34, ____, 36, ____, ____, 39

5. 89, ____, 91, ____, ____, 94, ☐

6. 44, 45, ☐ , 47, ____, ____, 50

T = 7	H = 22	R = 33	Y = 46	E = 50
I = 56	A = 69	G = 70	T = 95	K = 98

Match the numbers in the boxes to the letters.
Write the letters on the lines below to find the hidden word.

____   ____   ____   ____   ____   ____
1.   2.   3.   4.   5.   6.

Fishing for Pairs

Read the numbers.
Write the letter of the picture that matches the words.

6 tens and 5 ones G	A	5 tens and 3 ones ___	B
2 tens ___	C	4 tens and 1 one ___	D
3 tens and 2 ones ___	E	6 tens and 8 ones ___	F
8 tens ___	G	3 tens ___	H
1 ten and 4 ones ___	I	4 tens ___	J

© Harcourt

● Number Mix-Up

The shirts for three teams are mixed up.

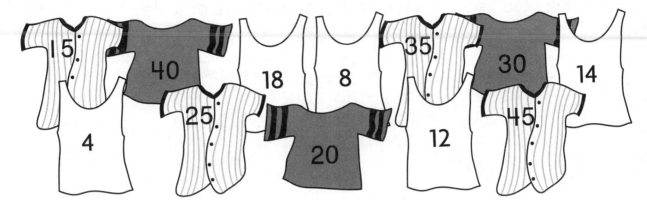

Put the shirts in order from least to greatest.

1. 2, 3, ___4___, 5, 6, 7, _____, 9,

 10, 11, _____, 13, _____, _____, 16, 17, _____, 19,

● _____, 21, 22, 23, 24, _____, 26, 27, 28, 29,

 _____, 31, 32, 33, 34, _____, 36, 37, 38, 39,

 _____, 41, 42, 43, 44, _____, 46, 47, 48, 49

Skip-count by twos, fives, or tens to find the numbers
on each team's shirts.

2. TEAM 1:

 5, 10, _____, 20, _____, 30, _____, 40, _____

3. TEAM 2:

 10, _____, _____, _____, 50, 60, 70, 80, 90

4. TEAM 3:

● 2, _____, 6, _____, 10, _____, _____, 16, _____

True or False Skip Counting

Follow the directions below. Cover the numbers with beans as you count. Read each question. Then circle true or false.

1	2	3	4	5	6	7	8	9	10
11	12	13	14	15	16	17	18	19	20
21	22	23	24	25	26	27	28	29	30
31	32	33	34	35	36	37	38	39	40
41	42	43	44	45	46	47	48	49	50
51	52	53	54	55	56	57	58	59	60
61	62	63	64	65	66	67	68	69	70
71	72	73	74	75	76	77	78	79	80
81	82	83	84	85	86	87	88	89	90
91	92	93	94	95	96	97	98	99	100

1. Skip count by 2's.
   All the even numbers are covered.   (true)   false

2. Skip count by 5's.
   Only numbers ending with 5's are covered.   true   false

3. Skip count by 10's.
   Even and odd numbers are covered.   true   false

4. Skip count by 5's.
   All numbers ending in zero are covered.   true   false

© Harcourt

Name _____

What Animal Am I?

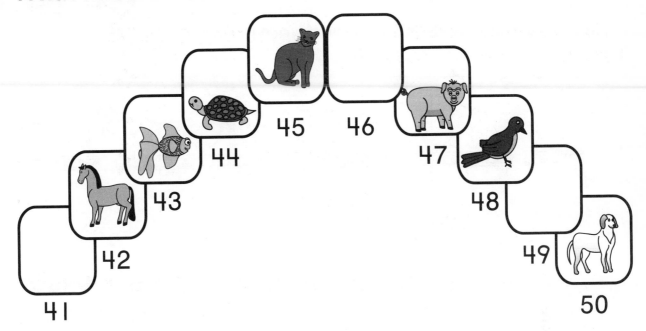

41   42   43   44   45   46   47   48   49   50

Circle the correct answer.

1. I am < 45.

2. I am = 43.

3. I am > 48.

4. I am < 49.

5. I am > 44.

6. I am = 42.

Color all the animal boxes that are circled.

What animal is left? _____

© Harcourt

Name _____

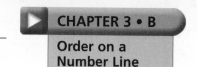
Lucky Duck Factory

Write the missing number on the duck that is
just before, between, or just after.

1.

6   7   8   9

2.

67   69   71

3.

93   94

4.

31   33

5.

77   79

6.

58   62

© Harcourt

Name _____

● Playground Picture Graphs

● 1. Sort the playground activities.
Color the children swinging red.
Color the children jumping rope blue.
Color the children on the slide green.

2. Use the picture to fill in the picture graph.
Draw 1 ⚲ for every child.

Playground Activities	
(swings)	
(jump rope)	
(slide)	

● © Harcourt

Name _____

Charting Colors

Which color do your classmates like best?
Fill in the tally table to show their answers.

blue	red	black	green	purple	orange

Use the tally table to fill in the graph.

Favorite Colors

Colors

blue	
red	
black	
green	
purple	
orange	

0   1   2   3   4   5   6   7   8   9   10

Number of Votes

Use the graph to answer the questions.

1. What is the favorite color of the most children? _____

2. What is the favorite color of the fewest children? _____

3. How many children in all like green best? _____

4. How many children in all like red best? _____

● Count Dot-to-Dot

Use the number line to count on.
Then connect the dots in order from least to greatest.

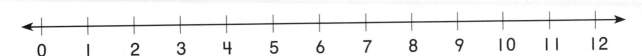

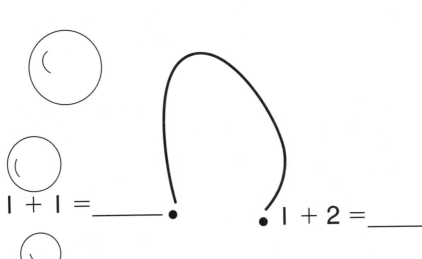

$1 + 1 =$ _____ • • $1 + 2 =$ _____

$0 + 1 =$ _____ $3 + 2 =$ _____

•**Start** ● $3 + 1 =$ _____ •

$3 + 3 =$ _____ •

• $7 + 3 =$ _____ $6 + 2 =$ _____

$8 + 1 =$ _____ $4 + 3 =$ _____

Name _____

Adding in Circles

Start at the top number.
Follow the arrows to add.
Write the sum.

1.

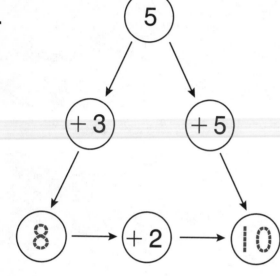

2.

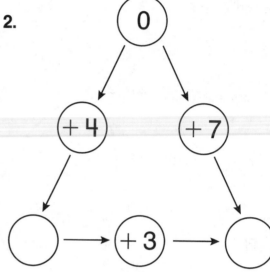

3.

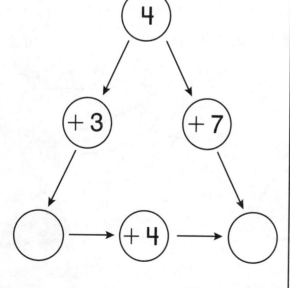

4.

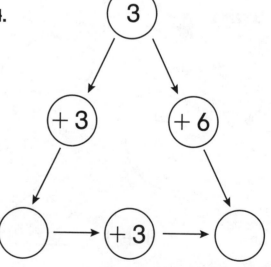

© Harcourt

IN382 Check What You Know Enrichment

Name _____

● Fact Match

Add and subtract.
Color the addition fact red.
Color the related subtraction fact blue.

1. $4 + 5 = \underline{9}$
   red

   $9 - 4 = \underline{5}$
   blue

   $4 - 3 = \underline{1}$

2. $6 - 3 = \underline{}$

   $3 - 3 = \underline{}$

   $3 + 3 = \underline{}$

3. $4 - 1 = \underline{}$

   $5 - 1 = \underline{}$

   $1 + 4 = \underline{}$

4. $7 - 3 = \underline{}$

   $5 - 2 = \underline{}$

   $2 + 3 = \underline{}$

Check What You Know Enrichment IN383

Name _____

Math Path

Use the number line to count back.
Then connect the 3's to find the path out of the maze.

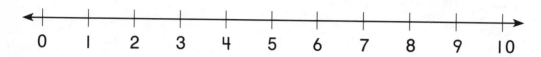

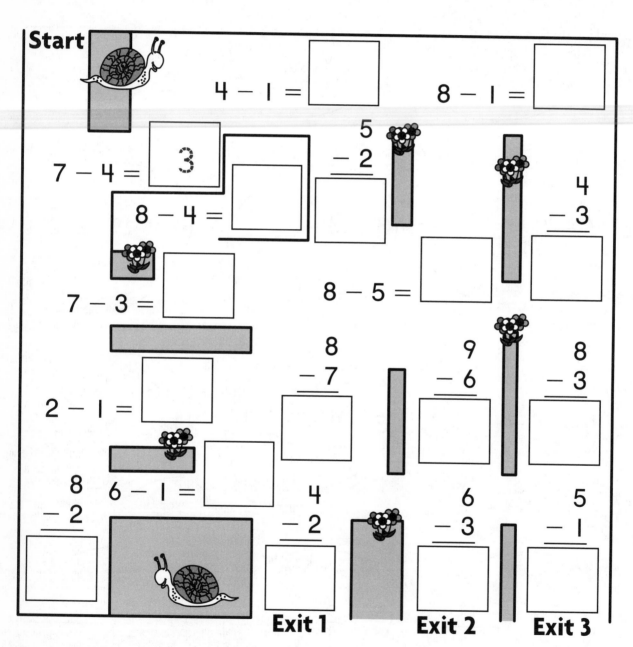

Start

4 − 1 = ☐

8 − 1 = ☐

7 − 4 = ☐ **3**

8 − 4 = ☐

5
− 2
‾‾‾‾
☐

4
− 3
‾‾‾‾
☐

7 − 3 = ☐

8 − 5 = ☐

2 − 1 = ☐

8
− 7
‾‾‾‾
☐

9
− 6
‾‾‾‾
☐

8
− 3
‾‾‾‾
☐

8
− 2
‾‾‾‾
☐

6 − 1 = ☐

4
− 2
‾‾‾‾
☐

6
− 3
‾‾‾‾
☐

5
− 1
‾‾‾‾
☐

Exit 1   **Exit 2**   **Exit 3**

What exit did you use? _____

© Harcourt

Name _____

Number Puzzle

Write the number.
Then write the number in the boxes to complete the puzzle.

1. | **Down**

eleven _____

4. | **Across** _____

2. | **Down** _____

5. | **Across** _____

3. | **Down** _____

6. | **Down** _____

eleven

twelve

thirteen

fourteen

fifteen

sixteen

seventeen

eighteen

nineteen

twenty

Check What You Know Enrichment IN385

Name _____

What's Missing?

Find the missing numbers.
Add across and down.

1.

10	20	30
30		40
	30	

2.

		60
20	12	
60	32	

3.

	4	
9		15
13		23

4.

12		42
	20	
22	50	

5.

3		9
	4	
11		21

6.

20		30
	20	
50	30	

IN386 Check What You Know Enrichment

Name _____

Secret Path

Add. Regroup if you need to.
Color the boxes where you regrouped
to find the path out of the maze.

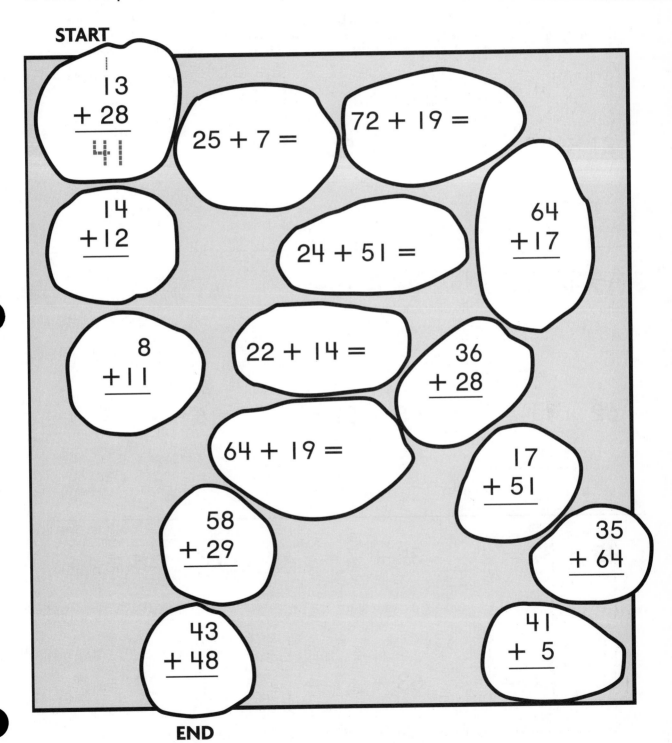

START

$$\begin{array}{r} 1\ 3 \\ +\ 28 \\ \hline 41 \end{array}$$

$$25 + 7 =$$

$$72 + 19 =$$

$$\begin{array}{r} 1\ 4 \\ +12 \\ \hline \end{array}$$

$$24 + 51 =$$

$$\begin{array}{r} 64 \\ +17 \\ \hline \end{array}$$

$$\begin{array}{r} 8 \\ +11 \\ \hline \end{array}$$

$$22 + 14 =$$

$$\begin{array}{r} 36 \\ +\ 28 \\ \hline \end{array}$$

$$64 + 19 =$$

$$\begin{array}{r} 17 \\ +\ 51 \\ \hline \end{array}$$

$$\begin{array}{r} 58 \\ +\ 29 \\ \hline \end{array}$$

$$\begin{array}{r} 35 \\ +\ 64 \\ \hline \end{array}$$

$$\begin{array}{r} 43 \\ +\ 48 \\ \hline \end{array}$$

$$\begin{array}{r} 4\ 1 \\ +\ 5 \\ \hline \end{array}$$

END

© Harcourt

Addition Pairs

Add.
Circle the addition sentences that have the same sum.

1. $54 + 27 = \underline{81}$ $12 + 49 = \underline{\hphantom{00}}$ $71 + 16 = \underline{\hphantom{00}}$

   $21 + 40 = \underline{\hphantom{00}}$ $16 + 56 = \underline{\hphantom{00}}$ $18 + 7 = \underline{\hphantom{00}}$

2. $17 + 34 = \underline{\hphantom{00}}$ $81 + 12 = \underline{\hphantom{00}}$ $61 + 9 = \underline{\hphantom{00}}$

   $62 + 11 = \underline{\hphantom{00}}$ $43 + 22 = \underline{\hphantom{00}}$ $26 + 44 = \underline{\hphantom{00}}$

3. $45 + 37 = \underline{\hphantom{00}}$ $34 + 7 = \underline{\hphantom{00}}$ $73 + 24 = \underline{\hphantom{00}}$

   $68 + 21 = \underline{\hphantom{00}}$ $63 + 19 = \underline{\hphantom{00}}$ $41 + 27 = \underline{\hphantom{00}}$

© Harcourt

Name _____

What Number Am I?

Read the clue.
Write the number sentence.
Circle the answer to the question.

1. If you subtract me from 11, the difference is 4. What number am I?

11 ◯— ⦅7⦆ ◯= 4

2. If you subtract 20 from me, the answer is 40. What number am I?

___ ◯ ___ ◯ ___

3. What number will you have if you subtract 20 from 70?

___ ◯ ___ ◯ ___

4. If you subtract 8 from me, the difference is 4. What number am I?

___ ◯ ___ ◯ ___

5. If you subtract 10 from me, the answer is 10. What number am I?

___ ◯ ___ ◯ ___

6. What number will you have if you subtract 50 from 90?

___ ◯ ___ ◯ ___

7. What number will you have if you subtract 9 from 17?

___ ◯ ___ ◯ ___

8. If you subtract 5 from me, the difference is 1. What number am I?

___ ◯ ___ ◯ ___

Check What You Know Enrichment IN389

How Many Are Left?

Store Item	Number on Shelf	Number Sold
cereal	46	4
milk	23	3
apples	57	30
crackers	84	40
juice	27	5

Use the table to write a subtraction sentence.
Find out how many items are left in the store.

1. cereal   46 − 4 = 42

2. milk   ____ − ____ = ____

3. apples   ____ − ____ = ____

4. crackers   ____ − ____ = ____

5. juice   ____ − ____ = ____

Name _____

Subtraction Riddle

Subtract.
Then match each answer to the letter.

1. 18 − 4 = 14

2. 26 − 9

3. 46 − 14

4. 75 − 14

5. 64 − 5

6. 45 − 4

7. 32 − 26

8. 67 − 48

9. 57 − 32

10. 17 − 14

11. 84 − 56

12. 79 − 53

13. 37 − 24

14. 47 − 38

15. 71 − 59

16. 62 − 16

3 = u	6 = o	9 = R	12 = e	13 = s	14 = T	17 = y	19 = s
25 = a	26 = u	28 = r	32 = r	41 = n	46 = x	59 = n	61 = a

What was the name of a dinosaur's dog?

1.	2.	3.	4.	5.	6.	7.	8.	9.	10.	11.	12.	13.		14.	15.	16.

© Harcourt

Check What You Know Enrichment IN391

Name _____

Compare Differences

Subtract.
Color the balloons.
Color differences between 0 and 30 red.
Color differences between 31 and 60 blue.
Color differences between 61 and 90 green.

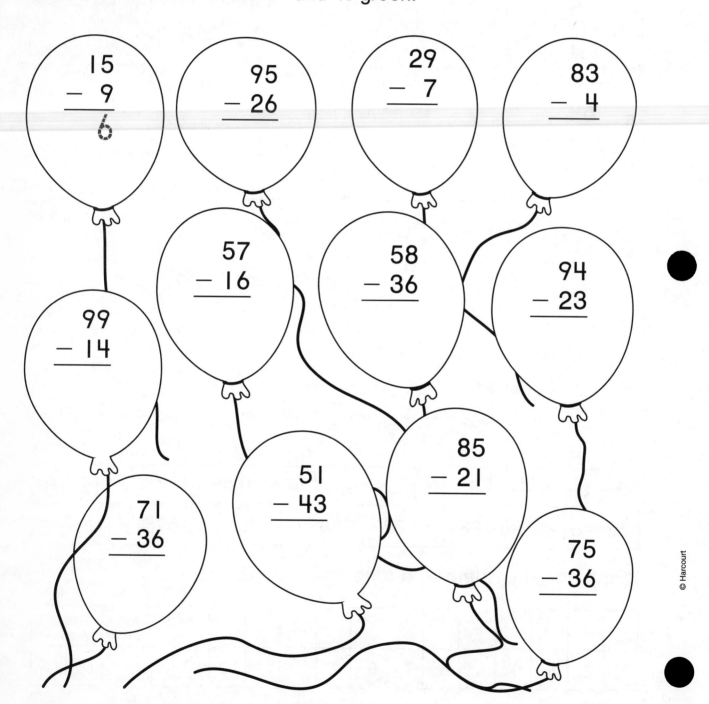

$$
\begin{array}{r} 15 \\ -\ 9 \\ \hline 6 \end{array}
\qquad
\begin{array}{r} 95 \\ -26 \\ \hline \end{array}
\qquad
\begin{array}{r} 29 \\ -\ 7 \\ \hline \end{array}
\qquad
\begin{array}{r} 83 \\ -\ 4 \\ \hline \end{array}
$$

$$
\begin{array}{r} 57 \\ -16 \\ \hline \end{array}
\qquad
\begin{array}{r} 58 \\ -36 \\ \hline \end{array}
\qquad
\begin{array}{r} 94 \\ -23 \\ \hline \end{array}
$$

$$
\begin{array}{r} 99 \\ -14 \\ \hline \end{array}
$$

$$
\begin{array}{r} 85 \\ -21 \\ \hline \end{array}
$$

$$
\begin{array}{r} 71 \\ -36 \\ \hline \end{array}
\qquad
\begin{array}{r} 51 \\ -43 \\ \hline \end{array}
\qquad
\begin{array}{r} 75 \\ -36 \\ \hline \end{array}
$$

© Harcourt

● Puzzling Addition

Use the numbers in the box to write two different addition sentences. Then add to find the sum.

1.

46		17
	22	
38		61

<u> 61 </u> + <u> 22 </u> = 83

_____ + _____ = 55

2.

9		43
	64	
40		18

_____ + _____ = 27

_____ + _____ = 83

3.

12		86
	39	
63		14

_____ + _____ = 75

_____ + _____ = 53

4.

57		31
	26	
48		79

_____ + _____ = 88

_____ + _____ = 74

Name _____

Subtraction Wheels

Subtract the number in the middle section
from the number in the center. Fill in each number.

1.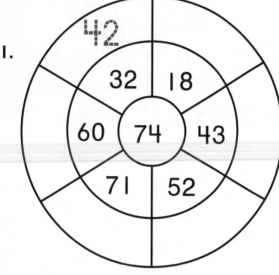

2.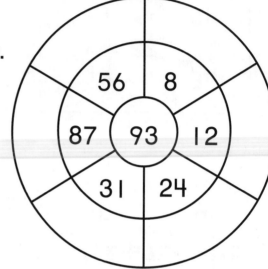

3.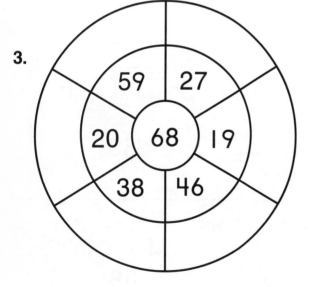

4.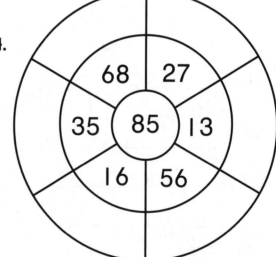

IN394 Check What You Know Enrichment

Name _____

Coin Values

Draw a line to match each coin to its value.

5¢

50¢

1¢

25¢

10¢

Do I Have Enough?

Count on to find the total amount.
Circle Yes or No to tell if you have enough money to buy the snack.

1.  23¢   (Yes) No

   __10__ ¢, __20__ ¢, __21__ ¢, __22__ ¢, __23__ ¢

2.  48¢    Yes No

   _____ ¢, _____ ¢, _____ ¢

3. 62¢   Yes No

   _____ ¢, _____ ¢, _____ ¢, _____ ¢, _____ ¢

4.  24¢   Yes No

   _____ ¢, _____ ¢, _____ ¢, _____ ¢

5.  22¢   Yes No

   _____ ¢, _____ ¢, _____ ¢, _____ ¢, _____ ¢

Name _____

● Coin Choices

Use coins.
Show the amount of money in two ways.
Draw and label each coin.

1.  △ 65¢ | |

2. 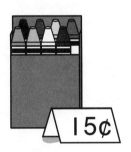 △ 15¢ | |

3.  △ 29¢ | |

© Harcourt

Name _____

How Can I Pay?

Write the amount.
Then show the same amount with different coins.
Draw and label each coin.

1.

2.

3.

Name _____

What Time Is It?

Match the clock to the correct time.

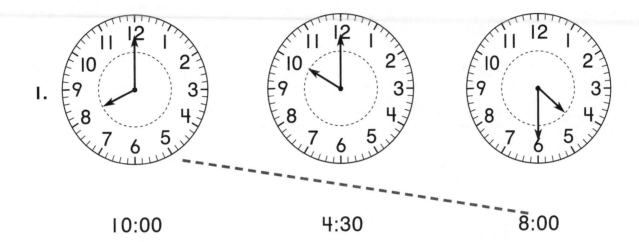

1.

10:00   4:30   8:00

2.

6:30   1:00   2:30

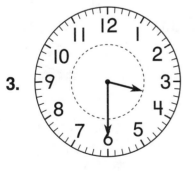

3.

5:00   3:30   12:00

© Harcourt

Check What You Know Enrichment IN399

Time to Begin

Activity	Start Time
Football Practice	2:00
Ballet Class	4:00
Soccer Game	6:00
Piano Lesson	8:00
Chorus	10:00
Book Club	12:00

Draw the hour hand and the minute hand
to show the time for each activity.

1. Book Club

2. Ballet Class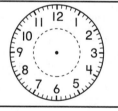

3. Football
   Practice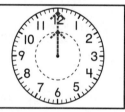

4. Soccer Game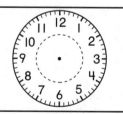

5. Chorus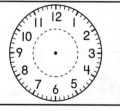

6. Piano Lesson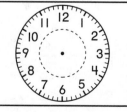

© Harcourt

Name _____

● Timing is Everything!

About how long would it take?
Circle the reasonable estimate.

1. to read a book

about 1 minute

(about 1 hour)

2. to walk to school

about 10 minutes

about 10 weeks

3. to drink some juice

about 5 hours

about 5 minutes

4. to ride a bike

about 1 day

about 1 hour

© Harcourt

Check What You Know Enrichment IN401

Pick a Day

Your family wants to go to the amusement park.
Find a date for the trip.
Read the clues.
Draw an X on any dates your family cannot go.
Circle the date for the trip.

MAY						
Sun	Mon	Tue	Wed	Thu	Fri	Sat
1	2	3	4	5	6	7
8	9	10	11	12	13	14
15	16	17	18	19	20	21
22	23	24	25	26	27	28
29	30	31				

1. The amusement park is closed on Mondays and Tuesdays.

2. You have a family picnic on May 5.

3. Your family is going on vacation the third week of May.

4. You can only go to the amusement park on a weekday.

5. You have a soccer game on the first and last Wednesday of the month.

6. There is chorus practice on May 26 and 27.

7. During the second week of May the park is closed for repairs.

What is the date of the trip to the amusement park? _____

© Harcourt

Map Maker

Suzy would like some help making a map of her neighborhood. Follow the directions below.

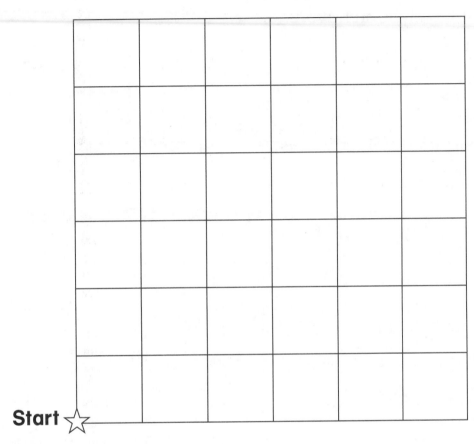

Start ☆

1. To get to Suzy's house, from start, go right 3 and up 4.
   Draw her house.

2. From Suzy's house, go right 2 and down 2 to get to the lake.
   Draw the lake.

3. Go to Suzy's school from the lake. Go up 4 and left 1.
   Draw the school.

4. To get to the woods from school, go left 3 and down 4.
   Draw the woods.

5. From the woods, the neighborhood playground is right 1 and up 3.
   Draw the playground.

Check What You Know Enrichment IN403

Jellybean Taste Test

Use the bar graph to answer the questions.
Number the jellybean jars from most favorite
to least favorite jellybean flavors.

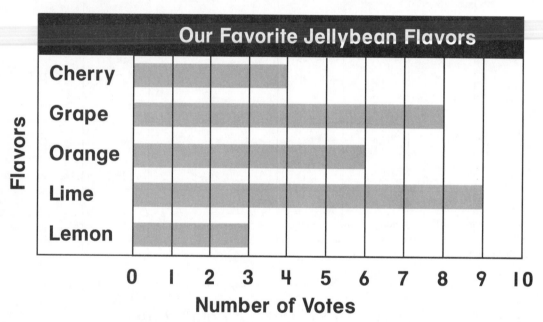

1. How many children like grape jellybeans best? _____

2. How many more like orange than lemon jellybeans? _____

3. How many children like cherry or lime jellybeans? _____

4. Do more children like lemon and lime or grape and orange
   jellybeans? Circle.

   lemon and lime   grape and orange

5. How many children voted in the jellybean taste test? _____

© Harcourt

Yes, Maybe, No

Read each sentence. If the statement is certain, put an X in the YES box. If it is possible, put an X in the MAYBE box. If it could never happen, put an X in the NO box.

	YES	MAYBE	NO
1. You will see a dog on the way home from school.		X	
2. You will go to sleep tonight.			
3. You will teach a cat to read three new words.			
4. You will see a friend at school.			
5. You will fly home from school this afternoon.			
6. You will drink some juice at breakfast time.			
7. You will do some homework after school.			
8. You will eat something for dinner.			

Name _____

Bag It!

Look at the contents of each snack bag.
Then read the questions. Circle your answer.

A

B

C

1. Mia likes pears. Which bag should she choose from?

   Bag A   (Bag B)   Bag C

2. Liz dislikes apples. Which bag should she choose from?

   Bag A   Bag B   Bag C

3. Mac dislikes grapes. Which bag should he choose from?

   Bag A   Bag B   Bag C

4. Chris dislikes pears and grapes. Which bag should he choose from?

   Bag A   Bag B   Bag C

5. Ellen likes apples. Which bag should she choose from?

   Bag A   Bag B   Bag C

6. Garrett likes pears and grapes. Which bag should he choose from?

   Bag A   Bag B   Bag C

Name _____

● Find the Shapes

Look for plane shapes.

Color the squares blue.

Color the rectangles red.

Color the circles yellow.

Color the triangles green.

Name _____

Draw the Shapes

1. Draw a square.

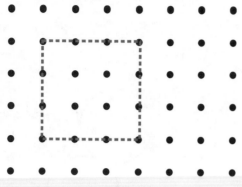

2. Draw a triangle.

3. Draw a rectangle.

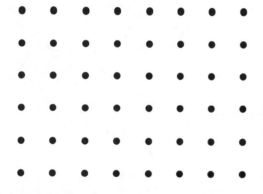

4. Draw a circle.

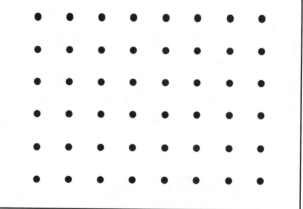

5. Draw a square and a triangle.

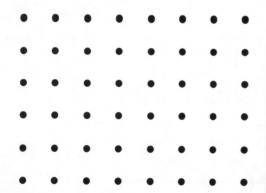

6. Draw a triangle and a rectangle.

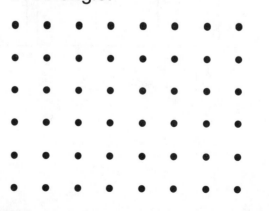

© Harcourt

Name _____

Solid Animals

Look for solid figures.
Color the spheres red.
Color the cones black.
Color the cylinders green.
Color the cubes blue.

Chart the Shapes

Complete the chart. Write how many.

Solid figure	Number of faces	Number of edges	Number of vertices
sphere	__0__ faces	__0__ edges	__0__ vertices
pyramid	___faces	___edges	___vertices
rectangular prism	___faces	___edges	___vertices
cube	___faces	___edges	___vertices

Name _____

● Slide and Turn It

Look at each figure in the first column. Draw the figure to show a slide in the second column. Then draw the figure to show a turn in the third column.

	SLIDE	TURN
1.		
2.		
3.		
4.		
5.		

Name _____

Symmetry Shelves

Look at each shelf. Find things that have symmetry.
Draw a line of symmetry and color the matching parts.

1.

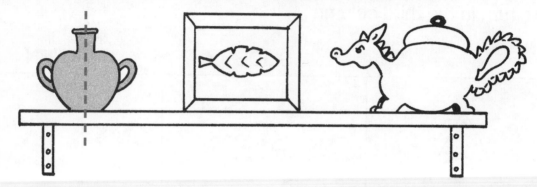

2.

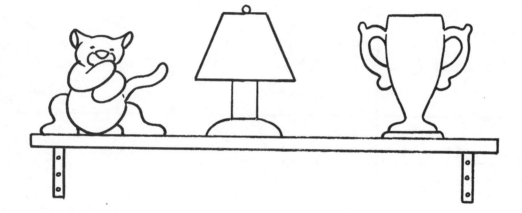

3.

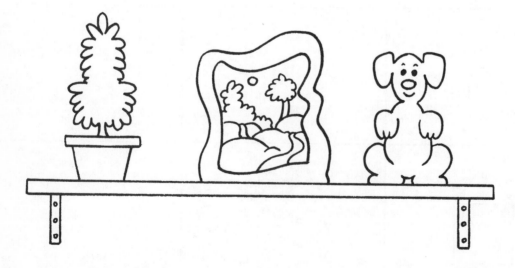

© Harcourt

Name _____

Whose Bracelet?

Draw a line to match the correct bracelet to each child.

1. My bracelet has a circle, square pattern.

2. My bracelet has a circle, square, triangle pattern.

3. My bracelet has a circle, triangle, triangle pattern.

4. My bracelet has a circle, circle, square, square pattern.

Necklace Makers

Oh no! The power is out and the necklace making machines have stopped. Extend the pattern to finish each necklace. Then color the beads.

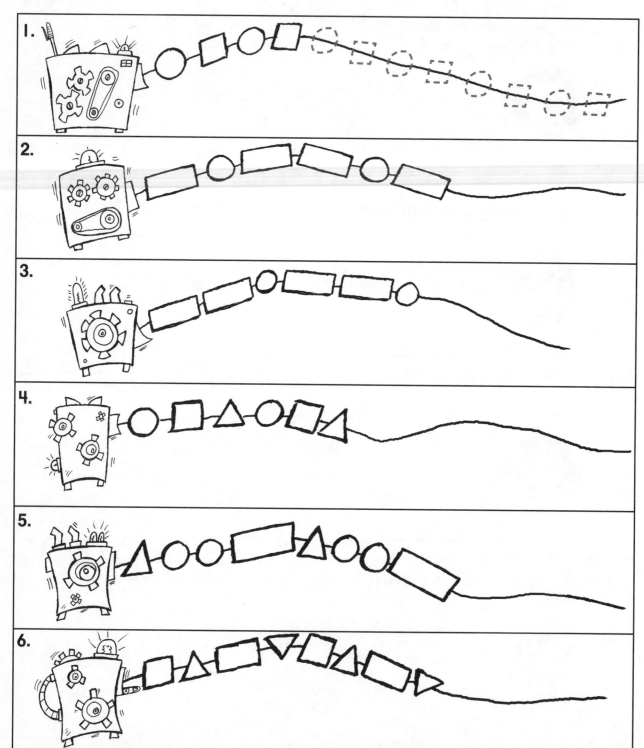

© Harcourt

Name _____

● Put Them in Order

Put the items in order from shortest to longest.
Write **1**, **2**, and **3** to show the order.

1.

   _2_   _1_   _3_

2.

   _____   _____   _____

3.

   _____   _____   _____

4.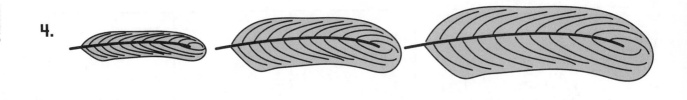

   _____   _____   _____

Check What You Know Enrichment IN415

Name _____

How Long Is It?

Use an inch ruler to measure.
Measure how long or how high the real object is.
Mark an **X** in the box to show the length.

	Less than 12 inches	About 12 inches	More than 12 inches
pencil	X		
desk			
book			
door			
chalk			

© Harcourt

How Much Can it Hold?

About how much does each container hold?
Circle the most reasonable answer.

1.

less than 1 cup
(about 1 cup)
more than 1 cup

2.

less than 1 cup
about 1 cup
more than 1 cup

3.

less than 1 cup
about 1 cup
more than 1 cup

4.

less than 1 cup
about 1 cup
more than 1 cup

5.

less than 1 cup
about 1 cup
more than 1 cup

6.

less than 1 cup
about 1 cup
more than 1 cup

7.

less than 1 cup
about 1 cup
more than 1 cup

8.

less than 1 cup
about 1 cup
more than 1 cup

Name _____

Weight Game

Look at the first object in each row.
Are the objects to the right heavier or lighter?
Circle the object that is heavier.
Draw an X on the object that is lighter.

1.		
2.		
3.		
4.		 
5.		

© Harcourt

Name _____

Small Measures

Circle the pictures that show things you would measure in centimeters. Cross out the pictures that you would not measure in centimeters. Give an estimate for each circled picture.

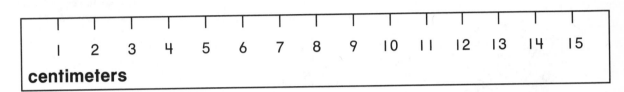

centimeters

1.

about _____ centimeters

2.

about _____ centimeters

3.

about _____ centimeter

4.

about _____ centimeters

5.

about _____ centimeters

6.

about _____ centimeters

Check What You Know Enrichment IN419

Measuring at the Library

Look at each item found in a library. Decide if
the pictured item measures less than, about
the same or more than 1 kilogram.
Circle your answer.

**A large book is
about 1 kilogram.**

1.

less than 1 kilogram
(about 1 kilogram)
more than 1 kilogram

2.

less than 1 kilogram
about 1 kilogram
more than 1 kilogram

3.

less than 1 kilogram
about 1 kilogram
more than 1 kilogram

4.

less than 1 kilogram
about 1 kilogram
more than 1 kilogram

5.

less than 1 kilogram
about 1 kilogram
more than 1 kilogram

6.

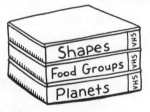

less than 1 kilogram
about 1 kilogram
more than 1 kilogram

Name _____

Addition A to Z

Start at A. Add the 3 numbers to the right of A.
Then cross them out. Find and circle the sum.

Add the 3 numbers to the right of the circled sum.
Then cross them out. Find and circle the sum.

Continue until you get to Z. Numbers that have
been crossed out or circled cannot be used again.

A	4	5	6	5	1	14	2	6	2
7	2	1	13	6	5	6	4	9	3
4	12	3	1	4	0	3	7	2	3
11	7	2	7	15	4	4	6	1	9
4	1	17	1	1	9	0	9	7	1
9	0	5	7	3	4	16	9	2	7
1	5	4	7	5	10	9	0	3	3
7	8	7	4	2	1	2	7	18	Z

1. $4 + 5 + 6 = 15$ 2. ___ + ___ + ___ = ___

3. ___ + ___ + ___ = ___ 4. ___ + ___ + ___ = ___

5. ___ + ___ + ___ = ___ 6. ___ + ___ + ___ = ___

7. ___ + ___ + ___ = ___ 8. ___ + ___ + ___ = ___

9. ___ + ___ + ___ = ___ 10. ___ + ___ + ___ = ___

Check What You Know Enrichment IN421

On a Roll

Count the dots on the number cubes.
Use them as addends.
Write as many number sentences as you can.

1.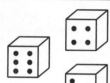

   $\underline{6} + \underline{4} + \underline{3} = \underline{13}$　　$\_ + \_ + \_ = \_$

   $\_ + \_ + \_ = \_$　　$\_ + \_ + \_ = \_$

   $\_ + \_ + \_ = \_$　　$\_ + \_ + \_ = \_$

2.

   $\_ + \_ + \_ = \_$　　$\_ + \_ + \_ = \_$

   $\_ + \_ + \_ = \_$

3.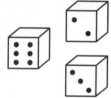

   $\_ + \_ + \_ = \_$　　$\_ + \_ + \_ = \_$

   $\_ + \_ + \_ = \_$　　$\_ + \_ + \_ = \_$

   $\_ + \_ + \_ = \_$　　$\_ + \_ + \_ = \_$

Now it's your turn. Roll 3 number cubes. Draw what you see.
How many number sentences can you make?

4.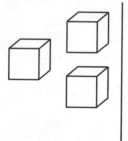

Name _____

Thirds, Halves, Fourths

Color one part red.
Write the fraction for the red part.

1.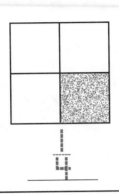

$\frac{1}{4}$

2.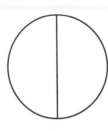

_____

3.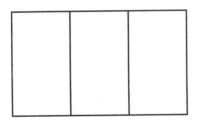

_____

4.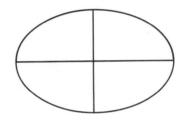

_____

5.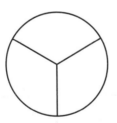

_____

6.

_____

7.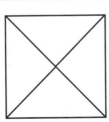

_____

8.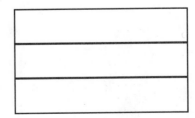

_____

Check What You Know Enrichment IN423

Name _____

Which One Is Right?

Circle the picture that shows the fraction.

1. $\frac{1}{2}$

 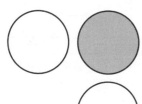

2. $\frac{1}{4}$

3. $\frac{1}{3}$

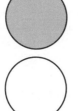 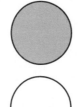

4. $\frac{1}{2}$

 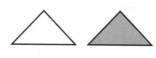

5. $\frac{1}{3}$

6. $\frac{1}{4}$

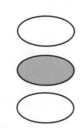 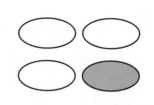

© Harcourt

IN424 Check What You Know Enrichment

Name _____

Ring the Numbers

Circle the number that tells how many.

1.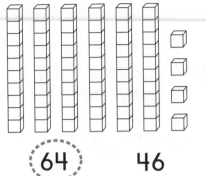

(64)   46

2.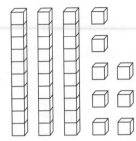

38   28

3.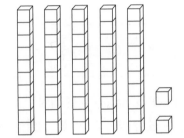

62   52

4.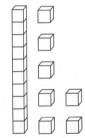

18   17

5.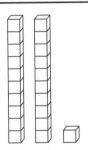

21   12

6.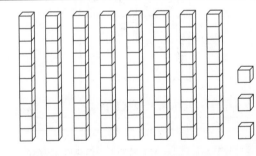

93   83

7.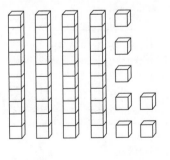

49   47

8.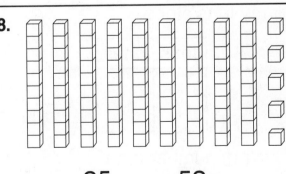

95   59

© Harcourt

Check What You Know Enrichment IN425

Name _____

Place Value Riddles

Read the clues. Write how many tens and ones.
Then write the number.

1. I have a 7 in my ones place
and a 2 in my tens place.

tens	ones
2	7

What number am I? _27_

2. I have an 8 in my tens
place and a number 1 greater
than 8 in my ones place.

tens	ones

What number am I? _____

3. I have 3 more than 2 in my
ones place and a 5 in my
tens place.

tens	ones

What number am I? _____

4. I have a 3 in my tens place
and an 8 in my ones place.

tens	ones

What number am I? _____

5. I have a 3 in my ones place
and I have 2 more than 5 in
my tens place.

tens	ones

What number am I? _____

6. I have 1 less than 7 in my
tens place and a 0 in my
ones place.

tens	ones

What number am I? _____

© Harcourt

Name _____

Get in Order!

Write the missing numbers.
Use  or a number line.

1.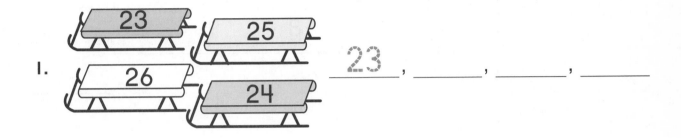

23 , _____ , _____ , _____

2.

_____ , _____ , _____ , _____

3.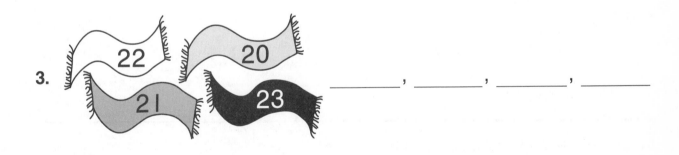

_____ , _____ , _____ , _____

4.

_____ , _____ , _____ , _____

© Harcourt

Check What You Know Enrichment IN427

You Make the Number

Use the numbers in the box below to build a
2-digit number that will make each sentence true.

4	6	1	8	9	0

1. 78 < _89_

2. _____ > 65

3. 38 > _____

4. _____ < 14

5. _____ > 89

6. 61 = _____

7. 46 < _____

8. _____ < 98

9. _____ < 56

10. 57 < _____

© Harcourt

Name _____

Number Play

Use the numbers on the houses to answer the questions.

1. The sum of these 2 numbers is 81.
   What are the two numbers?

   _67_ , _14_

2. The sum of these two numbers is 17.
   What are the two numbers?

   _____ , _____

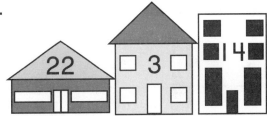

3. The sum of these two numbers is 99.
   What are the two numbers?

   _____ , _____

4. The sum of these two numbers is 51.
   What are the two numbers?

   _____ , _____

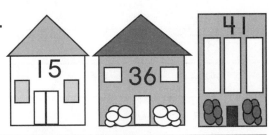

5. The sum of these two numbers is 88.
   What are the two numbers?

   _____ , _____

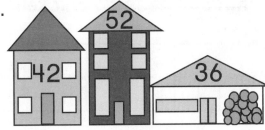

© Harcourt

Check What You Know Enrichment IN429

Name _____

Coded Subtraction

Subtract.
Then match each answer to the letter.
Write the letter on the line to answer the riddle.

1. $\begin{array}{r} {\scriptstyle 2\;16} \\ 3\!\!\!/6\!\!\!/ \\ -\;7 \\ \hline 29 \end{array}$

2. $\begin{array}{r} 78 \\ -\;50 \\ \hline \end{array}$

3. $\begin{array}{r} 45 \\ -\;26 \\ \hline \end{array}$

4. $\begin{array}{r} 62 \\ -\;34 \\ \hline \end{array}$

5. $\begin{array}{r} 28 \\ -\;15 \\ \hline \end{array}$

6. $\begin{array}{r} 49 \\ -\;21 \\ \hline \end{array}$

7. $\begin{array}{r} 97 \\ -\;58 \\ \hline \end{array}$

8. $\begin{array}{r} 75 \\ -\;43 \\ \hline \end{array}$

9. $\begin{array}{r} 87 \\ -\;68 \\ \hline \end{array}$

10. $\begin{array}{r} 82 \\ -\;24 \\ \hline \end{array}$

11. $\begin{array}{r} 47 \\ -\;28 \\ \hline \end{array}$

12. $\begin{array}{r} 45 \\ -\;6 \\ \hline \end{array}$

| 13=x | 19=e | 28=p | 29=h | 14=r |
| 32=t | 60=k | 39=o | 42=i | 58=l |

What sickness do chickens get?

| | | | | | | | | | | | | | |
|8.|1.|11.| |4.|9.|12.|6.|10.|3.| |2.|7.|5.|

© Harcourt

Name _____

Circus Ring Addition

Write an addition sentence for each drawing.

1.

__4__ + __4__ + __4__ + __4__ = __16__

2.

_____ + _____ + _____ = _____

3.

_____ + _____ + _____ + _____ + _____ = _____

4.

_____ + _____ + _____ + _____ + _____ = _____

Check What You Know Enrichment IN431

Name _____

Make Them Equal

Circle equal groups.
Write how many groups.

1. 2 equal groups

There are ___6___ in each group.

2. 3 equal groups

There are _____ in each group.

3. 6 equal groups

There are _____ in each group.

4. 4 equal groups

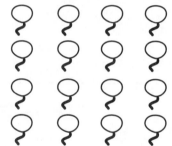

There are _____ in each group.

5. 5 equal groups

There are _____ in each group.

6. 2 equal groups

There are _____ in each group.

Name _____

Secret Numbers

Fill in the missing numbers.

1. _3_ , _4_ , 5, 6, [7] , 8, _9_

2. _16_ , 17, _18_ , _19_ , 20, 21, [22]

3. 51, _52_ , _53_ , 54, 55, [56] , _57_

4. [33] , 34, _35_ , 36, _37_ , _38_ , 39

5. 89, _90_ , 91, _92_ , _93_ , 94, [95]

6. 44, 45, [46] , 47, _48_ , _49_ , 50

T = 7	H = 22	R = 33	Y = 46	E = 50
I = 56	A = 69	G = 70	T = 95	K = 98

Match the numbers in the boxes to the letters.
Write the letters on the lines below to find the hidden word.

T   H   I   R   T   Y
1.   2.   3.   4.   5.   6.

Name _____

Fishing for Pairs

Read the numbers.
Write the letter of the picture that matches the words.

6 tens and 5 ones _G_	A	5 tens and 3 ones _H_	B
2 tens _A_	C	4 tens and 1 one _D_	D
3 tens and 2 ones _C_	E	6 tens and 8 ones _J_	F
8 tens _E_	G	3 tens _F_	H
1 ten and 4 ones _I_	I	4 tens _B_	J

Name _____

Number Mix-Up

The shirts for three teams are mixed up.

Put the shirts in order from least to greatest.

1. 2, 3, _4_ , 5, 6, 7, _8_ , 9,

10, 11, _12_ , 13, _14_ , _15_ , 16, 17, _18_ , 19,

_20_ , 21, 22, 23, 24, _25_ , 26, 27, 28, 29,

_30_ , 31, 32, 33, 34, _35_ , 36, 37, 38, 39,

_40_ , 41, 42, 43, 44, _45_ , 46, 47, 48, 49

Skip-count by twos, fives, or tens to find the numbers
on each team's shirts.

2. TEAM 1:

5, 10, _15_ , 20, _25_ , 30, _35_ , 40, _45_

3. TEAM 2:

10, _20_ , _30_ , _40_ , 50, 60, 70, 80, 90

4. TEAM 3:

2, _4_ , 6, _8_ , 10, _12_ , _14_ , 16, _18_

Name _____

True or False Skip Counting

Follow the directions below. Cover the numbers with beans as
you count. Read each question. Then circle true or false.

1	2	3	4	5	6	7	8	9	10
11	12	13	14	15	16	17	18	19	20
21	22	23	24	25	26	27	28	29	30
31	32	33	34	35	36	37	38	39	40
41	42	43	44	45	46	47	48	49	50
51	52	53	54	55	56	57	58	59	60
61	62	63	64	65	66	67	68	69	70
71	72	73	74	75	76	77	78	79	80
81	82	83	84	85	86	87	88	89	90
91	92	93	94	95	96	97	98	99	100

1. Skip count by 2's.
   All the even numbers are covered.   (true)   false

2. Skip count by 5's.
   Only numbers ending with 5's are covered.   true   (false)

3. Skip count by 10's.
   Even and odd numbers are covered.   true   (false)

4. Skip count by 5's.
   All numbers ending in zero are covered.   (true)   false

Intervention • Skills IN433

What Animal Am I?

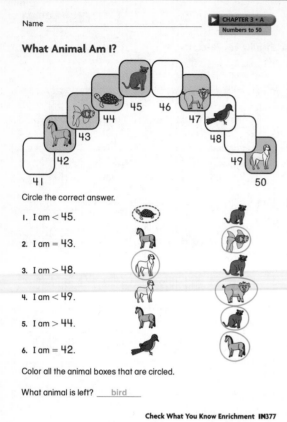

Circle the correct answer.

1. I am < 45.

2. I am = 43.

3. I am > 48.

4. I am < 49.

5. I am > 44.

6. I am = 42.

Color all the animal boxes that are circled.

What animal is left? ___bird___

Lucky Duck Factory

Write the missing number on the duck that is
just before, between, or just after.

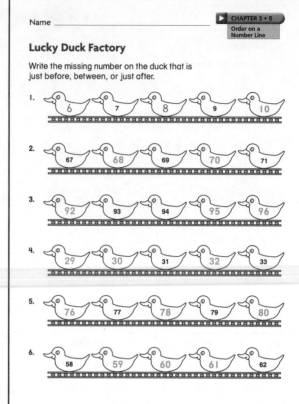

1. 6   7   8   9   10

2. 67   68   69   70   71

3. 92   93   94   95   96

4. 29   30   31   32   33

5. 76   77   78   79   80

6. 58   59   60   61   62

Playground Picture Graphs

1. Sort the playground activities.   Check children's work.
   Color the children swinging red.
   Color the children jumping rope blue.
   Color the children on the slide green.

2. Use the picture to fill in the picture graph.
   Draw 1 ⚲ for every child.

Playground Activities	
(swings)	⚲ ⚲ ⚲ ⚲
(jump rope)	⚲ ⚲
(slide)	⚲ ⚲ ⚲

Charting Colors

Which color do your classmates like best?
Fill in the tally table to show their answers. Answers will vary.

blue	red	black	green	purple	orange

Use the tally table to fill in the graph.

Favorite Colors										
blue										
red										
black										
green										
purple										
orange										
	0	1	2	3	4	5	6	7	8	9	10

Use the graph to answer the questions. Answers will vary.

1. What is the favorite color of the most children? _____

2. What is the favorite color of the fewest children? _____

3. How many children in all like green best? _____

4. How many children in all like red best? _____

© Harcourt

Count Dot-to-Dot

Use the number line to count on.
Then connect the dots in order from least to greatest.

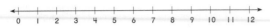

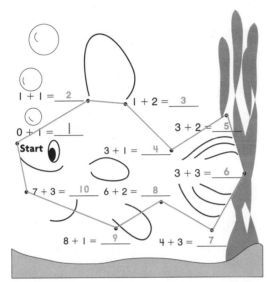

1 + 1 = __2__   1 + 2 = __3__

0 + 1 = __1__   3 + 2 = __5__

Start   3 + 1 = __4__

3 + 3 = __6__

7 + 3 = __10__   6 + 2 = __8__

8 + 1 = __9__   4 + 3 = __7__

Check What You Know Enrichment **IN381**

Adding in Circles

Start at the top number.
Follow the arrows to add.
Write the sum.

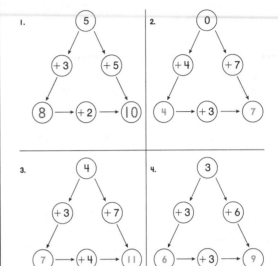

1. 5
   +3   +5
   8 → +2 → 10

2. 0
   +4   +7
   4 → +3 → 7

3. 4
   +3   +7
   7 → +4 → 11

4. 3
   +3   +6
   6 → +3 → 9

IN382 Check What You Know Enrichment

Fact Match

Add and subtract.
Color the addition fact red.
Color the related subtraction fact blue.

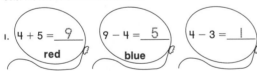

1. 4 + 5 = __9__   9 − 4 = __5__   4 − 3 = __1__
    red   **blue**

2. 6 − 3 = __3__   3 − 3 = __0__   3 + 3 = __6__
    blue   red

3. 4 − 1 = __3__   5 − 1 = __4__   1 + 4 = __5__
                     blue   red

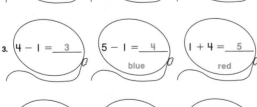

4. 7 − 3 = __4__   5 − 2 = __3__   2 + 3 = __5__
                     blue   red

Check What You Know Enrichment **IN383**

Math Path

Use the number line to count back.
Then connect the 3's to find the path out of the maze.

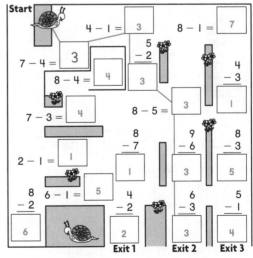

Start

4 − 1 = 3   8 − 1 = 7

7 − 4 = 3   5 − 2 = 3   4 − 3

8 − 4 = 4   3

7 − 3 = 4   8 − 5 = 3   1

2 − 1 = 1   8 − 7   9 − 6   8 − 3
            1   3   5

8 − 2   6 − 1 = 5   4 − 2   6 − 3   5 − 1
6   2   3   4

Exit 1   **Exit 2**   **Exit 3**

What exit did you use? __Exit 2__

IN384 Check What You Know Enrichment

© Harcourt

Number Puzzle

Write the number.
Then write the number in the boxes to complete the puzzle.

1. **Down**   eleven
4. **Across**   twelve
2. **Down**   twenty
5. **Across**   nineteen
3. **Down**   sixteen
6. **Down**   eighteen

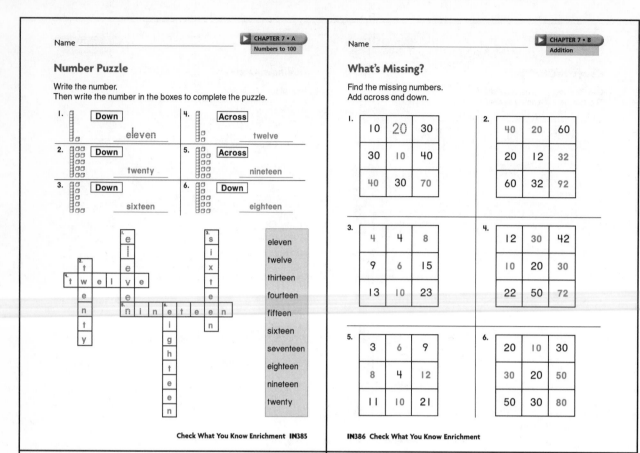

eleven
twelve
thirteen
fourteen
fifteen
sixteen
seventeen
eighteen
nineteen
twenty

Check What You Know Enrichment **IN385**

What's Missing?

Find the missing numbers.
Add across and down.

1.

10	20	30
30	10	40
40	30	70

2.

40	20	60
20	12	32
60	32	92

3.

4	4	8
9	6	15
13	10	23

4.

12	30	42
10	20	30
22	50	72

5.

3	6	9
8	4	12
11	10	21

6.

20	10	30
30	20	50
50	30	80

IN386 Check What You Know Enrichment

Secret Path

Add. Regroup if you need to.
Color the boxes where you regrouped
to find the path out of the maze.

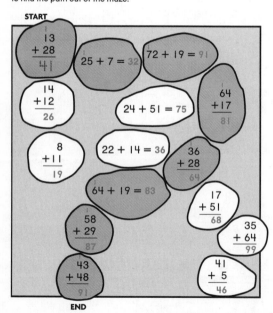

START

```
 13
+28
 41
```
25 + 7 = 32
72 + 19 = 91
```
 14
+12
 26
```
24 + 51 = 75
```
 64
+17
 81
```
```
  8
+11
 19
```
22 + 14 = 36
```
 36
+28
 64
```
64 + 19 = 83
```
 17
+51
 68
```
```
 58
+29
 87
```
```
 35
+64
 99
```
```
 43
+48
 91
```
```
 41
+ 5
 46
```

END

Check What You Know Enrichment **IN387**

Addition Pairs

Add.
Circle the addition sentences that have the same sum.

1. 54 + 27 = 81   (12 + 49 = 61)   71 + 16 = 87

   (21 + 40 = 61)   16 + 56 = 72   18 + 7 = 25

2. 17 + 34 = 51   81 + 12 = 93   (61 + 9 = 70)

   62 + 11 = 73   43 + 22 = 65   (26 + 44 = 70)

3. (45 + 37 = 82)   34 + 7 = 41   73 + 24 = 97

   68 + 21 = 89   (63 + 19 = 82)   41 + 27 = 68

IN388 Check What You Know Enrichment

Worksheet 1 (top left)

What Number Am I?

Read the clue.
Write the number sentence.
Circle the answer to the question.

1. If you subtract me from 11, the difference is 4. What number am I?

$$11 \;-\; \text{⑦} \;=\; 4$$

2. If you subtract 20 from me, the answer is 40. What number am I?

$$\text{㉖}\;-\;20\;=\;40$$

3. What number will you have if you subtract 20 from 70?

$$70\;-\;20\;=\;\text{㊿}$$

4. If you subtract 8 from me, the difference is 4. What number am I?

$$\text{⑫}\;-\;8\;=\;4$$

5. If you subtract 10 from me, the answer is 10. What number am I?

$$\text{⑳}\;-\;10\;=\;10$$

6. What number will you have if you subtract 50 from 90?

$$90\;-\;50\;=\;\text{㊵}$$

7. What number will you have if you subtract 9 from 17?

$$17\;-\;9\;=\;\text{⑧}$$

8. If you subtract 5 from me, the difference is 1. What number am I?

$$\text{⑥}\;-\;5\;=\;1$$

Worksheet 2 (top right)

How Many Are Left?

Store Item		Number on Shelf	Number Sold
	cereal	46	4
	milk	23	3
	apples	57	30
	crackers	84	40
	juice	27	5

Use the table to write a subtraction sentence.
Find out how many items are left in the store.

1. cereal $\quad 46 \;-\; 4 \;=\; 42$

2. milk $\quad 23 \;-\; 3 \;=\; 20$

3. apples $\quad 57 \;-\; 30 \;=\; 27$

4. crackers $\quad 84 \;-\; 40 \;=\; 44$

5. juice $\quad 27 \;-\; 5 \;=\; 22$

Worksheet 3 (bottom left)

Subtraction Riddle

Subtract.
Then match each answer to the letter.

1. $18 - 4 = 14$

2. $26 - 9 = 17$

3. $46 - 14 = 32$

4. $75 - 14 = 61$

5. $64 - 5 = 59$

6. $45 - 4 = 41$

7. $32 - 26 = 6$

8. $67 - 48 = 19$

9. $57 - 32 = 25$

10. $17 - 14 = 3$

11. $84 - 56 = 28$

12. $79 - 53 = 26$

13. $37 - 24 = 13$

14. $47 - 38 = 9$

15. $71 - 59 = 12$

16. $62 - 16 = 46$

3 = u	6 = o	9 = R	12 = e	13 = s	14 = T	17 = y	19 = s
25 = a	26 = u	28 = r	32 = r	41 = n	46 = x	59 = n	61 = a

What was the name of a dinosaur's dog?

T	y	r	a	n	n	o	s	a	u	r	u	s		R	e	x
1.	2.	3.	4.	5.	6.	7.	8.	9.	10.	11.	12.	13.		14.	15.	16.

Worksheet 4 (bottom right)

Compare Differences

Subtract.
Color the balloons.
Color differences between 0 and 30 red.
Color differences between 31 and 60 blue.
Color differences between 61 and 90 green.

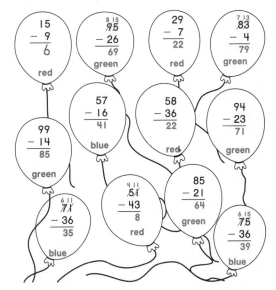

© Harcourt

Puzzling Addition

Use the numbers in the box to write two different addition sentences.
Then add to find the sum.   *Possible answers are given.*

1.
46	17
22	
38	61

$\underline{61} + \underline{22} = 83$

$\underline{38} + \underline{17} = 55$

2.
9	43
64	
40	18

$\underline{18} + \underline{9} = 27$

$\underline{40} + \underline{43} = 83$

3.
12	86
39	
63	14

$\underline{63} + \underline{12} = 75$

$\underline{39} + \underline{14} = 53$

4.
57	31
26	
48	79

$\underline{57} + \underline{31} = 88$

$\underline{48} + \underline{26} = 74$

Check What You Know Enrichment **IN393**

Subtraction Wheels

Subtract the number in the middle section
from the number in the center. Fill in each number.

1.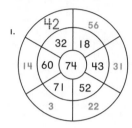

2.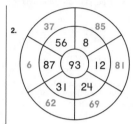

3.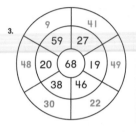

4.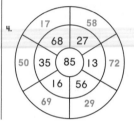

IN394 Check What You Know Enrichment

Coin Values

Draw a line to match each coin to its value.

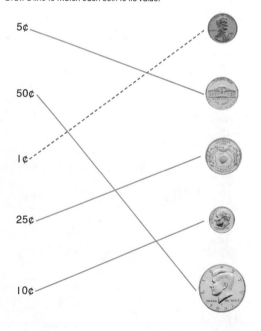

5¢

50¢

1¢

25¢

10¢

Check What You Know Enrichment **IN395**

Do I Have Enough?

Count on to find the total amount.
Circle Yes or No to tell if you have enough money to buy the snack.

1. (23¢)   (Yes)   No

$\underline{10}¢, \underline{20}¢, \underline{21}¢, \underline{22}¢, \underline{23}¢$

2. (48¢)   Yes   (No)

$\underline{25}¢, \underline{35}¢, \underline{36}¢$

3. (62¢)   (Yes)   No

$\underline{25}¢, \underline{50}¢, \underline{60}¢, \underline{61}¢, \underline{62}¢$

4. (24¢)   Yes   (No)

$\underline{5}¢, \underline{10}¢, \underline{15}¢, \underline{20}¢$

5. (juice 22¢)   (Yes)   No

$\underline{10}¢, \underline{15}¢, \underline{20}¢, \underline{21}¢, \underline{22}¢$

IN396 Check What You Know Enrichment

Coin Choices

Use coins.
Show the amount of money in two ways.
Draw and label each coin. Answers will vary.

1. 65¢ | 25¢ 25¢ 10¢ 5¢
2. 15¢ |
3. 29¢ |

How Can I Pay?

Write the amount.
Then show the same amount with different coins.
Draw and label each coin. Check children's work.

1. 27¢
2. 31¢
3. 59¢

What Time Is It?

Match the clock to the correct time.

1. 10:00   4:30   8:00
2. 6:30   1:00   2:30
3. 5:00   3:30   12:00

Time to Begin

Activity	Start Time
Football Practice	2:00
Ballet Class	4:00
Soccer Game	6:00
Piano Lesson	8:00
Chorus	10:00
Book Club	12:00

Draw the hour hand and the minute hand
to show the time for each activity.

1. Book Club
2. Ballet Class
3. Football Practice
4. Soccer Game
5. Chorus
6. Piano Lesson

© Harcourt

Timing is Everything!

Name _____

CHAPTER 15 • A
Time

About how long would it take?
Circle the reasonable estimate.

1. to read a book

about 1 minute
(about 1 hour)

2. to walk to school

(about 10 minutes)
about 10 weeks

3. to drink some juice

about 5 hours
(about 5 minutes)

4. to ride a bike

about 1 day
(about 1 hour)

Check What You Know Enrichment **IN401**

Name _____

CHAPTER 15 • B
Calendars

Pick a Day

Your family wants to go to the amusement park.
Find a date for the trip.
Read the clues.
Draw an X on any dates your family cannot go.
Circle the date for the trip.

MAY						
Sun	Mon	Tue	Wed	Thu	Fri	Sat
X͟1	X͟2	X͟3	X͟4	X͟5	⑥	X͟7
X͟8	X͟9	X͟10	X͟11	X͟12	X͟13	X͟14
X͟15	X͟16	X͟17	X͟18	X͟19	X͟20	X͟21
X͟22	X͟23	X͟24	X͟25	X͟26	X͟27	X͟28
X͟29	X͟30	X͟31				

1. The amusement park is closed on Mondays and Tuesdays.

2. You have a family picnic on May 5.

3. Your family is going on vacation the third week of May.

4. You can only go to the amusement park on a weekday.

5. You have a soccer game on the first and last Wednesday of the month.

6. There is chorus practice on May 26 and 27.

7. During the second week of May the park is closed for repairs.

What is the date of the trip to the amusement park? ___May 6___

IN402 Check What You Know Enrichment

Name _____

CHAPTER 16 • A
Follow Directions

Map Maker

Suzy would like some help making a map of her neighborhood. Follow the directions below.

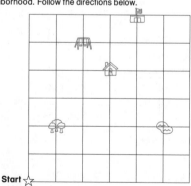

Start ☆

Check children's work.
1. To get to Suzy's house, from start, go right 3 and up 4.
   Draw her house. 🏠

2. From Suzy's house, go right 2 and down 2 to get to the lake.
   Draw the lake. ◌

3. Go to Suzy's school from the lake. Go up 4 and left 1.
   Draw the school. 🏫

4. To get to the woods from school, go left 3 and down 4.
   Draw the woods. 🌲

5. From the woods, the neighborhood playground is right 1 and up 3.
   Draw the playground. ⚙

Check What You Know Enrichment **IN403**

Name _____

CHAPTER 16 • B
Interpret Data

Jellybean Taste Test

Use the bar graph to answer the questions.
Number the jellybean jars from most favorite to least favorite jellybean flavors.

Cherry 4   Grape 2   Orange 3   Lime 1   Lemon 5

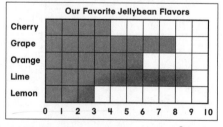

Our Favorite Jellybean Flavors

	0	1	2	3	4	5	6	7	8	9	10
Cherry											
Grape											
Orange											
Lime											
Lemon											

1. How many children like grape jellybeans best? ___8___

2. How many more like orange than lemon jellybeans? ___3___

3. How many children like cherry or lime jellybeans? ___13___

4. Do more children like lemon and lime or grape and orange jellybeans? Circle.

   lemon and lime   (grape and orange)

5. How many children voted in the jellybean taste test? ___30___

IN404 Check What You Know Enrichment

© Harcourt

Name _____

Yes, Maybe, No

Read each sentence. If the statement is certain, put
an X in the YES box. If it is possible, put an X in the
MAYBE box. If it could never happen, put an X in the
NO box.
Possible answers shown; accept reasonable responses.

	YES	MAYBE	NO
1. You will see a dog on the way home from school.		X	
2. You will go to sleep tonight.	X		
3. You will teach a cat to read three new words.			X
4. You will see a friend at school.	X		
5. You will fly home from school this afternoon.			X
6. You will drink some juice at breakfast time.		X	
7. You will do some homework after school.		X	
8. You will eat something for dinner.	X		

Check What You Know Enrichment **IN405**

Name _____

Bag It!

Look at the contents of each snack bag.
Then read the questions. Circle your answer.

A   B   C

1. Mia likes pears. Which bag should she choose from?

   Bag A   (Bag B)   Bag C

2. Liz dislikes apples. Which bag should she choose from?

   Bag A   Bag B   (Bag C)

3. Mac dislikes grapes. Which bag should he choose from?

   Bag A   (Bag B)   Bag C

4. Chris dislikes pears and grapes. Which bag should he choose from?

   (Bag A)   Bag B   Bag C

5. Ellen likes apples. Which bag should she choose from?

   (Bag A)   Bag B   Bag C

6. Garrett likes pears and grapes. Which bag should he choose from?

   Bag A   Bag B   (Bag C)

IN406 Check What You Know Enrichment

Name _____

Find the Shapes

Look for plane shapes.
Color the squares blue.
Color the rectangles red.
Color the circles yellow.
Color the triangles green.
Check children's work.

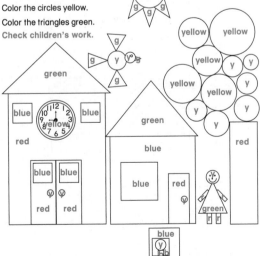

Check What You Know Enrichment **IN407**

Name _____

Draw the Shapes
Shapes will vary.

1. Draw a square.	2. Draw a triangle.
3. Draw a rectangle.	4. Draw a circle.
5. Draw a square and a triangle.	6. Draw a triangle and a rectangle.

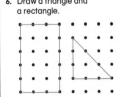

IN408 Check What You Know Enrichment

© Harcourt

Intervention • Skills **IN441**

Solid Animals

Look for solid figures.
Color the spheres red.
Color the cones black.
Color the cylinders green.
Color the cubes blue.
Check children's work.

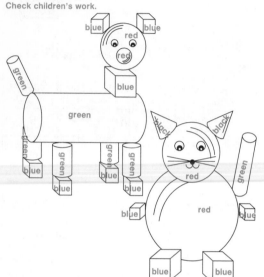

Chart the Shapes

Complete the chart. Write how many.

Solid figure	Number of faces	Number of edges	Number of vertices
sphere	0 faces	0 edges	0 vertices
pyramid	5 faces	8 edges	5 vertices
rectangular prism	6 faces	12 edges	8 vertices
cube	6 faces	12 edges	8 vertices

Slide and Turn It

Look at each figure in the first column. Draw the figure to show a slide in the second column. Then draw the figure to show a turn in the third column. Check children's work. Turns may vary.

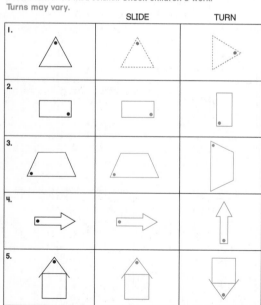

Symmetry Shelves

Look at each shelf. Find things that have symmetry.
Draw a line of symmetry and color the matching parts.

1.

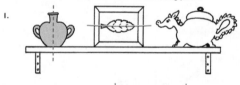

2.

3.

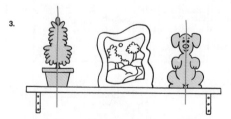

© Harcourt

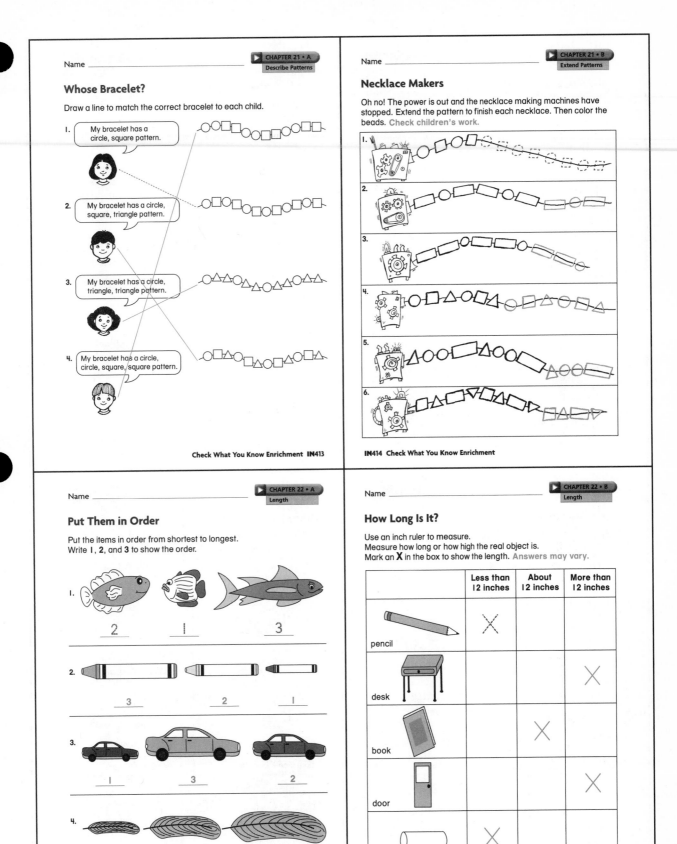

Whose Bracelet?

Name _____

Draw a line to match the correct bracelet to each child.

1. My bracelet has a circle, square pattern.

2. My bracelet has a circle, square, triangle pattern.

3. My bracelet has a circle, triangle, triangle pattern.

4. My bracelet has a circle, circle, square, square pattern.

Check What You Know Enrichment **IN413**

Necklace Makers

Name _____

Oh no! The power is out and the necklace making machines have stopped. Extend the pattern to finish each necklace. Then color the beads. Check children's work.

IN414 Check What You Know Enrichment

Put Them in Order

Name _____

Put the items in order from shortest to longest.
Write 1, 2, and 3 to show the order.

1.   2   1   3

2.   3   2   1

3.   1   3   2

4.   1   2   3

Check What You Know Enrichment **IN415**

How Long Is It?

Name _____

Use an inch ruler to measure.
Measure how long or how high the real object is.
Mark an **X** in the box to show the length. Answers may vary.

	Less than 12 inches	About 12 inches	More than 12 inches
pencil	X		
desk			X
book		X	
door			X
chalk	X		

IN416 Check What You Know Enrichment

© Harcourt

Intervention • Skills IN443

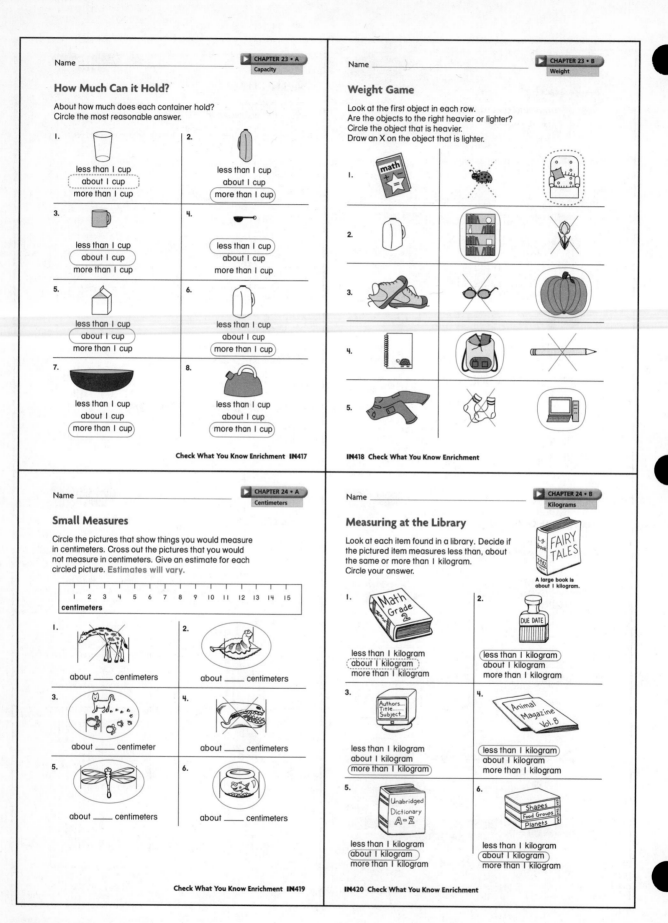

Name _____

How Much Can it Hold?

About how much does each container hold?
Circle the most reasonable answer.

1.
less than 1 cup
about 1 cup
more than 1 cup

2.
less than 1 cup
about 1 cup
more than 1 cup

3.
less than 1 cup
about 1 cup
more than 1 cup

4.
less than 1 cup
about 1 cup
more than 1 cup

5.
less than 1 cup
about 1 cup
more than 1 cup

6.
less than 1 cup
about 1 cup
more than 1 cup

7.
less than 1 cup
about 1 cup
more than 1 cup

8.
less than 1 cup
about 1 cup
more than 1 cup

Check What You Know Enrichment **IN417**

Name _____

Weight Game

Look at the first object in each row.
Are the objects to the right heavier or lighter?
Circle the object that is heavier.
Draw an X on the object that is lighter.

1.
2.
3.
4.
5.

IN418 Check What You Know Enrichment

Name _____

Small Measures

Circle the pictures that show things you would measure
in centimeters. Cross out the pictures that you would
not measure in centimeters. Give an estimate for each
circled picture. **Estimates will vary.**

1 2 3 4 5 6 7 8 9 10 11 12 13 14 15
centimeters

1.
about _____ centimeters

2.
about _____ centimeters

3.
about _____ centimeter

4.
about _____ centimeters

5.
about _____ centimeters

6.
about _____ centimeters

Check What You Know Enrichment **IN419**

Name _____

Measuring at the Library

Look at each item found in a library. Decide if
the pictured item measures less than, about
the same or more than 1 kilogram.
Circle your answer.

FAIRY TALES

**A large book is
about 1 kilogram.**

1.
less than 1 kilogram
about 1 kilogram
more than 1 kilogram

2.
less than 1 kilogram
about 1 kilogram
more than 1 kilogram

3.
less than 1 kilogram
about 1 kilogram
more than 1 kilogram

4.
less than 1 kilogram
about 1 kilogram
more than 1 kilogram

5.
less than 1 kilogram
about 1 kilogram
more than 1 kilogram

6.
less than 1 kilogram
about 1 kilogram
more than 1 kilogram

IN420 Check What You Know Enrichment

Addition A to Z

Start at A. Add the 3 numbers to the right of A.
Then cross them out. Find and circle the sum.

Add the 3 numbers to the right of the circled sum.
Then cross them out. Find and circle the sum.

Continue until you get to Z. Numbers that have
been crossed out or circled cannot be used again.

A	4	5	6	5	1	4	2	6	2
7	2	1	3	6	5	8	4	9	3
4	2	3	X	X	0	3	7	2	3
1	7	2	7	5	X	X	6	1	9
4	1	7	X	X	X	0	9	7	1
9	0	5	7	3	4	6	2	7	X
1	5	4	7	5	0	9	0	3	3
7	8	7	4	2	1	2	7	8	Z

1. $\underline{4} + \underline{5} + \underline{6} = \underline{15}$ 2. $\underline{4} + \underline{4} + \underline{6} = 14$

3. $\underline{2} + \underline{6} + \underline{2} = 10$ 4. $\underline{9} + \underline{0} + \underline{3} = 12$

5. $\underline{3} + \underline{1} + \underline{4} = 8$ 6. $\underline{7} + \underline{4} + \underline{2} = 13$

7. $\underline{6} + \underline{5} + \underline{6} = 17$ 8. $\underline{1} + \underline{1} + \underline{9} = 11$

9. $\underline{7} + \underline{2} + \underline{7} = 16$ 10. $\underline{9} + \underline{2} + \underline{7} = 18$

On a Roll

Count the dots on the number cubes.
Use them as addends.
Write as many number sentences as you can.

1. $\underline{6} + \underline{4} + \underline{3} = \underline{13}$ $6 + 3 + 4 = 13$

$\underline{4} + \underline{3} + \underline{6} = 13$ $4 + 6 + 3 = 13$

$\underline{3} + \underline{4} + \underline{6} = 13$ $3 + 6 + 4 = 13$

2. $\underline{5} + \underline{6} + \underline{5} = 16$ $5 + 5 + 6 = 16$

$\underline{6} + \underline{5} + \underline{5} = 16$

3. $\underline{6} + \underline{2} + \underline{3} = 11$ $6 + 3 + 2 = 11$

$\underline{2} + \underline{3} + \underline{6} = 11$ $2 + 6 + 3 = 11$

$\underline{3} + \underline{2} + \underline{6} = 11$ $3 + 6 + 2 = 11$

Now it's your turn. Roll 3 number cubes. Draw what you see.
How many number sentences can you make?
Check children's responses.

4.

Thirds, Halves, Fourths

Color one part red.
Write the fraction for the red part. Check children's work.

1. $\frac{1}{4}$ 2. $\frac{1}{2}$

3. 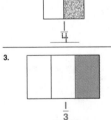 $\frac{1}{3}$ 4. 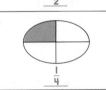 $\frac{1}{4}$

5. $\frac{1}{3}$ 6. $\frac{1}{2}$

7. $\frac{1}{4}$ 8. 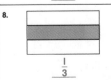 $\frac{1}{3}$

Which One Is Right?

Circle the picture that shows the fraction.

1. $\frac{1}{2}$ 2. $\frac{1}{4}$

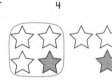

3. $\frac{1}{3}$ 4. $\frac{1}{2}$

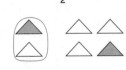

5. $\frac{1}{3}$ 6. $\frac{1}{4}$

Ring the Numbers

Circle the number that tells how many.

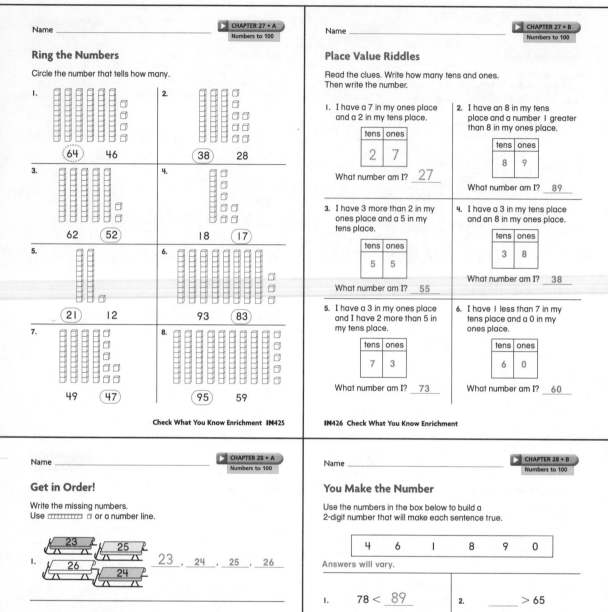

1. (64) 46
2. (38) 28
3. 62 (52)
4. 18 (17)
5. (21) 12
6. 93 (83)
7. 49 (47)
8. (95) 59

Place Value Riddles

Read the clues. Write how many tens and ones.
Then write the number.

1. I have a 7 in my ones place and a 2 in my tens place.

tens	ones
2	7

What number am I? _27_

2. I have an 8 in my tens place and a number 1 greater than 8 in my ones place.

tens	ones
8	9

What number am I? _89_

3. I have 3 more than 2 in my ones place and a 5 in my tens place.

tens	ones
5	5

What number am I? _55_

4. I have a 3 in my tens place and an 8 in my ones place.

tens	ones
3	8

What number am I? _38_

5. I have a 3 in my ones place and I have 2 more than 5 in my tens place.

tens	ones
7	3

What number am I? _73_

6. I have 1 less than 7 in my tens place and a 0 in my ones place.

tens	ones
6	0

What number am I? _60_

Get in Order!

Write the missing numbers.
Use ▭▭▭▭ ▭ or a number line.

1. _23_, _24_, _25_, _26_

2. _61_, _62_, _63_, _64_

3. _20_, _21_, _22_, _23_

4. _87_, _88_, _89_, _90_

You Make the Number

Use the numbers in the box below to build a
2-digit number that will make each sentence true.

4	6	1	8	9	0

Answers will vary.

1. 78 < _89_
2. ____ > 65
3. 38 > ____
4. ____ < 14
5. ____ > 89
6. 61 = ____
7. 46 < ____
8. ____ < 98
9. ____ < 56
10. 57 < ____

© Harcourt

Name _____

Number Play

Use the numbers on the houses to answer the questions.

1. The sum of these 2 numbers is 81.
What are the two numbers?

   _67_ , _14_

2. The sum of these two numbers is 17.
What are the two numbers?

   _14_ , _3_

3. The sum of these two numbers is 99.
What are the two numbers?

   _54_ , _45_

4. The sum of these two numbers is 51.
What are the two numbers?

   _15_ , _36_

5. The sum of these two numbers is 88.
What are the two numbers?

   _52_ , _36_

Check What You Know Enrichment **IN429**

Name _____

Coded Subtraction

Subtract.
Then match each answer to the letter.
Write the letter on the line to answer the riddle.

1. $\begin{array}{r} {}^{2\ 16}36 \\ -\ 7 \\ \hline 29 \end{array}$	2. $\begin{array}{r} 78 \\ -50 \\ \hline 28 \end{array}$	3. $\begin{array}{r} {}^{3\ 15}45 \\ -26 \\ \hline 19 \end{array}$	4. $\begin{array}{r} {}^{5\ 12}62 \\ -34 \\ \hline 28 \end{array}$
5. $\begin{array}{r} 28 \\ -15 \\ \hline 13 \end{array}$	6. $\begin{array}{r} 49 \\ -21 \\ \hline 28 \end{array}$	7. $\begin{array}{r} {}^{8\ 17}97 \\ -58 \\ \hline 39 \end{array}$	8. $\begin{array}{r} 75 \\ -43 \\ \hline 32 \end{array}$
9. $\begin{array}{r} {}^{7\ 17}87 \\ -68 \\ \hline 19 \end{array}$	10. $\begin{array}{r} {}^{7\ 12}82 \\ -24 \\ \hline 58 \end{array}$	11. $\begin{array}{r} {}^{3\ 17}47 \\ -28 \\ \hline 19 \end{array}$	12. $\begin{array}{r} {}^{3\ 15}45 \\ -\ 6 \\ \hline 39 \end{array}$

13=x	19=e	28=p	29=h	14=r
32=t	60=k	39=o	42=i	58=l

What sickness do chickens get?

t	h	e		p	e	o	p	l	e		p	o	x
8.	1.	11.		4.	9.	12.	6.	10.	3.		2.	7.	5.

IN430 Check What You Know Enrichment

Name _____

Circus Ring Addition

Write an addition sentence for each drawing.

1.

   _4_ + _4_ + _4_ + _4_ = _16_

2.

   _5_ + _5_ + _5_ = _15_

3.

   _3_ + _3_ + _3_ + _3_ + _3_ = _15_

4.

   _2_ + _2_ + _2_ + _2_ + _2_ = _10_

Check What You Know Enrichment **IN431**

Name _____

Make Them Equal

Circle equal groups.
Write how many groups.

1. 2 equal groups

There are _6_ in each group.

2. 3 equal groups

There are _2_ in each group.

3. 6 equal groups

There are _3_ in each group.

4. 4 equal groups

There are _4_ in each group.

5. 5 equal groups

There are _4_ in each group.

6. 2 equal groups

There are _6_ in each group.

IN432 Check What You Know Enrichment